Family Tree of
Queen Elizabeth the Queen *[Mother]*

Earls of Strathmore and Kinghorne

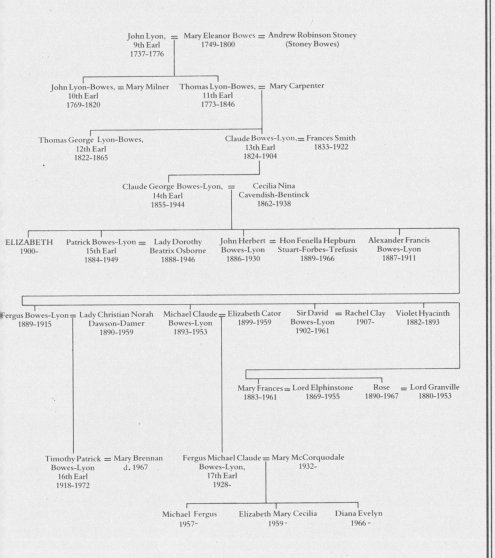

John Lyon, = Mary Eleanor Bowes = Andrew Robinson Stoney
9th Earl — 1749–1800 — (Stoney Bowes)
1737–1776

John Lyon–Bowes, = Mary Milner — Thomas Lyon–Bowes, = Mary Carpenter
10th Earl — 11th Earl
1769–1820 — 1773–1846

Thomas George Lyon–Bowes, — Claude Bowes-Lyon, = Frances Smith
12th Earl — 13th Earl — 1833–1922
1822–1865 — 1824–1904

Claude George Bowes-Lyon, = Cecilia Nina
14th Earl — Cavendish-Bentinck
1855–1944 — 1862–1938

ELIZABETH — Patrick Bowes-Lyon = Lady Dorothy — John Herbert = Hon Fenella Hepburn — Alexander Francis
1900- — 15th Earl — Beatrix Osborne — Bowes-Lyon — Stuart-Forbes-Trefusis — Bowes-Lyon
1884–1949 — 1888–1946 — 1886–1930 — 1889–1966 — 1887–1911

Fergus Bowes-Lyon = Lady Christian Norah — Michael Claude = Elizabeth Cator — Sir David = Rachel Clay — Violet Hyacinth
1889–1915 — Dawson-Damer — Bowes-Lyon — 1899–1959 — Bowes-Lyon — 1907- — 1882–1893
1890–1959 — 1893–1953 — 1902–1961

Mary Frances = Lord Elphinstone — Rose = Lord Granville
1883–1961 — 1869–1955 — 1890–1967 — 1880–1953

Timothy Patrick = Mary Brennan — Fergus Michael Claude = Mary McCorquodale
Bowes-Lyon — d. 1967 — Bowes-Lyon, — 1932-
16th Earl — 17th Earl
1918–1972 — 1928-

Michael Fergus — Elizabeth Mary Cecilia — Diana Evelyn
1957- — 1959- — 1966-

QUEEN ELIZABETH

A LIFE OF
THE QUEEN MOTHER

by
Penelope Mortimer

VIKING

VIKING

Penguin Books Ltd, Harmondsworth, Middlesex, England
Viking Penguin Inc., 40 West 23rd Street, New York, New York 10010, U.S.A.
Penguin Books Australia Ltd, Ringwood, Victoria, Australia
Penguin Books Canada Ltd, 2801 John Street, Markham, Ontario, Canada L3R 1B4
Penguin Books (N.Z.) Ltd, 182-190 Wairau Road, Auckland 10, New Zealand

First published 1986

This book was designed and produced by
The Rainbird Publishing Group
40 Park Street
London W1Y 4DE

Text set by SX Composing Ltd, Rayleigh, Essex, England
Printed and bound by Mackays, Chatham, Kent, England

British Library Cataloging in Publication Data

Mortimer, Penelope
    Queen Elizabeth: a life of the Queen Mother.—
    (Viking non-fiction)
    1. Elizabeth. *Queen, consort of George VI,*
    King of Great Britain   2. Great Britain—
    Queens—Biography
    I. Title
    941.084'092'4   DA585.A2

ISBN 0-670-81065-7

Illustration Acknowledgments

Reproduced by Gracious Permission of Her Majesty The Queen: 4; 17; 23;
BBC Hulton Picture Library: 13; 19; The Honourable Lady Bowes Lyon: 6;
7; 16; Tim Graham: 31; 32; John Topham Picture Library: 20; The Photo
Source: 12; 21; Popperfoto: 2; 9; 18; 22; 24; 25; 28; The Press Association: 14;
26; Syndication International: 1; 3; 5; 10; 11; 29; 30; Gerd Treuhaft: 15; 27
(Taken from Pathe Documentary Unit short film, *The King Who Loved His
Family*)

For Richard and Judy Hough

Nor do I apologise for my analyses of the Royal Family's circumstances and actions; we have no access to its members as real persons, and can only speculate. We can only chip away at the myths that encrust them, and look very carefully at the roles we force them to play. It is only hagiography that kills its subjects stone dead.

Lantern Lecture by Adam Mars-Jones, 1981

It has been my experience that the pleased incredulity with which the public reacts to the elementary demonstrations on the part of Royalty that they are, after all, like other people is matched by the public's firm refusal to accept them as such.

A King's Story, by HRH the Duke of Windsor, 1951

CONTENTS

ILLUSTRATIONS

INTRODUCTION

When in the late summer of 1983 I was asked to consider writing a biography of Queen Elizabeth the Queen Mother, the reason given by my prospective publisher was that he 'wanted particularly not to approach writers already associated with royalty, but rather a writer who could be counted on to write with style and imagination'. It seemed, however, a curious choice. I knew next to nothing about the Queen Mother or the Royal Family. I had never read a book about them and was unaware of the vast industry that thrives on their activities. I had therefore never read Frances Donaldson's comment in her Introduction to *Edward VIII*, that the task of the biographer is 'a desperate enterprise at the best of times . . . a hundred times worse when the subject is a member of the Royal Family.' As a novelist, I felt such a task would be both a challenge and a discipline.

As far as the events and personalities of the last eighty-six years are concerned, the research was pure pleasure. But what about the protagonist of the story? Frances Donaldson defines the 'desperate enterprise' of biography as endeavouring 'to seek out and represent as faithfully as possible the human being behind the history'. To paraphrase King George VI's remarks about the Duke of Windsor, most biographers' subjects are dead; the Queen Mother is not only alive, but very much so. She is also protected by a carapace of praise more impenetrable than the walls of the Royal Vault. There seemed at first to be no way, either by reading what had been written about her or by talking to people who claimed to know her, of discovering a credible human being behind the history.

'Do you get to see her?' I was constantly asked, with varying degrees of eagerness. The answer is No. Queen Elizabeth is inaccessible; more so, in fact, than she will be to future generations. There have been only two biographies written with her cooperation. In 1927 Lady Cynthia Asquith wrote *The Duchess of York* for serialisation in *The Woman's Journal*. She followed this in 1933 by *The Married Life of the Duchess of York* and this, in 1937, by *Queen Elizabeth*. They are all basically the same book, and all 'written and published with the personal approval' of Her Majesty. The fact that at her first interview Lady Cynthia 'immediately fell under the spell' put her in something of a quandary. 'How, unless I deliberately went in for understatement, could I hope to escape the charge of sycophancy? Unrelieved praise makes monotonous reading . . . Where (readers) would complain is the light and shade indispensable to good portraiture? Yet for the sake of safeguarding my book from the charge of sameness and insipidity, I could scarcely be expected to invent faults.'[1]

In 1966 Miss Dorothy Laird published *Queen Elizabeth The Queen Mother*, the second, and last, 'authorized biographical study of Her Majesty'. Miss Laird had none of Lady Cynthia's problems: she was already under the spell. In her foreword to this work she writes that she was offered 'the unusual privilege of an audience' but does not state that she actually had one.[2] However, she received much help from members of the family and Household and factually her book is invaluable. For the rest it is as spell-bound as all the others.

Apart from these 'authorized' works, there are literally scores of Queen Mother biographies ranging from distinguished pot-boilers to the most maudlin hagiography. None of them reveal more than the occasional flicker of a plausible human being. Neither did the majority of the people who, for the first six months or so, I spent my time interviewing. The interrogative adverb 'Why?' is unknown in royal circles. One charming elderly peer told me how the Queen Mother frequently insists on community singing round the post-prandial table. I asked him what happened if one of them didn't feel like singing; suppose he had a headache and wanted to go to bed? The old gentleman was not startled or put out; he simply didn't understand the question. 'Well,' he managed at last, gently blustering, 'one doesn't, it doesn't, I mean one simply *doesn't*. . .' Another, rather more articulate interviewee recorded vague pleasantries for half an hour and then, hearing the click as the tape ended, leaned forward and said in a much brisker voice 'As a matter of fact, I do think. . .' Perhaps such conversations told me more about the gentlemen concerned than about Queen Elizabeth, but nevertheless they provided infinitesimal clues to the character I was trying to seek out.

However, I soon found that the gossips talked too much, the others too little. Their anecdotes were all the same, so was their approach. On the rare occasions when I was told something new, it came with the stringent warning that it must on no account be used, or anyway attributed to the teller, in my book. I am not a professional journalist. Neither am I particularly interested in those aspects of royal life which most writers on the subject find so irresistible. I decided that trailing around the periphery of Clarence House, Windsor, Birkhall and the Castle of Mey was a waste of time. If this lays me open to criticism as a royal biographer, such criticism is based on the misconception that it is easier to find out the truth about a live person that it is about a dead one. As far as Royalty is concerned, it is virtually impossible.

I read, as everyone engaged in such a project must, ten times more than I actually used. I went through the various stages of her life with a toothcomb, following up apparently unrelated incidents, very often abandoning them. There were a lot of dead ends. I had no pre-conceived idea of the character I was looking for. As the clues began to accumulate I was frequently surprised at the shape that seemed to be emerging; and just as surprised when it changed. Contrary to my novelist's belief that character is responsible for history, rather than the reverse, I had to work from the facts inwards, instead of outwards from the character. I am aware that there are many discrepancies, many gaps, and I do not claim that the final picture is by any means entirely accurate. To combine 'a perfect little duck' with 'the most dangerous woman in Europe', or 'the perfect neighbour for a bunga-low' with 'the greatest Queen since Cleopatra' is difficult enough; to add one's own research, deduction and instinct to that combination makes the result even less predictable. I believe my portrait is valid. It may, indeed, have achieved the impossible and be almost right.

There has been a strong indication, long before publication, of the Establishment reaction. 'What would happen if I found something which was really damaging to the King?' Harold Nicolson asked Sir Owen Morshead, when Nicolson was engaged on his biography of King George V. If he was asked to cut such references out, could he resign the job? 'Your first duty will always be to the Monarchy,' Sir Owen replied primly. 'At which,' says Nicolson, 'all the contrariness in me surged up in a wave of sudden Republicanism.' His was an official biography and this one does not have to submit to such strictures. As far as the Queen Mother's countless admirers are con-cerned, I can only say 'If we offend, it is with our good will.'

Many of the people who have talked to me do not wish to be identi-fied. I must respect their wishes, while regretting their reasons, and thank them just the same. Among those who had no such reservations I would particularly like to thank Sir Martin Gilliat, Queen Elizabeth's Private Secretary, who had no idea what kind of book I was writing and was most helpful, agreeable and hospitable; the Rt Hon. Harold Macmillan, the Earl of Stockton, Elizabeth Longford, Frances Donaldson, James Lees-Milne, John Grigg, William Hamilton, M.P., John Piper; and Hugo Vickers, who was consistently patient and available.

Among those who declined to see me were HRH Princess Margaret ('The Princess personally feels that enough has been written about Her Majesty for the time being'), HRH Princess Alice, Duchess of Gloucester (regrets, which were mutual) and the Duke of Grafton (topic too personal).

I am also grateful to Elizabeth Blair, who had the thankless task of being my editor, to Polly Fisher for weeks spent in the British Library and Colindale, and to Thomas Blaikie, who also helped with the research; to my children for their unlikely interest, and above all to Richard and Judy Hough, to whom the book is dedicated, for their constant support and encouragement.

PART ONE

CHAPTER

1

The cool showery weather at the beginning of August 1900 must have come as a relief after July's heat wave, particularly to women like Cecilia, Lady Glamis, awaiting her ninth child in her parents' Grosvenor Gardens apartment. The last few weeks had brought a raffish, Mediterranean look to London. Horses had taken to sun-bonnets. Servants, too, had humanely been provided with straw hats, Homburg-shaped for butlers, boaters for footmen. The Great Canadian Water Shoot at the Earl's Court Woman's Exhibition was besieged by young people whose delighted screams through the splash and spray drowned the brave noise of the Swedish Hussar Ladies Band and The Maine Ladies Naval Orchestra. At the Royal Aquarium, 'London's largest, coolest Palace of Amusements', ladies fully dressed in stockings and elaborate bathing costumes swam slowly round and round, their heads held high. Grass was scorched as the South African veldt and at Church Parade in Hyde Park there were plenty of alpaca jackets, some slightly immodest gowns and a notice-able lack of gloves. Even the old Queen, who normally moved from place to place like clockwork, was rumoured to be feeling 'quite languid' at Osborne, and planning to go to Balmoral early if the intense heat persisted.

The weather, always a newsworthy subject, had temporarily taken over the headlines, competing with casualty lists from Frederickstad and the Chinese crisis and passionate arguments in Parliament concerning a statue of Oliver Cromwell. As it broke, there was a succession of notable deaths and disasters – first HRH Prince Alfred, Duke of Edinburgh and Duke of Saxe-Coburg-Gotha passed on from natural causes at Rosenau; then King Humbert of Italy was assassinated, followed four days later by an assassination attempt on the Shah of Persia. The *New York Herald* asserted that within the past few months twenty-seven anarchists had left America with the avowed purpose of laying low every crowned head in Europe.

It was once more a wet, windy, unreliable world. Cricket was interrupted by rain. Horses plodded bare-headed through the familiar drizzle. The Water Shoot lost customers to the Gravity Railway and

Mlle Marguerite's Performing Lions. Madame Tussaud's produced Lifelike and Realistic Portrait Models of the late Duke of Saxe-Coburg and the late King Humbert of Italy to show the crowds on Bank Holiday Monday, 6 August, by which time Lady Glamis's daughter was two days old.

Exactly where in London the future Queen Elizabeth the Queen Mother was born is the subject of mild speculation. There is a theory, current in recent years, that the event took place in an ambulance. As the first petrol-powered buses were not in operation until that year – and those, for some odd reason, in Norfolk – it is reasonable to assume that ambulances were still horse-drawn, and none too easy to summon in an emergency. It is, however, recorded that when Mrs Miller Mundy caught her foot in some matting at Earl's Court 'and one of her knee-caps broke right across, giving forth a loud report like that of a gun, and causing her excruciating pain', an ambulance was summoned to take the sufferer home, so it was obviously possible. Cabs were hailed by one's butler blowing a whistle – a single blast for a taxi, two for a hansom, three for a four-wheeler – so perhaps the same method applied. If that is what happened, and it arrived in time, did it clop calmly on through the traffic while Lady Glamis was delivered of her daughter or did it pull up in the Park? What was its intended destination, anyway? The official answer from Clarence House is that they have no idea. Queen Elizabeth has no interest in the subject. They have no interest in the subject. Anything is possible. An ambulance, you say? Well, well.

Still, wherever he left his wife and youngest daughter, we do know that Lord Glamis was in Scotland by 23 August, making nine runs out of his side's total of 303 for 9 declared in the Glamis v. Strathmore cricket match.[1] There he resolutely stayed until the third week in September. When he finally returned to the family home, St Paul's Walden Bury near Hitchin, the six-week-old Elizabeth was neither registered nor christened, non-existent in the eyes of God and man. Her father was immediately sent trotting to the Registrar's Office at Hitchin where he paid a fine of 7/6d for failing to report the birth on time. It was then – upset, perhaps, by this drain on his pocket and distraught by all the fuss and urgency – that he stated the child had been born at St Paul's Walden Bury. One must surely discount the wild suspicion that he himself was not at all certain where the birth had taken place, and perhaps this just seemed the easiest way out. Under the Forgery Act of 1861 he could have been sentenced to penal servitude for life. As nobody questioned the matter for the next eighty years, he got off, in this world at least, scot-free.

Next came the christening, which was performed by the Reverend Tristram Valentine, the incumbent of St Paul's Walden, after matins on Sunday, 23 September. As the godparents forgot to sign the register, all of them except Lord Glamis's spinster sister Maud from the Cotswolds and Lady Glamis's second cousin Mrs Arthur James have been forgotten. Venetia James and Cecilia shared the same great-grandfather, William, 3rd Duke of Portland, perhaps the only Prime Minister never to have made a speech in Parliament. Very much part of the *haute-monde*, which the Glamises and Bowes-Lyons were not, and a close friend of the Prince of Wales's future companion, Alice Keppel, Venetia also received her share of Royal attention until she made the mistake of concealing herself in a giant Easter egg, popping out with a whoop and a curtsy as the Prince and Princess of Wales were passing by. Edward was furious, Alexandra not amused.[2] For a time, Mrs Arthur James was under a cloud.

Venetia would become notoriously mean and rather severe in her later years, but in September 1900, as far as renouncing the vain pomp and glory of the world was concerned, she seems an improbable choice for a godmother. One imagines her wafting into the village church with her leghorn and her veils and her boa and her 16-in. waist, looking down her pretty little nose at the gawky Bowes-Lyon boys in their tweed knickerbockers and thoroughly upsetting the Reverend Valentine with her dimpled smile and flashing ankles. Perhaps this was one of the reasons why the christening had one or two tense moments. Mr Valentine misheard or misunderstood the infant's name – Elizabeth Angela Marguerite – and had to scratch about on the baptismal certificate to put it right; he omitted to state that the father was a Lord, and had to add that later. What with the business of the birth certificate and one thing and another, Lord Glamis must have heaved a sigh of relief when it was all over.

★   ★   ★

Queen Victoria died at Osborne on 22 January 1901. The Prince of Wales – now King Edward VII – travelled from his mother's deathbed to London on 25 January for his Accession Council and made history by rejecting the prepared speech and improvising his own. As nobody took down what he said, Lord Rosebery had to reconstruct it from memory for the records. That same day King Edward was proclaimed from St James's Palace with ritual that had not been used for over seventy-two years:

> Whereas it has pleased Almighty God to call to His Mercy Our Late Sovereign Lady Queen Victoria, of Blessed and Glorious Memory, by whose Decease the Imperial Crown of the United Kingdom of Great Britain and Ireland is solely and rightfully come to the High and Mighty Prince Albert Edward: We, therefore, the Lords Spiritual and Temporal of this Realm, being here assisted with these of Her late Majesty's Privy

Council, with Numbers of other Principal Gentlemen of Quality, with the Lord Mayor, Aldermen, and Citizens of London, do now hereby, with one Voice and Consent of Tongue and Heart, publish and proclaim, That the High and Mighty Prince Albert Edward, is now, by the Death of our late Sovereign of Happy Memory, become our only lawful and rightful Liege Lord Edward the Seventh, by the Grace of God, King of the United Kingdom of Great Britain and Ireland, Defender of the Faith, Emperor of India: To whom we do acknowledge all Faith and constant Obedience, with all hearty and humble Affection; beseeching God, by whom Kings and Queens do reign, to bless the Royal Prince Edward the Seventh, with long and happy Years to reign over Us. God save the King!

and the crowds roared in response, the trumpets sounded, the band played the National Anthem, a salute of guns boomed out from Hyde Park and the Tower. This event may have passed unnoticed by the five-month-old baby at St Paul's Walden Bury, but it would play a significant part in her future.

By the time Elizabeth was fourteen months old her mother was pregnant again. David Bowes-Lyon was born on 2 May 1902, four weeks before the end of the Boer War and eight weeks before the scheduled date for King Edward's Coronation. Unfortunately the King succumbed to acute appendicitis and the ceremony had to be postponed at the last minute, causing great inconvenience to foreign potentates and an unseemly riot in Hemel Hempstead, where the rustics felt cheated of a free dinner. The Coronation that finally took place on 9 August was celebrated with more jubilation by the troops just returned from South Africa than by the Almanac de Gotha, and this seemed appropriate to the dawn of a new era. Edward, the sunny King, rose benevolently over the first decade of the twentieth century and settled in what seemed to many people an eternal noon of peace and prosperity.

Of course there were skirmishes abroad and anarchists under the bed, deplorable goings-on in Russia and some very nasty murders. French aviators seemed to drop out of the sky like flies, the un-domesticated working classes were being troublesome and a few hysterical women, amusingly dubbed as 'fooligans', didn't seem to realize where their buttered bread came from. These, however, were little more than the midges and mosquitoes of a summer day. Real people, proper people, the sort of people one knows, never saw the dark or felt the cold. A million lights came on at dusk, and those who were not actually basking in the Royal Presence – the gentry, the respectable, affluent middle classes, domestic servants of superior rank and all good children – retired into their various fortresses, cosy and warm as Leonard Woolf's 'nursery with its great fire, when the curtains were pulled and the gas lit and Nurse settled down to her

18

reading, and occasionally far off could be heard the clop-clop of a horse in hansom-cab or four-wheeler...'[3] The sense of safety, of being protected from all outside worlds, may have been in direct proportion to the sense of peril, but few people said so.

In February 1904 the old Earl of Strathmore died and Elizabeth's father succeeded to the title, becoming the 14th Earl of Strathmore and Kinghorne, Viscount Lyon and Baron Glamis, Tannadyce, Sidlaw and Strathdichtie, Baron Bowes, of Streatlam Castle, County Durham, and Lunedale, County York. As a result of his considerable inheritance Lord Strathmore rented a splendid Adam mansion in St James's Square. Elizabeth and David, therefore, were the first of the family to grow up with a sense of relative wealth and privilege – a London home 'for the season', St Paul's Walden Bury and the vast folly of Glamis for the rest of the year. Elizabeth acquired a French governess, Mlle Lang, and attended Madame d'Egville's dancing class in Knightsbridge. She was small for her age, inclined to puppy-fat, with long dark hair tied back with a satin bow and an expression – in front of the camera, at any rate – of mischievousness alternating with wistful charm. She performed excellently, one-two-three-hopping through the polka, twirling to the waltz – if it had been allowed, she would probably have danced a vigorous can-can.

To her, and to all the other little Honourables skipping about the floor, London was an endless party. Soldiers wore scarlet when they came calling on housemaids; uniforms of every kind, from postmen to Field Marshals, were gilded and braided and bobbled; Peter Yapp's in Sloane Street sold sailor hats for children with HMS VICTORY emblazoned on the ribbon, surmounted by a gold star. If you were extremely grand, like the Buccleuchs of Montagu House or their neighbours, the Fitzwilliams, your prams were decorated with the family crest and painted in the family colours, and on special occasions you rode out with Mama and Papa in one of the family coaches: 'The harness was shining silver, and there were a wigged coachman and footman in front and two postillions behind all in livery, with red breeches and white stockings.'[4] Everything was remarkable to a child who had a firm grip on her governess's hand and muffins at home for tea: knife-grinders, crossing-sweepers, buskers, cripples, chimney sweeps, beggars, urchins, the whole colourful pageant of the un-washed poor; brass bands and barrel organs and parades, and perhaps, for a birthday treat, Mama might take you to the Coliseum if you're very good.

Whenever it was that Elizabeth saw her first music-hall, something about Vesta Tilley and Marie Lloyd and Gertie Millar struck a rousing chord in the little girl's fantasies – their clothes, their command of the stage, their glamour and vulgarity and rollicking good humour behind the impregnable footlights. Actresses had recently become socially acceptable, so much so that debutantes were rushing to the stage, happy to find that the theatre was almost indistinguishable from their daily lives. When Seymour Hicks rashly offered jobs to the twelve prettiest society girls to send him their photographs, he was inundated with replies.[5] Had she been a few years older, Elizabeth could easily have become another Zena Dare.

As it was, she used her talents effectively enough. Lord David Cecil remembers being introduced to her at a children's party at Lansdowne House: 'I turned and looked and was aware of a small, charming, rosy face around which twined and strayed rings and tendrils of silken hair, and a pair of dewy grey eyes. Her flower-like mouth parted in a grave, enchanting smile, and between the pearly teeth flowed out tones of drowsy melting sweetness that seemed to caress the words they uttered. From that moment my small damp hand clutched at hers and I never left her side ... Forgotten were all the pretenders to my heart. Here was the true heroine. She had come. I had seen and she had conquered.'[6]

The love that was more than love was loved for two golden summers: 'I remember her playing in the Park, racing beside her yellow-haired brother, her hair flying in the wind, her cheeks bright with the exercise, her clear infectious laugh ringing out; or sitting demurely at the tea-table; or best of all, at a fancy-dress party dressed as a Vandyck child, with high square bodice and stiff satin skirts, surrounded by a bevy of adorers...'[7] Remembered rapture so affected Lord David's prose style that it is hard to believe the child was real. If, in all this excitement, she occasionally wet her knickers, or sulked, or howled, or refused to eat her bread-and-butter pudding, her contemporaries have discreetly forgotten it.

After her younger brother was born their mother had engaged a new nursery maid, Clara Knight, one of those willing martyrs without whom the British aristocracy would never have survived. She was seventeen, a farmer's daughter from Hertfordshire, and was to spend the whole of her future life bringing up Strathmore children and grandchildren. For eight years Elizabeth and David spent most of their time under her care, and her effect on them must have been incalculable. Isolated by age from the rest of the family, adored and worried over by Clara, remote from their father, never hearing a cross word, both of them pretty as angels, the pair should by rights have had the sunny sanctity of a Margaret Tarrant print. But they don't. The early photographs remind me more of Henry James's Miles and Flora in *The Turn of the Screw* – dark backgrounds, solemn faces, a hint of innocence about to be corrupted or already, perhaps, doomed; good as gold and sly as little foxes; enchanting and yet, in their power to enchant obscurely dangerous. This, of course, is a more romantic view than most, but possibly more interesting.

★   ★   ★

Of all the Strathmore homes, St Paul's Walden Bury was best suited to an Edwardian childhood. There is nothing grand about it, like 20 St James's Square; nothing sinister, like Glamis. It is the sort of house that seems to bask, like a pretty old lady, in remembered summers – shabby, comfortable, taking its ageing beauty for granted. Both Elizabeth and her brother would write nostalgically about THE WOOD and THE HARNESS ROOM and, above all, THE FLEA HOUSE which 'could only be reached by a very rotten ladder, the rungs of which would certainly have broken if an adult had attempted the ascent. Consequently our nurse was unable to come up and retrieve us . . . In it we kept a regular store of forbidden delicacies, acquired by devious devices. This store consisted of apples, oranges, sugar, sweets, slabs of chocolate Meunier, matches and packets of Woodbines. Many other things there were besides, and to this blissful retreat we used . . . to have recourse whenever it seemed an agreeable plan to escape our morning lessons.'[8] Less agreeable, but perhaps more dramatic, were the secret hideouts and ghostly companions at Glamis.

Once they were installed in this remote fortress, Lady Strathmore would set about cheering the place up, though it must have been a dispiriting task what with the gloom and the bloodstains on the floor. Chips Channon remembered 'the whole castle heavy with atmosphere, sinister, lugubrious',[9] but Lord Gorrell, by temperament more inclined to look on the bright side, insists that 'it was all so friendly and so kind, days of such wholehearted and delightful youth under the gracious guidance of Lady Strathmore . . . the old castle re-echoed with fun and laughter.'[10] All the boys would be back from Eton and Oxford for the summer, except for Patrick, who was now Lord Glamis and a captain in the Scots Guards. According to one of their contemporaries the Strathmore sons were 'a wild lot'; the elder daughters, Mary and Rose, probably squealed a good deal and flounced off to their bedrooms, only to appear again, all smiles, as carriage-loads of visitors streamed through the lofty front door. Meanwhile, escaping from Clara and Mlle Lang, the two youngest children raced and toddled through spook-laden passages, past sealed-up doors behind which might be the Monster, mumbling and dribbling, or the Room of Skulls, in which a number of Ogilvys had been immured until, after eating the flesh off their own arms, they died of starvation and crumbled into a heap of bones.

'Was there a secret at Bly,' Henry James's heroine wondered anxiously, 'a mystery of Udolpho or an insane, unmentionable relative kept in unsuspected confinement?' There certainly was at Glamis. Thomas Lyon-Bowes, Lord Glamis, and his wife Charlotte had their first son and heir on 28 September 1822, or so the reference books – including Burke's Peerage – said. But was he their first? Debrett thought otherwise, and slipped in a son who was born, and reputedly died, on 18 October 1821. Luckier for him, and for all the succeeding Earls, if he had. The child was shaped like an egg, covered in hair, with spindly little arms and legs – according to the superstitions of the time, a monster. Unfortunately, hoping for a swift release and not wanting their little maverick to be eternally damned, the parents had the child baptized. He thrived, growing hairier and more egg-like every day. Now they had given him an immortal soul they couldn't just smother him or dump him in the river. What to do? The vast, largely uninhabited castle of Glamis provided the answer.

In 1684 the first Earl of Strathmore, a man with a passion for hiding, had built a secret room 'within the charter house', about ten feet wide by fifteen feet long. This dank and gloomy cell would become the rightful Lord Strathmore's home for, it is said, a hundred and fifty years. Only four men at a time knew of his existence or where he was kept: the current Earl, his eldest son, the family lawyer and the agent of the estate. In Elizabeth's grandfather's time, a tactless workman told the Clerk of the Works that he had found a door opening on to a long passage and didn't like the look of it. Before he knew where he was, he was pensioned off and dispatched to Australia. Rose Granville, Elizabeth's older sister, said in her old age, 'We were never allowed to talk about it . . . Our parents forbade us ever to discuss the matter or ask any questions about it. My father and grandfather absolutely refused to discuss it.'[11]

Whatever the fun and games indulged in by the women of the family and the younger boys, the Earls themselves were a melancholy lot. Each of them, on their succession, was taken by the lawyer and the agent through the secret door and down the long corridor to be introduced to the indestructible freak, its hair now grizzled, its antique rags smelling to high heaven. (This is my imagination, of course, but it serves.) According to various records, they never smiled again. Writing of his visit in 1877, Augustus Hare recounts that the Bishop of Brechin was so upset by Lord Strathmore's gloom that he offered his services as an ecclesiastic to try and dispel it. Lord Strathmore thanked him kindly, but said 'that in his most unfortunate position, no one could ever help him.' 'Silent and moody, with an anxious, scared look on his face,'[12] Elizabeth's grandfather must have made his brother's monstrous presence felt throughout the castle, even though his lips were sealed. It is said that Elizabeth's father was so alarmed by this that he himself 'absolutely refused to be enlightened' when the time came.

Whatever the truth of the matter, the idea of this unhappy, geriatric Monster lurking in their home must have affected the Strathmores profoundly. Perhaps he was, in his way, their most influential ancestor.

The place was packed with secrets and stories about secrets. No wonder the children whispered, darting quick looks over their shoulders to see if they were being overheard. The linen women and kitchen maids loved to tell the tale about a guest who, strolling on the lawn after dinner one night, saw a girl at one of the upstairs windows, gripping the bars and looking white-faced out into the darkness. As he watched, she disappeared. There was a piercing scream; then silence. It was one minute to midnight. A few minutes later the door of one of the towers opened and a hideous old woman 'with a fiendish face' staggered out with a sack on her back. At the sight of the guest she lolloped across the lawn and into the woods, her black cloak billowing, the sack bumping as she ran.

Years later, in a convent in Italy, the guest came across 'the girl at the Glamis window'. Her hands had been cut off and her tongue cut out – it had been discovered that she had stumbled on a family secret. Elizabeth was told that if she dared to look out of the night-nursery window late at night, she would see the tongueless woman running across the park, pointing in agony to her bleeding mouth. Struwelpeter was nothing to the dreadful warnings of the Strathmore ghosts. It was fearful fun, but the moral was clear: never admit to knowing secrets; never tell them.

★   ★   ★

In September 1908, with Mlle Lang on an extended holiday, there was a brief experiment of sending Elizabeth to school, accompanied, naturally, by the six-year-old David. They trotted off to Constance Goff's kindergarten in Marylebone High Street – curious that this should have seemed adequate for a girl of eight, but there it is – where they painted and modelled Plasticine and acted in little plays and dressed in identical tussore smocks. It didn't last long, interfering as it did with what Lady Strathmore considered to be the child's proper education. Elizabeth would obviously be much in demand as a bridesmaid now the six eldest siblings had reached a marriageable age (in November she gave an impeccable performance at brother Patrick's wedding in the Guards Chapel), and must have time for her social life – a far better insurance for the future than any amount of schooling. She had already met the young Wales children, David, Bertie, Georgie and Mary, at Lady Leicester's – palming off her crystallized cherries on to the speechless Bertie's plate, it was said – and the accomplishments of the eligible young lady she was to become were not part of the kindergarten curriculum. By the following Easter Mlle Lang had been recalled, piano lessons were begun at the Matilde Verne school in the Cromwell Road, visits were planned to Lady Strathmore's mother, who lived near Florence with her unmarried daughter Violet, an admirable person to introduce a girl to the more difficult aspects of Florentine art.

This suited Elizabeth very well. She was alone with David again, Clara in charge of their comforts, Mlle Lang fruitlessly imploring them from the bottom of the Flea House ladder. Christmas at Walden Bury, off to St James's Square for pantomimes and parties, starring in Madame Verne's children's concert, being lifted 'on and off the piano stool oftener than was necessary' by Madame Verne's sister, 'just because she was so nice to take hold of.'[13] Not that she was allowed to overlook the fact that she was unusually fortunate – Lady Strathmore was a devout Christian, and it was as necessary to support suitable charities as it was to be seen in the right place at the right time wearing the right clothes. Elizabeth was a tender-hearted child and would have been most upset, for instance, by the death from starvation and destitution of three-year-old Charles Leaning from Hoxton, if she had known about it. Mr Leaning, a scaffolder, had been out of work for nine weeks; his wife was earning five shillings a week making boxes, and on this the Leanings and their five children lived. Their rent was four shillings a week. When the child died his mother was at the police court being fined for not sending one of his brothers to school; as she was unable to pay the fine, Mr Leaning was sent to prison.[14] This happened at strawberry-time, a month before Elizabeth's ninth birthday, and was the sort of thing they prayed about most fervently, along with requests for the King's continued health and their own safety from damnation. 'The rich man in his castle/The poor man at his gate/God made them high or lowly/And ordered their estate/ALL things bright and beautiful...'

Back to Glamis again for the summer. Going to bed at Glamis might be perilous, but the ghosts, unlike those of Bly, considerately absented themselves during daylight hours. The children played cricket, rode their ponies, went on picnics, learned the mazurka and the minuet from old Mr Neal, who tucked his violin under a long white beard; they visited their neighbours and entertained their guests, among whom was the local minister. 'The countess sat down at the piano,' he recalled, 'and played a few bars of a quaint old minuet. Suddenly, as if by a magician's touch, two little figures seemed to rise from the floor and dance, with admirable precision and grace ... These little children were the Hon. David Lyon and Lady Elizabeth Lyon, the youngest son and daughter of the house. The former had donned part of the dress of the family jester and the latter had assumed the robe and cap of a little girl of the period of James I and VI.' After half an hour, ('Brief but supreme,' to the minister, at least), 'the music stopped and the little dancers, making a low bow and curtsey, clapped their hands with delight . . . Choruses of praise were heard on every side, and Lady Elizabeth, on being asked . . . the name of the character she had adopted, said with great *empressement*: "I call myself the Princess Elizabeth." '[15] The nine-year-old child had already set her sights higher than the Coliseum.

CHAPTER

2

At the end of April 1910, King Edward caught a cold. King Edward was ill; was dying, with his wife and Alice Keppel at his bedside; on 6 May King Edward was dead. Mourning was back after only nine years, though this time it took some bizarre forms. Alice Keppel threaded black ribbon through her daughter's underwear;[1] a desolate hostess tied a large black crêpe bow round a tree which the King had planted in her garden five years before; a grocer in Jermyn Street filled his window with black Bradenham hams.[2] At nine o'clock on the morning of 9 May King George V's accession was proclaimed from St James's Palace:

> Whereas it has pleased Almighty God to call to His Mercy our late Sovereign Lord King Edward the Seventh, of Blessed and Glorious Memory ... We, therefore, the Lords Spiritual and Temporal of this Realm ... with Numbers of other Principal Gentlemen of Quality ... do now hereby, with one Voice and Consent of Tongue and Heart, publish and proclaim That the High and Mighty Prince George Frederick Ernest Albert is now, by the Death of our late Sovereign of Happy Memory, become our only lawful rightful Liege Lord George the Fifth ... God Save the King!

and the crowds roared, the trumpets sounded, the band played the National Anthem, a salute of guns boomed out from Hyde Park and the Tower and the King's eldest sons, David and Bertie, watched it from the garden wall of Marlborough House. For the beginning of a new era it was more like a damp Sunday afternoon than a promising dawn. The lovely ladies, the gay blades, the gamblers and wealthy pimps, leaped with extraordinary alacrity into the shadows, leaving their places in the sun to the landed gentry, sporting peers, decorous dowagers and the clergy. God, a fitful element during King Edward's reign, rejoined the Monarchy in the social firmament. Respectable domesticity became the order of the day, the nights were long and peaceful. The widowed Queen, wandering disconsolately about Sandringham House wearing black and silver and a widow's cap, could not reconcile herself to it.[3] Georgie was not born to be King.*

* King Edward VII's eldest son, Albert Victor, Duke of Clarence and Avondale, died in 1892 at the age of twenty-eight. He was engaged to Mary of Tek who, eighteen months later, married his only brother, George.

May was a nice enough girl, but a poor relation after all. Encouraged by her sister Dagmar, Dowager Empress of All the Russias, Alexandra made it clear that she still considered herself to be First Lady in the land. To add to their recognizable image, King George V and Queen Mary had a mother-in-law problem.

The Coronation of King George V took place a year later, on 22 June 1911. Among the acts of God to mark this auspicious occasion were killer earthquakes in Turkestan, volcanic eruptions in Italy, Alaska and the Philippines, a Finnish village carried bodily out to sea, a 54 miles-per-hour gale and 1.1 in. of rainfall in fifteen minutes on a July day in London, a commander F. G. Brine washed overboard from his ship and drowned, and the shipwreck of the King's sister Louise and her husband off the coast of Morocco. The French Premier was shot at by a madman, the Russian premier was assassinated by an anarchist, and the Persian Minister of Finance was assassinated. Republics were proclaimed in Portugal and China, Italy declared war on Turkey, there was civil war in Mexico. Riots broke out for one reason or another in Bombay, Hankau, Liverpool, Rome, Tunis, Cardiff, Hull, Brazil, Dundee, Lisbon, Llanelly and Tredegar. In Britain, there were strikes of shipbuilders, seamen, dock labourers, railway workers, carmen, transport workers, postal employees, carters, taxi drivers and schoolboys.

Royalty had a bonanza. There was the Festival of Empire, the Coronation Exhibition, the Pageant of Empire, the Pageant of London, and the Coronation itself. Prince Edward received the Order of the Garter and was invested as Prince of Wales at Caernarvon, miserably dressed up in white satin breeches and a mantle and surcoat of purple velvet edged with ermine. ('Your friends will understand that as a Prince you are obliged to do certain things that may seem a little silly,' his mother said.)[4] The new King and Queen invited 100,000 children to tea at the Crystal Palace, which was later sold to Lord Plymouth for £210,000. Then there was the Durbar at Delhi, when Emperor George and Empress Mary sat 'on a lofty white many-tiered pedestal . . . on two golden thrones under a twenty-foot purple-and-gold canopy supported by twelve slender bronze columns and surmounted by a dazzling golden dome' and the Emperor's eagle eye noted that the Gaekwar of Baroda did not observe correct court etiquette when making his homage. King Vajiravudjh was crowned King of Siam at Bangkok. Unfortunately there was distinct coolness between King Alfonso of Spain and his aunt, the Infanta Eulalia owing to the publication of her autobiography.

Balloons were clearly out-dated – the remains of the 'Hilderbrandt', containing the bodies of two aeronauts, were found petrified under the ice in a Pomeranian lake. Among the relatively few aviators who had survived the last decade, M. Pierre Prier made history by flying from London to Paris without stopping. The first aerial post was inaugurated between Hendon and Windsor; whether this had any connection with a young French airman shooting the secretary of Hendon aerodrome, and then himself, is not clear. The Congress of International Law confirmed the right to use aerial warcraft in war, and its blessing resulted in a very entertaining demonstration of military aerobatics. Down to earth, the Reverend Swann and Mr E. Manning rowed across the Channel within days of each other, and Mr T. W. Burgess swam it. The *Lusitania* completed the round trip to New York and back in just over twelve days, and the first unsinkable liner, the *Titanic*, was launched from a British shipyard.

For the rest, suffragettes kept up their clamour as though nobody had anything better to think about; Members of Parliament voted to give themselves a salary for the first time; Winston Churchill became First Lord of the Admiralty; Dr Sun Yat Sen became President of China and abolished the pigtail. Prince Albert, aged fifteen, shot his first woodcock, his first partridge and his first grouse. In hindsight it is possible to see the shades of the prison house lengthening over Hitchin, St James's Square, Glamis and the British Empire.

On 1 January the previous year Patrick's wife had given birth to the first Strathmore grandson and Lady Strathmore had sacrificed Clara to the new baby. It must have been a traumatic parting, the worst for Elizabeth and David. Nannies must necessarily be fickle, soon comforted by another infant to be burped and dosed. Elizabeth should surely have outgrown the nursery anyway. A Scottish nursery maid, Catta McLean, took over at St Paul's Walden Bury. Maybe she was agile enough to climb the ladder to the Flea House.

The Bowes-Lyon children, cheering lustily, watched the Coronation procession, no doubt commenting on the costumes and deportment of the young Princes and Princess. Shortly afterwards, Elizabeth and David were taken by spinster Aunt Violet to stay with their maternal grandmother, Mrs Scott, at the Villa Caponi near Florence. Mrs Scott was very High Church and went in for incense and red damask wall-coverings in her private chapel. She was also the aunt of Ottoline Morrell and used to have her to tea with little Bertie Russell at her house on Ham Common, which reeked of tiger lilies.[5] Aunt Violet duly conducted the children to the Trecento frescos, the tombs of the Medicis, the Pitti Palace and the Boboli Gardens. They returned to Glamis at the height of the shooting season. On 19 October their twenty-four-year-old brother Alec died there, from an unspecified illness.

Almost a year later, in September 1912, David was sent off to prep school in Broadstairs, a bracing seaside resort mainly populated by small boys worrying their way to Eton, their knees chapped by the east wind and the necessity of constant prayer. Probably the establishment chosen by the Strathmores was St Peter's Court, already graced by the presence of the young Princes Henry and George. Elizabeth had been living with her parents' mourning all year; her own desolation was now extreme. 'David went to school for the first time on Friday,' she wrote to a friend, 'I miss him horribly.'[6] Smeared letters were sent off to Broadstairs by every post; she lost weight, looked peaky; her twelve-year-old heart was breaking. Mama, unused to this sort of thing from her youngest daughter, realized that something must be done.

If Elizabeth had been a boy, she too would have been preparing for Eton (her mother, if she had been a boy, would have been Duke of Portland, come to that). Indeed, the Buccleuchs of Montagu House were considering sending their two daughters, Alice and Sybil, to boarding school – not even to Heathfield, which would be proper, but to some insignificant institution in Malvern.[7] In spite of Elizabeth's loneliness, Lady Strathmore could not contemplate such a step. She finally and reluctantly decided on the Misses Birtwhistles' academy in Sloane Street as a passable, if temporary, distraction.

The Misses Birtwhistle took education seriously. They were both qualified and dedicated – intelligent, humorous spinsters trying to put ideas into their pupils' vapid little heads. It is recorded that during her eight months' schooling in Sloane Street Elizabeth won a literature prize, but otherwise, like most girls of her age, she undoubtedly giggled and bounced and stuffed herself with cream cakes and showed not the slightest interest in Girton or the intellectual development of her sex. Her eldest brother, the spitting image of his father, was nearly thirty; the next two, Jock and Fergus, were already in the army; Michael was up at Magdalen, Mary married to the 16th Baron Elphinstone – a good match. Twenty-three-year-old Rose was still at home, but she was a beauty and much occupied. Socially precocious, Elizabeth could be relied on to entertain distinguished old gentlemen like Lord Rosebery and Lord Curzon when they visited 20 St James's Square. She had already learned the knack of appearing to listen with sympathetic interest to crashing bores – 'the most astonishing child for knowing the right thing to say', a friend wrote to Cynthia Asquith. 'Had she been consciously rehearsing for her future she could hardly have practised her manners more assiduously.'[8]

School, in fact, was a waste of time. A temporary German governess, Fraulein Kathie Kuebler, was engaged to get the children through the Easter holidays in 1913, and, in 'Helen Cathcart's' words, 'Elizabeth stage-managed everything so admirably that Kathie ... agreed to stay as her permanent governess, taking over her entire teaching, from piano lessons to modern science.'[9] This was to be the extent of Elizabeth's education. Owing to Fraulein Kuebler's unhappy nationality the whole of it, modern science and all, was to be packed into less than eighteen months.

CHAPTER

3

'Never have the prospects for world peace been so bright. Never has the sky been more perfectly blue,' David Lloyd George, Chancellor of the Exchequer, declared on 1 January 1914. Such statements are always ominous. In fact, the war had been going on for some time. In the autumn of 1912 Serbia, Greece, Montenegro and Bulgaria had declared it on Turkey, who was already fighting it against the Italians in Tripoli. Making a hasty peace there, Turkey hurried home to declare it on Serbia and Bulgaria. Tsar Nicholas, one of King George's many cousins, took sides by sending a message of congratulation to King Peter on the successes of the Serbian army. Sir Edward Grey, the British Foreign Minister, said that the Powers could scarcely intervene unless requested by both Parties, though since there were half a dozen parties involved this seems unreasonable. Nevertheless, British battleships and destroyers were ordered to Turkish waters, just in case.

There were abortive Peace Conferences in St James's Palace: the war survived them. There were Imperial family get-togethers – George and Nicholas attended the wedding of their cousin Kaiser Wilhelm's daughter in Berlin, where George suspected that 'William's ear was glued to the keyhole' every time he and Nicholas tried to have a private chat.[1] There were diplomatic notes and ultimatums and blockades, and when the Turkish business seemed to be settled the war went on between the Balkan countries themselves. It was unstoppable, and sooner or later – or so it seemed to a few realists, if not to Lloyd George – Germany and Austro-Hungary would have to go to the defence of Turkey while Russia and her allies defended the Slav states.

By Christmas 1913 the Slavs hated each other. Everyone was out to get everyone else. In June 1914 Gustav Princip and his friend Cabrinovic, Bosnian Serb students who believed that a bullet in an Archduke was worth 10,000 casualties in war, were smuggled across the Drina from Belgrade equipped by the Serbian army with hand grenades and revolvers, and shot the Archduke Franz Ferdinand, heir to the throne of Austria, and his wife at Sarajevo.

Kaiser Wilhelm, racing at the Kiel Yachting Week, was very upset and went home to Berlin, but otherwise nothing much happened. King George and his son Bertie reviewed the fleet at Spithead as usual. M. Poincaré, the French President, was enjoying a series of brilliant State parties and preparing to visit St Petersburg. The Tsar was concerned with his son's illness, his wife pestering him to call in some crazy monk from the steppes. Glamis was getting ready for the Season, twenty-eight guest rooms to be polished as well as a dozen rooms for the ladies' maids in the service wing; the French chef was planning his menus, an army of local women scrubbing the blood-stains; the Monster twitched in its sleep, perhaps. Three and a half weeks of peace and quiet. Then on 23 July Austria-Hungary sent an ultimatum to Serbia charging her with tolerating terrorist propaganda against the Empire and accusing Serbian officers of planning the Sarajevo murders. The Emperor demanded that an inquiry, partially staffed by Austro-Hungarian officials, should be instituted forthwith. The time limit was forty-eight hours.

Serbia was reasonable, but stubborn, and offered to submit her case to the Hague Tribunal. On 26 July King George ominously cancelled his visit to Goodwood. On 28 July Franz Joseph declared war on Peter of Serbia. On 1 August Kaiser Wilhelm declared war on Tsar Nicholas. On 3 August Wilhelm declared war on M. Poincaré and marched into Belgium. On 4 August it was Elizabeth's fourteenth birthday. The family took her to the Coliseum to see Charles Hawtrey and Fedorovna, and the King wrote in his diary, 'I held a Council at 10.45 to declare war with Germany, it is a terrible catastrophe but it is not our fault ... the cheering was terrific'.[2]

* * *

There was no conscription, as in Germany and France, but any decent young man knew where his duty lay, and those who weren't so sure were soon shamed into it. The Bowes-Lyon boys and their contemporaries had no shadow of doubt. The three eldest sped back to their regiment; Michael abandoned Magdalen for the Royal Scots. David was only twelve (he was never to be a fighting man, anyway), and at Eton, where the Sixth Form soon dwindled to a few sickly intellectuals. The Glamis neighbours – the Dalhousies, Southesks, Butes, Monymusks, Douglases and Stuarts – became sonless almost overnight.

They did, however, gain a great many daughters-in-law. There was a lemming-like stampede to the altar. Fergus and Jock Bowes-Lyon were married within a fortnight of each other, one in Sussex and one (to a girl who sacrificed the name of Hepburn-Stuart-Forbes-Trefusis) in Scotland. One imagines first-class railway carriages full of slapdash bridesmaids and sniffling Mamas, all knitting against the clock. The clergy had never had it so good, turning out prospective widows every half an hour. The smaller jewellers ran out of stock of wedding rings, confetti was at a premium; no time for the niceties, just a brief collision to ensure an heir, then back to the barracks and to Mother.

Elizabeth later told Cynthia Asquith what she remembered of those suddenly purposeful days – 'the bustle of hurried visits to the chemists for outfits of every sort of medicine, and to the gunsmiths to buy all the things that people thought they wanted for a war, and found they didn't.'[3] It evokes a bizarre image of queues outside John Bell and Croydon and ladies staggering home with armfuls of rifles and ammunition. A week later, properly equipped, she and her mother set off for Glamis, leaving Rose to train as a nurse.

Glamis served as a hospital, and Elizabeth spent the next four years entertaining the troops with much success. Fraulein Kuebler had relinquished all hopes in the field of modern science and returned to Germany. She would have been pleased to know that her pupil passed the 'Oxford local' exam, presumably the School Certificate, or rough equivalent of O-level, but perhaps she was never told. An athletic Miss Boynard took over in the following spring. They played a great deal of tennis.

A young neighbour of the Strathmores, James Gray Stuart, third son of the 17th Earl of Moray, wrote an imaginative autobiography in the 1960s; as far as World War I is concerned, it seems safe to assume that his descriptions were largely accurate. 'I duly joined my battalion of the Royal Scots at Weymouth on 15 September,' he writes, 'and was happy to find a number of good friends from both Scotland and Eton among my comrades...'[4] They were toughened up on the parade ground for four months, route-marching round Portland Bill to harden their feet. 'It was a sketchy sort of training, but it was all we got and all there was time for.'[5] By the New Year of 1915 they were in the front line in Belgium. At Glamis, as in every other home in the kingdom, the main interest must have been in letters from overseas.

Those from the Bowes-Lyon sons and young Stuart are probably packed away in some attic or vault, but it isn't difficult, from other records, to deduce what they were like. Billy, the second son of the Duke of Buccleuch, wrote to his sister Alice that summer:

Dear Alice,
    You might let my father know that several articles arrived safely, viz 1 Fowl in tin; 2 tins of sardines; 3 tins of herrings; 1 tin of rolled ox tongue; many tins of cream cocoa etc, also such items as Dubbin.
    We live entirely on the tinned stuff from England as the only meat out here is pork and the ration beef is not very tempting.
    The asparagus is very good: but the best of all was the fowl in a tin.

What I particularly want is a tinned ham, or a big corned beef to have as a midday meal, and some *salad oil* or *mayonnaise sauce* would be very useful. Cakes are also very useful. In fact send the same as now only more. We have had a quiet time in the trenches with only a few casualties. I am only about 12-16 miles from Walter but cannot arrange to see him. Love from Billy.[6]

The Strathmores would have read *The Morning Post* and the discreet Scottish papers, so may at first have taken such letters at face value. The masses, who relied on news from Bert and Alf and the *Daily Express*, knew both more and less of the real truth: 'As they pressed forward to the attack they were suddenly swept by a diabolical fire from two machine-guns posted at either end of the German trench . . . In this zone no man could live. But . . . [they] . . . were men of grit. They did not stop. They got as far as the wire. They hacked at it, tore at it with their hands until they were raw and bleeding and their uniforms rent to tatters. From their starting point right up to the wire they left a deep lane of their dead and dying 120 yards long, a sight so poignant that men, coming suddenly on that bloody trail, broke down and wept at the sheer pity, the undying glory of it.'

Well-bred insouciance, sadistic jingoism, stupidity, courage, suffering, genocide – better, after all, to concentrate on young Lady Elizabeth among her wounded Tommies. There are many heart-warming descriptions of her life at this time – the sing-songs and whist, the way she wrote letters for them and bought their baccy at the village shop and asked them in 'that sweet quiet voice' 'How is your shoulder?', 'Do you sleep well?', 'Does it pain you?', 'Why are you not smoking your pipe?', 'Have you no tobacco?', 'You must tell me if you haven't and I'll get some for you' – a veritable phrasebook, she was, of the language of womanly concern. In fact, on the whole, she must have had a great time – with a score of lonely men to adore her, no competition, she would have been the envy of any teenaged girl. One day she dressed twelve-year-old David as a woman, in cloak, skirt, veils, furs and a becoming hat, and took him round the ward, introducing him as her cousin. He played his part with natural talent and they both much enjoyed the masquerade. Somehow that story seems the most significant of the Pollyanna tales.

In September 1915 Fergus came home on leave to spend his first wedding anniversary with his wife at Glamis, and to see his two-month-old daughter for the first time. He went back to France on Monday evening and was killed at the disastrously mismanaged Battle of Loos on Thursday. On the following Sunday the Revd J. Stirton's sermon at the parish church of Glamis was taken from John 14: 'I will not leave you comfortless; I will come to you. Yet a little while and the world seeth me no more; but ye see me; because I live, ye shall live also.' It is to be hoped that the comfort was not too long in coming, though the Almighty is notoriously dilatory in such matters. On 8 October the Glamis local paper, *Forfar Review and Advertiser*, published a long poem by one 'Walter C. Howdon':

> O brother mine, O comrade dead,
> O sunny-hearted son,
> What wreath shall crown your comely head
> When valour claims her own?
> Brother o' mine, twas ever yours
> To win the favoured goal;
> You had the courage that endures,
> The great all-conquering soul.
>
> Twas yours to join the great crusade,
> Twas mine to creep along;
> And while you flashed a radiant blade
> I spun an empty song.
> Twas yours to take the high lone road
> As mine to take the low,
> And the proud charger you bestrode
> Went where the God-led go.
>
> O brother mine, O comrade dead,
> O loyal-hearted son,
> What wreath more meet for your dear head
> Than the proud love you've won?
> And for your requiem ours to sing
> And that triumphantly –
> For you, O Death, where is thy sting?
> Grave, where thy victory?

While approving the sentiments, Lady Strathmore was unconvinced. She sensibly and quietly collapsed, leaving the running of the hospital and household to her daughter Rose, now a qualified nursing Sister, and the industrious Elizabeth. It was fairly strenuous, 'knitting, knitting, knitting . . . crumpling up tissue paper until it was so soft that it no longer crackled, to put in the lining of sleeping bags . . .'[7] Every morning, wearing little lace caps, Lady Strathmore and her youngest daughter prayed together in their private chapel. Elizabeth put her hair up and cut herself a whispy little fringe to complement the dewy, flirty eyes. If she was anything like a normal adolescent, the effect would, she hoped, make up for the fact that her legs were too short and plump. In truth, if photographs are anything to go by – and in those days they all had a strange, probably deceptive magic – Lady Elizabeth Bowes-Lyon was a tease, and very fetching in what looked like outfits from the local rummage sale – an Orphan Annie whose Daddy was worth well over £100,000 a year.

Fund-raising for the Red Cross, running the local Girl Guide company, strawberries and cream at Eton, champagne and white chiffon for Rose's wedding at St James's Piccadilly (Elizabeth and David gave the bride four silver toast racks and Venetia James parted with a Venetian mirror that had probably seen better days. Lady Sackville made do with a stamp-damper); Michael reported killed, and three months later found to be a prisoner – general rejoicing. It had at last been officially recognized that this was no gentleman's war. Heroes must be conscripted, even butlers and footmen and chauffeurs, unless they were mentally or physically deficient. The plight of the average Lady was piteous, 'There are only two housemaids,' Cynthia Asquith complained, 'so we can only have breakfast and tea in.'[8]

Still, the situation abroad was pretty grim too. The Battle of the Somme was an experience Jamie Stuart, and tens of thousands more, would never forget. At some places the Allies advanced seven miles; in others, not an inch. For these seven miles the British lost 420,000 young men and the French more than 200,000; German losses were given as 450,000,[9] but the equation was still rocky. America had joined in after nearly three years of shilly-shallying, but on the other hand Russia had more or less retired in order to have a Revolution. The terribly unfair thing, to a young girl just entering the marriage market, was that casualties were about three times heavier among junior officers than among common soldiers. The prospects as Elizabeth approached her eighteenth birthday seemed bleak.

The war ended in November 1918 exactly as it had begun, with cheering crowds and brass bands and balcony appearances and lumps in the throat. Perhaps the demonstrations were a little less sunny. A. J. P. Taylor writes that 'omnibuses were seized, and people in strange garments caroused on the open upper deck. A bonfire heaped against the plinth of Nelson's column in Trafalgar Square has left its mark to this day. Total strangers copulated in doorways and on pavements ... The celebrations ran on with increasing wildness for three days, when the police finally intervened and restored order.'[10] It is improbable that Elizabeth and her friends witnessed these Rabelaisian scenes; but there would be Victory balls and dances to look forward to, even if it wasn't easy to dance with a man with only three limbs, and she was determined to make the most of it. 'Elizabeth Lyon is out now, and Cecilia has had a dance for her,' wrote Lady Buxton to a friend, adding with a sigh, 'How many hearts Elizabeth will break.'[11]

CHAPTER

4

Albert Frederick Arthur George, the second son of George, Duke of
York and Princess Mary of Teck, was born on 14 December 1895 at
York Cottage, Sandringham. The only error his father made was not
to time things better. It was the thirty-fourth anniversary of the death
of the Prince Consort and the seventeenth anniversary of the death of
Princess Alice, a day dedicated to mourning at Windsor. George
waited anxiously for a reprimand, but although 'Gan-gan' Victoria let
it be known that she was 'rather distressed that this happy event
should have taken place on a darkly sad anniversary',[1] she bravely
looked on the bright side and gave the infant a bust of his sanctified
great-grandfather as a christening present. The ceremony went off
without a hitch, apart from one-year-old Prince Edward bursting into
howls of jealousy or boredom or prescient grief and having to be
removed to the vestry.

Some extraordinary combination of Teck and Wettin mixed with a
brew of Saxe-Coburg-Gothas and Wurttemburgs and Schleswig-
Holstein-Sonderburg-Glucksburgs had produced the exquisite
changeling Edward, known as David. Born a year later, his brother
Albert, known as Bertie, was to become a knock-kneed, stammering
second-best, with a chronic digestive complaint and an uncontrollable
temper. As a baby, he was stuck up on top of a pillar by Cosmo
Gordon Lang, who sourly remarked that the child 'was evidently not
accustomed to such robust amusement'.[2] Shortly after this terrifying
experience, his position in the family was made even more awkward
by the birth of a much-longed-for girl, Mary. The wretched Bertie
seemed doomed to a lifetime of vertigo in high places and mediocrity
everywhere else.

These children seldom saw their parents. On Bertie's fifth birthday
he received a letter from his father: 'Now that you are five years old, I
hope you will always try & be obedient & do at once what you are
told, as you will find it will come much easier to you the sooner you
begin. I always tried to do this when I was your age & found it made
me much happier.'[3] Presumably Bertie could read by then, and found
this a normal birthday greeting. It's all there was, anyway, unless he

was lucky enough to be staying with his grandparents. At Marl-borough House or Sandringham or Balmoral the indulgence and affection and fun were more than the repressed little boy could cope with. He became unruly, intoxicated by kisses and kind words, impossible to manage. The visits were curtailed, and the two elder boys turned over to an ex-footman called Frederick Finch. 'It was Finch who attended to their clothes and saw that they themselves were personally clean. It was Finch who heard their prayers morning and evening, and who tucked them up in bed, and it was Finch also who, when occasion demanded, administered condign chastisement upon their small persons.'[4] Luckily, they were both devoted to him. The 'handsome, stalwart, muscular'[5] Finch was the nearest thing to a natural parent they had ever known.

Even Finch, however, favoured the charismatic David and would later become his valet (concocting the 'pitiless remedy' for his young master's first hangover),[6] and then his butler. Very few people preferred Bertie. Among them, curiously enough, was Grandpa Edward, who wrote him countless encouraging notes beginning 'My dearest little Bertie',[7] and Lady Airlie, Princess May's lady-in-waiting: 'He made his first shy overture to me at Easter 1902 . . . when he presented me with an Easter card. It was his own work, and very well done for a child of six – a design of spring flowers and chicks, evidently cut out from a magazine, coloured in crayons, and pasted on cardboard. He was so anxious for me to receive it in time for Easter that he decided to deliver it in person. He waylaid me one morning when I came out of his mother's boudoir, but at the last moment his courage failed him, and thrusting the card into my hand without a word he darted away . . . When I succeeded later in gaining his confidence he talked to me quite normally, without stammering, and then I found that far from being backward he was an intelligent child, with more force of character than anyone suspected in those days.'[8] Mabell Airlie, a remarkable woman, was thirty-six at the time, a year older than Bertie's mother but an altogether more accessible character. She was a great friend of the then Lady Glamis. It would be nice to think that little Bertie sought refuge in her company.

But unlikely. He did not often brave his mother's boudoir, and had just come under the rule of his first tutor, Mr Hansell, a conscientious and high-minded person who would have disapproved of the six-year-old Prince dallying with the ladies. With the best will in the world, Mr Hansell set about teaching the left-handed child that left-handedness was a mortal sin, and showing his grieved disapproval when the stammer became worse. 'The work in simple division sums is most disheartening,' Mr Hansell reported, after he had been doing his best for a year. 'I really thought we had mastered division by 3 but division by 2 seems to be quite beyond [Prince Albert] now.' Six months later, 'I am very sorry to say that Prince Albert has caused two painful scenes in his bedroom this week. On the second occasion I understand that he narrowly escaped giving his brother a very severe kick, it being absolutely unprovoked & Finch being engaged in helping Prince Edward at the time.'[9] Bertie was caught in a vicious circle. The more he laboured to use his right hand and save his soul, the more inarticulate and stupid he became; the more stupid and inarticulate he became, the more his father upbraided him and his brothers and sister mocked; the more inferior and ridiculous he felt, the more obstreperous he was, raging and weeping at the slightest set-back or, almost worse, shouting and crashing about with manic exuberance, demonstrating something that his locked tongue couldn't say.

And yet, as Mabell Airlie discovered, the left-handed child who was trying to get out had a very modest, sensible attitude to life. Bertie's knees were the next target. (David had excellent knees.) Sir Francis Laking, Bt, GCVO, KCB, MD, devised a system of splints into which the child was strapped for certain periods during the day and, for a time, all night. 'This is an experiment,' Bertie wrote to his mother who, of course, was not at home. 'I am sitting in an armchair with my legs in the new splints . . . I have got an invalid table, which is splendid for reading but rather awkward for writing at present. I expect I shall get used to it.'[10]

His knees, in fact, improved. Nothing else did. He continued to let Mr Hansell down, and to burst into furious tears when presented with a simple equation. 'You must really give up losing your temper when you make a mistake in a sum,' wrote his father with a sort of bewildered concern. 'We all make mistakes sometimes, remember now you are nearly 12 years old & ought no longer to behave like a little child of 6.'[11] Somehow, this final admonishment worked. It seems incredible, but Bertie passed his Osborne examinations and entered the Royal Naval College in January 1909. David was already in his last term and the rigid etiquette of the school forbade him to be seen in the company of a new boy, even that of his own brother;[12] it was the first time Bertie had lived among other boys, let alone slept with them. His stammer was appalling, he was terrified, clumsy, and dreadfully homesick. After six months he caught whooping cough.

This would not seem such a remarkable event in the life of a normal fourteen-year-old. Bertie, however, after his whoops had been attended by the assistant medical officer of the College, one Surgeon-Lieutenant Louis Greig, was considered to need a long convalescence. For over three months the boy lived entirely on his own – apart from Finch to see to his socks and a Mr Watt to keep up the relentless tutoring – on an estate ten miles from Balmoral. What puzzled them was that he showed no signs of loneliness or boredom. A few Scottish miles to the south the Bowes-Lyon boys were racketing round the countryside and Elizabeth doing her royal impersonation. A few miles north and east and west children were working on trawlers and dressing up in their mothers' old clothes and being taken to America on sailing ships and putting in a ten-hour day in the shipyards and even – some of them – going to school. All Bertie wanted, then as later, was to be left in peace to shoot and fish and be cock of his own walk across the heather. Under these conditions his stammer became little more than a hesitation, the tension slackened; he was even happy.

His grandfather died the following year. There was now the added strain of being the King's son, and Bertie's place in his class at Osborne plummetted from bad to worse. 'My dear boy this will not do,' wrote his father desperately, 'if you go on like this you will be bottom of your Term ... It will be a great bore, but if I find that you have not worked well at the end of this term, I shall have to get a master for you to work with all the holidays & you will have no fun at all. Now remember, everything rests with you, & you are quite intelligent & can do very well if you like ...'[13] In vain. Bertie's final position in the term was 68th out of 68.

How he got into Dartmouth on these results is a mystery. His first term there was interrupted by measles, which necessitated another long convalescence at the Headlands Hotel, Newquay, under the supervision of Mr Hansell; his second by his father's Coronation. At the end of that term Bertie was placed 67th out of 68. Still, it was an improvement. Two years later, perhaps out of grim determination rather than aptitude, he passed out of Dartmouth in 61st place out of only 67 examinees, with a reference that stated he was 'quite unspoiled and a nice honest, clean-minded and excellent mannered boy'.[14] It was, perhaps, more than he had dared to hope for.

Bertie was now seventeen, an age at which, had he been a girl, he would have been beginning a strict training for marriage. The thought must have shuddered across his mind occasionally. Apart from his own inclinations, whatever they were, he was a Royal stallion and would have to be put out to stud sooner or later. It is hard to imagine what his sexual education could have been – probably a dutiful warning from Mr Hansell about the dangers of masturbation and homosexuality, vaguely mixed up with the Virgin birth and the habits of bees and the necessity of taking cold baths in emergencies. Even David at this time was diffident and socially immature, but his looks were so startling and in such contradiction to his exalted position as Prince of Wales that women were already staring and sighing and longing to touch the fragile manikin. Bertie was handsome enough, but unlike the precocious Lord David Cecil he was terrified of girls, particularly those surrounded by bevies of adorers. At the various balls which were given for the naval cadets when they were in Quebec nothing would induce him to dance; he dug himself into a corner and stayed there.

The Navy was the last career Bertie would have chosen for himself. Apart from being paralysed with shyness in every port, he suffered dreadfully from seasickness and disliked sailing. However, it did get him away from home, and there was a lot to broaden the mind and loosen the joints. By 24 November 1913 he was writing in his diary that he had danced nearly every dance at Lord Kitchener's ball in Alexandria and didn't get to bed until 3 a.m.[15] He was also coming into contact with the common people, an experience most necessary to Royal training: 'Last night I went to a ball given by the Municipality, which was a very funny affair,' he wrote to his mother from Toulon. 'There were 6000 guests, and it was in a theatre. There was no room to dance and you could not move at all. All the guests were ordinary people in the town and most of them got drunk at supper. I went away very early.'[16]

The Archduke Franz Ferdinand was shot at Sarajevo, but, like the rest of the world, the young midshipman took little notice. His remote relatives were constantly being assassinated, and although it was deplorable – 'What a good thing it was he was killed by the crowd' he had written to his father, after the lynching of 'one of these beastly anarchists' who had tried to kill the King of Italy[17] – it was not actually a case for mourning, as with poor Uncle Willy of Greece, who had been shot that spring while out for his morning stroll in Salonika. Fifty girls from Rodean visited Bertie's ship one afternoon, and they had a tea-dance.[18] A month later, Bertie carefully wrote in his diary, 'I got up at 11.45 and kept middle watch until 4.0. War was declared between us and Germany at 2 a.m. I turned in again at 4.0 till 7.15 . . . Papa sent a most interesting telegram to the fleet. I put it down in words.'[19]

Apart from whooping cough and measles and seasickness, Bertie's health seems to have been better during these years than it had been when he was small. Three weeks after the declaration of war, he was attacked by violent pains in the stomach and had great difficulty breathing. The *Rohilla* was recalled from active service in the North Sea to take him to Aberdeen, where he was operated on for appendicitis. After three months' convalescence, when he was due to rejoin his ship, the pain recurred. With everyone else occupied, he hung about, trailing from Sandringham to Buckingham Palace and back again, miserably depressed and no use to anybody. They gave him a job in the Admiralty, but it was only a sinecure and he had nothing to do. David had already succeeded in getting himself sent overseas. 'What does it matter if I'm killed?', he had demanded of Kitchener. 'I have four brothers.'*[20] He was dashing about boosting morale and being consulted by French generals. Bertie's morale was lower than it had ever been.

At last he was allowed to return to sea, though forbidden to play football or hockey or to do any gymnastic exercises. Three months later the pain came back. He was transferred to a hospital ship for observation and the doctors sadly concluded that Prince Albert was unfit for active service. Such a humiliating and indeed unthinkable idea had never occurred to King George. He was horrified. '. . . the idea of the Prince's not being allowed to proceed into action with his ship would prey on his mind and undo all the good effects of his treatment,' Lord Stamfordham wrote to His Majesty's passionate dictation. 'Therefore HM cannot agree to Dr Sutton's sugges-tion . . . the King would prefer to run the risk of Prince Albert's health suffering than that he should endure the bitter and lasting disappoint-ment of not being in his ship in the battle line.'[21]

But in spite of what amounted to an order, Bertie was unable to get better. His complaint had been diagnosed as caused by the weakening of the muscular wall of the stomach and a consequent catarrhal con-dition; the treatment was a quiet life, careful dieting, and an enema every night,[22] all of which would have been hard to provide in the middle of a naval battle. He was transferred to yet another hospital ship and, inevitably, finished up on the Balmoral estate in the care of the perennial Mr Hansell and a naval doctor. He did not return to sea until the following May, by which time almost half the war was over.

Bertie was, however, to have one moment of glory. At 2 p.m. on Wednesday, 31 May 1916 he was in the sick-bay of the *Collingwood* 'in a state of acute depression'.[23] Suddenly he heard shouts of 'Action!' and 'Full speed ahead!' He leaped out of his hammock and scrambled to his turret, where he stayed until 9 p.m. and the Battle of Jutland was over. 'When I was on top of the turret,' he wrote afterwards to David, 'I never felt any fear of shells or anything else. It seems curious but all sense of danger and everything else goes except the one longing to deal death in every possible way to the enemy.'[24]

'In a single summer afternoon,' states Prince Albert's biographer, 'he had passed into the full dignity of manhood.' Whatever that means, Bertie was certainly tremendously excited by the experience. 'In a war on such a scale as this,' he told David, with the wisdom of a veteran, 'of course we must have casualties and lose ships & men, but there is no need for everyone at home to bemoan their loss when they

* The fourth brother was Prince John, who was ten years old at the time and an epileptic.

are proud to die for their country. They don't know what war is, several generations have come and gone since the last great battles.'[25] Prince Albert was among those officers commended for their services by Admiral Sir John Jellicoe in his dispatch. His health improved quite dramatically. 'Though his food that evening and night was of an unusual description,' Captain Ley wrote to King George, 'I am glad to tell your Majesty that he has been quite well since and *looks* quite well again!'[26]

Three months later Bertie was back at Windsor suffering from a duodenal ulcer. The doctors, as usual, prescribed a prolonged period of rest. He rested until the following May, his only excitements being a trip in a submarine on the Solent and receiving the Order of the Garter from his father. ('I cannot thank you enough for having made me a Knight of the Garter. I feel very proud to have it, and will always try to live up to it,' Bertie wrote. 'I am glad you say you will try & live up to the Garter,' the King replied.)[27] Back to sea for another three months, then back to Windsor for more rest and quiet. Even Bertie began to see the endlessly repeating pattern. Surgeon-Lieutenant Louis Greig from Osborne had turned up again, and in spite of the fact that he was now second surgeon on the battleship *Malaya* strings had been pulled to send him home with Bertie. Perhaps it was he who sensibly persuaded the Prince to give up the Navy. In any case, with considerable courage Bertie wrote to his father that he felt that he was not fit for service at sea. During four years of what he considered to be his country's heroic struggle he had managed to stay afloat for twenty-two months.

The operation performed at the end of November 1917, though two years overdue, appeared to be successful, and by the beginning of 1918 Bertie and Dr Greig ('He is a perfect topper')[28] were moved to the Royal Naval Air Service, pending its amalgamation with the RAF. A fortnight before the Armistice they were posted to General Trenchard's staff at the Headquarters of the RAF at Autigny. Bertie was in France at last, albeit nowhere near the front line. In what sounds like a desperate effort to assert himself again, he immediately started pontificating. 'General Trenchard won't allow anybody to talk about peace here,' he informed his father only a few days before the final shot was fired. 'I have never seen a man more engrossed in his command ... He fairly keeps everybody up to their work.'[29] Unfortunately there was very little work left. Bertie and Greig found themselves staying peacefully and comfortably at the British Embassy in Paris, waiting to be told what to do.

They were sent, as we shall see, to Brussels. Immediately after that, George himself visited France and took both his elder sons on a tour of the battlefields, war cemeteries and devastated villages. It was decided that Bertie should remain in France for a while, in case the relatives of those who had been proud to die for their country should start asking awkward questions. 'Bertie can be of far more use in this way than sitting in England where he has spent most of the war not that this was his fault!!', David scribbled to his mother. 'But by remaining with the armies till peace is signed he will entirely erase any of the unfair questions some nasty people asked last year as to what he was doing you will remember.'[30] Undoubtedly Queen Mary did remember. She was feeling very distressed by the death of her youngest son, 'poor darling little Johnnie', and wished David would come home instead of planning to 'rush about' the world, which would only make it harder for him to settle down when the time came. Harry seemed steady enough, but she had to confess she found him extremely dull. Bertie's health was a constant worry. George, in his first year at Dartmouth, was the only son with whom she was quite satisfied. If only she could find suitable wives to take them all off her hands. In the meanwhile, sending Christmas greetings to Bertie at Spa in Belgium, she would have recalled that it was once the most fashionable spa in Europe and that many of her relatives had benefited greatly from the efficacy of its waters.

CHAPTER

5

James Stuart, last seen on the Belgian front in 1914, had survived the war to become a Brigade Major MC (with bar). This he seems to have achieved by strolling about No-Man's-Land unarmed ('I couldn't be bothered carrying arms')[1] and using his own initiative when given orders that were 'too boring' to obey. In November 1918 he was keeping a military eye on Brussels and having a good time. There, according to his autobiography, he was detailed to keep the Prince of Wales and Prince Albert amused in their spare time when they arrived for the Belgian victory celebrations. In spite of the years of devastation, restaurants in Brussels served magnificent food and the Burgundy was excellent. Stuart recalls that they took a couple of pipers with them to 'The Merry Grill' and Highland flung on the dance floor, presumably careening back to the Palace in the small hours. 'We had a great deal of fun,' he writes succinctly.

His memory, however, is incorrect. One good time, after all, is much like another, and possibly he and David had done their share of painting Brussels red during the war years. But the Prince of Wales was now attached to the headquarters staff of the Canadian Corps and had duties, according to his father, that he must not neglect. For the first time it was Bertie alone who was chosen for the limelight, and it must have been for Bertie alone that the pipers played. 'The entry into Brussels went off very well today,' Prince Albert wrote to his father. 'I met the King and Queen outside the town this morning and rode in with them. The King told me how delighted he was that you had sent me to represent you. I rode on his right side.'[2] There is no trace of a hangover, or of David. As Stuart was to write that he found Bertie 'not an easy man to know or handle', whatever fun there was must have been a little strained.

However, Louis Greig, by now Bertie's constant companion and mentor, was something of a hero to Jamie, having been Scotland's rugby captain at one time. His presence must have made the chore of entertaining the Prince somewhat easier. Greig's rôle of Royal Nanny was exhausting and time-consuming, whatever affection and loyalty he felt towards his difficult charge, and he may already have been on the look-out for some assistance. Greig's greatest ambition was to 'put steel into' Prince Albert.[3] Jamie's courage, his war record and his *savoir-faire* were just what was needed. Major Stuart, who seemed to have no particular plans for his future, might come in very useful.

Meanwhile, Jamie went home to Edinburgh to read law and play golf and lead the life of an eligible young bachelor in Scottish society. Elizabeth, 'a noticeable debutante' said Lord David Cecil with remarkable restraint, who dressed 'picturesquely, unfashionably'[4] – she was given to wearing sunbonnets and homespun skirts – was also doing the seasonal rounds. She was at Ascot, and probably gave her little wave to Princess Mary in the Royal Box, quickly assessing her 'sweet frock of filmy georgette, with touches of the pale blue that is so becoming to our blue-eyed Princess' and the 'large hat of white crinoline straw with one large pink rose reposing on the brim'.[5] Some biographers believe that she popped into the Palace from time to time to dance to Mary's gramophone. Be that as it may, she was having a wonderful time. 'All the men were at her feet,'[6] says Lady Longford, and her feet were twinkling and *chassé*-ing in most of the exclusive ballrooms south and north of the border.

Dancing was no longer a formal pastime. It was a way of life, and Elizabeth was very good at it. You could dance through lunch, through tea, through dinner, and on until breakfast. You could dance in clubs and pubs and restaurants, on roof tops and river boats and trains. It was a kind of energetic, extended foreplay, all the healthy exercise of sex with none of its unpleasantness. Self-styled moralists thundered their outrage at the 'Twinkle' and the 'Missouri Walk', the 'Elfreda', the 'Jog Trot' and the 'Shimmy'. The music, in fact, was brazenly innocent, 'heavily punctuated, relentless rhythm, with drums, rattles, bells, whistles, hooters and twanging banjoes'.[7] Of course anything could be done with the tango, and often was, but the Blues, with its disturbing, wailing melodies, was still to come; so were the tribal dances of the Bright Young Things, the Charleston and the Black Bottom.

Prince Albert was a nifty dancer, almost as agile on the ballroom floor as he was on the tennis court. Since so few facts are known about Elizabeth's success at this time in breaking hearts, some romantically minded biographers have assumed or hoped that they came to know each other while they were both, so to speak, on the trot in 1919 and early 1920. Bertie was a Squadron Leader in the RAF and a token undergraduate at Trinity, Cambridge, during that winter. With his elder brother out of the country for four months in 1919 and seven months in 1920, he was also called upon to do a number of royal chores. While it could not be said that these employed him for 247 days a year, 8 hours a day, give or take the odd Bank Holiday, he was reasonably busy. Elizabeth was delightfully occupied with a dozen flirtations, more and less serious. While they must have seen each other occasionally – an awkward acknowledgment from Bertie, a cool flutter of eyelashes from Elizabeth – they had little in common. She was probably less aware of Bertie than she was of David, Prince of Wales, whose name was on every girl's lips and in every mother's dreams. He was being seen everywhere with Mrs Freda Dudley Ward, but it was well known that she was *persona non grata* with the King and Queen and such a liaison couldn't possibly last. What was it about Freda that attracted him? None of them could understand it, they said. That the very qualities which made Elizabeth 'irresistible to men'[8] were those that made her so resistible to the Prince of Wales may have rankled a little, even then.

She was small, wistful, yielding, an instinctive mistress of the arts and crafts that please. '. . . mildly flirtatious in a very proper romantic old-fashioned Valentine sort of way . . . She makes every man feel chivalrous and gallant towards her,[9] wrote Chips Channon. She was, the highest accolade at that time, dainty.* Her contemporaries might crop their hair and drink Sidecars and smoke De Reszke cigarettes and fling their silk-stockinged legs about, but all they got for it was a slap on the back and the endearment 'good sport', 'ripper', even 'good chap'. Elizabeth, though she would have been shocked at the familiarity, was pattable, a pet, a positive darling. The young men in her circle, back from the stench and squalor of the trenches, wanted nothing better. 'I was madly in love with her. Everything at Glamis was beautiful, perfect. Being there was like living in a Van Dyke picture . . . I fell *madly* in love. They all did.'[10]

We don't know, of course, who wrote this, any more than we can be sure of the identity of the suitor who serenaded her by cracking his hunting whip under her window half the night. 'What a happy group we were,' Channon sighed. 'Paul . . . Gage and me, the Queen, others . . .'[11] There are a good many dots and gaps, and a great deal of editing. The young men crowded round her in the photographs are now dead, and probably their grandchildren would be unable to recognize their kilted or tweeded figures, moustached, jaunty, wrinkling their eyes against the sun. We could, however, identify James Stuart. Like his ancestor the bonny Earl of Moray, he looked 'a braw gallant'. Unfortunately his evidence, as we know, is unreliable. Since

* OD: choice morsel. *The Lady*, in a single issue during 1919, lists Dainty dance frocks at Peter Robinsons, Dainty tea frocks at Debenham and Freebody's, Dainty dishes, recipes for, Dainty sewing for odd moments, Dainty trifles for Odds & Ends, Dainty voile frocks for warmer days, Dainty wear for Nursery Folk, Dainties for Invalids, Dainty lingerie, the Daintie Hair Net and the Daintiness of Aertex Cellular Clothing.

he has been almost completely overlooked by previous biographers, it is necessary to read between his lines in order to understand the sequence of events in Elizabeth's life over the next three years.

★   ★   ★

Early in 1920, in James Stuart's own words, 'my whole life changed. I was asked by Louis Greig to come to London to see him. Prince Albert had gone to Cambridge after the war and the suggestion was that I should join him there about a month before he came down and started his official career. I was to be his first Equerry. Such a thought had never entered my head.'[12] If he did join Bertie at Cambridge, he forgets to mention it in his autobiography. By the beginning of May, however, cross and lonely and not a little homesick, Jamie was installed on the schoolroom floor of Buckingham Palace along with Mary, Harry, and his new 'master'.

Elizabeth was also in London that May, which must have been a compensation. On the 20th, Lord and Lady Farquhar gave a ball at 7 Grosvenor Square to which Prince Albert, and, naturally, his equerry, were invited. Among the other guests were Lord and Lady Annaly, chaperoning 'the youngest Strathmore girl'. Perhaps Jamie and Elizabeth danced together sufficiently often for Bertie to take notice. Long afterwards, he told Lady Airlie 'that he had fallen in love that evening, although he did not realize it until later'. There is no convincing evidence that he even asked Elizabeth for a foxtrot, with or without twinkle.★

At the beginning of June Bertie was made Baron Killarney, Earl of Inverness and Duke of York in the Birthday Honours List. ('I must write and thank you again ever so very much for having made me Duke of York,' he wrote to his father, '. . . and I hope I shall live up to it in every way.') Almost more encouraging, he and Louis Greig won the finals of the RAF Doubles Competition at Wimbledon. Bertie must have been in a sunny mood. Quite suddenly, with no reasonable explanation whatever, we find him visiting St Paul's Walden Bury and 'basking' in Elizabeth's 'radiant vitality'.[13]

The theory seems to be either that Prince Albert unaccountably remembered that he was 'a friend of her many brothers',[14] or that Elizabeth's 'close friendship' with his sister Mary somehow brought these visits about. Bertie's friendship with the Bowes-Lyon brothers

---

★ James Stuart writes in his autobiography (p 57) that he introduced Elizabeth to Bertie at the Royal Air Force Ball at the Ritz in the summer of 1921. This cannot be correct, as Bertie had already visited Glamis in October 1920. Stuart's claim that he introduced them is equally unlikely – Bertie certainly knew who she was, if only through her acquaintance with his sister Mary. I therefore rely on John Wheeler-Bennett's *George VI* and Elizabeth Longford's *Queen Mother* (p 18) for my dates.

has not been mentioned anywhere else. He never went to school; none of them were up at Cambridge with him; their careers had been totally different; of the surviving three sons, only Michael was an approximate contemporary. As for Princess Mary, while she and Elizabeth were certainly acquainted on a basis of juvenile thés-dansants, society weddings and a mutual enthusiasm for the Girl Guides, 'close friendships' are not indulged in by the Royal Family.★ There is nothing to indicate that, as children or young women, they ever visited each other's homes, and certainly they never went out alone together. Added to this, Lord and Lady Strathmore were by no means enamoured of Royalty; he had thoroughly disapproved of the Prince of Wales's dissipation back at the turn of the century and always swore that 'if there is one thing I have determined for my children, it is that they shall never have any post about the Court';[15] she, disgusted by the rapaciousness of some society hostesses, had been heard to murmur, 'Some people, dear, have to be fed royalty like sea-lions with fish.'[16] They were not the sort to invite Prince Albert for the weekend on the strength of a brief meeting at the Farquhars' dance.

Prince Albert's equerry, on the other hand, was an old friend. If Bertie had fancied Elizabeth at the Farquhars', and learned that Jamie was going to stay, what more natural than to take advantage of it? An equerry cannot refuse a command however reluctant he may be. That Bertie 'basked' at St Paul's Walden Bury may be true. What Captain James Stuart and Lady Elizabeth thought about it is not known.

The exodus to Scotland took place as usual, the Strathmores to Glamis, Bertie to the Ancasters at Drummond Castle. By the end of August all the Royals were at Balmoral except David, steaming towards Honolulu on HMS *Renown*, and Mary, who was staying with Lady Airlie at Cortachy Castle. Jamie rather enjoyed Balmoral, even if he did have to dance with the Queen at the Ghillies Ball and play golf on a course that more closely resembled a hayfield.[17] Of course he went over to Glamis; and inevitably he took the now eager Duke with him. Elizabeth made the best of it. One evening, according to one biographer, there was a dance, and Elizabeth wore 'a rose brocade Van Dyke dress with pearls in her hair'.[18] She may have been in love, but not, I think, with Bertie.

Shortly after this the Duke of York and his brother Harry went south for the required round of country house visits, which consisted of shooting a great many birds and inspecting the indigenous

★ 'You are right to be civil & friendly to the young girls you may occasionally meet, & to see them sometimes – but *never* make *friendships*; girls' friendships and intimacies are very bad & often lead to great mischief ... Besides ... you are so many of yourselves that you *want no one* else.' Letter from Queen Victoria to her seventeen-year-old granddaughter, Princess Victoria, 8 December 1880.

debutantes. They were entertained by Miss Edwina Ashley at her grandfather's shoot near Newbury and by the Pembrokes at Wilton, where 'the lovely Bath girl, Lady Mary Thynne, *and* the youngest and only unmarried Cadogan girl'[19] were among the guests. Meanwhile Jamie kicked his heels at Balmoral and visited Glamis as much as he could. The *Tatler* for 27 October 1920 contains a picture taken during the lunch interval at a Glamis Shoot in which Elizabeth, wearing a baggy tweed coat and skirt, embroidered jumper and sensible felt hat, looks demure; Jamie, even tweedier, stalwart; Miss Elizabeth Cator of Woodbiswick (a friend from the distant Birtwhistle days) is engulfed in a kind of blown-up bowler, and Lady Strathmore wears a magnificently unsuitable black feathered helmet. The rest of them, Captain and Miss Malcolm, Mary and Lord Elphinstone and Lord Strathmore, have the uneasy look of people unaccustomed to the camera. For some reason – perhaps to be on the safe side – there is an individual snap of Jamie which shows him smiling behind his pipe, his flat cap giving him a comfortably squirarchal air – a man, one feels, who finds everything going his way and is enjoying it.

★   ★   ★

With the migration of those wild geese that had survived the season's slaughter everyone moved south. The castles and country houses were left empty except for servants and factors and major-domos. Armies of carpenters, plumbers, masons, painters and upholsterers moved in to repair the damage; gunsmiths oiled and polished; poachers set about stocking up their cottage larders with the 'rubbish' – exhausted stags, wounded rabbits – that remained. The lease of 20 St James's Square having lapsed, the Strathmores took possession of 17 Bruton Street, off Berkeley Square. The Prince of Wales was home again, which added a *frisson* of excitement to dances and dinners. The Twenties were in their infancy, but there was change in the wind already: new sounds, new experiences, with any luck a new life. The *jeunesse dorée* glittered by Royal Command.

The more decorous aristocratic circles, to which the Strathmores belonged, followed the prescribed circuit of charity lunches and charity balls and sales of needlework. 'There are, it seems,' wrote *The Lady* with a sob in her throat, '4,600 little souls (Waifs and Strays) being cared for at the moment and what do you think it would cost to buy them two handkerchiefs each? I am sure you would never guess! £115! But it just gives one some little idea of what it must cost to keep the tiny folk in other things.' Handkerchiefs for the Waifs and Strays was a good enough cause for a fancy dress party or a smallish dance, or for girlfriends to get together and eat prodigious amounts of trifle and cream cakes, when the gossip would concern the Duke of Westminster's new bride: 'My dear, you know what she was wearing? Brown spats!'; and the extraordinary case of Miss Radclyffe Hall appearing in court in men's clothes: 'He'd accused her of coming between him and his wife! Well, I don't see *how*, do you? She does look very odd, but after all . . .' and the latest rumours of marriage plans, which concerned them greatly. The humiliation of going through one's second season unmarried was too dreadful to contemplate; at the third, one would be forced to flee to India, or worse. The heady business of being adored by the few young men who were left was all the more intoxicating for being so brief. They were butterflies preening themselves in the last patch of sunlight, anxious to be caught before dark.

Elizabeth, we are told, had no such fears. Much has been written about her high standards and the seriousness with which, at twenty, she regarded the marriage vows. She would only commit herself, it is said, to a man who was kind and brave, unswervingly loyal and honest, unimpeachably virtuous and deeply religious. 'There was one immensely attractive man, the son of a neighbour, who kept on trying. But he also had flirtations in between, and she wouldn't have that . . . More than any of her friends she knew what she really wanted and that was absolute purity.'[20] Anyone, short of the Prince Consort of blessed memory, would have had a hard time living up to such expectations.

A more plausible reason for rejecting all the suitors who clamoured to bestow on her their considerable worldly goods was that she was already in love. Then why didn't she say so? Perhaps there were unusual complications. Perhaps Lady Strathmore had begun to have different ideas. Elizabeth seems to have lacked all the normal instincts for rebellion, or anyway for expressing them. Instead, she resorted to passive resistance, which in a few years would take the form of minor illnesses whenever a crisis loomed. This was made much easier if she refused to recognize that anything difficult or unpleasant was happening. With luck, things would sort themselves out without involving her. And so they did, though not quite in the way she expected.

Bertie had now seen enough of her to be catastrophically in love, and unable to keep quiet about it. His equerry must have had some trying moments. Queen Mary was delighted, though cautious. 'I have discovered that he is very much attracted to Lady Elizabeth Bowes-Lyon,' she told Mabell Airlie while they were taking a drive one afternoon. 'He's always talking about her. She seems a charming girl but I don't know her very well.' Mabell understood immediately. She replied that she had known Elizabeth all her life, and could say nothing but good of her.[21] No more was needed. The two ladies drove on, bright-eyed and smiling under their toques.

CHAPTER

6

That Christmas at St Paul's Walden Bury was the usual riot of innocent fun – brothers and sisters and in-laws, nephews and nieces, unattached guests with no home to go to and guests who hoped to consider the Bury as home. Elizabeth entertained by singing popular songs with the words adapted to suit the personalities and idiosyncracies of the company;[1] she could do a lot with 'And her mother came too' and 'Ma, he's making eyes at me' but may have been stumped by 'Look for the silver lining'. Her favourites, of course, came from the music-hall, and a spirited rendering of 'My old man said follow the van' would have been the high spot of the evening. According to his book, Jamie too had a weakness for these songs and knew most of them by heart. From the look of him, he had a fine baritone.

Meanwhile at Sandringham the slow, costive festivities plodded through their usual routine, the young men restive, archbishops and dowagers discreetly breaking wind on their hard, upright chairs, Queen Mary planning a little chat with her second son when the appropriate occasion arose. As for him, he had been unsettled by his glimpses of life at Glamis and St Paul's Walden Bury and had actually been heard to grumble about things at home: 'No new blood is ever introduced ... no originality in the talk – nothing but a dreary acquiescence ... No one has the exciting feeling that if they shine they will be asked again ... they know they will be automatically, as long as they're alive. Traditionalism is all very well, but too much of it leads to dry rot.'[2] Strong words for a young man whose reflex action to his very existence seemed to be to thank his father. His youngest brother, Georgie, was equally glum. He hated the Navy and found the endless anecdotes about shooting, which he hated just as much, intolerably boring. David couldn't wait to get back to London. Only Harry's neighing giggle broke the hush – he enjoyed a state of semi-concussion most of the time and didn't notice a thing. On Christmas morning he was the only one to sing 'God rest you merry, gentlemen' with any kind of verve.

Bertie had his chat with Mama, and was greatly relieved. She approved of Elizabeth, with the proviso that she would of course have

52

to meet the girl properly before anything could be decided. Bertie, knowing his mother's eagerness to get her sons settled, and what a powerful ally she was, announced that he was going to propose anyway. 'You'll be a lucky fellow if she accepts you,'[3] his father growled, though whether this was because he believed in Elizabeth's virtues or because he had such a low opinion of his son is not clear.

Bertie had at last found a job he liked doing, and perhaps it was this, as much as the conduciveness of the season, that made him wait until spring before confronting Elizabeth. In May 1919 he had been asked to become President of the Boys' Welfare Association – soon to be renamed the Industrial Welfare Society – 'an organization through which industry itself might be responsible for ... the betterment of working conditions, the setting up of works' committees, the provision of health centres and canteens in factories, and of proper facilities for the maximum of enjoyment in the workers' free time.'[4] This may smack of Handkerchiefs for the Waifs and Strays to us, but in the early 1920s it soon commanded 'the interest, respect and commendation of over a hundred firms',[5] though certain elements in management bellowed Bolshevism and some Trades Unionists deplored the idea of Labour lying down with Capital.

In spite of his serious intentions, Bertie was like a small boy on the spree. He went down coal mines, clambered up scaffolding, drove locomotives and trucks and, once, a tram-car through the crowded streets of Glasgow. He poured molten metal from crucibles, pressed a button to blast thousands of tons of rock, walked unflinchingly through glue factories. For the first time in his life he talked to working-class men, and although the conversations were necessarily brief and one-sided, he learned more than he had done in the whole of his twenty-five years about the way that 99 per cent of his countrymen looked and spoke and survived. They saw him at his best, because he was enjoying himself. 'Of all the many visitors we had here,' said one manager, 'I never met one who asked more sensible questions or showed greater understanding of our fundamental problems. He does like getting to the bottom of things.'[6] The Labour politician Miss Margaret Bondfield once remarked that Queen Mary would have made an excellent factory inspector.[7] Her second son, who is invariably regarded as a replica of his father, inherited much more from his mother than is generally recognized.

Apart from the fact that he was relatively busy, Bertie was in no tearing hurry to propose, now that he had his parents' qualified blessing. He had no doubt of the result. Possibly the prospect of leaving his awful home after all these years was, illogically, a little daunting. There would be such a fuss over the wedding, and what if he couldn't get the words out? This is the sort of thing that worries anyone on a sleepless night. Come the first crocus, Bertie made his proposal. And was refused.

Why? The answer is obvious: Elizabeth didn't want to marry Bertie. Because, I suppose, such a self-evident fact is too embarrassing to contemplate, all her biographers have relied on some fiction about her being nervous of everything such a marriage would entail – the public life, the responsibility of being royal and so on. Elizabeth had been training herself for public life since she was nine years old, if not longer. Performing to an audience – the smiles, the waves, the applause – was second nature to her. She was confident of her ability to enchant, entertain, be adored. The role of Duchess of York, though one step down from Princess of Wales, would suit her admirably. There was only one thing wrong with the proposition – the Duke. It is a biographer of Queen Mary who writes that '[Elizabeth's] resistance to Bertie had much more to do with her royal suitor himself. Apart from his extreme moodiness, Bertie was not of a strong constitution and he was disconcertingly nervous. He had a serious speech impediment and numerous twitches, sometimes blinking his eyes with too much frequency and unable to control the muscles around his mouth. In addition, his drinking problem, though thought to be kept secret, had grown worse . . .'[8] Far from her ideal hero, and a poor alternative to some of his competitors.

Queen Victoria firmly believed that 'if two eligible young people were pushed into a double bedroom, love would be sure to follow', and if it didn't, any well-brought-up gal would be happy to make the best of it. Elizabeth, it seems, had not yet realized the cynicism and ruthlessness of Royalty's attitude to marriage – it was very nice that Bertie was so much in love, but the important thing was that Elizabeth seemed a suitable mare, and mares did not have opinions. King George's doubts about his son's acceptability were not, of course, intended to be taken seriously. It was unthinkable that the girl should refuse such a catch.

Wanting to please everyone, and inevitably a little flattered, Elizabeth could hardly have told Bertie that he didn't live up to her standards of the perfect husband. Anyway, she may have quite liked him by now – it it hard, though by no means impossible, to dislike someone who adores you, and Bertie certainly had likeable qualities once you got to know him. What did she say? Sorry, but I hope we can be friends – the classic put-down? Even that must have needed considerable courage. She had said it often enough before, but those occasions hadn't involved royal disapproval and turning down a good part. Unless she had a better alternative, Bertie must have been exceptionally undesirable.

The Duke of York was desolate, in spite of everyone's sympathy. 'I do hope he will find a nice wife who will make him happy,' Lady Strathmore wrote to Mabell Airlie. 'I like him so much and he is a man who will be made or marred by his wife.' Prescient, but little comfort. Neither were the high spirits of his equerry.

Bertie did not take failure lightly. He was too familiar with it. A report of a reception given for him that spring presents a sad picture: 'The Duke of York seemed, perhaps, the least enthusiastic ... Poor dear, it can't be really very amusing to be continually surrounded with pomp and ceremony...'[9] Not only did he have to contend with his own humiliation, his father's jokes and his mother's outrage, but he was being pitied by the Press.

Dutifully, he soldiered on. He hunted with the Quorn, and appeared at Grafton Hunt 'Chases' with his two younger brothers, all identical in grey herringbone tweed. He climbed ladders and inspected nuts and bolts. Then, inevitably, it was Cowes Week with the Barings and Edwina Ashley and his cousin Louis Mountbatten, and Greig snapping 'Behave yourself, Sir!'[10] when he lost his temper on the tennis court, which didn't help much. 'Such a collection of youth and beauty at Nubia House,' enthused the gossip-writers, 'Lady Crewe ... Sir Harry and Lady Mainwaring, Captain James Stuart, Lord Moray's youngest son, who is generally with the Duke of York...'[11] What did the two men talk about? Certainly not Elizabeth, though perhaps they politely agreed that they were concerned about her mother's health.★

There were additional complications. Elizabeth had danced on through the spring and early summer, by now 'the pretty Strathmore girl',[12] she had been noticed at Lady Astor's, the Caledonian Ball, and the requisite number of country houses. If she was at Ascot – and nothing but illness would have prevented her – she probably chatted with Bertie, David and Harry in their toppers and tails; and perhaps, out of the corner of her eye, noticed Jamie's interest in the Cavendish girl, Rachel, just back from Canada where her father was Governor-General.† Perhaps he didn't realize that of all the impractical virtues that Elizabeth said she demanded, unimpeachable morals – in other words, total fidelity to herself – were the most essential. Like many daughters of elderly, indulgent parents, she was capable of virulent jealousy, and always would be. The scales may have tipped that day in Bertie's favour, but none of them were aware of it.

There are various versions of the subsequent events. Captain Stuart is not mentioned in any of them. In August 1921, Queen Mary descended on Lady Airlie at Cortachy Castle, accompanied by

★ Viscount Stuart of Findhorn overlooks the year 1921 in his autobiography, except for the inaccurately dated episode already mentioned.
† Viscount Stuart of Findhorn places this meeting in the summer of 1920.

Princess Mary, a gentleman in waiting and his servant, two dressers, a detective, a footman, a chauffeur and an under-chauffeur. It was a small castle. The Queen's excuse was that she could no longer go abroad to stay with the old Grand Duchess of Mecklenburg-Strelitz, as she used to do, and needed a 'real holiday'.[13] In fact, her objective was to inspect the Strathmore girl who had been causing Bertie so much trouble. According to most biographers, Bertie was staying at Glamis. He was certainly shooting there, with Michael and David, in late September,[14] but at this point, according to Lady Airlie, he escorted his mother when she set off in her two-chauffeured motor car on the fateful visit to Glamis. When they arrived they found Lady Strathmore ill in bed and young Elizabeth acting as hostess. If it had been planned, it couldn't have been more successful. Elizabeth soared to the occasion.

Bertie's mother or no, this was Queen Mary. Metaphorically, Elizabeth turned on all the lights. She was charming, she was exquisitely polite, she was in command, she was properly humble. She smiled the whole time, and asked the right questions, and showed considerable knowledge of the history of her rather draughty castle. The Queen departed with a glint in her eye. She had decided that this was 'the one girl who could make Bertie happy'. Perhaps it would be as well if something were done about that surly young man lurking in the background. 'But,' the old hypocrite added swiftly, 'I shall say nothing to either of them. Mothers should never meddle in their children's love affairs.'[15]

Early in the New year of 1922 Jamie left England for the oil-fields of Oklahoma.*

---

* Ernest King, in his book *The Green Baize Door*, says that Queen Mary 'had made quite certain of her second son's marriage to present Queen Elizabeth the Queen Mother when she was Lady Elizabeth Bowes-Lyon. A possible rival had quickly found himself appointed to the Governor-General's staff in Canada.' The Governor General was Jamie's future father-in-law. Mr King, perhaps, confused fact with probability.

CHAPTER

7

London: The paper 'London Gossip' printed . . . this
morning . . . that the Duke of York . . . was engaged to
Lady Elizabeth Bowes-Lyon, daughter of the Earl of
Strathmore. It is stated on authority here that the report is
entirely without foundation. Gossip on this matter was
prevalent in London a month or so ago, when it was also
said that the Duke of York's wishes to enter upon the
engagement had brought him into conflict with his
father. Inquiries at the time failed to obtain any information tending to corroborate these reports . . .

New York Times, 4 February 1920

The hue and cry had begun, but Elizabeth made no attempt to escape.
She was still refusing Bertie and would continue to do so for another
year, but it was beyond her to refuse Queen Mary. Bewildered,
unhappy – entirely my own view, of course – she did everything she
was told except give in to marriage. 'Holding hands in a boat',[1]
according to the famous lines quoted by Robert Lacey, was Bertie's
idea of courtship. Elizabeth pulled her hand away and kept him
waiting when he came to call.[2] This could have been her natural
flirtatiousness, but it seems unlikely. In the photographs of that period
she looks wan, almost bedraggled. Who did she confide in, apart from
close friends now dead and eternally discreet? Helen Hardinge, sister-
in-law of Elizabeth's young confidante Diamond and herself a lady
who would play a significant role in later years, tells the usual tale:
'Lady Elizabeth had nothing against the Duke himself; but . . . having
been so happy in her own family, it was hard for her to have to face a
situation in which privacy would have to take second place to her
husband's work for the nation.'[3] Yes, yes. In fact Elizabeth knew that
the temptation to gossip was irresistible, and that unless you happened
to be a Strathmore secrets were hard to keep. Because the Royal
Family was involved, an official explanation for the delay was necessary. It would hardly have been possible to excuse her reluctance on
the grounds that she was waiting for another man.

Meanwhile Queen Mary who, being no fool, probably understood the situation arranged for her to be seen with the right people. A photograph taken in the autumn of 1921 at Brechin Castle shows Elizabeth for the first time in a group surrounding the majestic figure of her would-be mother-in-law.[4] The next step was to include her among the bridesmaids for Mary's wedding to Viscount Lascelles on 28 February 1922. Among the other seven blue-blooded misses was Lady Rachel Cavendish.

In spite of much public rejoicing, this sounds a gloomy occasion. Mary's bridegroom was fifteen years older than herself, and not the most immediately desirable of men. King George, though he put on a brave face at the ceremony, had 'quite broken down' when he went to her room to take leave of his virgin child before escorting her to the Abbey. David, who might have provided the necessary light relief, was in India. The bridesmaids were decked out in silver – silver roses worn at hip-level and tied with lovers' knots, diadems of silver rose leaves. From the wedding picture, they all looked perfectly awful: sullen and dowdy, with a hint of acne here and there. Elizabeth came off worst, being almost hidden in the back row, her expression, as seen by one of her biographers, 'pensive, if not anxious'.[5] Her expression as seen by everybody else was one of wretchedness and fury. When the official portrait of the wedding group was painted she got left out altogether. The excuse was that there was no room on the canvas, but it seems more likely that the painter felt he could do nothing to make her look even tolerably joyful.

Describing the festivities to her eldest son, Queen Mary might have been telling him about a funeral: 'Mary is married & has flown from her home leaving a terrible blank behind her as you can well imagine. Papa & I are feeling very low & sad without her especially as Georgie had to return to Malta yesterday while Harry has at last joined the 10th Hussars at Canterbury & Bertie has gone hunting for a few days . . . Papa & I felt miserable at parting, poor Papa broke down, but I mercifully managed to keep up as I so much feared Mary wld break down. However she was very brave . . .'[6] The gloom deepened. Three weeks later she was writing 'There has been a perfect epidemic of deaths. Ly Farquahar's, Col: Erskine's mother Ly Horatia Erskine, Dow: Ly Derby, Bertha's Aunt, Wigram's brother in law, then Leopold & then Ly Stamfordham who as you know has been ill since last July – It is all rather sad & depressing & this added to the most odious cold dull rainy weather makes life almost intolerable.'[7]

Insensitive to the depression settled over Windsor and Glamis, social vultures and hangers-on were meddling under the guise of being helpful. Venetia James, by now a pillar of Belgravia Establishment, encouraged Bertie with little dinner parties and stringent hospitality ('She would pass a note to her butler with DCSC scribbled on it, which meant Don't Cut Second Chicken.')[8] So did Mrs Ronnie Greville, another well-preserved and powerful relic of Edwardian days and one of the greatest snobs of the century. It was not a question of taking sides, since apart from her inexplicable obstinacy Elizabeth was unimportant, but of making sure they were in at the kill, whoever the victim might be. With David away, and finding himself surrounded by sympathy and concern as well as the odious cold dull rainy weather and his parents' low spirits, Bertie held the stage for a while. 'Those close to him were alarmed at these times at how much whisky he drank. His stuttering was worse than ever.'[9] One way and another, it sounds a bad patch.

After the Lascelles wedding, Elizabeth disappears from the records for over six months. Bertie staggered on. He deputized for his father at the wedding of Princess Marie of Roumania to King Alexander of the Serbs, Croats and Slovenes, riding an 'excessively restive horse' through the streets of Belgrade and scattering handfuls of coins to children who had been taught to chant, 'O Koom, your purse is burning.'[10] He was a great success, but it didn't relieve his misery. Hardly was he home, but the *Daily Chronicle* announced his engagement to Lady May Cambridge, basing this information on the fact that the King, accompanied by the Duke of York and Lady May, had galloped for an hour in Windsor Great Park. Earlier in the year, he had been married off in the Press to Mary Ashley, Edwina's sister. It was all getting too much. Louis Greig, once more responsible for Bertie's welfare, was at his wits' end. Before the Duke set off for Dunkirk on 25 July to lay the foundation stone for a War Memorial, Greig telephoned Viscount Davidson, a young man of whom King George apparently approved, asking him to make a point of attending the ceremony. The implication was that Greig himself was no longer able to cope.

Davidson was Conservative M.P. for Hemel Hempstead, only six years older than Bertie but, from the sound of him, extremely staid and a great respecter of all Royalty except the Prince of Wales, whom he thought 'an obstinate, but really a weak man, in whose pastimes I could have taken no share, and whose friends, male and female, I would not wish to have known intimately.'[11] A more suitable influence, perhaps, than Jamie Stuart. Davidson duly arranged to sail in the specially chartered ship which was to take members of both Houses of Parliament from Harwich to Dunkirk, and after the ceremony 'loitered by the gangway' until Greig turned up to take him on board the royal destroyer for the return journey. '. . . directly she cast off he took me down to the wardroom where I was presented to His Royal Highness, with whom I remained alone for nearly three hours.'[12]

As they chugged homeward, Bertie bared his soul. 'He seemed to have reached a crisis in his life, and wanted someone to whom he could unburden himself without reserve. He dwelt upon the difficulties which surrounded a King's son in contrast with men like myself who had always had greater freedom at school and university to make their own friends ... We discussed friendship, and the relative value of brains and character, and all the sort of things that young men do talk about in the abstract ... I sensed that he was working up to something important. I felt moved with a great desire to help him if I could, he was so simple and frank and forthcoming.

'Then out it came. He declared that he was desperately in love, but that he was in despair for it seemed quite certain that he had lost the only woman he would ever marry.' Davidson replied, man to man, that however black the situation he mustn't give up hope, his own wife had constantly refused him before she finally said yes. This, understandably, irritated Bertie. Whatever Davidson's troubles had been, the situation was quite different. 'The King's son,' the Duke explained, 'cannot propose to the girl he loves, since custom requires that he must not place himself in the position of being refused, and to that ancient custom the King, his father, firmly adhered. Worse still, I gathered that an emissary had already been sent to ascertain whether the girl was prepared to marry him, and that it had failed. The question was, what was he to do?'[13]

The advice Davidson ventured to give him was simple. 'I suggested that in the Year of Grace 1922 no high-spirited girl of character was likely to accept a proposal made at second hand; if she was as fond of him as he thought she was' – did he? – 'he must propose to her himself ... His mood when we parted was much brighter and more buoyant than at the beginning of our talk.'[14]

Had Bertie in fact been relying on a third party to do his proposing for him? It seems almost incredible; and yet, according to Robert Sencourt, the Prince of Wales had told Elizabeth, 'You'd better take him, and go in the end to Buck House.'[15] Is it conceivable that Bertie had asked his brother to sound her out, at least? If so, and she was genuinely fearful of taking on the responsibilities of royalty, this advice would have been the worst he could have given.

It is all so unlikely, in view of the subsequent relationship between Elizabeth and David, that their characters suddenly become unrecognizable. At the same time their real natures, behind the accumulated veneer of history and myth, probably are unrecognizable. If David volunteered as go-between; if Elizabeth confided in him ... All we know is that David found the formality of his father's Court intolerable and the stodginess of family life almost equally so, and that he thought Elizabeth provided 'a lively and refreshing spirit'.[16] We know that Elizabeth had strong reservations about marrying Bertie, whether they were caused by Bertie himself or by taking on the role of Duchess of York, and that in her old age, according to Lady Donaldson, she wistfully remembered that David had been 'such fun'.[17] In short, marriage into the Royal Family would be a great deal more bearable if David were around; and if he didn't marry – a possibility, even then – she would be the first lady in the land after Queen Mary's death. Such an arrangement, though second best, might have something to recommend it? She couldn't go on much longer hoping for the best. Something was needed to catapult her into a decision.

★   ★   ★

Daily News, Friday, 5 January 1923:

SCOTTISH BRIDE FOR PRINCE OF WALES
HEIR TO THRONE TO WED PEER'S DAUGHTER

AN OFFICIAL ANNOUNCEMENT IMMINENT
HAPPY CHOICE
ONE OF THE CLOSEST FRIENDS OF PRINCESS MARY

The formal announcement of the engagement of the Prince of Wales to a young Scottish lady of noble birth will be made within the next two or three months.

. . . The future Queen of England is the daughter of a well-known Scottish peer, who is the owner of castles both north and south of the Tweed . . . A happy feature of the engagement is that the girl of the Prince's choice is one of the closest friends of his sister, Princess Mary.

Elizabeth was staying with her old friend George Gage in Sussex. Among the guests was the ubiquitous Chips Channon, who wrote post-haste in his diary: 'The evening papers have announced her engagement to the Prince of Wales. So we all bowed and bobbed and teased her, calling her 'Ma'am': I am not sure that she enjoyed it. It couldn't be true, but how delighted everyone would be! She certainly has something on her mind . . . She is more gentle, lovely and exquisite than any woman alive, but this evening I thought her unhappy and distraite. I longed to tell her I would die for her, although I am not in love with her. Poor Gage is desperately fond of her – in vain, but he is far too heavy, too Tudor and squirarchal for so rare and patrician a creature as Elizabeth.'[18]

I don't believe that this was the first shock of Elizabeth's New Year. If it was, she would surely have laughed it off – almost everyone, after all, had been marked down as the Prince of Wales's intended at one time or another. Bertie's continuous pestering may have worried her, and pressure from both their mothers would naturally make her anxious – but 'unhappy and distraite' indicates something more personal that had nothing to do with threats and blandishments from Windsor and Sandringham and which, in the ordinary course of events, would have been of little interest to the newspapers. Perhaps Elizabeth herself had been turned down. She had, from the sound of it, already lost heart by the time she made her first headline.

Bertie was staying with the Drummonds at Pitsford Hall, where the news would have been received with much expostulation and, on the Duke of York's part, rage. It was one thing to excite sympathy in his unjust predicament; quite another to be ousted from the scene altogether in favour of his eldest brother. If they wanted to print their damnable lies why not at least pick on the right man?

The reaction at Windsor must be invented to be believed. Up until now the situation might have been unfortunate and inexplicable, but at least it had been managed with a certain decorum. Now the tiresome girl had got herself into the gutter press. Something had to be done, and quickly. In the Royal backwaters there were peremptory commands for Action, Full Steam Ahead. Elizabeth Bowes-Lyon had met her Waterloo.

The Prince of Wales contented himself with a patient, slightly ironical denial. 'A few days ago the *Daily News* announced the forthcoming engagement of the Prince of Wales to an Italian Princess. Today the same journal states on what is claimed to be unquestionable authority that the formal announcement of His Royal Highness's engagement to a daughter of a Scottish peer will be made within the next two or three months. We are officially authorized to say that this report is as devoid of foundation as was the previous . . .' The papers quickly turned over their headlines to Tutankhamun's tomb and the imminent execution of Frederick Bywaters and Edith Thompson.

Sometime in the following week Elizabeth went to tea with Lady Airlie. This was not unusual. Mabell, humorous, cosy, wise, discreet, was the confidante of all the Royal children – except possibly Harry, who had nothing much to confide – and had known Elizabeth since she was a baby. In the preceding months both Bertie and Elizabeth – though always separately – had used her as a sounding-board. Out of affection for the small boy who had made her an Easter card, and perhaps, too, out of loyalty to her old friend Queen Mary, Mabell had gently been pleading Bertie's cause. This had shown no effect, and after the unfortunate publicity of the weekend she 'meant to make a final effort'.[19] But Elizabeth was already expert at deflecting conversation from unpleasant topics, and Lady Airlie found herself talking about her own marriage instead.

Mabell, the girl who loved to spend days alone on the Irish moors with her sketch book, who was 'not a success' at the children's parties at Marlborough House and who was quite sure she would never get married, did in fact marry David William Stanley, sixth Earl of Airlie, on 19 January 1886. He was a cavalry officer, 'essentially a product of the soldiering, Empire-building Britain... He might have been a prototype of Rider Haggard's Englishman – brave, honourable, chivalrous, with a simple faith in God and the infallibility of British rule'[20] – and he adored her. Mabell, however, was miserable. She found herself reduced to a nobody by her mother-in-law;[21] when they got away, to Aldershot, it was nothing but exercises and manoeuvres and polo; she felt excluded from army life, and detested getting pregnant;[22] she was continually pregnant. She wrote a pamphlet entitled *The Real Rights of Women* which, as far as her social world was concerned, was a mistake. She was lonely and self-pitying. 'It was an unsettled phase for both of us,' she told Elizabeth, 'and one that I imagine a great many young couples must pass through. But in my youth there were no easy divorces – even a separation was considered a terrible disgrace.' She and David were forced to have patience with each other. After the early quarrels 'resulting from the clash of two undisciplined personalities'[23] they found a *modus vivendi*, which turned into a mutually rewarding, loving partnership. And that, Mabell implied, was worth all the agitation and inevitable disillusion of being 'in love'.

Whether she also told Elizabeth that it was the birth of a son, after three girls, and her decision to 'follow the drum' – galloping in a cavalry ccharge across Salisbury Plain, wearing a straw boater or, in bad weather, a fetching billy-cock – that solved the problem, is unlikely. She simply said how much she had hated the life at first, and how she had grown to enjoy it. 'After she had gone,' Mabell remembered, 'I feared I might have bored her by bringing up a chapter of my past which had closed before she was born, and wished that I had talked more of the Duke.'[24]

In Elizabeth's world people so seldom talked about their feelings that in fact Lady Airlie's story was something of a revelation. Her own mother, surely, had never admitted to a moment's unhappiness in her marriage. One simply didn't. It wouldn't be helpful. The idea that someone of her mother's generation, a woman she had been brought up to admire and respect, could cheerfully confess to having been discontented with her husband was both shocking and oddly encouraging. Perhaps everything might come right in the end. And what, after all, was the alternative? Whether or not she had discussed the problem with David, a lot of apparently disconnected arguments were weighing the scales in Bertie's favour.

At the end of that week the Duke of York arrived at St Paul's

Walden Bury with his jaw bones pumping and a glint in his eye. On Saturday he proposed once more. Elizabeth accepted him. The Press would concoct an unconvincing version of the scene. 'If you are going to keep it up for ever,' she is reputed to have said, laughing merrily, 'I might as well say "Yes" now.' With one word she had prescribed her future until her dying day. She was twenty-two years old.

CHAPTER

8

Nobody marries one person. Even an orphaned bridegroom or bride carries a huge lump of history which is dumped, sooner or later, in their spouse's lap. When Elizabeth Bowes-Lyon accepted Albert, Duke of York she took on an entire species.

Although in this last quarter of the twentieth century it is hard to believe that one group of people can be considered genetically superior to the rest, the Houses of Windsor, Saxe-Coburg and Gotha, Denmark and Wurttemburg were certainly distinctive. George, Elizabeth's prospective father-in-law, was the thirty-seventh British monarch since the Norman Conquest and eighth in descent from the Electress Sophia of Hanover, mother of George I, who had been presented with the British throne as a sort of self-assembly package by the Act of Settlement. To placate those who might consider the Hanovers mere upstarts, he could also claim to be twenty-ninth in line from William the Conqueror (the bastard son of Robert the Devil of Normandy and a tanner's daughter from Falaise) and thirty-sixth from Alfred the Great, who was born in Wantage. According to the genealogists, Charlemagne, Barbarossa, Rodrigo the Cid, Egbert King of Wessex, Cadwaller, Vortigern, Neill of the Nine Hostages, the High Kings of Erin and even Mahomet had contributed drops of variously coloured blood to this choleric old Norfolk squire and his barely literate children.

Elizabeth would not have to take these remote ancestors into account very often. They just hovered in case of trouble. It was when Bertie's great-great-grandfather on the distaff side married his, Bertie's, great-grandfather's sister that the complications really began. Their only child was Alexandrina Victoria, a very fecund Queen.

Of the nine children she bore to Prince Albert of Saxe-Coburg-Gotha, seven married into the royal houses of Europe and one, after marrying Princess Alexandra of Denmark, became King Edward VII of England. Among George's more familiar relatives were Aunt Vicky and Uncle Frederick, Empress and Emperor of Germany; Aunt Alice and Uncle Louis of Hesse and the Rhine; Uncle Alfred Edinburgh and Saxe-Coburg-Gotha (who died, you may remember, at the end of the 1900 heat-wave); Aunt Helena and Uncle Christian Schleswig-Holstein; Aunt Louise and Uncle John Argyll; Uncle Arthur Connaught and Aunt Louise Prussia; Uncle Leopold and Aunt Helen Waldeck and Aunt Beatrice and Uncle Harry Battenberg. Those who were not actually reigning sovereigns were, of course, Princes or Princesses or Grand Dukes or Duchesses. To their descendants, and for the purposes of this book, that goes without saying.

On his mother's side there was Uncle Frederick VIII Denmark and Aunt Louise Sweden; Uncle Willy (who became George) and Aunt Olga Greece; Aunt Dagmar (alias Marie Feodorovna) and Uncle Alex Russia; Aunt Thyra and Uncle Ernest Cumberland and Hanover; Uncle Valdemar Denmark and his Roman Catholic wife.

This little lot – 'little', that is, compared with the rest of the population – ran Europe as though it were a group of country estates, constantly visiting each other, writing letters to each other, marrying each other, involving themselves in each other's weddings and christenings and funerals, easing the way for their politicians by family chat over brandy and cigars, getting terribly upset when the politicians imposed squabbles on them or gave one of them the sack. The catastrophic row of the Great War had been a family disaster. Queen Mary's sister-in-law, Princess Alice, Countess of Athlone (*née* Princess of Albany) found that most of her mother's relations, and many of her father's, were on the German side. So, of course, was her husband's family, the Wurttemburgs. The confused Princess Alice's affections, though never her loyalty, were split between these close German relatives and her cousins King George of England and the Empress Alexandra of Russia, not to mention the cousins who, at the start of the disagreement, professed themselves neutral – Queen Ena of Spain, Queen Maud of Norway, Queen Sophie of the Hellenes and Crown Princess Marie of Rumania. 'Overnight, close, dearly-loved relatives had to be treated as enemies; princes who had grown up together now faced each other across the firing line.'[1] And why? 'To have to go to war on account of tiresome Servia beggars belief!'[2] Queen Mary, whose family connections were similarly complicated, wrote in a moment of exasperated honesty. By the time it was all over, those who had survived the shock were pulling themselves together – perhaps 'huddling' would be a more accurate term – and looking about for young members of the aristocracy to breed from, since the old dynastic blood was running thin.

Even so, in 1923 Bertie's cousins, either directly or by marriage, still included six operational or semi-operational Kings – Greece, Sweden, Denmark, Norway, Rumania and Yugoslavia; five Queens – Spain, Sweden, Yugoslavia, Greece and Rumania; the Prince of Monaco, the

Prince of Liechtenstein, Princess Marina of Greece, various Counts, Hereditary Grand Dukes, Marquesses, Viscounts, Earls and Dukes; and Louis Mountbatten who would become Burma, to name but a few. Most of them were a little younger than Bertie and some of them had already started having children. The one word that never passed their lips was ominously similar in all their languages: Republic.

In spite of their divine right, their ceremonial and rigmarole, their unshakeable belief in themselves, this vast, homogenous family had lived for years in increasing fear. They were sitting ducks for the *battue* conducted by unsportsmanlike anarchists, Bolshevists, lunatics of all kinds. 'These are among the little uncertainties of our profession,' Humbert of Italy had said before he was shot through the head at Monza. That may have been so, but when the entire Russian contingent was wiped out overnight, only five years before Elizabeth became engaged to Bertie, the news had shaken Buckingham Palace to its foundations. 'The news were confirmed of poor Nicky of Russia having been shot by those brutes of Bolsheviks last week,' Queen Mary wrote in her diary. 'It is too horrible and heartless – Mama and Toria came to tea, terribly upset . . .'

Their stoicism, however, was amazing. When poor Ena and Alfonso were blown up, though fortunately not fatally, at their wedding, everyone was naturally a little *distrait*, but Aunt Marie Edinburgh-Coburg had been heard to murmur disdainfully, *'Moi, je suis tellement accoutumée a ces sortes de chose.'* They were all used to it, but it was still upsetting. Only the other day, on 29 January 1923, a small man with a club foot tried to strike King George with his crutch at St Pancras and George remarked bravely that he supposed the poor fellow was suffering from shell-shock. People must be deranged to attack the Monarch: it was the only explanation. One had to pity them, dispose of them, and rise above it.

★   ★   ★

King Edward VII, more worldly than most Sovereigns, had once introduced his son George as 'the future last King of England'. Such an idea was unthinkable to George himself. He benefited from a total lack of imagination. A simpleton in some ways, his honesty and straightforwardness were natural characteristics rather than acquired virtues. He had no inner censor, no protective mechanism – except, of course, his rank – to prevent him from speaking his mind. 'He was sometimes too outspoken,' his wife said ruefully. 'I remember that I once had a lady-in-waiting who was a fool and used to ask indiscreet questions of my husband in the motor car. He always answered exactly what he thought. I had to get rid of the woman.'[3] In politics, too, he was unable to dissemble. When Lloyd George talked him into giving secret guarantees to create new peers if the Parliament Bill were vetoed in the Lords, he was horribly uncomfortable. 'I have never in my life done anything I was ashamed to confess,' he grumbled. 'And I have never been accustomed to concealing things.'[4] This was not boasting; it was more of a statement of fact, like being allergic to cats. The King 'never liked going round and round'[5] and Lloyd George was particularly circuitous. When George was still Prince of Wales he had leaned across the dinner table one night and bellowed at the Permanent Secretary of the Treasury, 'I can't think . . . how you can go on serving that damned fellow Lloyd George!',[6] and some years later, forgetting that the lady he was addressing was the wife of an eminent Cabinet Minister, he 'poured into her astonished ear terrific denunciations of Lloyd George on the subject of pheasants and mangold-worzels',[7] a subject about which the King knew a good deal and his Chancellor of the Exchequer patently nothing.

If it is normal to be circumspect and approach the truth with care, George was an eccentric. When he came to the throne, he had dealt with rumours of his drunkenness by instructing the Dean of Norwich publicly to refute them. The Dean, in all good conscience, did so. The rumours stopped. He had never made any bones about the fact that as a young man he had kept a girl in Southsea and another, whom he shared with his brother, in St John's Wood. He cheerfully admitted that he had been much taken with a Miss Julie Stonor,[8] and would have married her if he could, and that his cousin 'Missy' had also been the object of his affections for a while. But when he was accused of bigamy by a republican called E. F. Mylius (damned foreigner, of course), George did not issue an official denial or pretend it wasn't happening – he had the man sued, and himself sent a statement to Court saying that Mylius's story was a load of rubbish and that he would have given evidence himself had not the Law Officers advised him that it was unconstitutional for a Sovereign to appear in the witness-box.[9] That such naïvety could remain intact in the centre of diplomatic subterfuge, political manoeuvre and family pressure is remarkable. Though it would have astonished him if he had known it, George Windsor was a good man.

His goodness, unfortunately, paved much of the hell of his sons' childhoods. There was something about them – indeed, about all growing boys – that he found irresistibly contemptible. He lost no opportunity of guffawing at their weaknesses and bellowing at their shortcomings. During an inspection of the fleet he caused agonies of shame to the future Lord Mountbatten by loudly inquiring about a rag doll which the young midshipman had dearly loved in childhood.[10] There must have been a sexual element in this, a need to emasculate young male competition, for once his sons had proved themselves capable of providing him with legitimate grandchildren the baiting stopped and they all got on quite amicably.

★   ★   ★

Bertie's mother was a very different proposition. Queen Mary was fifty-eight when Elizabeth entered the family. As Chips Channon described 'her appearance was formidable, her manner – well, it was like talking to St Paul's Cathedral...'[11] She inspired fear without even trying. Her grandfather, Alexander, Duke of Wurttemburg, had made a morganatic marriage, thereby tainting the Wurttemburg blood and adding considerably to their intelligence. Perhaps May was compensating for this slip-up with her all-consuming passion for the Monarchy and the families that embodied it – in any case there was nothing about the genealogy of Europe's aristocracy that she didn't know. Minor off-shoots, like the Strathmores, were immediately investigated. In Elizabeth's case, when the Queen spotted Robert Bruce (also a distant ancestor of her husband's) she was reasonably satisfied.

Like the iceberg she frequently resembled, the greater part of the Queen's personality was submerged in the chill waters of duty. She had 'sacrificed everything to [George's] needs and to the preservation of his peace of mind, thinking of him before she thought of anyone else, her children and, of course, herself, included.'[12] Her appearance, for instance, was created from top to toe by her husband, and this, however much his dreary taste might be regretted, she felt proper. Her biographer's theory is that George wished his wife to grow old looking exactly as she had done when they had first become engaged;[13] and so, with the addition of a few million pounds' worth of diamonds, she did. Lady Airlie recalls one brave effort to keep up with the times: 'Having been gifted with perfect legs, she once tentatively suggested to me in the 1920s that we might both shorten our skirts by a modest two or three inches...' Mabell was to be the guinea pig in this experiment. It was not a success. Mabell let down her hem again with all speed and May's legs remained the exclusive property of the Crown.[14] Around the same time – was it something to do with feeling distanced from her sons? – the Queen shyly asked Sir Frederick Ponsonby to teach her some of the new dance steps. The lesson was interrupted by the entry of the King, who expressed himself so violently that she never ventured to repeat it.[15]

One of those ubiquitous 'members of the household' once commented that 'the royal family were not given to talking things out, even *en famille*. If anything was wrong, the subject was carefully avoided. They would talk about shooting, the weather, a friend's marriage, the shocking behaviour of the French – but never a word about the subject gnawing at their souls.'[16] After thirty years of this, May was probably incapable of an intimate conversation with anyone, even Mabell Airlie. As a young woman she had still been able to confide in her much-loved governess, Helene Bricka. At the age of twenty-five, unmarried and apparently overwhelmed by her ebullient mother, she wrote to Helene: '. . . sometimes I grumble at my life, at the waste of time, at the *petitesse de la vie* when one feels capable of greater things.'[17] Fifteen years later, as Princess of Wales: 'So many things appear futile, frivolous, waste of time & energy, yet they must be done as long as the world is as civilization (?) has made it, of course one often rebels *mais que faire?*'[18] Her complaints and her rebellion had to be packed away, 'Not Wanted On The Voyage' on which, as fiancée to Prince Albert Frederick and wife to his brother, she had embarked. If she had not opened them up from time to time for Helene Bricka, no one would ever have known they were there. Her natural high spirits suffered the same fate. 'In youth she was gay and amusing and would often be in fits of laughter,' her sister-in-law Princess Alice remembered. 'As Queen she was so sedate, so *posée*.'[19] She did add that after George's death his wife 'blossomed out once more and all her great worth was revealed', but no one was to know this in 1923, least of all Queen Mary.

Could she honestly, and without reservation, encourage her daughter-in-law to follow such an example? *Mais que faire?* What other way was there? Queen Mary's 'real world' was what James Pope-Hennessy describes as 'the calm, doomed world of privilege' and she knew no other. Her husband was also her King. Whatever drawbacks he may have had as a man, the fact remained that according to her beliefs he could do no wrong. That this ceaseless juggling with square pegs and round holes required 'a constant and dramatic exercise of imagination, foresight and control' was something she might have admitted to Helene Bricka (unfortunately dead by now) but not – at least explicitly – to Elizabeth. The girl had a good pedigree, she had been well reared and her sense of duty, if not love, would find a way to placate and manage Bertie. She was not, after all, going to be Queen (or did the old lady have a shrewd suspicion, even then?) and the job of Duchess of York was not particularly onerous. Once she had satisfied herself that those little signs of obstinacy and wilfulness had been ironed out and that Elizabeth had received proper instruction in protocol and family history, the Queen probably did little more than keep a watchful eye. Emotionally, she had no resources left to deal with other people's problems.

★   ★   ★

Of all Elizabeth's contemporaries in the Royal family, Princess Mary is the most shadowy. At the age of six, according to Mr Hansell, her disposition had been 'mercurial; one can enforce discipline and order of a sort but the fact remains that, so long as she is in the room, her brothers cannot concentrate their attention on any serious work.'[20] She was soon removed from the schoolroom and put under the stricter supervision of a Mlle José Dussau. What happened to her between then and her emergence as a keen enthusiast in the activities of Brown and Tawny Owls is obscure. Lady Airlie writes that as the girl was her father's favourite, she was 'the least inhibited' of the children;[21] but by the time she was twenty-two there were signs that even this relatively tolerable home life left a lot to be desired. Her father was possessive and jealous, her mother incapable of communicating except in the most oblique way. 'I don't feel she's happy,' the Prince of Wales told Mabell. 'If she'd confide in me I might be able to do something. But she never complains. The trouble is that she's far too unselfish and conscientious. That's why she was so overworked at her lessons. When my brothers and I wanted her to play tennis she used to refuse because she had her French translation to do, or she hadn't read *The Times* for the day. Is that normal for a girl?'[22]

Not, certainly, for a daughter of King George V. Perhaps Mary would have been charming, and might have been extremely happy if the misfortune of her birth had not condemned her to the severe and miserable existence of being a princess. She occupied herself laying foundation stones and opening memorial clubs and being President of charitable institutions until she married the elderly, but at least reasonably cultivated, Lord Lascelles. Then, with time off for giving birth to two sons, she seems to have gone on being President of charitable institutions and opening memorial clubs and laying foundation stones. Apart from one long out-of-print biography★ written in 1922 there is very little record of her life and little, apart from the admirable Lord George Harewood, to commemorate it.

★   ★   ★

When David Prince of Wales was twelve years old, Lord Esher remarked that he could not trace 'the look of Weltschmerz' in the boy's eyes to any ancestor of the House of Hanover.[23] To his mother, he was not only 'winning, intelligent and handsome, he had . . . the further and supreme merit of looking like "the old Royal Family".'[24] Whether his Uncle Frank, one of Queen Mary's three brothers, had this particular characteristic or not, there is at least more superficial similarity between him and his nephew than there is between David and the Guelphs. Frank was handsome, irreverent, a glamorous ne'er-

★ *Princess Mary* by M. C. Carey Nisbet & Co.

do-well loved by his family against their better judgment. He kept an elderly married mistress and died, himself unmarried, in 1910. The obvious difference between them is that Frank seems to have been born a black sheep, whereas it took David over half his life to become one.

In 1923, when Elizabeth joined the family, he had hardly begun. On the contrary, apart from a certain carelessness over his dress and an engaging informality in public, he was a star Royal performer, combining duty and spontaneity with unprecedented success. His war record had shown just the right amount of bravado. He had traipsed, apparently indefatigable, through one-horse towns in Canada and Australia, had been caressed black and blue in Melbourne and practically stripped in Quebec; he had driven through Bombay in a horse-drawn carriage with a Kitmatgar holding a gold-embroidered umbrella over his head and won the light-weight hog-hunter's race at Lucknow. 'Statesmanlike . . . gracious . . . tactful . . . courageous . . . a true leader of men' were some of the accolades bestowed on him by the Press and the Government. Even his father expressed qualified approval.

Nevertheless, it was 'the look of Weltschmerz' that gave him his charisma. He came and left unpredictably, lonely, excited, nervous, melancholy, jaunty, a pint-sized Prince or elderly *gamin* but never, in his father's terms, anyway, a man. Some people, Noel Coward among them, believed he was homosexual,[25] but while David himself wrote that he was 'full of curiosity, and there were few experiences open to a young man of my day that I did not savour'[26] it seems improbable that straight homosexuality was among them. There were 'moments of tenderness, even enchantment, without which a Princely existence would have been almost intolerable',[27] but like most 'rebels' of his day, he was basically conservative, a protestant against manners rather than morals. On the other hand what Lady Donaldson terms his 'special affinity of tastes'[28] with his younger brother George might be taken to indicate some sort of deviation from the accepted norm. Isolated from all contacts outside the family, poorly educated and yet plagued with unattainable standards of virtue and nobility, it is surprising that the royal brothers were normal in any way. It doesn't really matter, except that it must have been frustrating for girls to find the Prince of Wales impervious to their strenuously cultivated charms. 'I danced with a man who danced with a girl who danced with the Prince of Wales' was the nearest most of them could get to him, even in bed.

David himself considered that he was 'a product of the war';[29] Lady Donaldson thinks that he was 'a genuine product of his period' – 'bereaved and uprooted and emotionally exhausted but with an entirely new freedom from convention . . . '[30] If this is so, would it not apply equally to Bertie, only a year his junior? Neither of them had been bereaved or uprooted. Emotional exhaustion, particularly in a family noted for the lassitude and apathy of its young men, can be caused by having insufficient emotion to draw on, as well as by excessive use of it. David at twenty-nine and Bertie at twenty-eight were the very dissimilar products of something much older and more powerful than the post-war mood, to which Elizabeth, incidentally, though a contemporary of Poppy Baring, Audrey James, and all the other Bright Young Things, seems to have been immune.

In any case, David's fidelity to Freda Dudley Ward had made her accepted as another Alice Keppel by everyone except his parents. As he lived at York House with the genial company of Captain 'Fruity' Metcalfe and the rather suspect Brigadier-General Trotter, their disapproval could not have worried him unduly. Elizabeth was just right for his rather dull brother. She was sweet and appealing, comical and decorative. Between them, they might liven the old place up a bit. David himself was unmoved.

★   ★   ★

Unfortunately, according to the Duke of Gloucester's biographer, 'Prince Henry was a little slow, when told by his brother, Prince Albert, of his engagement to Lady Elizabeth Bowes-Lyon, to appreciate his brother's discernment, maturity and good fortune.'[31] It is hard to believe that Harry had any perceptive criticism or reason to dislike the girl. Perhaps it simply means that Prince Henry was a little slow. In a large family there is often one member who gets lumbered with the prefix 'poor', and poor Harry certainly earned it. He had a worse temper than Bertie, was more stupid and, almost incredibly, even more sickly. He also spent much of his childhood in splints, having weak legs as well as knock-knees, and suffered from what his mother called the 'tiresome nervous habit' of bursting into tears on the slightest provocation. He was also subject to uncontrollable fits of giggling for which, since his fancy was tickled by disaster, there was plenty of cause.

Theoretically, at least, he had an advantage over his elder brothers in being sent to school, though with one thing and another he hardly led the life of a normal schoolboy. At Eton he had endless colds ('You always seem to have one which is tiresome,' wrote Queen Mary)[32] and spent many of his holidays in rented houses with his old tutor, Hansell, knitting comforts for the troops. From Eton he did a stint at Sandhurst and at Trinity College, Cambridge, before becoming a cavalry officer attached to the 13th Hussars. To those who could appreciate his good intentions he was endearing. 'Prince Henry,'

Diana Cooper, a fellow guest at Belvoir Castle, wrote to her husband in the winter of 1919, 'is not half bad. I sat next to him at deenah. The Prince arrived sans equerry, sans clothes, sans valet, sans everything . . . I am favourably impressed with him.'[33]

★   ★   ★

There remains George, the only son who has never had, or never been allowed to have, a biographer. He, too, had been sent to school where, unlike poor Harry, he was an immediate success. 'Superficially much more charming than Prince Henry, he was also intellectually far more gifted; in fact, academically, musically and culturally in general he was streets ahead of anyone else in the family circle.'[34] Queen Mary found him 'a great comfort'. She could 'talk to him openly and with ease, the 2 other sons' – Bertie and Harry – 'are *boutonnés,*'[35] she remarked.

George was twenty-one when Elizabeth became engaged to his brother, and already in the Navy he hated. In the future he would pass under various clouds and emerge married to the stylish Marina of Greece, to become one of the leaders of a social set far removed from Elizabeth and Bertie's orbit. He had recently joined his brother David at York House, after Louis Mountbatten moved out on his marriage to Edwina Ashley. Georgie probably seemed to Elizabeth a nice boy, only a year younger than herself but, as women tend to believe, aeons away in wisdom and experience.

PART TWO

CHAPTER

9

COURT CIRCULAR

YORK COTTAGE, Sandringham

15 January: The Duke of York, attended by Wing Commander Louis Greig, has arrived at York Cottage.

It is with the greatest pleasure that the King and Queen announce the betrothal of their beloved son the Duke of York to the Lady Elizabeth Bowes-Lyon, daughter of the Earl and Countess of Strathmore, to which union the King has gladly given his consent.

'I was so startled and almost fell out of bed when I read the Court Circular, Chips Channon wrote in his diary. 'We have all hoped, waited, so long for this romance to prosper, that we had begun to despair that she would ever accept him ... He is the luckiest of men, and there's not a man in England today who doesn't envy him. The clubs are in gloom.'[1]

Chips, of course, wrote his diary with both ears cocked for posterity, and it is hard to believe that people genuinely devoted to Elizabeth felt such whole-hearted delight at the match. As for the entire male population of England nursing its broken heart, that was simply the beginning of the hyperbole that would obscure her from view for the rest of her life.

The papers couldn't think of much to say at first. There had been brief interest in the girl at the beginning of the month, but after the Prince of Wales's denial she had been dropped and nobody seemed to know much about her. 'She has been described as one of the most beautiful and popular young women at Court,'[2] the *Daily News* hazarded hopefully and inaccurately. Glamis was a help: a sixteenth-century ancestor had been burned as a witch, Macbeth was vaguely associated with the castle (let's say he owned it) and the Monster was good for a few lines. The front page photograph in the *Daily News* looked as though they were both direct descendants of the egg-shaped

Earl. Headlines in the *Daily Sketch* announced that Bertie had fought at Jutland and was a fluent speaker. By the following day, Wednesday, reporters were queuing outside 17 Bruton Street. Elizabeth happily gave the first and last personal interview of her life.

Lady Elizabeth is seated at a little writing desk, pen in hand, a pile of letters and telegrams before her. She is wearing a morning frock of greyish blue edged with fur, and round her neck is a double string of pearls. The bride-elect is very petite and has a magnetic personality.

Elizabeth: How very kind of you to come. And I am so happy – as you can see for yourself. You ask where is the Duke? Well, Bertie – you know everybody calls him Prince Bertie – has gone out hunting and he won't be back until this evening, when I've no doubt [with a smile] I shall see him.

Interviewer: You are fond of hunting, too?

Elizabeth: Oh yes, but I have done little lately. I play golf – badly – and I am fond of lawn tennis.

Interviewer: And so many people know what a beautiful dancer you are.

Elizabeth: That *is* kind of you to say that ... You see how busy I am trying to answer all these! I had no idea our engagement meant so much hard work. I think telegrams have come either here or to Buckingham Palace from all parts of the world. I had not the remotest idea everybody would be so interested or so extraordinarily kind. Edinburgh and Glasgow lead the public bodies in sending congratulations: it is altogether impossible to give anything like a list.

Interviewer: Has the Prime Minister sent a message?

Elizabeth: Not yet.

Interviewer: You are not wearing your engagement ring?

Elizabeth (laughing): No. It is to be made of sapphires.

Interviewer: And what are your immediate plans?

Elizabeth: First of all, I'm staying indoors today to deal with this correspondence. Of course, no wedding date has been fixed or where we are to live. I think we shall go down to Sandringham this coming weekend when all the wedding plans will be discussed. The visit to Sandringham is for that express purpose.

Interviewer: What were the circumstances surrounding the Duke's proposal?

Elizabeth (with great composure): Yes, it is true that he proposed in the garden at Welwyn on Sunday. But the story that he proposed or had to propose three times – well, it amused me, and it was news to me.

Interviewer: Princess Mary and Viscount Lascelles drove through the West End the afternoon after their engagement was announced. Do the Duke and yourself contemplate following that example?

Elizabeth: I don't know, but perhaps not just yet. He has a banquet at the Savoy tomorrow night. I am not [with another merry laugh] going to that. [Enter further telegrams and a message to say that the photographers are ready upstairs.]

Elizabeth: Thank you so much. I am sorry there is so little I can tell you.[3]

Such candour, such radiant charm. Fleet Street was captivated. No one was going to point out that her account of Bertie's proposal was unrelated to the facts, which were that Bertie had proposed for the umpteenth time on Saturday. No one except her parents knew that her birth certificate, already lodged with the appropriate authorities, could have been considered a felonius document. 'ALL THE WORLD LOVES A LOVER' the *Daily Sketch* declared, eagerly recording its share of the prattle: 'It's so very embarrassing,' said Lady Elizabeth, with a captivating smile. 'I've never been in such demand before, and it takes a little while to get used to it . . . Do people really want to know about my ring? . . . I can't realize that what is being written in the newspapers refers to me. I read it all quite impersonally as though it were about somebody I do not even know. I simply can't accustom myself to being the centre of such enormous public interest . . . Do they want to photograph me?' she broke off in a surprised tone, glancing out of the window at a score of photographers who had been waiting outside the house for an hour or more. 'That's an ordeal I shrink from, especially indoors. I hate flashlight photographs. Wouldn't it do if just *one* of them took me?'[4]

Friends and relations also had their say. 'Oh, she didn't bother about it,' her sister Rose remarked, when asked about the reputed engagement to the Prince of Wales. 'I don't think she paid the slightest attention to it.'[5] Lord Strathmore, 'laughing happily' (perhaps the most bizarre notion of all), said that his daughter's friendship with the Duke dated from early childhood: 'As to when and where the wedding will take place, I can tell you nothing. You must go to the womenfolk for that.'[6]

This naïve garrulity was short lived. 'The interviews granted to the Press, for which, let me add, both Press and public are duly grateful, by Lady Elizabeth Bowes-Lyon are surely without precedent. Never before has the bride-to-be of a prince of the blood-royal established such a link between the teeming millions and the private affairs of the exalted few. But I shouldn't be at all surprised to find a complete cessation of these interviews in the very near future.'[7] For once, the prognosis was correct. Elizabeth's innocent prattle was cut short by an edict from Sandringham, where the King and Queen had difficulty in surviving the shock of such outrageous publicity. Her talents in future would be restricted to mime.

Perhaps it was just as well. Her enterprising attitude to the truth, and the gullibility of the popular Press, led to one of the few public reprimands she would ever receive. 'One may be pardoned for imagining that Lady Elizabeth Bowes-Lyon was, when her engagement was first made public, quite a novice in the art of being interviewed,' wrote the *Illustrated London News*. 'Intent on being nice to everyone, she agreed to all that was suggested, even to the Duke of York being "quite as surprised as she was when he proposed!" This is assuredly not at all what she meant. Smiles were almost audible at the naïve statement that the Countess of Strathmore came into the room and the interview closed. I should say it did!'[8] On the other hand, when she had been effectively silenced and forced to rely entirely on the smile, the cheekily cocked head, the fluent wave, she wasn't at first entirely successful, 'people averring that it was impossible for her to be so permanently good natured as she would lead them to believe by her everlasting smile, which must surely be put on for the benefit of the public, and that when she got home it fell from her like a mask, to be replaced by a perfectly vile temper, and the unkindest behaviour to all around her. Her pink and white complexion was also made the target for unkind remarks...'[9] Elizabeth, in short, was still considered a human being.

No doubt she continued to be one. It becomes increasingly difficult to sympathize and identify with her as she moves from place to place, wearing this or that, waving from trains, opening a Sale of Work in aid of the National Orthopaedic Hospital, supporting the Duchess of Portland's 'At Home' to benefit the Nottingham lace industry, attending a performance of *Elijah* at Eton to patronize the St George's Chapel Restoration Fund, showing no preferences, expressing no dislikes, always predictable even in the moments of calculated spontaneity. This is Royalty's job, as digging holes is a road-mender's job, and it is extremely tedious. My task is not to report on the performance but to try to discover who, behind all that, was doing the performing.

She was seen dancing at Claridges, 'charmingly dressed in ivory laces [sic], the low waist finished on one side with a shower posy of blush roses ... She is decidedly petite, with small feet, and dances well.' This item of news from *The Lady* finishes with a puzzling postscript:

> 'Marriage the happiest bond of love might be
> If hands were only joined where hearts agree'

says the poet. Then, on the other hand, an old proverb tells us that we should 'Marry first and love will follow'.

She was photographed choosing the wedding cake at McVitie and Price, Bakers and Confectioners and Purveyors By Appointment to His Majesty the King, in Edinburgh, a firm whose latest biscuit tin was decorated with a portrait of her future father-in-law and a less profound but much cheerier verse:

Prince of sportsmen
Peerless shot
But happiest
Aboard his yacht.

She stood for hours while the Convocation of Canterbury, the City Corporation, the Convocation of York, London University, Cambridge University, the representative Ministers of the General Body of Protestant Dissenting Ministers of the Three Denominations and the Deputies of Protestant Dissenters presented their Loyal Addresses to the King on the occasion of his son's engagement, and the King answered them all one by one. And always, whatever she was doing, there was Bertie by her side, looking grateful.

★   ★   ★

Much though he wanted his sons to settle down, George had not looked forward to having a daughter-in-law. 'He disapproved,' wrote his eldest son, 'of . . . painted fingernails, women who smoked in public, cocktails, frivolous hats, American jazz, and the growing habit of going away for weekends.'[10] Most young women nowadays seemed inclined towards all those things. It was a great relief to find that Mabell Airlie's description of Bertie's girl as 'a born home-maker'[11] was less than adequate. She was soft and cuddly, tractable and yet the tiniest bit naughty, 'a perfect little duck,' chortled Admiral Beatty.[12] The King fell slightly in love with her himself. He made excuses for her unpunctuality, kept his temper in her company and patted her affectionately whenever the opportunity offered. Queen Mary, well satisfied with the outcome of all her hard work, wrote primly to her brother, 'Elizabeth is with us now, perfectly charming, so well brought-up, a great addition to the family.'[13]

'The cat is now completely out of the bag and there is no possibility of stuffing him back,' Elizabeth wrote to a friend[14] a few weeks earlier – a clumsy image which the Queen, had she known of it, would have found out of character. No point, therefore, in crying over spilt milk. Elizabeth set about learning her new job.

Life at St Paul's Walden Bury, Glamis and Bruton Street had been positively Bohemian compared with the clockwork ceremonial of Windsor and Sandringham. She had probably hoped that Helen Hardinge, now married to the King's assistant private secretary, would show her the ropes and share a few giggles, but Helen was inexplicably distant. Elizabeth was unaware at first that 'one or two of the older members of Queen Mary's entourage' – not, surely, Mabell Airlie – had 'said that it was thought wise that Lady Elizabeth should not see too much of her old friends . . .'[15] The future Duchess of York must learn that Royalty did not have friends.

As we have seen, Elizabeth was no rebel. She did not confront Helen, or tell the old ladies to mind their own business. The important thing, now as always, was to stay with the winning side. Like Helen, she quickly learned that 'to feel reasonably secure, one just had to learn the rules – it was rather like . . . keeping out of trouble in the army'. [16] She noted that the King liked the ladies to remove their long white gloves at dinner, rather than poking their hands through the wrists, as they usually did. Perhaps the cumbersome unrolling and unravelling was a nostalgic reminder of that nice little gal in Southsea, though the arms revealed were hardly as graceful. At the end of the meal they would all get dressed again, led by Queen Mary. As the gloves reached up to their armpits, it must have taken a considerable time. For these elaborate dinners the King and the Prince of Wales wore the 'Windsor uniform' designed by George III – dark blue tail coat with red collar and cuffs, breeches, and a white tie and white waistcoat. [17] The meal was accompanied by selections from such works as *The Merry Widow* and *No, No, Nanette* played by a string orchestra hidden behind a grille of fine wire gauze[18] – a humanitarian innovation since Queen Mary had discovered that for years the musicians had been crammed into an airless cupboard, [19] with the result that many of them collapsed unconscious over their violins.

Precisely one hour after they all sat down, the Queen would rise, followed by the women, each of whom curtsied to the King as they backed out of the room. They would then proceed to the Green Drawing Room, where the Queen sat bolt upright on her sofa and received the ladies, one by one, for a brief chat. The rest of them stood about swallowing their yawns. Exactly twenty minutes later, the King and his gentlemen appeared. There might then be a short gramophone concert – Caruso singing Handel's 'Largo', followed by the 'Hallelujah Chorus' and ending with a record of the Aldershot Military Tattoo, or perhaps the King's favourite, 'a sentimental yet stirring piece' entitled 'The Departure of the Troopship'. [20] The recital ended with the National Anthem, during which everybody, including the King and Queen, stood to attention. On the stroke of eleven, Their Majesties and the members of their family said goodnight to their guests – another lengthy ceremony – and went to bed. [21]

It is hardly surprising that night after night of this absurd and joyless ceremonial led to digestive complaints and, in some of them, a desperate longing for depravity. One evening David, Bertie, Harry and Georgie told the orchestra to wait for them in the Green Drawing Room after the old people had gone to bed. Collecting the younger members of the party – Elizabeth, perhaps, among them – they crept back to the drawing room after lights-out, rolled back the rugs, and tried to have a party. '. . . the musicians, more familiar with classical music and martial airs, made an earnest attempt to cope with out-moded foxtrots, which were as close as they could come to jazz', but it was a hopeless failure. 'The ancient walls seemed to exude dis-approval,' David recalled sadly. 'We never tried it again.'[22]

★   ★   ★

The wedding was announced for Thursday, 26 April 1923, and during that month James Stuart returned from America. Whatever Elizabeth was feeling – regretful, relieved, optimistic, doubtful – she looked much perkier than she had the year before. Her new '*café-au-lait* brown duvetyn skirt and loose Russian-shaped coat to match' and 'big black straw hat trimmed with soft black and gold ribbon' were most successful – presumably the Russian in question had been very short and plump, while 'soft black' became the rage overnight – and a girl is always happy thinking about her trousseau. Van loads of presents were arriving at 17 Bruton Street and the Palace. At the Archbishop of Canterbury's Faculty Office the veteran clerk, a Mr Bull, spent three days in a locked room engrossing the marriage licence on a roll of parchment nearly a yard square, using twenty quill pens of various thicknesses.[23] Court officials were working night and day on sensi-tive problems of protocol and precedence. Invitations were sent out to 3,000 guests, among whom were thirty 'factory boys', all of whom had to be provided with new suits.[24] Scores of seamstresses were snipping and stitching; hundreds more women and men were employed preparing the Abbey, rehearsing the procession, polishing buttons and harness, baking, decorating, cleaning up the streets, hurrying purposefully from place to place with sacks of letters, packages, flowers, buckets, ladders, potted palms, bandboxes. When she wasn't on call at the Palace or Windsor, Elizabeth spent hours with Madame Handley Seymour and her girls, being fitted for the wedding dress and trousseau. She had, it seemed, made the final decision of her life. She was a new comer and a commoner. Nobody was going to ask for her opinion.

On 24 April George and Mary gave an after-dinner party for 600 guests, who were required to spend most of it surveying a selection of wedding presents. 'I went in my knee breeches and medals after dinner to Buckingham Palace,' Herbert Asquith recorded, 'where the rooms big as they are were very nearly crowded. There were huge glass cases like you see in Bond Street shops, filled with jewels and every kind of gilt and silver ware: not a thing did I see that I would have cared to have or give. The poor little bride, everyone says, is full of charm and stood in a row with the King and Queen and the bridegroom, and was completely overshadowed.'[25] Possibly Elizabeth was wondering what on earth she could do with a thousand gold-eyed needles from the Livery Company of Needlemakers, and the English oak chest stacked with twenty-four pairs of wellington boots and galoshes from the Pattenmakers ('I look forward to an opportunity of putting to a practical test the contents of this beautiful chest which you have so generously given me,' she said).

On the morning of 25 April, *The Times* announced the engagement of Captain the Hon. James Gray Stuart, MVO, MC, formerly Equerry to the Duke of York, third and youngest son of the Earl and Countess of Moray, to Lady Rachel Cavendish, fourth daughter of the Duke and Duchess of Devonshire. Photographs of the couple shared a page with photographs of Elizabeth's wedding presents: a pearl necklace with heart-shaped pendant of amethyst set in brilliants from Queen Alexandra; two hideous vases, no doubt of great worth, from the Prince Regent of Japan; a necklace of diamonds and sapphires with a bracelet, ring and pendant to match from Queen Mary; a diamond necklace and pendant from Bertie and a diamond bandeau from Lord Strathmore. To fill up the page there was J. S. Helier's winsome portrait of the Prince of Wales which was to be exhibited at the Paris Salon, and a photograph of Signor Mussolini and General Diaz, Italian Minister for War, taking the salute at the Fascisti procession to celebrate the founding of Rome in 753 BC.

The great news in the world of charity was Pencil Week, the object of which was to sell a million pencils to raise funds for 'welfare work with mothers and babies'. A concert in aid of this estimable cause was held at the Mountbatten residence, Brook House, in Park Lane. Everybody bought a pencil and Miss Violet Vanbrugh recited Shelley's 'Arethusa'.[26] On the same day, 25 April, *The Tatler* came out with a full-plate colour portrait of Elizabeth looking infinitely wistful.

Elizabeth Bowes-Lyon and Prince Albert, Duke of York, were married next day in Westminster Abbey by Randall Davidson, Archbishop of Canterbury, and Cosmo Gordon Lang, Archbishop of York, assisted by Bishop Herbert Edward Ryle, Dean of Westminster, and the Most Reverend Walter John Forbes Robberds, Bishop of Brechin and Primus of the Scottish Episcopal Church.

CHAPTER

10

The York-Bowes-Lyon wedding was not broadcast, as the Archbishop of Canterbury feared that men in pubs might listen to it with their hats on. In every other way it was much like any Royal wedding in living memory. Traffic in the West End was disrupted. Fifty different 'bus routes were diverted and it was estimated that the Underground would have to carry over one million more than its daily number of passengers. Arrangements were made for both 'buses and trains to run 50,000 miles in excess of their normal day. 'Fabulously large crowds ... assembled, or tried to assemble, in Whitehall. There, perhaps, the soldiers ... and the police had to be more genially firm, or, rather firmly genial, than anywhere,' reported *The Times*. 'It was fortunate, too, that the weather was no more than fitfully fine, or the stream of ambulances in and out of Scotland Yard might have been really embarrassing.'

Superior journalism of those days reads as though the reporters were eager young graduates anxious to exploit the latest literary fashion. The historic present was much in favour. Inside the Abbey there 'is the ceaseless clank of swords and tinkle of spurs; the rustle of silks and chink of medal on medal; sailors stiff with gold lace, soldiers in scarlet and green and gold, divines in their robes, great men of law in wigs and gowns; orders, ribbons...' When the bride arrives on the arm of her father, 'an immense beadle, or other officer, garbed in a huge, scarlet gown, comes softly up to her. From his great hand dangles a little, white, very feminine object – a handkerchief bag, we judge it – which the bride has left in her carriage...' Elizabeth takes the bag with a grateful smile, then steps forward and puts her bouquet on the tomb of the Unknown Warrior, thereby sensibly solving the problem of holding two things at once.

The bride is dressed in fine chiffon moire, the colour of old ivory, embroidered with silver thread and pearls, with long medieval sleeves of fine Nottingham lace. Her train, lent by her mother-in-law, is made of point de Flandres lace mounted on tulle and her shoes are ivory moire embroidered with silver roses. She is attended by eight bridesmaids – the Ladies May and Mary Cambridge, Katharine Hamilton and Mary Thynne, the Misses Diamond Hardinge and Betty Cator, and her two nieces Elizabeth Elphinstone and Cecilia Bowes-Lyon. The bridegroom is in the uniform of a Group Captain of the RAF with the Garter Riband and Star and his recently acquired Thistle Star; the gold aiguillettes over his right shoulder show that he is a Personal Aide-de-Camp to the Sovereign and his single row of medals include his Service Medals from the Great War. His best man, or supporter, the Prince of Wales, wears the scarlet uniform of the Grenadier Guards. King George is impeccable as Admiral of the Fleet, Harry trussed into the uniform of the Tenth Hussars and Georgie miserably got up as a naval cadet. The mother of the bride is wearing a handsome gown of black marocain and georgette embroidered in jet and blue paillettes, with a cloak of black lace and marocain, the collar composed of shaded blue roses; the mother of the bridegroom is in aquamarine blue and silver, to which an iridescent effect has been added by showers of aquamarine blue crystals that sparkle on the skirt and corsage. Queen Alexandra wears purple velvet trimmed with gold lace. The Marchioness of Lansdowne is in pearl grey embroidered in cut steel. She wears badges which include the Royal Order of Victoria and Albert, the Imperial Order of the Crown of India, the Companion of Honour, the Lady of Justice of the Order of St John of Jerusalem in England and the ribbon and star of the Order of the British Empire, as well as a quantity of diamond and pearl knickknacks.

There are dark tortoishell paillettes and cabochans over heavy self-coloured satin beauté, draped bleu de soir chiffon velvet and crêpe marocain with old Carrickmatcross lace, oxidised and lie du vin woven drape d'argent bouclé with embroideries in claire de lune colourings, shot green and brown taffeta, giving the effect of beetle wings, Persian designs in multi-silks and metal thread. There are picture hats of cream-coloured lace straw trimmed with large cockades of gardenias and foliage, hats of fine crinoline with shaded ostrich feathers falling at one side, small hats of auburn-hued velvet decorated with sweeping aquamarine feathers, turban hats of almond-green embossed satin adorned with bunches of green feathers. There are gris fume fox collars and sable wraps, diamonds, amethysts, sapphires, emeralds and the Lesser Star of Africa. Dr Lang, in his customary inspiring manner, told the couple, 'You will not think so much of enjoyment as of achievement . . . it is to yourselves, as simple man and maid . . . that our heart turns as you go forth to meet the years that are to come. On behalf of a nation happy in your joy, we bid you Godspeed.'

There was, of course, no just cause or impediment why the simple man and maid should not be joined together in holy matrimony. The only recorded mishap was when a cleric in the bride's procession fainted, although the two smaller bridesmaids had a few awkward moments when Queen Alexandra and Queen Mary converged for a chat on either side of the bride's train and the children, holding the end of it, were left stranded. However, they gallantly fought their way through the purple velvet and the showers of aquamarine crystals and emerged, still clasping the train, triumphant. Apart from these minor crises the production went smoothly, accompanied by Elgar, Parry, Stanford and Mendelssohn, and even the Registers were correctly signed and witnessed. 'There is but one wedding,' *The Times* pronounced solemnly, 'to which [the public] look forward with still deeper interest – the wedding which will give a wife to the Heir to the Throne, and, in the course of nature, a future Queen to England and to the British people.'

★   ★   ★

As Elizabeth up to this point had been a commoner (i.e. below the rank of peeress), she had of course driven to the Abbey in an ordinary State landau, escorted only by four mounted police; the troops lining the route had not been required to present arms as she passed. So much for the common people. On her return as Duchess of York she rode with her husband in a scarlet and gold coach escorted by cavalry, followed by the King and Queen, the Princes, the Princess and the Viscount, Queen Alexandra, the Strathmores, and carriages full of royal relics. Behind them came six ambassadors, thirteen foreign ministers, six chargés d'affaires, the Prime Minister, the Baldwins, the Neville Chamberlains, the Lloyd Georges, the Asquiths, the Winston Churchills, the Clyneses and Mr Ramsay Macdonald M.P. The troops saluted as she passed, and the common people yelled their delight at her elevation. She looked, not surprisingly, radiant.

When the procession had finally disappeared into the inner quadrangle the troops were withdrawn and the crowds made a concerted rush to Buckingham Palace. The sun came out, well-polished tubas and bassoons and trumpets hooted and tooted merrily across the Park, people swarmed over the Victoria Memorial and clung to the Palace railings. At 1.15 the windows of the Balcony Room opened and the minuscule couple, like a pair of distant puppets, appeared behind draped red velvet followed by the King and Queen, Queen Alexandra and the Strathmores. Cheering resounded down the Mall, across Green Park and St James's Park and Constitution Hill. After five minutes, Alexandra 'stole away' and the parents stepped back. Bertie stood stiffly, looking a little dazed, but Elizabeth gave her benediction again and again, north, south, east and west, repeating 'Thank you ... thank you.' The audience roared. Paradoxically, the act that isolated her from them had made them feel that they now owned her.

The gesticulating, inaudible little figure on the balcony suddenly 'belonged'. If she had actually been one of them, a twenty-two-year-old girl hanging on to her husband's arm, she would have been a stranger.

The menu for the eight-course wedding breakfast included Consommé à la Windsor, Supreme de saumon Reine Mary, Cotelettes d'agneau Prince Albert, Chapons à la Strathmore and, very suitably, Fraises Duchesse Elizabeth. There were no speeches, but the bride prettily mimed cutting one of the pre-sliced wedding cakes. Meanwhile the rain had started again, a worry for those who were responsible for the next procession but surely no great matter of concern to the Royal party. The wedding pictures, nevertheless, are joyless. The newly-weds look stuffed, the bridesmaids like ghoulish wax-works. Recklessly contradicting the evidence, the papers asserted that Elizabeth's 'happiness infected everyone, and happiest of all was the bridegroom'. Their appearance of gloomy fortitude must have been caused by the restraint of the occasion or the inadequacy of the photographers.

Luckily the rain had stopped by the time they climbed into the open landau which was to take them to Waterloo. They were pelted instead with 'favours' hurled by the three mischievous Royal brothers, one of whom – Harry? – moulded confetti and bag into a lethal ball which he aimed at the bridegroom. For a split second it looked as though there might be a nasty scene. Fortunately their mother and sister and Aunt Vicky began wafting rose petals – made by blind workers for the occasion – from the balcony; Elizabeth bowed and waved and smiled, Bertie was distracted and the onlookers roared their approval. No sooner had the landau and its four greys trotted off down the Mall than the Prince of Wales bundled into his car and was gone, with only a peremptory salute to the crowd.

At Waterloo the couple were received by Sir Herbert Walker, an official of the Southern Railway, Mr Szlumper, chief engineer, and Mr Bushrod, acting superintendent of the line. The platform barrier, normally jammed with commuters, was decorated with palms, hydrangeas and rhododendrons. They were conducted to their special train by Sir Herbert, Mr Szlumper and Mr Bushrod, who no doubt informed them that they were due at Bookham at 17.10 or, as they said in those days, ten minutes past five. Their saloon carriage was upholstered in old gold brocade and decked with white roses, white heather, white carnations and lilies of the valley. Mr Szlumper or Mr Bushrod blew the whistle, the signals came down and Driver Wiggs, with a celebratory blast on the hooter, steamed off in the direction of Surrey.

Did they kick their shoes off, puff and groan, fall into each other's arms, or did they sit decorously looking out of the window, making small talk as the miles chuntered by? One should be able to hazard a guess by now, having lived with them so long, but it's impossible. Holding hands in a boat may suddenly have seemed inadequate preparation for the immediate future. Luckily Bookham is not very far – slightly north-east of Guildford, in fact. Unless someone had provided them with a thermos, they must have been longing for a cup of tea.

Arrived at Bookham, they were received by the Chief Constable of Surrey and a posse of officials. No tea. After the usual speeches of welcome, they drove out of the station yard, through a modest crowd of cheering natives, proceeded a couple of hundred yards and stopped. Elizabeth was presented with a bouquet by the daughter of a works-manager, a child who could not, it seems, toddle as far as the station. Elizabeth thanked her for the bouquet. They drove on as far as the church. No tea, but 300 schoolchildren, Girl Guides and Boy Scouts lined up and smartly polished, together with the Chairman of the Parish Council and his fellow Councillors. The Chairman presented a short but painstakingly rehearsed speech of welcome and stood back, humbly expectant. Bertie summoned the spirit of Jutland: politely but firmly he thanked the Chairman, pointed out that it had been a tiring day, and propelled Elizabeth towards the car. A moment's dismay, then fifteen-year-old Jean McFarlane pelted after them with a bouquet of red roses tied up in a long streamer of Strathmore tartan. Elizabeth thanked her for the bouquet. At last they were free to drive the mile and a half to Polesden Lacey, lent for their honeymoon by the ecstatically flattered Mrs Ronnie Greville.

On 28 April the *London Gazette* announced:

> that, in accordance with the settled general rule that a wife takes the status of her husband, Lady Elizabeth Bowes-Lyon on her marriage has become HRH Duchess of York, with the status of a Princess.

CHAPTER

11

Polesden Lacey had none of the comforts of home, as Bertie and Elizabeth understood them. There were seven self-contained guest suites, each with its own bathroom – remarkable in those days – and 'an unobtrusive luxury' that even Osbert Sitwell said he had never encountered elsewhere. Apart from this opportunity for indulgence, it is hard to know how the Yorks could put up with Mrs Greville, who in years to come would complain, 'I was so happy in the days when they used to run in and out of my house as if they were my own children.'[1] Her only admirers were royalty, which is by its very exclusiveness ignorant or naïve, and Sir Osbert, who was neither. Harold Nicolson, no mean snob himself, called her 'nothing more than a fat slug filled with venom', Sacheverell Sitwell thought she was 'sheer hell', Lady Leslie said she would rather have an open sewer in her drawing room than Maggie Greville. The young Yorks, revelling in the unaccustomed fleshpots, were her prize protégés. When she died in 1942, leaving an estate of around £2 million, she bequeathed Marie Antoinette's priceless jewels to Elizabeth, £20,000 to Elizabeth's younger daughter and £25,000 to the Queen of Spain. Having no heirs, she left Polesden Lacey to the National Trust. One can't help suspecting that this last thought was wily rather than magnanimous.

It is not recorded whether Mrs Greville's two unreliable butlers, Boles and Bacon, remained to attend on the honeymoon couple. If so, there must have been some hilarious meals. Both retainers were constantly as drunk as the lords they waited on, but oblivious to reprimand and never, for some curious reason, sacked. Boles, who claimed to be a communist, had been known to eat the entire dish he was about to serve; Bacon, on receiving a furious note from Mrs Greville saying 'You're drunk. Leave the room at once,' placed it on a silver salver and carried it unsteadily down the table to Sir Austen Chamberlain, who was astounded. Whether or not they were present during the honeymoon, on later visits this raffish pair became very attached to Elizabeth. 'All the butlers were drunk,' Osbert Sitwell wrote of one dinner party, '...bobbing up every minute during dinner to offer the Duchess of York whisky.'[2] What with Bertie's predilection for alcohol, and this kind of service, it would be nice to think that the first ten days of the Yorks' honeymoon passed in a state of innocent inebriation.

Next they went to Glamis, where Elizabeth succumbed to whooping cough – where she could have caught it, heaven knows. Bertie, in spite of his own experience of the complaint, was unsympathetic. 'So unromantic to catch whooping cough on your honeymoon,' he wrote to Queen Mary, who merely thought it tactless. A new bathroom had been installed in their honour, but after the luxuries of Polesden Lacey Bertie was not impressed. The weather was appalling, there was nothing to do, and Elizabeth lay in the ancestral four-poster whooping like an expiring sheep. 'It must have been with a pang that you left your home after 27 years,' his father had written after the wedding. Perhaps even Bertie had felt that this was hardly the thing to say to a newly married son. At Glamis, just for a day or two, he wondered whether the old man was more perceptive than he seemed.

A fortnight later they travelled south again, to Frogmore House in Windsor Great Park. In spite of the glum connection between his birthday and 'Mausoleum Day', and the close proximity of his dead great-grandparents, Bertie was happy at Frogmore. In his childhood there had been a single bathroom on the ground floor, poor lighting, bad drainage, inadequate plumbing and very little heat; it had been crammed with commemorative statuettes, miniatures, gold lockets containing strands of hair from the dear departed, letter-weights of bronze hands modelled after death.[3] There is no reason to suppose that it was very different in 1923. Nobody had actually lived there since George V came to the throne, though Queen Mary often came across from the Castle to spend summer afternoons in the garden and it was sometimes lent to exiled royal relatives, which Her Majesty found 'a decided bore'.[4] Elizabeth was familiar with ghosts, but hers were a disreputable lot compared with the stodgy Hanovers and their memorabilia. It was like spending your honeymoon in a cross between a furniture repository and a necropolis.

Not, however, to Bertie. The further he got from his childhood, the more golden it seemed. The schoolroom was just the same, even the ink stains on the table. This is where he and David and sister Mary drilled with midget bayonets, that's the statue of great-great-Grandpa – we had a footman called Smithson who looked just like him, and (they were now in the dining room) I'll never forget when poor old Hua took his first mouthful of tadpoles on toast, we'd caught them in the lake and got the kitchen to serve them up – he thought they were frogs' legs,[5] we nearly died laughing. Smiling, exclaiming, asking questions, taking it all in for future reference, Elizabeth was the perfect companion.

At the beginning of June, the honeymoon over, they moved into White Lodge in Richmond Park, 'a shallow and impermanent-feeling house', according to Pope-Hennessy, built as a hunting lodge by George II and much enlarged by his daughter Amelia. When Queen Mary was two years old, the house had been given to her parents. It was, therefore, her childhood home; her father and mother had died there and her eldest son had been born there. Not surprisingly, she wished to 'keep it in the family'. Forgetting how upset she had been to find York Cottage fully furnished when she moved in as a young bride (George, with the best intentions, had given the whole place over to a 'Maple's man' without consulting her), she had happily supervised the decoration and furnishing of White Lodge while her son and daughter-in-law were away. Elizabeth, the 'born home-maker', found that there was precious little to do, apart from rearranging the knickknacks and making room for twenty-four pairs of wellington boots.

Still, they were lumbered with it. Alone at last – apart, that is, from cooks, butlers, footmen, parlourmaids, housemaids, kitchen maids, ladies maids, valets, bootboys, chauffeurs, grooms, gardeners, ladies-in-waiting and equerries – the newly-weds made themselves as cosy as possible in their eighteen reception rooms, only one of which was large enough to receive in, and their warren of bedrooms, only one of which was large enough for the ducal bed. Their estate was a miserable five acres. On holidays and at weekends they were peered at by sightseers. Although the Duchess of Teck, Queen Mary's mother, had 'found it quite possible to conduct a social life from Richmond if one had plenty of good horses and carriages', the Yorks in their Daimler found it exhausting. The climate in Richmond Park seemed particularly inclement and the central heating broke down. Altogether it was hardly a propitious start to married life.

★   ★   ★

On 9 June, two days after they moved in, Princess Christian of Schleswig-Holstein-Sonderburg-Augustenburg (known as 'Lenchen', to which her mother usually added the prefix 'poor') died in London. Nobody had any great reason to mourn her. The third daughter of Queen Victoria, she had behaved very badly back in the 1890s when Mary of Teck became engaged to the Prince of Wales; apparently she thought that her own daughters, Marie Louise ('Louie') or Helena Victoria ('The Snipe') had a greater claim to Prince Eddy's affections. Royal memories are long, and Queen Mary never quite forgave her for this indiscretion. Nevertheless, the Court plunged into its familiar black and the Yorks' holiday was extended for a further month. When it was all over, Elizabeth found that the bulk of poor Lenchen's official duties had been bequeathed to herself.

I cannot improve on Lady Cynthia Asquith's summing up of this amorphous employment: 'Each day she was asked to become Patroness of several societies, to visit hospitals, to lay foundation stones. Every sort of appeal poured in, and each one had to be seriously considered and answered. The daily post became a very formidable factor in her life. Then there were Court Functions to attend, and visits to be paid with her husband to Industrial Centres, visits that sometimes involved a stay of two days.' The first of these, described as 'a round of duties', was to Liverpool at the end of July.

They did not, of course, stay in Liverpool, but as guests of Lord Derby at Knowstey. Elizabeth smeared a blob of cement on the foundation stone of the new Nurses' Home at the Royal Infirmary, and was warmly applauded. She then stood on the balcony of the Town Hall and watched the inspection of the Guard of Honour. Bertie gave a bronze medallion to an X-ray pioneer and unveiled some frescos in the Memorial Hall. Next day they boarded the tender *Galatea* and chugged up the Mersey. Elizabeth stayed in the saloon, since it was raining, but later joined Bertie on deck to wave and bow to the damp crowds lining the banks. Then they took a brisk look at the excavations at Gladstone Dock, drove to Aintree to watch the racing, and returned to London.

She was now 'very tired', according to Lady Cynthia, and in need of a break. Bertie took her to Balmoral. She was marched up a nearby mountain by Princess Alice, Countess of Athlone, where they got stuck in a snowstorm. Alice, reputed to be the only woman in history who could knit and mountaineer at the same time,[6] probably finished a sock or two. In September they moved from Balmoral to Holwick Hall, one of the Strathmore properties in County Durham, for the shooting. They had barely settled down before Bertie received a telegram ordering him to go to Belgrade in October to stand god-father to King Alexander's infant son and to represent King George at the wedding of Prince Paul of Yugoslavia to Princess Olga of Greece.

Bertie was furious. He was a married man now, with responsibilities. They were having a well-earned rest, and he was fed up with the bloody Balkans anyway. 'Curzon should be drowned for giving me such short notice,' he raged to the long-suffering Greig, '... he must know things are different now.'[7] The culpable Foreign Secretary being unavailable, the house-party, which included most of the Strathmore family, went through a short period of stress. Perhaps this was the first time Elizabeth had to use all her wiles to restore order, but she managed it. On 27 September Bertie had 'a very nice day' – three rabbits, one snipe, two black game and three hundred and fifty-four grouse hit the heather.[8] On 18 October they set off to attend one of the final performances of European monarchy.

★   ★   ★

When Elizabeth was two days old, on 6 August 1900, *The Times* published the following leader:

> The marriage of King Alexander of Servia and Mme Draga Maschlin was solemnized yesterday at Belgrade 'with much ceremony' we are told. On the more personal aspects of this marriage to which grave exception has been taken in Servia, not merely on account of the great disparity of age between the young bridegroom and his matronly bride, we do not propose to dwell. The Obkenovitch family is neither of such ancient nor of such illustrious origin that the term mesalliance must necessarily be applied to the union of the King with one of his subjects, were there no other objection to the choice which he has made but that of the lady's social standing. From that point of view King Alexander might appeal with no little force to the example set to him by his father when he raised the daughter of an army contractor to the throne. Rightly or wrongly, however, the announcement that Mme Maschlin's notorious influence over the young sovereign was to be tightened by a matrimonial alliance provoked at the outset such widespread disapproval as to threaten serious consequences for the tranquillity of Servia and even for the peace of the Balkan peninsular.
>
> King Milan, in whom his son could hardly have expected to find so stern a censor, marked his paternal displeasure by throwing up ostentatiously the post of Commander-in-chief of the Servian army; the Servian Cabinet handed in its resignation, and the Pretender, Prince Peter Karageorgevitch, son-in-law of the Prince of Montenegro, was reported to be holding himself in readiness on the frontier for any opportunity which popular disturbance might offer . . .

Almost three years later, on 10 June 1903, King Alexander and Queen Draga were assassinated – or perhaps 'lynched' is more accurate, for it was a nasty killing – in Belgrade. Peter Karageorgevitch's chance had come, and he was unanimously elected King of the Serbs, Croats and Slovenes.

His eldest son George abdicated his right of succession owing to the report that he had mortally wounded his valet in a fit of passion. It was, therefore, the younger son, Alexander, three years Bertie's junior, who was appointed Regent in 1913 when his father became too ill for the job. Alexander fought with proper heroism in the Great War and succeeded to the throne in 1921. A year later he married Princess Marie of Rumania (known as 'Mignon'), the daughter of King Ferdinand and Princess Marie of Edinburgh (known as 'Missy'), who was herself the daughter of Princess Marie of Russia (known as 'Aunt

Marie') and Queen Victoria's son Alfred, Duke of Edinburgh and Saxe-Coburg-Gotha, who died on page one of this book in the summer of 1900. Bertie, you may remember, attended the Yugoslav wedding in 1922 when he was at his lowest ebb; the baby to whom he was now to stand godfather was born on 6 September 1923 and would be called Peter.

As for Prince Paul and Princess Olga, whose nuptials were to take place the day after Peter's christening, he was the son of Prince Arsene Karageorgevitch and a cousin of King Alexander; she was the grand-daughter of Queen Alexandra's brother King George I of Greece (known as 'Uncle Willy') – the one who was assassinated in 1913 while taking his morning stroll in Salonika. She was also the sister of Marina, who would later rescue Bertie's youngest brother from what Robert Sencourt calls 'an errant love'.[9] Paul had been up at Oxford with the Prince of Wales and, as Chips Channon repeatedly re-members, was part of what Chips liked to think of as the Channon-Elizabeth-Gage clique in Elizabeth's debutante days.

Both ceremonies were intended to demonstrate that the House of Karageorgevitch was securely in possession of the Yugoslav throne, and to strengthen the dynastic ties that were supposed to bind the Balkan royal families together. The entire clan, regnant and exiled, would be present. Perhaps it is now clear why George V was so anxious to be represented.

When the special train pulled in at Belgrade on the evening of 20 October and Elizabeth saw the whole chorus lined up on the platform, her heart, if it was anything like a normal heart, sank. She triumphed of course. 'They were all enchanted with Elizabeth especially Cousin Missie [sic],' Bertie wrote proudly to his parents. 'She was wonderful with all of them & they were all strangers except two Paul and Olga.[10] The Palace was overcrowded, there was no hot water, Kings and Queens, Archdukes and Grand Duchesses, scurried about on a hopeless search for a lavatory, a hot water bottle, someone to sew on a button. At the christening the ancient Patriarch lost his grip on the Crown Prince, who sank, bubbling, to the bottom of the font. Bertie, with great presence of mind, scooped him out just as the whole of the infant's short life was passing before his eyes. The House of Kara-georgevitch, temporarily saved from extinction, breathed again.

Blue in the face and bawling murder, the child was then placed on a cushion and carried by Bertie three times round the altar, preceded by a deacon with a thurible emitting clouds of incense. The chapel, unlike the Palace, was as hot as a sauna. Sweating under their gold braid and ribbons and orders and hardware, choked by the fumes and deafened by the Crown Prince's protests, the nobility of Europe somehow survived the ordeal. The following day they all watched while

Princess Olga stepped over a strip of cloth, symbolizing the moat of her husband's house, scattered corn and kissed a boy baby.[11] As things turned out, she would have been wiser to slip away incognito to Buenos Aires.

They were all, except for Elizabeth and Bertie, doomed. Alexander was assassinated by a Croat in Marseilles eleven years later. Paul was then appointed Regent, but understandably collapsed under German pressure and bolted in 1941, after which he and Olga were dispatched in disgrace to South Africa by the British Government. Peter, left to cope with the German invasion as best he might, was rescued by the RAF and eventually brought to England. 'Missy', who had already suffered greatly through her son Carol's elopement with the notorious Magda Lupescu, not to mention his two divorces, would in a couple of months' time see her second daughter, the Queen of Greece, exiled. Of the twenty-four representatives of European royalty to attend Elizabeth's eldest daughter's wedding in 1947, fourteen would in fact be exiles, their titles as meaningless as the Emperor's new clothes. As I write, eighty-two-year-old Princess Olga, eighty-five-year-old Elizabeth and her eighty-four-year-old sister-in-law Alice, Duchess of Gloucester, are among the very few who can vouch for the existence of that long, elaborate tragi-comedy.

1. Queen Victoria with some of her family at Osborne House, *circa* 1899. Bertie stands with his father, the then Duke of York. The Duchess of York (*third left*) holds Princess Mary with David standing beside her.

2. The Earl and Countess of Strathmore with their nine children, *circa* 1904. The Countess holds David and Elizabeth stands by her side.

3. LEFT David (*left*) and Bertie with their tutor.

4. BELOW Elizabeth and her brother David at Glamis, 1909.

5. OPPOSITE ABOVE Queen Alexandra (*centre*) with her son, King George V, and Queen Mary as they leave St Margaret's, Westminster after the wedding of Louis Mountbatten and Edwina Ashley, 1922.

6. OPPOSITE BELOW David Bowes-Lyon's (*centre back*) family photograph of Queen Mary's visit to Glamis, 1920. Elizabeth (*middle row, centre*) stands next to her father and Queen Mary is seated next to Lady Airlie (*far left*) with the Countess of Strathmore and Princess Mary on the right.

7. ABOVE LEFT A private family photograph of Elizabeth with Bertie (*left*) and David.

8. ABOVE RIGHT James Stuart as a captain in the Royal Scots, March, 1918.

9. RIGHT Elizabeth and Bertie, 1923.

10. RIGHT Lady Elizabeth photographed with her father the Earl of Strathmore and her eldest brother, Lord Glamis, just before her marriage to the Duke of York.

11. BELOW The Duke and Duchess of York leave the courtyard of Buckingham Palace in an open landau for their honeymoon at Polesden Lacey, 1923.

12. OPPOSITE ABOVE The Duke of York (*centre*) with his brothers, the Prince of Wales (*left*) and the Duke of Gloucester at a point–to–point meeting, 1924.

13. OPPOSITE BELOW The Duchess of York drives with her mother, the Countess of Strathmore, to the opening of the British Empire Exhibition at Wembley, 1925.

14. RIGHT The Prince of Wales kisses the Duchess of York before the Duke and Duchess leave for their World Tour, 1927.

15. BELOW The Duchess of York with King George V at a charity fête in the grounds of Balmoral, 1927. They are accompanied by Princess Elizabeth, Queen Mary and the Duke of York.

16. Elizabeth with her mother the Countess of Strathmore, her brother David Bowes-Lyon and her daughter Princess Elizabeth.

CHAPTER

12

Elizabeth's sense of theatre must have been roused by the Belgrade shenanigans. It was hard to settle down to the rigours of White Lodge, the staid English Court, the daily grind. Fortunately there was the wedding of Louise Mountbatten and Crown Prince Gustav of Sweden to look forward to – with two working kings, four queens, six princes and ten princesses among the guests it was almost as good as the Balkans. A week later, on 12 November 1923, they were off to the Guards Chapel for the marriage of Bertie's cousin Maud to Lord Carnegie. Maud's Uncle George was not present at this relatively homely affair. He was sitting at home trying to persuade Stanley Baldwin not to dissolve Parliament and call a General Election. He failed. Baldwin was heavily defeated at the polls on 8 December. 'The result of the General Election must be very worrying to Papa now,' Bertie wrote nervously to his mother, 'I wonder what is going to happen.'[1] On 22 January 1924 King George handed over the government of his country and Empire to the Labour Party for the first time in history.

Anyone who thinks that politics have no place in Elizabeth's story lacks imagination. In the experience of her husband's family, Socialism was the beginning of the end, and a very nasty end at that. Every creak in the corridors, every rustle in the rhododendrons, might mean their hour had come. Fog lay heavily on Windsor and Richmond Parks. They appeared to be empty, but who knew what was lurking out there? The mob had already sung the Red Flag in the Albert Hall, of all places. They waited, in the dripping silence, for the sound of tumbrils.

But nothing happened. It seemed that the only people who believed in the logical consequences of Socialism were those who, theoretically, should have been its first victims. These regicides and rabble-rousers were, thank God, British. 'As we stood waiting for His Majesty amid the gold and crimson magnificence of the Palace,' the new Lord Privy Seal recalled in his memoirs, 'I could not help marvelling at the strange turn of Fortune's wheel, which had brought Macdonald the starvelling clerk, Thomas the engine driver, Henderson the foundry labourer and Clynes the mill-hand to this pinnacle beside the man whose forbears had been Kings for so many splendid generations...'[2]

The contrast between a thriving aristocracy and the men in bowler hats who now governed them gave a curious twist to British snobbery at both ends of the scale. It was said that Co-op vans were now delivering provisions to 10 Downing Street. The Dowager Countess of Warwick threw open her stately home, Easton Lodge, as a rest home for Labour Members of Parliament. There was a brief scandal about Ramsay Macdonald holding 30,000 £1 shares in McVitie and Price. The first State ball at the Palace started disastrously, all the guests standing about as though at a village hop. 'At last,' Chips Channon recorded, 'the Prince of Wales opened the ball with the Duchess of York and soon everyone was dancing.'[3] No other couple in the family, or in the Court, could have saved that situation.

The Government lasted for nine months, during which time the only new legislation that had anything to do with Socialism was Wheatley's Housing Act. King George liked Mr Wheatley: 'He is an extreme Socialist and comes from Glasgow. I had a very interesting conversation with him.[4] He also admired Ramsay Macdonald with reservations. But the Bolshevik the King became most attached to was Jim Thomas, the engine driver, who was invited to stay every year at Balmoral: 'Well, it's a bloody dull 'ouse, of course, and I told the King so. 'E was regretting that the young Princes didn't like the place. So I said, "I don't wonder at that, Sir. It's a bloody dull 'ouse...".'[5]

They did, it's true, recognize the Soviet Union. The King confined himself to hoping that the Soviet representative would be a Minister, whom he could ignore, rather than an Ambassador, who would have to be asked to dinner. The most pressing problem, however, was sartorial. Would the starvelling clerk and the foundry labourer agree to wear Court dress? Of course they would. But could they afford it? Tactful inquiries were made, and Moss Bros. offered to provide regulation trousers, coat, cocked-hat and sword for a mere £30 the set. It soon became difficult to distinguish between Conservatives and Socialists, until they opened their mouths. 'Baldwin would have been at home leading the Labour Party, and Macdonald, with his romantic cast of mind, was well suited to lead the Conservatives,'[6] writes A. J. P. Taylor. It all came to the same thing in the end.

The point was, the Royal family insisted, that although there was undoubtedly a most worthy side to Socialism – they were nothing if not fair – it simply wasn't *necessary* in Britain. *Everyone* was deeply concerned with welfare and improving the lot of the poor – the young Yorks, for instance, in spite of their gruelling round of official duties and the inconveniences of their domestic life had found time to attend the 'Banquet for Little Londoners and a distribution of Hampers to Crippled Children' just before Christmas. An orchestra played while the children enjoyed their roast beef and potatoes, and after that there was community singing. The Duke and Duchess watched from the gallery. Later they talked to the children, who had each been given a packet of food to which the Duke and Duchess had contributed biscuits.

This, surely, was practical Socialism. As for all the nonsense about privilege, the Family was feeling the pinch as much as anyone. £360,000 of the King's annual income was spent on maintaining the functions of monarchy, leaving him only £110,000 for his personal use. Even with the additional revenue from the Duchy of Lancaster – a mere £44,000 – it didn't go very far. The Queen, it's true, received £10,000 a year, but surely she earned it? The Queen Dowager, they had to admit, was a liability. The country gave her an annual £70,000, but even with the interest on the fortune bequeathed to her by her dead husband she couldn't seem to make ends meet – generous to a fault, that was Motherdear's trouble. Her affairs had been investigated by the Treasury, and to everyone's horror it was discovered that the old lady had been paying tax. That was soon put right. After all, the State could surely afford to pay its widows 10/- a week without robbing the Queen Dowager. As for the younger generation, they worked hard for their living. The Prince of Wales got nothing at all except the revenue from the Duchy of Cornwall, and Bertie certainly earned every penny of his £25,000 a year.

Complacently, though not without a certain amused sympathy, the Royal Family watched the Labour Government's ineffectual attempts to undermine British capitalism. By the end of October it had admitted defeat. On 7 November Stanley Baldwin, Lord Curzon, Viscount Cave, Lord Salisbury and Lord Birkenhead, together with an assortment of knights and distinguished Members, put on their own Court dress once more and set out for the familiar Palace. The Yorks, badly in need of a holiday after such a nerve-wracking year, left for four months' big-game shooting in Africa. 'I don't think I really thanked you properly for allowing Elizabeth & me to go,' Bertie wrote hurriedly to his father.[7]

I certainly don't intend to follow the Yorks' every move, but this trip shows them at play, which is unusual. They ate in the open and slept under canvas, watched tribal dances ('some of which were very weird,' wrote Bertie),[8] were offered a farm, which the King told them not to accept ('What would you do if the farm didn't pay?'),[9] were taken on safari by a Portuguese white hunter known as 'The Hoot'. Elizabeth wore an untypical but fetching get-up of pants, belted shirt and felt bush-hat. With her 0.275 Rigby rifle she bagged a rhinoceros, a buffalo, a waterbuck, an oryx, a Grant's gazelle, an antelope, a Kenya hartebeest, a steinbuck, a water-hog and a jackal. In Uganda, Bertie, intrepidly hunting on foot, shot an elephant whose tusks weighed 90 lb each: 'It was very lucky as there are not many very big ones left.' He killed a smaller one two days later, 'so we did well in the home of the elephant.'[10] It didn't compare, of course, with his father's and brother's hauls in India – thirty-nine tigers in one day, not to mention panthers, bears, and most of the remaining lions – but he felt it was a pretty respectable score.

They returned home on 19 April 1925 to face what was, for Bertie, a major ordeal. The British Empire Exhibition at Wembley had been opened by the King the previous summer – an historic occasion, as it was the first time that the Emperor's voice had been broadcast, the apparatus and microphones cunningly concealed among the cinerarias on the Royal Dais. This year, Bertie succeeded David as President of the Exhibition, which was due to re-open on 10 May. The most popular exhibits on the 220-acre showground were Queen Mary's dolls'-house, the tomb of Tutankhamun and an effigy of the Prince of Wales made out of butter. There was a coal mine with real pit ponies – I don't know if there were real miners – and a reproduction of Niagara Falls; an entire Maori village, complete with authentic Maoris, and a Palace of Engineering six and a half time the size of Trafalgar Square. 'The British Empire Exhibition aims to complete in 1925 the educational work for Empire unity and Empire trade so well begun in 1924,' Bertie's official announcement read. Saying it through a microphone in front of his father and thousands of spectators, not to mention the unseen millions of listeners, was a different matter. 'I do hope I shall do it well,' he wrote to the King. 'But I shall be very frightened as you have never heard me speak & the loud speakers are apt to put one off as well. So I hope you will understand that I am bound to be more nervous than I usually am.'[11]

It was an agonizing experience for everyone. Elizabeth might smile and smile at the inarticulate, struggling man on the Dais, but it was no use. 'Bertie got through his speech all right, but there were some rather long pauses,'[12] the King wrote gloomily to Georgie the following day. There was grave disquiet in the family circle. Could Bertie really be counted on? He was inadequate in public and even his private abilities seemed open to doubt. He had been married for two and a half years, and not a sign of an heir. Had they been mistaken in Elizabeth? Backed the wrong horse? One didn't discuss such things, naturally, but there was an aura of failure round the Duke of York which nobody cared for, least of all his wife.

Something must be done. Somehow, between unveiling a stained glass window in York Minster, attending the Railways Centenary celebrations in Darlington, dining with the African Society and touring the Kodak works at Wealdstone, it was. By the time they left for Glamis and Balmoral in August, Elizabeth was pregnant. 'Alge and I are thrilled over your news of Elizabeth's hopes; thank God,' Alice Athlone wrote fervently to Queen Mary, adding rather wildly, 'Kenya is famous for having that effect on people, I hear!'[13]

CHAPTER

13

In November 1925 Queen Alexandra died at Sandringham. The decorative, silly, kind-hearted old lady, no deafer now than she had been in life, was stowed away in the Memorial Chapel at Windsor. The King was downcast, experiencing at the age of sixty 'that stark moment of abandonment when a man realizes that he is no longer a son.'[1] He felt lonely. Some damned scribblers, he heard, were criticizing the Prince of Wales. Goodwood had been spoiled by a threatened coal strike. He had protested to Baldwin about the Prime Minister's flippancy and disregard of parliamentary decorum, which had brought a sharp reminder 'that one of the earliest historical objects of the House of Commons was to exclude the Crown from interfering in its proceedings.'[2] There hadn't been anything like that under the Labour chaps. He missed Jim Thomas. He didn't feel well. Elizabeth's pregnancy was the only bright spot on the horizon.

The Yorks were now living in Curzon House, Curzon Street. During that winter Elizabeth sometimes helped her mother-in-law with the task of sorting out Queen Alexandra's vast accumulation of treasures and junk in Marlborough House, though with constant reminders not to lift anything. Neither Queen Mary nor King George could understand what she had against White Lodge. It was quite obviously the place for Bertie's heir to be born and they refused to consider any alternative. In desperation, Bertie arranged to rent a house in Grosvenor Square from a Mrs Hoffmann,[3] at which Lady Strathmore offered them the Strathmore residence in Bruton Street. Elizabeth, at last, seemed satisfied, and Bertie moved in with his in-laws. Nevertheless, it was clearly a temporary arrangement. People were beginning to think it odd that the Yorks had been married for nearly three years and still had no house of their own. The White Lodge situation was ridiculous; but if Elizabeth didn't want to live there, she wouldn't, and that was that. She wanted to live in Carlton House Terrace, but nobody died in Carlton House Terrace, nobody was even hopefully poorly, and eviction was out of the question. They considered Norfolk House in Norfolk Street, Mayfair, but it wasn't right. Then Elizabeth heard about 145 Piccadilly, an imposing but dilapidated Crown Property backing on to Hyde Park. In 1921, the estate agent advertisement ran, 'This important mansion . . . which is approached by a carriage drive used jointly with No. 144 Piccadilly, contains spacious and well-lighted accommodation, including entrance hall, principal staircase hall, a secondary staircase with electric passenger lift, drawing room, dining room, ballroom, study, library, about 25 bedrooms, conservatory etc . . .' It was still empty in 1926, and Elizabeth set her heart on it. Anxious to keep his pregnant darling happy – though possibly with some misgivings, since he was a practical man – Bertie entered into protracted negotiations with the Crown Estates Office and Buckingham Palace, and finally obtained a yearly lease on the property. The Crown Estates Office would, of course, pay for the renovation, adding a fire escape to the nursery floor, carrying out 'various necessary and overdue repairs' and decorating the whole place in the new, fashionable pastel shades. Bertie generously offered to pay for the construction of an extra bedroom. With a growing family, approximately twenty-five bedrooms was scarcely enough. Although it was termed a 'grace-and-favour residence' Bertie also promised to contribute the rent. Any sacrifice, Elizabeth said, was worth the chance to get out of White Lodge.

Once all that was settled, she could turn her attention to the matter in hand. Clara Knight was summoned to report back for duty in time to take over the Royal Heir. Her latest charge, Elizabeth's niece, was only nine months old and there were some ineffectual protests. 'She was mine first!' the Duchess declared, stamping her size 3½ foot. For a short while it looked as though sawdust Clara might be torn limb from limb.

Although tiny and dainty and all the rest, Elizabeth was a healthy Scottish lass who could, it seems, survive most physical rigours without much fuss. Presumably the doctors discovered the child was a breech[4] when it was too late, for some reason, to turn the foetus. In any case, after she had been in labour all day on 20 April, it was decided to perform a Caesarian section. To undergo such an operation in a private house appears extraordinary to us now, but in 1926 it was still considered *infra dig* for a royal person to attend hospital in anything but a charitable capacity. If there was the slightest likelihood of dying, the correct thing was to do it in the room, preferably the bed, in which one had been born; failing this, then at least in familiar surroundings where proper provision could be made for mourners and the necessary officials. Even without such gloomy forebodings, a royal birth needed the presence of the Home Secretary and a whole gaggle of relations. To facilitate matters, the surgeon, Sir Henry Simpson, and the obstetrician, Walter Jagger, Consultant at the Samaritan Hospital for Women, were installed in the house. Their first mystifying bulletin announced that they were going to follow 'a certain line of treatment'; their next, that 'Her Royal Highness the Duchess of York was safely delivered of a Princess at 2.40 a.m. this morning, April 21st'. It sounds, for some reason, more painful than having a daughter.

Ten days later, on 1 May, a national coal strike began; the following evening a General Strike was proclaimed. Thick, drizzling fog and bitter cold must have added to the misery, but no, all the accounts are of courage, ingenuity, and a good time had by all. 'Our old country can well be proud of itself,' the King wrote in his diary when the crisis was officially over, 'as during the last nine days there has been a strike in which 4 million men have been affected; not a shot has been fired & no one killed; it shows what a wonderful people we are...'[5] The miners, in fact, held out for another six months before they were driven by starvation to accept longer hours and lower wages. The Archbishop of Canterbury, preaching at St Martin in the Fields, took his timely text from Ephesians iv 1: 'Walk worthy of the vocation wherewith ye are called,' to which Bertie and Elizabeth responded with a devout Amen.

Elizabeth had provided a third successor to the throne; everyone else moved down a peg. The next thing on her agenda was Bertie's stammer. They were due to go on a World Tour in January 1927 and knew that the Australian Premier, Stanley Bruce, had forcibly expressed his doubts about what was known as the Duke of York's 'affliction'. The King, too, was uneasy, and Bertie even more so. They were told that an Australian called Lionel Logue, an ex-engineer with no medical qualifications but a remarkably successful record in faith-healing, was practising in Harley Street. Bertie was sceptical. There had been too many 'cures', too many failures. Whatever form Elizabeth's insistence took – persuasion, nagging, rational argument, subtle blackmail or simple command – Bertie went to Harley Street. He 'entered my consulting room at three o'clock in the afternoon,' Logue recorded, 'a slim, quiet man, with tired eyes and all the symptoms of the man upon whom habitual speech defect had begun to set the sign. When he left at five o'clock, you could see that there was hope once more in his heart.'[6]

Hope, as Logue knew, was half the battle. The actual treatment consisted of being taught to breathe correctly, to develop the lungs and control the rhythm of the diaphragm. There was no instant miracle, but Bertie's new optimism and Elizabeth's determination had a considerable effect. For two and a half months they visited Harley Street almost daily. By 6 January 1927, when they sailed for New Zealand en route for Australia, Bertie could claim that he was 'full of confidence'. Elizabeth, on the other hand, was in tears. Lilibet was nine months old and they would be away until June. '*Mais que faire?*' as her mother-in-law had so frequently asked. Australia, it seemed, needed her more.

The World Tour, like every other World Tour, was accounted a great success. There was some bad feeling in Melbourne about the fact that they had chosen to go to New Zealand first, but that was ignored. Two Labour M.P.s, Mr Ammon and Mr David Kirkwood, tactlessly suggested in the House of Commons that 'a pleasure trip of this kind' should not have been undertaken at a time of industrial depression; in spite of the country's distress 'it can afford to vote £7,000 to send out their Royal Highnesses to the uttermost parts of the earth, and it would not matter one iota to the welfare of the country supposing they never returned!'[7] Baldwin, as usual, regarded this as a joke. The King was not amused: 'His Majesty takes a graver view of these flippant, discourteous, if not insulting allusions to his Family...' Mr Ammon and Mr Kirkwood clearly had no conception of the 'almost terrifying schedule of dinners, receptions, garden-parties, balls and other official duties – relieved by brief fishing excursions'[8] which the Duke and Duchess were enduring. Cantankerous letters from his father didn't make Bertie's task any easier: 'I send you a picture of you inspecting the Gd of Honour (I don't think much of their dressing) with yr Equerry walking on yr right side next to the Gd & you ignoring the Officer entirely. Yr Equerry should be outside & behind, it certainly doesn't look well.' 'I had finished inspecting the guard of honour,' Bertie explained laboriously, '& was walking back to join Elizabeth ... It was an unfortunate moment for the photograph to be taken...'[9] However, the new Parliament at Canberra was duly opened – the purpose of the trip – and Australia conquered. Although Bertie endured a terrible ten days alone, while Elizabeth withdrew with tonsillitis, she achieved 'the responsibility of having a continent in love with her',[10] and probably the Governor as well. She also accumulated three tons of toys and twenty live parrots for the Princess.[11] At Portsmouth on 27 June they were met by David, Harry, George, and instructions from the King regarding their reunion at Victoria: 'We will not embrace at the station before so many people. When you kiss Mama take yr hat off.'[12]

Lilibet was now over a year old. It must have been a bewildering day for her, what with the hugs and kisses and being held up on the balcony like a football cup, the crowd roaring below. Eventually the reunited family drove through more crowds to 145 Piccadilly – home at last – where they were welcomed by Captain Basil Brooke, their Comptroller, Mr Ainslie, the butler, Mrs Macdonald, the cook, and Mrs Evans, the housekeeper. To fill up some of the empty spaces there were an under-butler, two footmen, an odd man, a steward's room boy, three housemaids, three kitchen maids, a nursery maid, a dresser, a valet, an RAF orderly, a night watchman, and a Boy Scout to operate the telephone.[13]

★   ★   ★

The glowing accounts of the Yorks' World Tour, their connubial bliss, impeccable morals and sense of duty provided a happy contrast to the increasing flightiness of the bachelor brothers. London's Bright Young Things, led by the thirty-four-year-old Prince of Wales, were dancing the Charleston dressed up as babies or tramps or Japanese coolies, careering about on paper chases and treasure hunts, drinking quantities of Manhattans and Sidecars and Bronxes, doing their utmost to give the decade a bad name. Unlike their Sixties grand-children they really believed, with a delicious *frisson* of guilt, that they were damned. Evelyn Waugh was their Savonarola, Noel Coward their St Paul:

> Poor little rich girl,
> You're a bewitched girl.
> Better beware!

While Bertie and Elizabeth were slogging round New Zealand in the rain, Prince George had been enjoying a relatively trouble-free affair with one of these doomed debutantes. So far every effort he had made to follow his own inclinations had ended in squalor and scandal. His more unacceptable girlfriends were chased out of the country by Scotland Yard and the few who might pass muster at Cowes or Ascot had been turned down flat by his parents. The progress of his affair with Miss Poppy Baring was watched with keen interest by his friend Duff Cooper: '8 January 1927: Poppy sleeping peacefully in the arms of Prince George . . . 14 January: there is talk of marriage. I hope it comes off . . . [Poppy] says she couldn't bear the Royal Family. I said it wan't much worse than other families . . . 29 January: the great news was that Prince George had been to see his parents and told them he wanted to marry Poppy. They had taken it wonderfully and raised hardly any objection . . . 8 February: [Prince George] was afraid it was all off. Unfavourable reports about poor Poppy appear to have reach-ed His Majesty's ears . . . So the girl's sunk.'[14] To say that Georgie's parents drove him to homosexuality and drugs is perhaps going too far, but they certainly didn't allow him any satisfactory alternative until, six years later, they produced Princess Marina of Greece. That summer the unpredictable Prince of Wales spent a bucket-and-spade holiday at Sandwich with Freda Dudley Ward and her two young daughters. A few weeks later Stanley Baldwin accompanied both Princes to Canada for the Diamond Jubilee celebrations, and regretted it. They both behaved abominably.

The York star rose ever higher in the royal firmament. Little Lilibet was wheeled round Hamilton Gardens in the Royal Perambulator every afternoon, unless a royal carriage drawn by a pair of bay horses, with a coachman and footman on the box, arrived to take her for a drive. Elizabeth, when she was not on view accepting brooches from her Regiments or dolls from such generous institutions as the Sunshine Guild or the Streatham Hospital for Incurables, occupied herself like any other housewife with routine desk work and general household decisions. Miss Dorothy Laird tells us that the Duchess was most interested in the well-being of her staff and had taken the trouble to learn all their names. Looking back it seems strange that the events of 1936 were not a foregone conclusion.

★   ★   ★

Late at night on 22 October 1928, in total darkness, the remains of eight unidentified members of the Royal Family were removed from the Royal Vault of St George's Chapel, Windsor, and re-interred at Frogmore. It was rumoured that one of the coffins had exploded during Evensong, but the official explanation for the move – though not for the bizarre way it was conducted – was that in future only Sovereigns would be buried at Windsor. It was ominous that four weeks later Queen Mary should be writing in her diary, 'George had a chill & had to go to bed – too tiresome.'[15]

A week later the Prince of Wales, big-game hunting in East Africa with Thelma Furness and brother Harry, received a cable telling him to return home immediately. With assistance from Mussolini, who sent his own train to meet the ship at Brindisi and ordered the tracks to be cleared at the Swiss frontier, David made the 7,000-mile journey in nine days.[16] He found his father barely conscious. Bertie did not sound unduly concerned. 'There is a lovely story going about which emanated from the East End,' he had written to his brother, 'that the reason of your rushing home is that in the event of anything happening to Papa I am going to bag the Throne in your absence!!!! Just like the Middle Ages...'[17] He had been appointed a Counsellor of State and was, perhaps, a little intoxicated by his new authority.

The King had acute septicaemia; his heart was growing weaker. He was operated on. Licensing hours for prayer were relaxed and the churches stayed open twenty-four hours a day. Christmas was gloomy. The old man battled through, and by February 1929 was well enough to be moved for his convalescence to a house near Bognor. In March Lilibet went to stay, attended by Clara, while her parents attended the wedding of Crown Prince Olav of Norway, the only child of King Haakon and their Aunt Maud (known as Harry) to Princess Martha of Sweden, an occasion that does not seem to have been intended to demonstrate anything in particular. 'On their way home' from Oslo (rather a devious route, surely?), they stayed at the British Embassy in Berlin and were taken to lunch at the golf club by Harold Nicolson. Elizabeth's perception astounded him. Not only had she read his book *Some People*, she understood it. 'You choose your colours so carefully,' she told him. 'That bit about the Palace in Madrid was done in grey and chalk-white; the Constantinople bits in blue and green; the desert bits in blue and orange.' What an amazing woman! 'If Harold was over-estimating her intellect,' writes Nicolson's biographer, 'he could not exaggerate her charm. It was overwhelming. The Duke's,' he adds laconically, 'was less evident.'[18]

They returned home to find that the King had been much amused by his granddaughter. He was rapidly losing faith in David and already beginning to think what he would so vehemently say in a few years' time: 'I pray to God that my eldest son will never marry and have children, and that nothing will come between Bertie and Lilibet and the throne!'[19] Bertie was praying equally fervently for the exact opposite. The choice must have been based on precedence, I suppose.

That summer the Labour Party scraped in again with a bare majority. No one was unduly alarmed. The King, wearing a Chinese dressing gown, received his old friend Jim Thomas and the rest in his bedroom at Windsor.[20] Jim went to Canada and came back announcing that he had found 'the complete cure' for unemployment. Unemployment rose by 8 per cent. A Thanksgiving Service was held for the King's recovery on 7 July, but a few days later he laughed so heartily at one of Jim's ribald jokes that he had a relapse and was operated on for the removal of a rib. As for the Yorks, Elizabeth had every reason to congratulate herself, and did. Lilibet was a success and Bertie's stammer was under control: 'Through all this nervous strain my speech has *not* been affected one atom,' he wrote proudly to Lionel Logue.[21] What could be done now, to consolidate their position?

CHAPTER
14

For the past four years Bertie had slogged on conscientiously through his assignments as his father's representative and his elder brother's understudy. 'When his photograph appeared in the Press it either showed him inspecting a factory, playing games with the boys at his camps or, more often, playing second fiddle to his wife and daughter.'[1] He had played second fiddle all his life, and was good at it. The trouble arose on the rare occasions when he had to perform a solo.

In January 1930 the Crown Prince of Italy, young Umberto, was to marry Princess Marie-Jose of Belgium in the Pauline Chapel of the Palace of the Quirinal in Rome. Like the Belgrade wedding seven years before, this was an important political alliance, intended (rather obscurely) to demonstrate the reconciliation of the House of the Savoy and the Italian State – Benito Mussolini, Knight Grand Cross of the Order of the Bath[2] (1923) – with the Vatican. The Yorks, as usual, had been told to attend. Elizabeth, however, was feeling poorly – bronchitis, she said. Bertie, with growling reluctance, had to go alone.

Elizabeth was not only his lifeline, she was an addiction. He was helpless without her, and on top of that he had a terrrible cold. The Ambassador Sir Ronald Graham and his wife, with whom Bertie was staying, found that he 'appeared to be in a perpetual state of discontent and ill-humour'. When Lady Sybil's small dog snuffled under the breakfast table one morning, Bertie 'touched it with his foot, perhaps more forcibly than he had intended'. The dog yelped. Lady Sybil turned pale. 'How republican one feels near certain royals!'[3] she was heard to mutter as she cradled her innocent pooch.

At the wedding itself the *placements* had been arranged by the Grand Master of Ceremonies, Duke Borea d'Olmo, who was approaching his hundredth birthday and no longer seemed able to distinguish between black and white. Bertie was placed after ex-King Amanullah of Afghanistan, a nice enough fellow (he had visited Windsor the year before and given the Princess Royal a massive gramophone in a mahogany case)[4] but a nigger nevertheless. Rumour had it that the Duke of York never forgot this slight. The crowning insult was that he was offered the Grand Cross of San Maurizio e Lazzare instead of the Ordine dell' Annunziata, or Italian equivalent of the Garter. And why? Because David had already been given the Ordine dell' Annunziata, and no two members of the same family were permitted to wear it.[5] If Elizabeth had been with him, he raged, none of this would have happened; and he was probably right. No wonder he kicked the bloody dog.

Soon after his return from this calamitous visit, Elizabeth's secret was out – another little successor to the throne was on the way. In spite of her first experience, she was determined to have this baby at Glamis, at extreme inconvenience to everybody, particularly the Home Secretary and the Ceremonial Secretary at the Home Office, both of whom had to be present. As always, however, the Little Duchess got her way. The baby was said to be due between 6 August and the 12th; on the morning of the 5th Mr Clynes, the Home Secretary, and Mr Boyd, the Ceremonial Secretary, arrived at Cortachy Castle, where they were to be guests of Lady Airlie.

Lady Airlie's description in her memoirs of this visit is impossible to improve on. Any precis is bound to bungle the nuances, but I shall do my best. Mr Boyd was 'a small anxious-looking man, meticulously neat in his dress and movements, who had spent many years of his life in China.' He was obsessed with the fear that because the Duchess had decided to have her baby at Glamis there might be some impression that the affair was going to be conducted in 'an irregular, hole and corner way'. It had been suggested to him that he and the Home Secretary might book into a hotel in Perth, and that two sleepers should be reserved for them on every night train from London until the event was over, but the implications horrified him. What if the birth should take place in the early hours of the morning and the Home Secretary could not get to Glamis in time? (In his agitation he sprang out of his chair and paced up and down Lady Airlie's sitting room.) If the birth was not properly witnessed, its legal right might be questioned. The child would be in direct succession to the Throne. Look at what had happened at the birth of the son of James II and Mary of Modena. (He had brought the book with him, the relevant passages underlined in red ink.) By offering her hospitality, Lady Airlie saved the throne of England from dishonour.

Mr Clynes was a small man, very quiet and shy, dressed in a rather ill-fitting suit and a grey Homburg hat. He talked very little, in contrast to Mr Boyd, who fidgeted incessantly and still seemed pre-occupied with the fear of some plot. 'I could not help feeling,' remarks Lady Airlie, 'that his long residence in China was inclining him to view the situation in too oriental a light.' A single telephone wire had been installed from Airlie to Glamis and a dispatch rider was available at Glamis day and night in case the wire broke down. All they could do was wait. Mr Clynes went for walks, and admired the scenery. Mr Boyd's anxiety developed into frenzy. On hearing from Sir Henry Simpson that the event could not be later than 11 August, they sat up all night, 'sustained by frequent cups of coffee'. Not a word. By the 14th Mr Boyd was in a panic and lost his temper with Mr Clynes when the latter was on the point of going out for a tranquil drive with Lady Airlie. On the following day Mr Clynes and Lady Airlie resumed their pleasant excursions. Mr Clynes even made an impromptu speech at the Airlie Flower Show. On the morning of 21 August 1930, Boyd, 'wild-eyed and haggard after sitting up all night', telephoned Glamis. No news. He dashed out into the garden and kicked a few stones.

That evening, as Lady Airlie was dressing for dinner, Admiral Brooke rang, asking in an agitated voice for Mr Boyd. Mabell bundled into her dressing gown and banged on Mr Boyd's door. 'Telephone! From Glamis!'

She heard a tremendous opening and shutting of wardrobes, then a wail of anguish: 'I can't go downstairs, I'm not dressed and I can't find my suit.'

'Never mind!' bawled the noble lady, 'Take the call in my room! I'm not dressed either but it doesn't matter!'

Mr Boyd rushed out of his bedroom in a dark blue kimono, and into Lady Airlie's. 'What! In an hour?. . . We must start at once!' He renewed the frantic search for his suit. Lady Airlie ordered sandwiches. When they got downstairs Mr Clynes was calmly waiting at the door in his big coat and Homburg hat. He pointed to the sunset. 'Just look at that, Boyd,' he said. 'In such a night did Dido from the walls of Carthage . . .' Mr Boyd pushed Mr Clynes into the car. They arrived at Glamis with half an hour to spare.[6] So was the birth of Princess Margaret honourably, if euphemistically, witnessed and passed into history. Mr Clynes returned to recoup what he could of his interrupted holiday in Brighton with his wife and children. No one cared very much what happened to Mr Boyd.

On 7 March that year Mrs Ronald Armstrong-Jones had given birth to a boy, Antony, in Eaton Terrace, Belgravia. The biggest hit of the theatre season was Noel Coward's *Private Lives*, which proved that even the Elyots and Amandas of this world have hearts of gold. There was a craze for midget golf; everyone owned a yo-yo; a motor yacht for a Greek millionaire was the only ship being built in the Clyde shipyards and the dole queues lengthened by half a million. The Prince of Wales, perhaps a little envious of Bertie's domesticity, asked his father to give him 'a castellated conglomeration' called Fort Belvedere near Sunningdale. 'What could you possibly want that queer old place for?' the King asked. 'Those damn weekends, I suppose.'[7] Freda helped with the alterations and decorations while David worked in the garden. There seemed to be signs that the Prince of Wales was settling for bachelorhood. In November, while staying with Thelma Furness and her husband at Melton Mowbray, he was introduced to Mrs Wallis Simpson.

★   ★   ★

By 1931 Elizabeth had put on a good deal of weight; her face was rounder, her eyes smaller; she was no longer a wistful waif, a Barrie heroine, but a pneumatic mother of two with a roguish twinkle. Nobody directly mentions her sex appeal, but sexuality was her most formidable characteristic. This doesn't mean that she invited anyone to bed. On the contrary. High moral principles, by inhibiting activity, produce an enormous reserve of sexual power. It was this power that transformed Bertie from an inarticulate nobody into a man of some stature, hypnotized the general public and eventually reinstated the throne in the public's fantasy. Without it, for all her virtues, she would be remembered as little more than a stop-gap between her romantic brother-in-law and her worthy elder daughter. On a more obvious level, people succumbed in their thousands to 'the drowsy caressing voice, the slow sweet smile, the delicious gurgle of laughter, the soft eyes glowing, etc.' and to the inappropriate message all this seemed to convey. They still do. She is the most successful sex-symbol that British royalty has ever known.

In the summer of 1931 the Duke and Duchess of York went to Paris to open 'British week'. While they were there they visited the Colonial Exhibition, presided over by the brilliant old French colonial administrator Marshal Lyautey. According to Rebecca West, the Marshal was 'sustained by male vanity in its most beneficent form. It was not that he looked down on anybody; he looked up at the sun and congratulated it on having an object like himself who was worthy to be shone on by its rays.'[8] A challenge, in fact.

That afternoon the old man seemed tired and sombre as he showed them round. Elizabeth suggested they should stop for a cup of tea in one of the cafés. Then, turning the full battery of her charm on the Marshal, she murmured 'Monsieur le Marechal, you are so powerful, you created the beautiful country of Morocco and you have made this fine exhibition – would you do something for me?' (I imagine this sounded more appealing in French.)

'For you, Madame? But what can I do for Your Royal Highness?'

'Why, this. The sun is in my eyes, Monsieur le Marechal. Will you make it disappear?' At that moment the sun went behind a cloud. 'Thank you, Monsieur le Marechal,' said Elizabeth, 'I knew you could do anything.' The old man, vanquished, smiled and relaxed. Even Bertie, who must have been used to such demonstrations by now, was astounded. 'I saw the cloud coming,'[9] she murmured, her expression of admiring gratitude unchanged.

Perhaps the story would be better without the final line, but there it is. Could such an actress be trusted? Did it matter? The elementary magic worked, that was the point. The whole thing was a splendid collusion, hoaxed and hoaxers indistinguishable from each other. Her younger daughter would attempt to emulate her mother's performance and fail. Her elder never even tried.

Altogether, 1931 was a year of incident and drama. The Yorks had Charlie Chaplin to lunch; he may have proved a tougher nut even than the Marshal. Mrs Wallis Simpson was presented at Court, wearing Thelma Furness's train, feathers and fan. The Prince of Wales and his brother George spent the early months of the year on a semi-official tour of South America, 'poking around department stores and wholesale mercantile establishments',[10] addressing Chambers of Commerce, inspecting factories and avoiding revolutions. A suggestion was made that Bertie should become Governor-General of Canada. Before Elizabeth had made up her mind, Jim Thomas vetoed the idea on the untenable grounds that the Canadians didn't like Royalty. Lord and Lady Strathmore celebrated their Golden Wedding at Glamis, the two little York girls adding footnotes to the family photograph. An apparently insignificant bank, the Credit Anstaldt in Vienna, locked its doors and the entire Western economy toppled. By August the crisis was so acute that the King, on reaching Balmoral, had to turn straight round and go back to London. 'I *will* not be left sitting on a mountain!' Queen Mary exclaimed.[11] Gandhi arrived in London for the second Round Table Conference. The King and Queen gave a teaparty for the delegates, at which the Mahatma in his loin-cloth failed to remind them of the splendours of the Durbar.

The crisis escalated. America refused to help. Ramsay Macdonald flung out of the Cabinet Room in a state of extreme agitation. 'I am off to the Palace,' he shouted, 'to throw in my hand!' Instead, he found himself heading a National Government. The King worked hard that day. After seeing Macdonald he had King George of the Hellenes to lunch and his aunt Princess Louise to tea and Lord Cromer to dinner, visited Harry in hospital, worked on his boxes and spent some time on his stamp collection. 'Our Captain played one of his best innings with a very straight bat,' said his Private Secretary. 'He stopped the rot and saved his side. He was not-out at the end and had hardly turned a hair, or shown any signs of fatigue.'[12] The British had two identical sides to their coin of fortune: triumph and Triumph. Whichever way it spun, the result was always a certainty.

Not that things weren't a little unstable meanwhile. Direct taxes were increased by £51½ million; beer, tobacco and petrol by £24 million. Teachers' salaries were reduced by 15 per cent, unemployment rates cut by 10 per cent and the rate of contribution increased. Then there was a minor mutiny in the British Navy, which shook the faith of foreign investors – £33 million in gold were withdrawn from the Bank of England in one week. On 21 September Britain went off the Gold Standard. King George gave up £50,000 from his annual Civil List for as long as the emergency lasted. David contributed £50,000 from the Duchy of Cornwall to the National Exchequer. Bertie, with a wife and two daughters to keep, gave up hunting with the Pytchley and sold his six hunters for a miserable 965 guineas. 'This is the worst part of all,' he wrote to the Master, 'and the parting with them will be terrible.'[13] It must have been the Coburg in him coming out. Bertie could never look on the bright side.

Even as all this stringent tightening of belts was going on, the King offered the Yorks a grace-and-favour country house, the Royal Lodge, in Windsor Park. David, after all, had Fort Belvedere. Perhaps a breath of fresh air would compensate for the loss of the hunters. The place was, of course, uninhabitable. Concerned as they were about the financial crisis, they contented themselves to begin with by restoring the great Wyatville Saloon, building a new wing and putting in a few bathrooms.

CHAPTER
15

By the spring of 1932 the Yorks were installed in the Royal Lodge, and just before Easter the children's first governess arrived. Marion Crawford was twenty-two, an Eton-cropped graduate of the Moray House Training College in Edinburgh. Her ambition, she says, was to be a child psychologist. With that urge for self-annihilation – or aggrandizement – so necessary to some women, she was to devote the next seventeen years of her life to Lilibet and Margaret, providing hearty, cheerful good sense in a household that was rapidly coming to resemble its public image. Elizabeth was enchanted with the image. She 'had a definite idea of the sort of training she wished her daughters to receive, and pursued her course untroubled by other people's doubts'.[1] She wanted them to spend as much time as possible in the open air; to acquire good manners and perfect deportment, and to cultivate all the distinctively feminine graces, 'for', writes Dermot Morrah, 'she is one of those whose natural instinct is to emphasize the contrast between the sexes rather than seek to assimilate them to one another.'[2] As far as the rest of their education was concerned, she agreed that 'her children should gain as much reasonable book-learning as might prove to be within their capacity; but this she regarded as only one of several branches of education, to be kept in proper proportion with the rest and in subordination to the whole.'[3] When it became clear that Lilibet's capacity for mathematics was extremely limited, it was Miss Crawford who worried, not the Duchess. There were hilarious bath-times and hopscotch and hide-and-seek, endless grooming of ponies and mucking out of stables, but nobody had any ideas or bothered to make any mundane decisions. Queen Mary was the only person, if such a term is not *lèse-majesté*, to give the governess any practical support.

The bankrupt and mostly unemployed Welsh had given Lilibet a house for her sixth birthday. It was, of course, child-sized. Her grandmother insisted on inspecting it on her hands and knees, a regal Alice whose toque alone was as high as the chimney. She satisfied herself that the plumbing was in good order and the kitchen well stocked. Meanwhile Uncle George was involved in a blackmail scandal – something to do with letters to a young man in Paris,[4] but of course it was never mentioned. David's friends the Simpsons spent their first weekend at nearby Fort Belvedere. Thelma Furness seemed to have supplanted Freda in David's affections; Elizabeth very much enjoyed visiting the Fort. One evening Bertie and his brother had great fun hurling David's new unbreakable plastic records across the Terrace. 'Come on, David, let's see if these are really unbreakable, as the label says,' cried Bertie. 'While the brothers roared with laughter,' wrote Thelma, 'the Duke had us ducking and dodging like rabbits. Unfortunately the records didn't break, and the game went on until we all fled inside. They followed us in and continued their sport in the drawing room until one of the Prince's most treasured lamps was bowled over by a direct hit...'[5]

Then there was the weekend when Virginia Water froze and they all went skating, Thelma and Elizabeth hanging on to a couple of old kitchen chairs and both 'in gales of laughter'. 'If ever I had to live in a bungalow in a small town,' Thelma thought, 'this is the woman I would most like to have as a next-door neighbour to gossip with while hanging out the washing in our backyards.'[6] Thelma was the first person to insist on having a Christmas tree at the Fort, with ornaments from Selfridges and all the trimmings.[7] Part of her charm, no doubt, was her vivid imagination.

On the afternoon of Christmas Day King George made his first broadcast from Sandringham. The script had been written by his friend Rudyard Kipling. 'I speak now from my home and from my heart to you all; to men and women so cut off by the snows, the desert, or the sea, that only voices out of the air can reach them...' Monarchy's Prospero, the old man touched the most cynical of listeners.

★   ★   ★

'1933,' according to Lady Longford, 'was the year of the corgi.'[8] There were a few secondary events, such as Hitler becoming Reich Chancellor, the Reichstag Fire, a demonstration by 30,000 Jews from Stepney and the Oxford Union's decision that it would in no circumstances fight for King and Country, but it was 'Dookie' who made the news at the Royal Lodge. The animal, unfortunately, emulated the less pleasing aspects of the royal temperament. Members of the Household gallantly hid their bleeding hands while passing the time of day with the Princesses; the staff went in constant fear of hydrophobia. This angry animal was soon joined by Jane, Mimsy, Stiffy, Scrummy and Choo Choo. The last four were not corgis. They were golden labradors and a Tibetan lion dog.

★   ★   ★

In November 1934 Prince George, recently made Duke of Kent, married Marina of Greece who, as we know, was the granddaughter of Queen Alexandra's brother George ('Uncle Willy') and first cousin to thirteen-year-old Prince Philip of Greece. The story went that she had been brought over to England the previous year in the hope that she would do for the Prince of Wales who was, as usual, stubbornly uninterested. Aristocratic, chic, with no pretensions to cleverness, she was the ideal wife for George, if he had to have one at all. Queen Mary had high hopes of her, which were somewhat dashed when the Princess turned up at the Palace with red fingernails.

'I'm afraid the King doesn't like painted nails,' the Queen said icily. 'Can you do something about it?'

'Your George may not,' Marina replied, equally regal. 'But mine does.'[9]

Such *hauteur* did not endear her to Elizabeth, who is said to have been referred to by Marina as 'that common little Scottish girl'. An added irritant was that King George – always appreciating a pretty gal, whatever the colour of her fingernails – was much taken by his new daughter-in-law, cheerfully overlooking the fact that she had spent most of her adult life as an itinerant exile and had no money. Elizabeth, who could have given Marina much advice and encouragement, was uncooperative: 'The Duchess of York's serene professionalism,' writes Marina's biographer, 'was so far ahead of everybody else that instead of helping by its example she set a standard that seemed almost impossible to reach.'[10] The impeccable commoner and the royal amateur did not, in short, feel warmly towards each other.

A State reception was held at Buckingham Palace two days before the wedding, to which the Prince of Wales invited Ernest and Wallis Simpson. They were, after all, close friends of Marina's sister Olga and her brother-in-law Prince Paul. Nevertheless, their presence raised a few courtly eyebrows. Wallis, small, flat as a board, with her big head and labourer's hands and noisy chatter, wore a violet lamé dress with a vivid green sash: 'the most striking gown in the room,' said Prince Paul sincerely.

★   ★   ★

1935 was the year of King George's Silver Jubilee, and for the first few months there wasn't a cloud in the sky. Elizabeth wore pink at Lady Astor's ball and danced with Anthony Eden, George Gage and Duff Cooper.[11] David went ski-ing in Kitzbuhl with a group of friends that included Mrs Simpson. On 6 May the Yorks rode in an open landau to St Paul's for the Jubilee Thanksgiving Service, 'the two tiny pink children', as Channon described them, waving more energetically than their parents. 'Wonderful service,' the King told the Dean.

'. . . Just one thing wrong with it – too many parsons getting in the way. I didn't know there were so many damn parsons in England.'[12] Every day there were processions and fireworks and brass bands and illuminations, all night the crowds sang and cheered – gratifying, of course, but impossible to get a wink of sleep. On Jubilee Day itself, Lady Alice Montagu-Douglas-Scott, daughter of the 7th Duke of Buccleuch, left Mombasa for England. She had gone to Kenya 'for a last taste of freedom before abandoning a truly private life for ever'.[13] Harry had decided to marry her. She was thirty-four years old, and would in future sound a small, calm note of sanity whenever she made an appearance in the royal drama. The York princesses were brides-maids at her wedding, wearing truncated Kate Greenaway dresses. 'I want to see their pretty little knees,' the King explained to Norman Hartnell.[14] His wife may have wryly recalled the fuss there was when she thought of showing her pretty little ankles. 'May God bless the dear couple,' she wrote in her diary on their wedding night. As far as she could see, He was certainly not blessing the Prince of Wales.

There was no good reason for David inviting the Simpsons to the first State ball of the Jubilee season, but there they were. By now everyone knew that Ernest had not accompanied his wife to Kitzbuhl and that she and the Prince had gone on together to waltz in Vienna and csardas in Budapest. Foxtrotting in Buckingham Palace, in front of the family, was going too far. We don't know what Wallis wore – something a little more restrained, I suspect – but we know what she felt: 'As David and I danced past [the King and Queen], I thought I felt the King's eyes rest searchingly on me. Something in his look made me feel that all this graciousness and pageantry were but the glittering tip of an iceberg that extended down into unseen depths . . . depths filled with an icy menace for such as me.'[15] She would have seen the same expression in the Duchess of York's normally soft and sym-pathetic eyes if she had glanced round for a moment.

I imagine Elizabeth, an incandescent blur of tulle and diamonds, gracefully turning her back on the dancers; then, lightly resting a tiny jewelled hand on some gold-braided sleeve, moving off among the guests with fury in her heart. Eleven years had gone by since she had opened the Ball with David. She had worked unceasingly since then to establish herself as the power behind the future throne. She had made herself the embodiment of all royal virtues, the unchallenged star. ('How lovely to see you – *such* fun!') Did David really think that she would take second place to that vulgar, hideously unattractive, American nobody? ('Quite delicious, don't you think? *Such* fun!') If so, he was reckoning without her Highland blood. He would regret it.

If the Duchess of York felt none of these things on this occasion, she had every reason to do so. My means may be a little devious, but the end was history.

CHAPTER

16

On 16 January 1936 King George complained of a cold and stayed in his room all day. This time the Queen was worried. She sent for Bertie to help her with the Sandringham houseparty, and wrote a note to David saying 'I think you ought to know that Papa is not very well'.[1] Although Elizabeth's 'flu had turned to pneumonia, Bertie was at Sandringham by late afternoon. David flew there next day in his new De Havilland Gypsy Moth. That night the old man wrote shakily in his diary, 'A little snow & wind. Dawson arrived this evening. I saw him & feel rotten'.[2]

On Sunday, 19 January, the Archbishop of Canterbury, Cosmo Gordon Lang, arrived. Bertie and David flew to London and 'informed the Prime Minister that [the King] was not expected to live more than two or three days'[3] – grim news that could not, apparently, be mentioned over the telephone. Presumably Bertie stayed the night at 145 Piccadilly and saw his sick wife, for the brothers did not fly back until Monday afternoon. That morning, a Privy Council was held at Sandringham to appoint Counsellors of State. 'We were summoned to the sick room...,' wrote the Archbishop. 'The King was in his chair, looking pathetically weak and frail, but fully conscious ... The President read the Order in Council. With a clear voice the King gave the reply so familiar to him, "Approved." Then Dawson, kneeling at his feet and watching his face, said, "Sir, do you wish to sign yourself?" "Yes," said the King ... "I have always signed in my own hand." Dawson tried to put the pen in his fingers, but owing to the failure of circulation they could not hold it. Then the hands moved most pathetically over the paper in the effort to sign. This took some minutes. Then the King turned to his Counsellors and said, "I am very sorry to keep you waiting so long"; adding shortly after, "You see, I can't concentrate." Once again the hands moved impotently up and down. Then, with great adroitness, Dawson put the pen in his hand and guided it, saying, "Make a mark, Sir, and you may sign afterwards." So two marks, XX, were made. Then the King turned again to his Counsellors and dismissed them with the old kind, kingly smile...'[4]

The family had tea together, 'the Prince of Wales full of vitality and talk, and touchingly attentive to the Queen',[5] and waited. At 11.15 the Archbishop put on his cassock and went to the King's room. 'The Queen and Princess Mary were there, with the doctors and nurses. The sons were together downstairs. No one seemed to think of calling them, and for this I was sorry.' The Archbishop then read the Twenty Third Psalm, 'The Lord is my shepherd', and some passages from the Bible, 'and then, going to the King's side, I said the Commendatory Prayers – 'Go forth, O Christian Soul' – with a final Benediction. As it was plain that the King's life could only last for a few minutes, I felt that I must leave the Queen and her family alone, and retired. I was told afterwards that the sons, especially the Prince of Wales, were painfully upset. . .'[6] At five minutes to midnight George V died.

When Louis Mountbatten's father died in 1921, David said to his cousin, 'I envy you a father whom you could love. If my father died, we should have felt nothing but relief.'[7] That was fifteen years ago. Now, writes Helen Hardinge, 'his grief was frantic and unreasonable. In its outward manifestations, it far exceeded that of his mother and his three brothers, although they had loved King George V at least as much as he had.'[8] She does not say how much grief she considers 'reasonable' for a son to feel on the death of his father, or how she knew the relative amounts of grief felt by the family. In six months time the Hardinges would be among the new King's most virulent enemies; everything Lady Hardinge writes about David's reign is embittered by wifely loyalty and womanly outrage. It is not un-reasonable to think of her as a spokeswoman for her friend the Duchess of York.

On 21 January Bertie and King Edward VIII flew to London for the Accession meeting of the Privy Council at St James's Palace. '. . . I place my reliance upon the loyalty and affection of my peoples throughout the Empire, and upon the wisdom of their Parliaments, to support me in this heavy task,' the King told them, 'and I pray God will guide me to perform it.'[9] Bertie went home, and David rushed to the Ritz to meet Wallis Simpson. She was ten minutes late, and Lord Charles Montagu saw the King 'stamping up and down the long corridor, looking angry and anxious till she came in and joined him.'[10] The idea of our present Queen meeting a lover in the Ritz on the day of her Accession to the throne is so bizarre that this story is hard to believe. Either they were both out of the minds, or times have changed even more radically than we think. The Yorks, who had never kept such an assignation in their lives, were horrified. That night, while Bertie and Elizabeth were discussing the mournful events of the week and speculating about the even more mournful events of the future, David dined with Wallis.[11]

While the Accession was being proclaimed from St James's Palace the next day, mourning for King George V was temporarily suspended to allow for official jubilation:

Whereas it has pleased almighty God ... We, therefore, the Lords Spiritual and Temporal of this Realm ... with one Voice and Consent of Tongue and Heart publish and proclaim that the High and Mighty Prince Edward Albert Christian George Andrew Patrick David is now, by the Death of our late Sovereign of Happy Memory ... God Save the King!

The crowds roared, trumpets blew, the band played the National Anthem, a salute of guns boomed out from Hyde Park and the Tower and the King himself, accompanied by Mrs Wallis Simpson and a group of friends, watched the ceremony from a room in the Palace overlooking Friary Court. 'It was all very moving,' said Wallis. 'But it has also made me realize how different your life is going to be.'[12] To which the King replied, 'Wallis, there will be a difference, of course. But nothing can ever change my feelings towards you.'[13]

It is unlikely that this conversation was overheard, but the story was all round London in no time. 'We are all riveted by the position of Mrs S –,' Channon wrote in his diary that night. 'No man has ever been so in love as the present King; but can she be another Mrs Fitzherbert? If he drops her she will fall – fall – into the nothingness from whence she came, but I hope he will not, for she is a good, kindly woman, who has had an excellent influence on the young Monarch.'[14] The Times, still maintaining that a King could do no wrong, surpassed itself for this occasion: 'The King's son was proclaimed ... with a glow of heraldic pageantry, like the light of dawn seen upon distant mountain tops from a valley still wrapped in the shadows.'[15]

The following day, 22 January, David and Bertie returned to Sandringham with Elizabeth and the Gloucesters. On the morning of 23 January the body of King George was taken on a gun-carriage from Sandringham Church to Wolferton Station. The weather was fine and frosty, the procession moved at the quick-march pace of the contingent of the Guards preceding the coffin. Behind the coffin walked the King, looking grim, and his three brothers and brother-in-law wearing identical black overcoats and carrying their silk hats. Behind them came a closed carriage containing Queen Mary, Elizabeth and the Princess Royal; after that, a similar carriage with Alice, Duchess of Gloucester, Marina, Duchess of Kent and two ladies-in-waiting. Then, an imaginative touch, George's shooting pony, Jock, riderless, phlegmatic, followed by a group of sombre officials; behind them, the local dignitaries, mayors and mace-bearers, and then a trudging phalanx of tenants, servants, beaters, keepers – countrymen, well-booted, wearing their tweeds and deer-stalkers and gaiters. The King's Piper, Forsyth, brought up the rear, the plaintive wheeze of 'Flowers of the Forest' accompanying the muffled sound of clopping horses, creaking carriages and hundreds of footsteps. 'Just as we topped the last hill above the station,' the new King recalled, 'the stillness of the morning was broken by a wild, familiar sound – the crow of a cock pheasant . . . The thought occurred to all of us that . . . he would have chosen something like that: a pheasant travelling high and fast on the wind, the kind of shot he loved.'[16]

By five o'clock that evening, the dead King was alone in Westminster Hall except for the four Yeoman guarding the coffin and the few officers charged with special duties. Over the next four days well over half a million people shuffled past the catafalque; some waited all night, equipped with camp stools and thermoses, others queued for hours in the rain. By Saturday, queues extended as far as St Thomas's Hospital and it was taking seven hours or more to cover the distance to Westminster Hall along both banks of the river. Members of English and foreign royalty crept in and out under the impression that they were not noticed. At 6 o'clock on the evening of Monday, 27 January, Queen Mary arrived with Lilibet, followed by Bertie and Elizabeth, Harry and Alice Gloucester, George Kent, the Princess Royal and her husband the Earl of Harewood, the King and Queen of Norway, Prince Olaf, the King of Denmark, the King of Belgium, the Crown Prince of Italy, Prince Axel of Denmark, the Comte de Flandres, Prince Ernest Augustus of Hanover, Prince Frederick of Prussia, Prince George and Prince Nicholas of Greece. 'The Royal party came in so unobtrusively that many then inside the hall did not realize that they were present,' reported *The Times* blandly. Just after the changing of the guard had taken place that night, an officer saluted the Colour lying on the catafalque and removed it. From the entrance of the Guards' officers' quarters marched the King, in the uniform of the Welsh Guards; the Duke of York, in the uniform of the Scots Guards; the Duke of Gloucester in the uniform of the 10th Hussars; and the Duke of Kent in naval uniform. The four brothers took up position between the Guards already on duty and remained motionless, resting on their swords, for about a quarter of an hour. It was, as Queen Mary said, 'a very touching thought'. She commissioned Mr E. E. Beresford to paint a picture of it called *The Vigil of the Princes*. The family gave it to David for his forty-second birthday in June.

The following day George V was taken to Windsor, via Paddington Station. The procession from Westminster Hall, miles long, included everyone from Mr T. Tubb, the Sergeant Footman, to Commander Funpapzeanu of the Rumanian Army. The royal brothers walked behind the coffin, followed by twenty-eight royal foreign colleagues and the President of the French Republic. Among the former were the King of Rumania, the King of the Bulgarians, HRH Prince Chakradongse, HRH The Duke of Saxe-Coburg and Gotha, HRH the Hereditary Grand Duke of Hesse, HRH the Duc de Nemours, HRH the Prince of Said, Prince Frederick of Prussia, HRH the Duke of Braganza, HRH the Infante Alfonso of Spain, HRH Prince Alvaro of Orleans-Bourbon, the Grand Duke Dimitri of Russia, and a Prince Salih. A procession of ghosts, compared with the lively mourners in Norfolk, but it had become impossible to be too discriminating. Lord Louis Mountbatten KCVO and the Duke of Beaufort GCVO were among the more corporeal figures to attend them. Next came Queen Mary in a glass coach accompanied by Elizabeth, HM Queen Maud of Norway and HRH the Princess Royal. Behind them, the procession stretched in doleful splendour to a detachment from the London Fire Brigade. The whole cortège moved slowly and solemnly towards Paddington Station. Wallis Simpson watched it from a window in a room at St James's Palace that had until recently been occupied by Sir Frederick Ponsonby, Queen Victoria's Private Secretary. What 'affected [her] profoundly' was the sight of the heavily veiled royal women,[17] though the nature of this affect is not disclosed.

Lilibet was waiting at Paddington with her governess – they occupied the time by playing 'endless games of noughts and crosses on GWR notepaper'[18] and joined her strangely shrouded mother for the journey to Windsor. There, after more than a week of being bumped about and stared at, the old King was finally laid to rest. 'I had the uneasy sensation,' David wrote, 'of being left alone on a vast stage, a stage that was the British Empire, to play a part not yet written.'[19] His sister-in-law Elizabeth, now the wife of the Heir Presumptive and, until Queen Mary emerged from her mourning, effectively the first lady in the land, possibly felt much the same.

CHAPTER

17

For the Yorks, King George's death was an appalling loss. They had flourished under his benevolent autocracy, become his favourites, responsible for maintaining the high standards of mediocrity that were characteristic of his reign. Now, overnight, they were cut adrift, spiritually exiled. Elizabeth went into a temporary decline. She had been very ill, and the strain of the funeral had been too much for her. Bertie, eager to support his brother, went off for a fortnight to Sandringham to conduct an inquiry into the whole economy of 'the voracious white elephant'[1] that had been his father's favourite home. Putting aside his own fond memories of the place, resolutely refusing to listen to the old mole under the floorboards, he produced a report which, says his biographer, in its 'clarity and common sense ... would have done credit to his great-grandfather, the Prince Consort'.[2] While sitting about miserably at home, Elizabeth heard gossip from well-meaning friends: at the Brownlows – Perry Brownlow was Lord-in-Waiting to the King – Mrs Simpson had rocked the room by declaring that she hadn't worn black stockings since she gave up the can-can;[3] The King, like any business man, was stopping by at Mrs Simpson's flat in Bryanston Court on his way home from work, for a cocktail and a brief chat; he had taken her to Windsor Castle, and she was at Fort Belvedere every weekend. Bertie, over-concerned with his brother's ridiculous schemes, didn't seem to understand how serious this was; he tittered, shrugged it off, said that was just like David. It was a relief sometimes to go out and see sympathetic people like Lady Maureen Stanley and Harold Nicolson[4] who, although he was a friend of the dreadful Lady Cunard, had the right instincts about David and Mrs S. He did not, he said, feel at ease in such company.[5]

As official mourning gave them six months off work, when Bertie had finished his Sandringham survey he took the family to stay at one of the Duke of Devonshire's houses, Compton Place, at Eastbourne, hoping the sea air would buck Elizabeth up a little. 'I miss him [King George] dreadfully,' she wrote to Lord Dawson. 'Unlike his own children, I was never afraid of him, and in all the twelve years of having me as a daughter-in-law he never spoke one unkind or abrupt word to me...'[6] But that wasn't all. 'I am only suffering, I think, from the effects of a family break-up, which always happens when the head of a family goes. Outwardly one's life goes on the same, yet everything is different, especially mentally and spiritually. I don't know if it is the result of being ill but I mind things that I don't like more than before.'[7] After this lapse into confidence she added briskly, 'But it will be very good for me to pull myself together and try to collect a little will power...'

Perhaps she had not collected enough by the afternoon in April when David brought Wallis over to the Royal Lodge for tea. Apart from the two occasions at the Palace, Wallis says that she had 'seen the Duchess of York ... on several occasions at the Fort and at York House'.[8] Presumably this means they were on speaking terms, though the choice of the word 'seen' is curious. Wallis must have been nervous. She was already beginning to experience the appalling manners of the British upper classes. 'I had one friend who absolutely refused to shake hands with her,' Lady Hardinge writes with relish, "What did you do?" I asked her ... "Oh," she replied, "it was quite easy. I dropped my handbag just as she got to me, so I had to stoop down to find it".'[9] However unappealing Wallis Simpson may have been to some people, the Baltimore divorcée knew how to behave in company; as far as I know there is not one incident to demonstrate that she was ever guilty of the incivility she received from others. She must have known by now how much Elizabeth disliked her. She just hoped, for David's sake, that the Duchess's well-known good breeding would save the day. It seems she was disappointed.

There are only two eye-witness accounts of this meeting, one Wallis's and the other Marion Crawford's. Neither is entirely convincing. David had just bought a new American station wagon, which he wanted to show Bertie. On one of his sudden whims, he piled his houseparty into the car and drove over to the Royal Lodge, swinging round the circular driveway in great style and pulling up at the front door with a flourish. He must have telephoned first, as Bertie and Elizabeth were waiting to greet him. 'It was amusing to observe the contrast between the two brothers,' Wallis wrote, 'David all enthusiasm and volubility ... the Duke of York quiet, shy, obviously dubious of this newfangled American contrivance.'[10] The brothers went off in the car, leaving the women alone. There is then a gap in the story. As far as anyone knows, they could have remained petrified, holding their smiles rigid until, 'after a few minutes', the men returned. Anyone showing off his new car takes longer than a few minutes to demonstrate its speed and convenience and beauty, and while it is unlikely that either Elizabeth or Wallis said anything of the slightest significance it was the first time they had been left more or less alone (we are not told what happened to the rest of the party) and it would be interesting to know what they said to each other.

After the men came back, they all walked through the garden. The Duchess of York's 'justly famous charm was highly evident' says Wallis.[11] They discussed the merits of the garden at the Fort and the garden at the Royal Lodge. Then they went indoors for tea, where they were joined by Lilibet, Margaret and Miss Crawford. The two children 'were both so blonde, so beautifully mannered, so brightly scrubbed, that they might have stepped straight from the pages of a picture book'[12] thought the childless Wallis, who clearly did not find small girls very interesting. David and Elizabeth carried on the conversation, with Bertie contributing very little. 'It was a pleasant hour; but I left with a distinct impression that while the Duke of York was sold on the American station wagon, the Duchess was not sold on David's other American interest.'[13]

Anyone who cares to know Miss Crawford's version of that afternoon will not find it in the English edition of her book. It is hard to understand why it was censored (and by whom?), but it was apparently deemed improper for the British public to know that Mrs Simpson '. . . appeared to be entirely at her ease; if anything, rather too much so,' and that 'she had a distinctly proprietary way of speaking to the new King. I remember she drew him to the window and suggested how certain trees might be moved, and a part of a hill taken away to improve the view.'[14] Nor must it be known that Crawfie 'never admired the Duke and Duchess more than on that afternoon. With quiet and charming dignity they made the best of this awkward occasion'[15] – why, one can't help wondering, did it have to be an awkward occasion? – 'and gave no sign whatever of their feelings. But the atmosphere was not a comfortable one.' Elizabeth then suggested that the governess should take the children 'into the woods' for a while, and as they were leaving the house Lilibet asked, rather naturally, 'Crawfie, who is she?'[16] It is Miss Crawford herself who describes this question as 'uneasy'. When an incident is written about in hindsight it is only too tempting to colour it in the lurid light of subsequent events. My guess is that it was a more or less normal afternoon at the Royal Lodge: a little stiff, rather boring, enlivened only by David's manic prattle. 'No one alluded to that visit when we met later in the evening,' Crawfie writes ominously. '. . . Maybe the general hope was still that if nothing was said, the whole business would blow over.'[17] Except for Elizabeth, with her new vulnerability, everyone had probably forgotten it.

There is no knowing what Bertie thought of Mrs Simpson at this time. He himself had suffered from the stuffiness and tedium of the old Court, and must always have had a sneaking admiration for David's glamorous cronies. He knew they found him dull – 'uninteresting and unintellectual, but doubtless well-meaning'[18] was Chips Channon's verdict – and they were probably right. Anyway, none of them were such good shots as he was, and he could beat them hollow at tennis. Wallis wasn't so easy to get on with as Freda or Thelma, but she obviously made David happy – where was the harm? It was a pity that his brother's behaviour as King was so erratic, but it was early days, he couldn't be expected to change overnight. If it hadn't been for Elizabeth, Bertie would have enjoyed going over to the Fort more often – have a few drinks, listen to the gossip, admire the new gadgets. Harry and Alice were often there, and you couldn't find a more respectable couple than the Gloucesters. George and Marina got on well with Wallis and saw both Wallis and David constantly. Bertie felt excluded. He would never do anything to upset Elizabeth, but all the same, it was a pity she couldn't see things as Alice did. 'We were as unhappy with the liaison as the rest of the family,' the Duchess of Gloucester wrote in her memoirs, 'but as a brother Prince Henry felt obliged to go. Mrs Simpson was always charming and friendly and, being American, also a wonderful hostess. After dinner we would play vingt-et-un or rummy or watch a film. It was very informal and they were most loving together.'[19] If the Duchess of York had been equally understanding, future events might have been no different, but they would have been a lot less painful.

David, unaware of anything except his all-consuming love affair, seems to have had no idea of the Yorks' feelings. On 9 July he invited them to a dinner party at York House in honour of Sir Samuel Hoare, the First Lord of the Admiralty. Among the guests were the Viceroy of India, Lord Willingdon, Margot Asquith, the Winston Churchills, Sir Philip Sassoon, Alec and Helen Hardinge and, naturally, Wallis Simpson. The fact that she was there alone, without her husband, was the cause of much disapproval among the ladies. Helen Hardinge wrote with her usual prim venom, 'Winston Churchill was one of the few people around the dinner table that night who found Mrs Simpson acceptable. Curiously enough, he considered that she just did not matter and had no great significance; he believed that, in the ultimate analysis of the Monarchy, she simply did not count one way or the other.'[20]

In so far as Churchill believed the doctrine that the King is an eternal concept and never dies, majesty being transferred to the heir the moment its previous embodiment ceases to live, he was perfectly right. Mrs Simpson could not disturb the Monarchy any more than she could disturb God. But she could, and did, disturb royalties and bishops.

Churchill was out to make mischief that night. After dinner he plumped himself down on a sofa next to Elizabeth and embarked on a long diatribe about the Prince of Wales (later George IV) and Maria Fitzherbert, a Roman Catholic widow whom the Prince had secretly married in defiance of the Act of Settlement and the Royal Marriage Act. Whether this was intended as an example or a dire warning to the King is not clear, or even whether Elizabeth got the point, whatever it was. Finally she commented rather absently, 'Well, that was a *long* time ago.'[21] (In spite of the many elaborate interpretations of this conversation, it sounds to me as though she could hardly keep awake. Urgent signals across the room: we must *go*, Bertie.) Undaunted, Churchill started on the Wars of the Roses – red Lancaster at logger-heads with white York – to which she could only reply, 'That was a very, very long time ago.'[22] Elizabeth was in exceptionally bad form that night. In contrast, Mrs Simpson, 'enthusiastically moving into the regal role into which she had cast herself' [Lady Hardinge again], caused Sir Samuel Hoare to comment 'not only on her sparkling talk, but also her sparkling jewels with up-to-date Cartier settings. Wallis Simpson was, he said, 'very attractive and intelligent'.[23] For the Duchess of York, an unhappy evening.

The next morning, as though the dinner for the First Sea Lord had been a ceremony to propitiate Neptune, George V's much-loved *Britannia*, which had sailed in 569 races in her 43 years and won 231 first prizes for her Commander, was towed out to a point south of the Isle of Wight and scuttled in deep water,[24] to Bertie, a further cause for mourning. Almost a week later, on 16 July, an exhibitionist threw a loaded revolver at the King's horse as he and Bertie were riding down Constitution Hill on their way back from presenting new colours to the Brigade of Guards. 'Apart from a muttered remark from the King and an answering grin from the Duke of York, neither checked his horse nor showed any sign of concern'.[25]* Hitler sent a telegram saying 'I have just received the news of the execrable attempted attack on your Majesty. I beg to tender to your Majesty my heartiest congratulations on your escape from this danger.' Mussolini telephoned. On 21 July there was an afternoon reception in the gardens of Buckingham Palace, 'the first occasion in history', said *The Times*, 'on which debutantes have curtsied to their Sovereign in mackintoshes'. When only half of the 600 or more ladies in 'decorative rainproofs' had sunk gracefully to the mud, a cloud burst. David immediately gave orders that 'those ladies ... who were unable to

---

* The following day Chips Channon met the King at Mrs Simpson's and was told that he had said, 'Is it a bomb? Will it go off?' – in which case Bertie's answering grin was out of place. The King himself says that he turned to General Sergison-Brooke, 'a man without fear', and remarked, 'Boy, I don't know what that thing was; but if it had gone off, it would have made a nasty mess of us.' *King's Story*, 298.

pass the King's presence will be considered as having been officially presented at Court' and disappeared into the Palace. Mothers raged, daughters wept. Elizabeth, in a long, black and white flowered dress, silver fox cape and large damp hat, did her best.

It was a relief when the King set off with a group of friends and Wallis to cruise along the Dalmatian coast in Lady Yule's *Nahlin*. 'I am glad you have chartered a yacht,' Queen Mary wrote to him from Sandringham, '& I hope you will find sunshine & good weather abroad & be able to get out to Venice or wherever you join the yacht in comfort, I hope too that this autumn may be free from complications of which we have had more than our share for years. It was a nice day today & less cold & no rain for a wonder.'[26] The Yorks went to stay with Mr J. P. Morgan, the American financier, at Cannochy for Elizabeth's thirty-sixth birthday, then eagerly on to Glamis.

CHAPTER
18

Queen Mary's hopes were not fulfilled; from the moment David returned from the Nahlin cruise complication followed complication. The Archbishop of Canterbury, who had already taken it on himself to give the King a paternal talking-to, did not receive the customary invitation to Balmoral. Instead, 'the kind Yorks' invited him to Birkhall, about eight miles away. Their nearest neighbours were the ubiquitous Hardinges. While David and Wallis, tanned by the Mediterranean sun and in high spirits, entertained their friends at Balmoral – cocktails and three-decker sandwiches and the gramophone playing 'These Foolish Things' – the Birkhall and Altnaguibhsach contingent 'walked over the hills, lit bonfires round the house to keep the midges away, sketched the view, fished for trout and salmon, tended the kitchen garden ... small things which made up a simple pleasant life.'[1] The Princesses performed action-songs, and the Archbishop refrained from putting Margaret on top of a pillar. On the Sunday before the King and his entourage arrived, the Minister at Craithie Church preached on the subject of Nero.[2]

The King, predictably, didn't ease the situation. He had turned down a request to open new buildings at Aberdeen Royal Infirmary that September, on the grounds that he would still be in mourning. The official mourning period had ended in July. Bertie was asked to do the job for him, regardless of the fact that the same lame excuse would apply to him. On 23 September, therefore, Bertie and Elizabeth dressed up and traipsed to Aberdeen and did their duty. At the same time David, in motoring goggles, was hanging about Aberdeen Station waiting for Wallis Simpson's train to arrive.[3] He was, of course, recognized, and 'although the news was neither broadcast nor published in the papers ... it spread all over Scotland within forty-eight hours,'[4] helped, no doubt, by Lady Hardinge and other well-wishers. It was a silly thing to do, but did it really deserve such outrage? Would the medical treatment in the Infirmary have suffered if the buildings hadn't been 'opened' at all? The Establishment's priorities were, in their own way, just as unreal as the King's. Its instinct was always to haul him up on the carpet and demand, 'What would happen if everybody behaved like that?' Unfortunately, far from finding the question unanswerable, the King invariably replied, 'Everybody does.'

Elizabeth was not the only one to think that David was, in fact, a little mad. It seemed the only explanation. Even apart from his obsession with Mrs Simpson, his behaviour was bizarre: he had walked from Buckingham Palace to the office of the Duchy of Cornwall without telling his chauffeur; he insisted on making his own 'phone calls, which led to confusion and panic on the switchboard;[5] he wandered about playing his bagpipes; his clothes, off duty, were embarrassing; he was unpredictable in every way. Even Bertie, for all his loyalty, was becoming uneasy. David and 'that woman' between them had made changes in the running of Balmoral without consulting him, and he was deeply hurt. Blithely unaware, David once more invited the Yorks to dinner. This time, greeted by Mrs Simpson as hostess, Elizabeth 'openly showed her resentment'[6] and the evening was a dreadful failure. What she hoped to gain by such behaviour, heaven knows. David's instant conversion? Wallis, reduced to tears, packing her bags and creeping away? If they noticed it at all, it only confirmed their view that the Duchess of York was sanctimonious and absurd, and consequently made things even more difficult for her husband.

The British Press, meanwhile, looked the other way. Foreign papers arrived on the bookstalls with every reference to Mrs Simpson cut out. The authorities seemed to think that no one would notice. They also had to overlook the fact that foreign newspapers arrived in their hundreds through the post, and that boatloads of indiscreet travellers returned every day, only too anxious to spread the news that the King of England was intending to marry an American divorcee. For that, in a nutshell, was the story. Still nobody would confront the King, least of all his brothers. 'I have been meaning to come and see you,' Bertie wrote plaintively to his mother, 'but I wanted to see David first. He is very difficult to see and when one does he wants to talk about other matters. It is all so worrying and I feel we live a life of conjecture; never knowing what will happen tomorrow, and then the unexpected comes...'[7]

Nothing, now, could have been unexpected to anyone of normal discernment. On 15 October the Press Association telephoned Alec Hardinge at the Palace and told him that Mrs Simpson's divorce case was to be heard at Ipswich Assizes on 27 October. It occurred to Hardinge – a bolt from the blue – that once Mrs Simpson was free, and in a position to marry the King, 'grave constitutional – and not only moral – issues might only too easily arise.'[8] He therefore lost no time in writing to Stanley Baldwin: the Prime Minister must, he implored, 'see the King and ask if these proceedings could not be stopped, for the danger in which they placed him (HM) was becoming every day greater'.[9]

Baldwin happened to be staying the weekend at Cumberland Lodge in Windsor Park, so he asked the Hardinges over to lunch. Major Hardinge arrived with a sheaf of carefully prepared notes (I feel he had something in common with Mr Boyd, the Ceremonial Secretary) with the help of which he hoped to persuade the Prime Minister to advise the King to stop the divorce proceedings and to stop 'flaunting' Mrs Simpson in public, particularly in the Court Circular. Baldwin was dubious, but eventually agreed. However, where was the King? Lost. He wasn't at the Fort: he wasn't at Sandringham. Major Hardinge's telephone calls became ever more frantic, his messages increasingly desperate. Mrs Simpson had taken a house at Felixstowe, conveniently near the Ipswich Assizes. The King, rather obviously, was at Felixstowe. However, he 'phoned Hardinge back at nine o'clock on Monday morning from Sandringham. Hardinge said his piece, and was horrified to be told that Mrs Simpson's divorce was her own business and that neither the King nor the Prime Minister nor the Archbishop of Canterbury nor anyone else had the right to intervene.[10] However, if the old boy wanted to see him, let him come to Sandringham. Impossible, Hardinge expostulated, the meeting must be in *complete privacy*, he must stress the importance of *secrecy*.[11] Perplexed by all this drama, the King agreed to meet Baldwin at the Fort the following morning. 'Plainly a crisis of some kind was imminent in my personal affairs'[12] was his laconic comment.

The meeting was not a success. The King stubbornly refused to hide his friendship with Mrs Simpson or to interfere in any way with her divorce. He was, nevertheless, perturbed: 'A friendship which so far had remained within the sheltered realm of my private solicitude' (a pretty phrase, but not quite accurate) 'was manifestly about to become an affair of State . . . along with the air estimates, the Polish corridor, the civil war in Spain and the value of the pound sterling.'[13] It was absurd, but perhaps he needed advice. He decided to ask his old friend Walter Monckton, the former Attorney-General, to lunch.

A few days later he and Monckton were strolling under the cedar trees at Fort Belvedere. David suddenly stopped short. 'Listen, Walter, one doesn't know how things are going to turn out. I'm beginning to wonder whether I really am the kind of king they want . . . Well, there's my brother Bertie . . .'[14]

CHAPTER
19

Major Hardinge sped to 145 Piccadilly immediately he had heard Baldwin's account of his fruitless interview with the King. The divorce would go through; provided there were no obstructions, Mrs Simpson would receive her decree absolute on 27 April, just in time for the King to marry her before the Coronation in May. It went without saying that such a disaster would necessitate the King's abdication. The Duke and Duchess of York must prepare themselves to take over. Having delivered himself of this bombshell he dashed off to spread the feeling of impending disaster through Whitehall.

On 26 October *The New York Journal* printed an article under the headline 'KING WILL WED WALLY' in which it cited the example of the Duke of York marrying 'a commoner, so-called' and stated categorically that eight months after the divorce Edward would marry Mrs Simpson and that after the Coronation she would become his consort.[1] Anyone who could count would be puzzled by the fact that in this case they would marry in June, a month after the Coronation, but never mind, the gist of it must be true because William Randolph Hearst, the owner of the *Journal*, was believed to have visited Fort Belvedere recently and must have heard it from the King himself. On the same day, after a satisfactorily gloomy meeting with the Archbishop of Canterbury, Major Hardinge received Geoffrey Dawson, Editor of *The Times*. Mr Dawson brought with him a very long and extremely pompous letter railing against the King, which he had received from a British resident in the United States who signed himself BRITANNICUS IN PARTIBUS INFIDELIUM. The letter was scurrilous and abusive, but the use to which it was put gave it some dubious historical importance. 'It may be presumptuous, and even impertinent, for a person far removed from the centre of events to suggest a remedy,' the presumptuous and impertinent expatriate concluded his diatribe, 'but I cannot refrain from saying that nothing would please me more than to hear that Edward VIII had abdicated his rights in favour of the Heir Presumptive, who I am confident would be prepared to carry on in the sterling tradition established by his father. In my view it would be well to have such a change take place while it is still a matter of individuals, and before the disquiet has progressed to the point of calling in question the institution of monarchy itself.'[2]

'For some months,' Lady Hardinge writes with pride, 'my husband had ... been forwarding to the King samples of similar letters from abroad ... in order that the King should be under no illusion about public opinion overseas.'[3] It was, of course, his duty to keep the King informed; but this sort of thing could hardly be classed as 'information'. Major Hardinge eagerly agreed with Geoffrey Dawson's request that he should pass it on. It would be untrue to say that a poison-pen letter decided the futures of at least six people (never forgetting the Little Princesses), but it was effectively used with that end in view. To the Yorks, who undoubtedly received a copy post-haste, it was a confirmation of all Elizabeth's views and Bertie's fears. On 27 October, as predicted, Mrs Simpson received her decree nisi on the grounds of her husband's adultery with one Buttercup Kennedy (who was not named) at the Hotel de Paris, Bray, near Maidenhead,.

On 3 November King Edward opened Parliament with, as was to be expected, several irregularities. It was pouring with rain, so, 'to the disappointment of my children, among others',[4] commented Lady Hardinge, the King drove to the House of Lords in a closed Daimler instead of the customary State coach. As he had not yet been crowned, he decided to wear the cocked hat of the Admiral of the Fleet instead of 'the massive bejewelled headgear of kingship' (his father used to say that he knew of few worse ordeals than being obliged to read some-body else's speech while at the same time balancing a 2½ lb gold crown on his head).[5] As he was a bachelor, there was only one throne under the canopy behind the Woolsack. His Private Secretary was not alone in visualizing another beside it, occupied by the whore of Babylon.

In their issue of 9 November *Time* magazine claimed that Mr J. P. Morgan, with whom the Yorks had stayed during the summer, was likely to intervene 'at the personal request of the Duke and Duchess of York' over American Press stories about the King and Mrs Simpson.[6] Was this, if true, a sign of hope? Of support? Of what? A month later the same paper was to report that 'Her Royal Highness the Duchess of York, weekending with the Earl and Countess of Pembroke, reacted with hard gaiety on Sunday to the cautious question by a titled guest as to whether the King is resolved to marry Mrs Simpson. "Everyone knows more than we do," replied the Duchess of York. "We know nothing. Nothing!" Her Royal Highness followed this by a brittle laugh.'[7] When the 'delicious gurgle' that had enslaved Lord David Cecil could be described, even by hearsay, as 'brittle' it was clear something had gone very wrong with Elizabeth's performance.

The drama inched forward to its climax. On 12 November the King left for two days with the Home Fleet, far from domestic squabbles, the Prime Minister, the Archbishop and, he foolishly thought, the Hardinges. On the evening of 13 November he arrived back from Portland at the Fort, exhausted, cold, pleased with himself and long-ing for a hot bath. He was met by his butler, who told him that there was an urgent letter from Major Hardinge; and there indeed it was, 'Urgent and Confidential', on top of the pile of dispatch boxes. He took it upstairs and ran his bath (it's safe to assume that he turned on his own taps, considering his attitude to the telephone) and opened the letter. 'An instant later I was confronted by the most serious crisis of my life.'[8]

For the first time, in fact, he was confronted by the reality of the situation as seen by Major Hardinge, Stanley Baldwin, the Lords Spiritual, their supporters, and his own family. The letter made three main points: 1) that the silence of the British Press would not be maintained much longer. 'It is probably only a matter of days before the outburst begins. Judging by the letters from British subjects living in foreign countries . . . the effect will be calamitous'; 2) that the Prime Minister and senior members of the Government 'are meeting today (13 November) to discuss what action should be taken'. The resignation of the Government – 'an eventuality which can by no means be excluded' – would mean that the King would have to find someone else capable of forming a government which the present House of Commons would support. Major Hardinge had 'reason to know that, in view of the feeling prevalent among members of the House of Commons of all parties, this is hardly within the bounds of possibility.' The alternative would be a dissolution and a General Election fought on the marriage issue, which would, in Major Hardinge's opinion, irreparably damage the Crown, 'the corner-stone on which the whole Empire rests'; 3) the only way of avoiding this situation was for Mrs Simpson to go abroad *without further delay*. Major Hardinge *begged* His Majesty to give this proposal his earnest consideration before the position became irretrievable, and had the honour etc. etc. of being . . .'[9] This letter, Lady Hardinge maintains, was 'a last bid to enable the King to remain on the throne'.[10]

David, alone in his bathroom, suddenly felt like a king. How dared this upstart suggest that 'I should send from my land, my realm, the woman I intended to marry'? His first instinct was to seize the tele-phone.[11] Then he thought better of it, and took his bath instead. When he joined Wallis and her Aunt Bessie downstairs, Wallis knew that something was seriously wrong, but during the evening he cheered up and they all played three-handed rummy.[12]

What the King did not know at this time – but Major Hardinge's confidantes undoubtedly did – was that Baldwin had been asking the opinions of Clement Attlee, Leader of the Opposition, and Sir Walter Citrine, the general secretary of the T.U.C., and both had agreed that the Labour voters in the country would not countenance Mrs Simpson becoming Queen.[13] Neither did he know that representatives of the Civil Service had composed a draft ultimatum so harsh in its wording that Baldwin took it to Chequers with him and somehow mislaid it.[14] Nor had he been informed that Baldwin had sounded out the Dominions, and that both Lord Tweedsmuir, the Governor-General of Canada, and Stanley Bruce, the High Commissioner for Australia, were dead set against any possibility of a Queen Wallis. On that very day, in fact – the ill-omened Friday the 13th – his indefatigable Private Secretary had lunched with the High Commissioner, as a result of which Bruce sent a stern memo to Baldwin itemizing all the points that Baldwin had failed to make in his meeting with the King three weeks before. If the King seriously intended marriage, Bruce instructed the Prime Minister, 'you would be compelled to advise him to abdicate, and unless he accepted such advice you would be unable to continue as his adviser and would tender the resignation of the Government'.[15] As Hardinge mentioned none of this in his letter – though the implications of 'I have reason to know' might suggest something even more ominous – it was understandable that the single-minded King took it as a personal attack. He decided that it would be impossible to continue negotiations with the Government through Hardinge, and again contacted Walter Monckton. This naturally increased the bitterness in what was now called the Roundhead faction. Elizabeth and Lady Hardinge spent much time on the telephone. Anonymous abuse arrived daily in the Cavaliers' mail. 'You old bitch,' Lady Cunard read with alarm, 'trying to make up to Mrs Simpson, in order to curry favour with the King . . .'[16] It was learned that two affidavits had been filed demanding the intervention of the King's Proctor in Simpson v. Simpson, on the grounds of collusion.[17]

In the maelstrom of gossip, rumour and, perhaps, intrigue, one thing that indubitably did not happen was Elizabeth asking Wallis round for a cup of tea and a chat, which might have saved everyone a great deal of anguish and expense. According to Wallis's autobiography, David had friends at the Fort for lunch and dinner on Saturday, 14 November. On Sunday they were invited to tea by Marina and George at Coppins and David said that he wanted to call by Windsor Castle on the way to rehang some portraits, though he admitted to Wallis later that he had met Walter Monckton there 'for a private talk about a serious matter'. On their return to the Fort, David, presumably on Monckton's advice, showed her Hardinge's letter. Wallis was 'stunned'. Her first instinct was to leave the country immediately, as Hardinge had suggested. 'You'll do no such thing,' David said peremptorily. 'I won't have it. This letter is an impertinence.'[18] 'To use a good American expression,' Wallis said, 'they're about to give me the works. They want me to give you up.'[19] 'They can't stop me,' David said. 'On the Throne or off, I'm going to marry you.'[20]

Wallis was frightened. What had started as a challenging flirtation was now far beyond her control. She had inadvertently opened Pandora's box – bits of the ancient throne, shreds of the British Constitution, ghoulies and ghosties and long-legged beasties from dead Parliaments and deserted churches whirled into her trivial, well-ordered life; most frightening of all, perhaps, was the unrecognizable animus of her funny little Prince, released from centuries of inhibition and frustration, deaf to reason, wild, formidable and grim. If she followed her instinct and bolted, he would simply come after her. As an individual, she no longer mattered. She had become a cause.

The following evening the King summoned Baldwin to the Palace and told him categorically that he intended to marry Wallis as soon as she was free. Baldwin then propounded the curious but, he clearly thought, irrefutable theory that 'in the choice of a Queen, the voice of the people must be heard'.[21] As it had previously been maintained that an election on the marriage issue would be disastrous this seems inconsistent, unless by 'the people' he meant their political representatives, who had other irons in the fire. The King, however, was past arguing. 'I have made up my mind and nothing will alter it – I have looked at it from all sides – and I mean to abdicate to marry Mrs Simpson.' 'Sir,' said Baldwin, 'this is a very grave decision and I am deeply grieved.'[22]

As almost all the accounts are at variance with each other, it is not surprising that the Yorks were in a state of confusion and panic. Alec Hardinge, their only direct contact with the King, had been dismissed from the affair. Bertie, the Heir Presumptive, had so far been told nothing by his brother, and everything else was speculation. They heard that Mrs Simpson had told Lady Colefax that David had never mentioned marriage to her at all.[23] Could that be possible? There was a rumour that Lady Colefax had contacted Neville Chamberlain. But Mr Chamberlain was stricken with gout, and incommunicado. On the other hand they heard that Lord Willingdon had told his niece that if the King insisted on marrying, the Privy Council would assemble and insist that he either abdicated or they resigned. If David had never even asked Mrs Simpson to marry him, what could that mean? 'I believe quite sincerely,' wrote Harold Nicolson in his diary, 'that the King has proposed to Mr Baldwin and has not proposed to Wallis.'[24] In the centre of all this Queen Mary seemed to tower in dignified dependability, as Chips Channon said she looked – like the Jungfrau. 'Thank God we have all got you as a central point,' Elizabeth is reputed to have written to her, 'because without that point it [the Family] might easily disintegrate.'

That night, Monday, 16 November, David's intentions, at least, were finally made clear. He had invited himself to dinner at Marlborough House, (he 'suddenly appeared after dinner,' writes the Duchess of Gloucester).[25] Wearing white tie and tails, he went into his mother's boudoir and was glad to find his sister Mary there as well ('having asked that his sister Mary should be present,' says Lady Donaldson,[26] whose account is probably the more reliable of the two). David was 'somewhat nonplussed', however, to find his sister-in-law Alice also present. She had only been married to Harry for a year, 'almost a stranger to the family'. Queen Mary, he says, put both of them at their ease by announcing with a reassuring smile that Alice was tired and would go to bed directly after dinner. ('He was in a great state of agitation,' wrote Alice, 'and asked his mother if I could leave the room ... Queen Mary was discernibly angered by this request, but with many apologies she asked me to go, which of course I did'.)[27] The meal seemed endless. They discussed the London Needlework Guild, the painting of the outside of Buckingham Palace, the Newmarket Sales. David felt especially sorry for Alice (if she was there). 'Never loquacious, this evening she uttered not a word. And when at last we got up to leave the table ... she almost fled from the room.[28]

David then informed his mother and sister that he was in love with Wallis, determined to marry her, and aware of the fact that he would probably have to abdicate. There was no mention of Bertie's, or indeed Mrs Simpson's, possible reluctance to go along with this plan. It was to be two years before Queen Mary would be able to put her feelings that night into coherent words. At the time, shock as a believer in the infallibility of the Monarchy, shock as a supporter of the highest moral standards and shock as a proud and loving mother almost paralysed her. The next day she stepped briskly into the room to greet Mr Baldwin with the words, 'Well, Prime Minister – here's a pretty kettle of fish!'[29] What more was there to say?

On Wednesday, 18 November the King was due to go on a tour of South Wales; he therefore only had Tuesday in which to inform his brothers of his decision. Harry, as usual, 'appeared little moved',[30] just disgruntled at the idea that if he had to become Regent Designate he would have to give up the Army, and that would be damn rotten, old boy. George, according to David's own account, 'was reconciled to my decision';[31] according to Chips Channon, the Kents' neighbour in Belgrave Square, he was desolate. And Bertie?

'Bertie was so taken aback by my news that in his shy way he could not bring himself to express his innermost feelings at the time.' Did he get a chance to do so? After a few days Bertie 'wrote that he longed for me to be happy, adding that he of all people should be able to understand my feelings; he was sure that whatever I decided would be in the best interests of the country and Empire.'[32] So much is missing that this confrontation, in some ways the most dramatic in the entire story, dwindles to a stammering, self-pitying mumble from Bertie and a complaisant sigh of relief from his brother. The situation presented by such scanty evidence is too unreal to justify any speculation as to what really happened.

What was Elizabeth's reaction? She had missed her opportunity of establishing, or at least making an effort to establish, a diplomatic entente with Wallis Simpson. Her overt hostility had added to the brothers' lack of mutual understanding and would destroy what remained of brotherly affection. She was left with the prospect of being married to an unwilling and possibly incompetent King, and of herself wearing the crown that she had considered too sacrosanct to be worn by David's mistress. '. . . the agony of it all has been beyond words,' she wrote to Victor Cazalet a few weeks later. 'And the melancholy fact remains still at the present moment that he for whom we agonized is the one person it did not touch. Poor soul, a fearful awakening is awaiting his completely blinded reason before very long.'[33] Was this a threat, or simply a prediction? I can only turn to Miss Laird, who presumably knows. 'Once she realizes that . . . trust has been misplaced, the wound goes deep; she can forgive any act but treachery, but then she is implacable as any Scot.'[34]

The Yorks were due to leave for Edinburgh on 29 November, in order that Bertie might take over David's position as Grand Master Mason of Scotland. During the intervening week, the Duke of York was by no means idle. He went to see Queen Mary on Wednesday, the Prime Minister and Queen Mary again on Thursday, down to the Royal Lodge for the weekend, Queen Mary on Monday, David on Tuesday evening. The following day he wrote to Sir Godfrey Thomas, the King's Assistant Private Secretary, 'If the worst happens & I have to take over, you can be assured that I will do my best to clear up the inevitable mess, if the whole fabric does not crumble under the shock and strain of it all.'[35] Meanwhile a new complication had arisen; the proposal that the King should contract a morganatic marriage. Perhaps it was this suggestion that made Queen Mary, herself very sensitive to being the descendant of such a marriage, to explode 'Really! This might be Rumania!'[36] The whole thing had gone too far. 'I hate going to Scotland to do what I have to do as I am so worried over this whole matter,' Bertie wrote. 'I feel like the proverbial "sheep being led to the slaughter", which is not a comfortable feeling.' He and his wife rattled north in (I imagine) despondent silence; and Chips wrote gleefully in his diary, 'The Royal entourage must indeed be in a stew and turmoil today.'[37]

CHAPTER

20

> The Simpson crisis has been a great delight to everyone.
> At Maidie's nursing home they report a pronounced turn
> for the better in all adult patients. There can seldom have
> been an event that has caused so much general delight and
> so little pain...
>
> *Evelyn Waugh's Diary*
> Friday 4 December–Tuesday 8 December 1936[1]

As the Yorks stepped out of their sleeping car at Euston station on the morning of Thursday, 3 December they were confronted by newspaper posters proclaiming 'THE KING'S MARRIAGE' in letters a foot high. The news was out, the barriers down. Now, perhaps, it could be left to the people.

The days that followed were without doubt the most dreadful of Bertie's entire life. He spent that Thursday hurrying between his mother at Marlborough House and David and Walter Monckton at the Palace, ending up with nothing more concrete than an arrangement to see David at Fort Belvedere the following day. In the morning, before leaving 145 Piccadilly, he telephoned the Fort to be told that David could not see him until Saturday. On Saturday Bertie and Elizabeth drove to the Royal Lodge. On their arrival Bertie immediately 'phoned David and was told not to go and see him until Sunday. 'I will see you and tell you my decision when I have made up my mind,' said the King. Bertie 'phoned on Sunday to be told that the King was in conference, but would call him back later. Prince Paul went to tea at the Royal Lodge that afternoon and found that the Yorks were completely in the dark about what might happen. 'The Duke of York is miserable, does not want the throne, and is imploring his brother to stay.'[2] David did not 'phone back that day. On Monday, 7 December Bertie waited until lunchtime, then rang again. David said he might be able to see him that evening. With more than a touch of brusqueness, Bertie said he had to go to London, but immediately regretted it and called back to leave a message that he was still at the Royal Lodge. At 6.50 p.m. David 'phoned and asked him to go over to the Fort after dinner. 'No,' said Bertie, 'I will come and see you at once,' and was at the Fort by 7 o'clock.

Both the Duke of Windsor and Chips Channon say that the Duke of Kent was with the King that weekend, 'never leaving him for a second and trying by every means in his power to persuade him to stay', according to Channon.[3] There is a theory that Kent was being considered as an alternative successor to the Duke of York; if so, and this was being discussed, Bertie's presence might have been awkward, however reluctant he was to take over the Crown. The Kents had obvious advantages, not least of which was a son. Marina was royal by birth and George had none of Bertie's handicaps. On the other hand there was his past to consider, and the last thing the Establishment wanted was another flighty King on the throne. All things considered, there really was no alternative to Bertie.

This was the decision the Duke of York was told when he arrived at the Fort that evening. There is no record of his reply. He went back to the Royal Lodge for dinner with Elizabeth, then returned to the Fort. Late that night he and Elizabeth returned to London.

The following day, Tuesday, 8 December, Elizabeth took to her bed with an attack of 'flu. She would remain there until things were sorted out. Bertie went to see his mother, then met Walter Monckton, who explained all the facts of the situation to him, and returned to his mother to explain them to her. Then he drove down to the Royal Lodge to meet Harry, with whom he went to the Fort to see David and Stanley Baldwin. The Duke of Kent was already there and the four brothers, Baldwin, Monckton and some other advisers, all had dinner together, 'A dinner I am never likely to forget,' Bertie wrote. 'While the rest of us were very sad . . . my brother was the life & soul of the party, telling the P.M. things I am sure he had never heard before about unemployment centres etc . . . I whispered to W.M. "& this is the man we are going to lose"'. One couldn't, nobody could, believe it.'[4] Then he went back to London. The next day, after seeing Queen Mary and Baldwin and two different sets of lawyers, he took his mother to the Royal Lodge for a meeting with David – she would not, it seems, meet him in his own home – and then went to the Fort to see David and more lawyers. After driving back to London he went to see his mother again and 'broke down and sobbed like a child'.[5] A few minutes later he was told by Downing Street that he was wanted to witness his brother's instrument of abdication at 10 o'clock the following morning at Fort Belvedere.

On Thursday, 10 December he was at the Fort all morning and afternoon. The tension was unbearable and he went over to the Royal Lodge for a rest. But Bertie found he could not rest alone, and was back at the Fort by 5.45. When he eventually got back to London he found a large crowd outside 145 Piccadilly 'cheering madly'. He was overwhelmed. He went to see Queen Mary.[6]

On Friday, 11 December he was busy arranging details of his own Accession Council and seeing Crown lawyers about David's title. By the time he arrived at the Fort with Harry at 7 p.m. he was King of England. All David's servants called him His Majesty. Sir John Reith wished to announce David as Mr E. Windsor for his broadcast. 'I soon put that right. One other matter I settled too.'

Queen Mary, David, Mary, Harry, George, Aunt Alice, Uncle Algy and Bertie all had dinner together.* When David and Bertie said goodbye they kissed, parted as freemasons, '& he bowed to me as his King'.[7]

At 2 a.m. on the morning of Saturday, 12 December, His Royal Highness Prince Edward sailed for Boulogne on the destroyer *Fury*. At 11 a.m. Bertie, looking haggard and desperate, attended his Accession Council. 'With my wife and helpmeet at my side,' he said slowly, 'I take up the heavy task which lies before me...' The Accession was proclaimed that afternoon. During the few hours that it took to read the Proclamation over the length and breadth of Britain, gossip about the departed King was suspended and everyone became discreetly loyal. Bertie, his mother and his two daughters watched the ceremony at St James's Palace from a room overlooking Friary Court.

> Whereas by an Instrument of Abdication dated the tenth day of December instant His former Majesty King Edward the Eighth did declare His irrevocable Determination to renounce the throne for Himself and His Descendants, and the said Instrument of Abdication has now taken effect whereby the Imperial Crown of Great Britain, Ireland and all other His former Majesty's dominions is now solely and rightfully come to the High and Mighty Prince Albert Frederick Arthur George: We, therefore, the Lords Spiritual and Temporal of this Realm ... with the Principal Gentlemen of Quality ... do now hereby with one voice and Consent of Tongue and Heart publish and proclaim ... God Save the King!

There was a little indecisive cheering, the band played the National Anthem, the guns boomed out from Hyde Park and the Tower and Elizabeth, hearing them, shut her eyes in prayer. For the country, the drama was over. For King George VI and Queen Elizabeth the long, laborious sequel was about to begin.

Later that day the new King and Queen received a telegram through the Admiralty:

> Have had a good crossing. Glad to hear this morning's ceremony went off so well. Hope Elizabeth better. Best love and best luck to you both. David.[8]

* According to Elizabeth Longford (*Elizabeth R*, 286) '... the Queen Mother could never forget the horror of Abdication week. "That last family dinner party was too awful," she said to a friend years later, shuddering at the memory of her husband's agonies. "Thank goodness I had flu and couldn't go."'

PART THREE

CHAPTER

21

The idea of Wallis on the throne, even to those who think of it as an unnecessary piece of furniture, was, and is, preposterous. Harold Nicolson, after attending an official dinner at Buckingham Palace on 17 March 1937, wrote in his diary: 'The Queen ... wears upon her face a faint smile indicative of how much she would have liked her dinner party were it not for the fact that she was Queen of England. Nothing could exceed the charm or dignity which she displays, and I cannot help feeling what a mess poor Mrs Simpson would have made of such an occasion. It demonstrates to us more than anything else how wholly impossible that marriage would have been.'[1] Whatever other accomplishments Wallis may have had she was a dreadful actress, incapable of appearing as anything but her unfortunate self – quite wrong for the part. It only needed a dinner party to prove that the Abdication had been inevitable.

Elizabeth, therefore, started off with an enormous advantage. But what about Bertie? Not only did he have less experience and less theoretical knowledge of the job than David – 'I never wanted this to happen; I'm quite unprepared for it. David has been trained for this all his life. I've never even seen a State Paper ...,' he protested[2] – but he had no hope of competing with his brother's charisma. Nobody was really going to be inspired by his enthusiasm for Boys' Camps, his proficiency with a tennis racquet or the fact that he was still 'a nice, honest, clean-minded and excellent mannered boy'. And that, when it came down to it, was all anyone could find to say in his favour. When he drove out to take his first levee at St James's, there was only a handful of spectators – 'Not many of them, are there, my Lady?'[3] one of the maids said with gloomy relish to a Lady-in-Waiting. Warren Bradley Wells of the *New York Herald Tribune* noted that when the family left for Sandringham at Christmas:

King George VI, hat in hand, bowed right and left automatically as he drove up. Scarcely a hat was raised in reply ... [The King] and his family walked bowing across the platform. Perhaps half the men in the little throng raised their hats. There was a subdued murmur which might have been a suppressed cheer – or might not. In short, on his first public appearance after his succession to his brother, King George VI was given an extremely cold shoulder.[4]

Even *The Times* was not much of an improvement. Elizabeth and the children had a sentimental appeal, but Bertie was an anti-climax. The Archbishop of Canterbury had done his best; as usual, this made everything worse:

> When his people listen to him, they will note an occasional and momentary hesitation in his speech. But he has brought it into full control, and to those who hear it need cause no sort of embarrassment...[5]

Everyone promptly prepared to be embarrassed. The papers, under the guise of staunchly denying rumours of the King's incapacity, publicized all his weaknesses: 'King George, according to those who know him best, has not so great a capacity for endurance as his brother ... and it is felt that any undue strain might have unfortunate consequences,' said the *News Chronicle*, after pointing out that the Coronation programme would be, 'in the words of a high Court official ... "almost too much to expect of any man".'[6] The *Sunday Referee* came out with an indignant banner headline: 'WHISPERING AGAINST THE KING.' After attributing such whispers to 'Communists and Mayfairites', the loyal editorial continued:

> The reason why the King has not appeared in public much since his Accession is that he is fully occupied learning the complicated job of kingship. His brother, as Prince of Wales, spent forty years of his life being groomed for stardom ... The fact that he (the King) did not broadcast a Christmas message; that he has paid only one visit to the British Industries Fair; that the Durbar in India has been postponed; all have been worked up by those who 'love a bit of gossip' into alarming stories of the King's health ... Once the Coronation is over, the King will appear more frequently in public; not so much as did King Edward, for he is naturally of a more reserved and conservative disposition...[7]

Time magazine for March 1937 quoted the King as saying, 'according to the papers, I am supposed to be unable to speak without stammering, to have fits, and to die in two years. All in all, I seem to be a crock!'[8] With such supporters, the unfortunate monarch did not need enemies.

Since the Heir Apparent was a minor, it was necessary to appoint a new Regency Council. This led to a lengthy and stormy debate in the House of Commons on who should decide whether a reigning monarch was capable of performing his duties. The troublesome Mr Gallacher from West Fife declared:

> As a matter of fact, this is a bill directed against the present Monarch. Before the Coronation takes place, we are already discussing how we can

substitute him ... It is the present occupant of the throne who is suspect and for whom all this preparation has got to be made, and it is not in any way intended to apply to any future reign.[9]

The cries of 'No, No!' were not heard outside the House. What could be done to save the situation? It was up to Elizabeth. Bertie would do whatever she said, and present whatever image she decided to give him. But they needed time.

Even if Elizabeth had not read Bagehot's *English Constitution* (and by now she probably had), she knew that the real strength of the Crown lay in 'the labourers of Somersetshire', the 'credulous obedience of enormous masses'. It was on that huge, faceless substructure of society that she had to smile, while at the same time keeping Bertie safely on a pedestal far above their reach. She knew too that her greatest support in achieving this would come from the old hands, those whose conservatism and reliable absence of originality had sustained her father-in-law's regime, and not from the fashionable fly-by-nights who had decorated David's court. The few who were of any use – Churchill, the Duff Coopers – must be won over. The rest must go.

It is hard for any normal person to appreciate the extent of Royalty's paranoia. They have little first-hand experience of human nature, and their collective unconscious is crammed with battle, murder and sudden death. Elizabeth's own history, reaching far back into the Scottish mists of time, was full of peril – banditry, feuds, vendettas, Jacobite plots and violent ends. Their imagination was, and perhaps still is, far more sensitive in this respect than that of your man or woman in the street, doggedly plodding from cradle to grave in the hope of not being knocked down by a 'bus. The first sign of the purge, just before Christmas 1936, was the overnight dismissal of Lord Brownlow from his position as Lord-in-Waiting.

Perry Brownlow's crime was that he had been detailed by David to accompany Wallis to France, where he had done his best to persuade her to take a fast boat to China, even booking her a state-room and drafting her farewell message to the King.[10] Foolishly, Brownlow considered that he had done his best for his country, and expected a hero's welcome on his return. He was due to go into Waiting on 21 December, but was told that he needn't bother as Bertie was only receiving the Archbishop of Canterbury that afternoon for an informal meeting at 145 Piccadilly. The next morning Brownlow read in the Court Circular that Lord Dufferin and Ava had succeeded as Lord-in-Waiting. 'He rang up the Palace, and was told that his name could never appear in the Court Circular again and that "his resignation had been accepted". "Am I to be turned away," he asked, "like a dishonest servant with no notice, no warning, no thanks, when all I did was to obey my Master, the late King?" "Yes," was Lord Cromer's answer.[11]

Later both Lord Cromer and Lord Wigram – Private Secretary to George V and now Permanent Lord-in-Waiting – telephoned him to say that his dismissal had not been at the King's request. Of course not. The King was on his pedestal, smiling at grief, and responsible for nothing but keeping quiet. As Chips Channon wrote uneasily,

> I feel this means there is to be a 'Black List' and the Court will try to damage everyone who was a friend of the late King ... A foolish, small-minded policy, as it will only create enemies to the new regime and make their difficult roles still more so. Are we all on the 'Black List'? ... I cannot believe that it is Queen Elizabeth's doing. She is not so foolish.[12]

Elizabeth was seldom foolish. It had been at the Brownlows' that Wallis had made her unforgivable wisecrack about the black stockings.

There were occasions, particularly within the family, when Bertie had to be seen to step down and voice an opinion. This was considered necessary over Emerald Cunard, a leading society hostess and one of David's most eloquent sympathizers, who had been on Queen Mary's black list for years. The Queen Dowager wrote to Prince Paul:

> ... the other day in my presence, Bertie told George he wished him and Marina never to see Lady Cunard again and George said he would not do so. I fear she has *done David a great deal of harm* as there is no doubt she was great friends with Mrs S at one time ... Under the circumstances I feel none of us, in fact people in society, should meet her ... and I am hoping that George and Marina will no longer see certain people who alas were friends of Mrs S and Lady Cunard's and also David's...[13]

It would be hard to believe that this was any great deprivation to Lady Cunard if we did not have Harold Nicolson's evidence that, on meeting Maggie Greville soon after the Abdication, Emerald, without batting a bird-like eyelid, said 'Maggie, darling, do tell me about this Mrs Simpson – I've only just met her.'[14] Mrs Greville herself, that 'galumphing, greedy, snobbish old toad who watered at the chops at the sight of royalty and the Prince of Wales's set',[15] would soon tell Harold Nicolson that David 'was the only one of the family with whom she was never intimate'.[16] If a cock had crowed with every treachery, the Accession of good, simple, devout King George VI would have sounded like a barnyard at dawn.

Do such trivialities matter? They do to the people with whom we are concerned. Nor was the threat entirely imaginary, regardless of the subversive guests round Lady Cunard's dinner table. A King's Party had indeed existed by the end of the previous November.[17] It seems to have consisted of a few excitable politicians eating a prodigious number of meals – Esmond Harmsworth lunched with Mrs Simpson and with Lord Lothian, Sir Samuel Hoare lunched with Lord Beaverbrook and David Margesson lunched with Churchill; Tom Jones, declaring wildly that 'the country is split in two' had breakfast with Baldwin. In a few days, 'Margesson reported a thickening of the Churchill-Beaverbrook brew and a small group of M.P.s wrote to the King offering their support; a potential "King's Party" of, at this stage, about forty M.P.s could be said to exist.'[18] On Friday, 4 December, Channon reported that 'London is now properly divided and the King's faction grows; people process the streets singing "God Save the King" and assemble outside Buckingham Palace, they parade all night.' Channon, an American convert to what he considered to be the British way of life, 'personally lost my temper with any Roundhead I could see, and hurled abuse at them in my Royalist fury'.[19] By the weekend of 5 December 1936 there had been the alarming makings of a King's Party of substantial size. Sir Reginald Blaker, a Middlesex M.P., said on the Sunday that a group of Conservative M.P.s had formed to keep the King on the throne. Such talk was dangerous.[20]

David himself would more or less sum all this up with the wry remark that 'an Irish baronet of ancient lineage and antique gallantry offered to place his sword at my service in this menacing hour.'[21] His brother and sister-in-law, temporarily devoid of even their own sense of humour, might well have purged the Irish aristocracy if they had known. As it was, thanks to the deep lassitude that descends over all professional men except clergymen over the English weekend, the King's Party was dead by Monday, 7 December. Nevertheless, it would haunt Bertie and Elizabeth for the next sixteen years, undimmed by World War II and the huge increase in their own popularity. They and the Nazi Government were perhaps the only people ever to think of the Duke of Windsor as a potential revolutionary.

A further threat revived over the Abdication – that of abolishing the monarchy altogether – could never have been taken seriously by anyone except the Royal Family, but since they are the dramatis personae of this tale we should take a brief look at the arguments that worried them at the end of Edward's reign. Many relatively sane people were in favour of a change within the Monarchical system – the Leader of the Labour Party, for instance, an ex-pupil of Haileybury and quite a gentleman (he was born in Putney) said, 'I hope we shall see a new start being made. I believe this is necessary if constitutional monarchy is to survive in the present age.' That kind of comment could be overlooked. But what about the Honourable Member for West Fife?

No one can go out before the people of the country and give any justification for clinging to the Monarchy. You all know it. You will not be able, no matter what you do, to repair the damage that has been done to the Monarchical institution. If you allow things to go on as they are going, you will encourage factions to grow, and factions will grow, of a dangerous and desperate character...

What about the Honourable Member for Bridgeton?

We are doing a wrong and foolish thing if, as a House, we do not seize the opportunity with which circumstances have presented us of establishing in our land a completely democratic form of government which does away with all the Monarchical institutions and the hereditary principle . . . .

And the Honourable Member for Gorbals:

. . . instead of having the ordinary frailties that all of us have, they will have this additional one, of being surrounded with a set of flunkeys who refuse to let them know the truth as others do. Tomorrow I will willingly take the step of going out and saying it is time the people ceased to trust these folk, but only trust their own power and their own elected authority.

What about the Honourable Member for Calachie, who baldly announced 'It is time to put an end to all this flummery'?[22] One expected this sort of thing from Communists and intellectuals, but these were representatives of the people – and, most hurtful of all, Scottish people. Never mind. Elizabeth would smile at them and, eventually, they would come to heel. Just over forty years later, Willie Hamilton M.P., Britain's last official republican, wrote an eightieth birthday greeting to Elizabeth in the *Sunday Mirror*:

. . . my hatchet is buried. My venom dissipated. I am glad to salute a remarkable old lady. Long may she live to be the pride of her family. And may God understand and forgive me if I have been ensnared and corrupted, if only briefly, by this superb Royal trouper.[23]

Clearly that particular conquest took a little time. The few politically important figures in David's circle were easier to win over. Duff Cooper, Secretary of State for War, and his wife Diana had actually accompanied David and Wallis on the *Nahlin* cruise; Duff was known to have told David that if only he would wait a year, perhaps they could make Wallis Queen;[24] Diana, it was reported, had only recently curtsied to the woman. Surely they, if anyone, were for the block? On the contrary. In April 1937, Coronation year, the Coopers were invited to Windsor. Duff, it seems, had 'idolized' Elizabeth for many years.[25] That being so, why not forgive and forget? After Duff had been closeted with the Queen in her boudoir for over an hour, 'the Coopers left Windsor with the impression that things would do a lot better under the new regime.'[26]

The same approach could hardly be used with Churchill. He had been shouted down in the Commons for his apparently unwavering support of the ex-King and he was at the nadir of his career; even so, he was a significant figure and might well come in useful. This was Bertie's department. On 18 May, six days after his Coronation, he wrote:

My dear Mr Churchill,

I am writing to thank you for your very nice letter to me. I know how devoted you have been, and still are, to my dear brother, and I feel touched beyond words by your sympathy and understanding in the very difficult problems that have arisen since he left us in December. I fully realize the great responsibilities and cares that I have taken on as King, and I feel most encouraged to receive your good wishes, as one of our great statesmen, and from one who has served his country so faithfully. I can only hope and trust that the good feeling and hope that exists in the Country and Empire now will prove a good example to other Nations in the world.

Believe me,

Yours very sincerely,

George R.I.[27]

Winston soon saw the error of his ways. Four years later, as one of the most powerful Prime Ministers the country has ever known, he wrote to Their Majesties that they were 'more beloved by all classes and conditions than any of the princes of the past'.[28]

CHAPTER

22

Coronations, like Royal weddings, are all much the same. The only thing that was unique about the crowning of George VI and Elizabeth was that their predecessor listened to it on the radio.[1] To provide this facility, the BBC moved twelve tons of equipment and 472 miles of wire into Westminster Abbey, and at the end of the ceremony inadvertently broadcast to the world an agitated official crying, 'What are we to do? The Barons are on the hoof, and we haven't got the Earls away yet!',[2] a question that remained for ever unanswered. The Archbishop of Canterbury, 'ever vigilant of public interest and good taste', bustled down to British Movietone News in Soho during the evening to see the news films and cut out anything which he considered unsuitable for the public at large to see. The result was that they saw very little but horses.

Since then television has enabled us to see Royals in close-up, warts and all. In 1937 relatively few people had ever seen one at all, except on black and white newsreels of official occasions, when everyone seemed to be in an enormous hurry. The previous Coronation, though only a quarter of a century before, had taken place in a strange pre-war world with very little motor transport and no media except an awe-struck Press. This time, fleets of charabancs, special 'buses and private cars poured into London; 1,000 special trains were laid on for Coronation Day itself; the Office of Works provided seating for 90,000 people, made from 850 tons of Columbian pine (though the exact nature and source of the wood kept the House of Commons happy for days) and 3 million feet of tubing. Statistics, as usual, were employed to strike amazement in the minds of the simple public. The Procession would be 3,500 yards long and would take 40 minutes to pass any given point; 800 Peers wearing their coronets and ceremonial robes would pay 3d a head to travel in a special Underground train from Kensington High Street to Westminster (London 'bus drivers had taken the opportunity to go on strike). The lead hand horse in the Procession, ridden by the head Royal Postilion, was to be a Windsor grey named Silver Fox (known as Dawey) which would be paired by a mare named Angela; there would be seventy Royal Cleveland bays, and the ones with nonconformist white legs would be painted with lampblack; it would take two hours to prepare each animal, twenty-two yards of red or blue satin ribbon would be plaited into their manes and each set of state harness weighed 128 lbs. The cost of the whole thing was left, broadly speaking, to the imagination.

None of this meant very much to the chief performers. Elizabeth had to organize the move to Buckingham Palace, get a new crown, decide on her robes, sort out the Crown jewels, appoint a new household staff, take instruction from the Archbishop, entertain wives, learn her part, try to find time for the children. Her mother-in-law was a great help, giving Elizabeth the Koh-i-Noor from her own crown, taking the children out, and always ready with advice. Miss Crawford and Clara, on the other hand, were not as supportive as one might have hoped. 'The little girls' lives were all upset,' Crawfie complained. 'They were always being taken from lessons to try on clothes or to have a look at something their parents felt they ought not to miss.'[3] Everybody looked forward to the day when the ceremony would be over and they could all settle down to a quiet reign.

It was important, in all this whirl of activity, to have some normal family get-togethers. There was no empty place laid at the family lunch on 10 May; no mention of an absent son or brother or uncle. Walter Monckton had at last persuaded David to stop telephoning Bertie with advice on questions of the day,[4] and he and his brother were no longer communicating. Queen Mary wrote her eldest son occasional little notes, stiffly chatty: 'I went to 2 premieres last week in aid of charities & have also been to 2 plays ... I was interested in reading you drove through Gmunden, where in 1884 my parents Alge & I spent 2 months with the Cumberlands ... as far as I remember & I did go to Ischl once,'[5] but this was no time for saying she wished he was here. After lunch, they all gave each other presents – a gold teaset which had belonged to the Duke of Cumberland, a tortoiseshell and diamond fan for Elizabeth, miniatures and ribbons and Orders. A few souvenir shops outside the Palace gates displayed plaster busts of Edward VIII marked '1/6 to Clear'. Nobody bought them.[6]

Of the many descriptions of this Coronation, Bertie's is the only one to show the slightest humour. To the Archbishop of Canterbury, who felt he was 'sustained by some Higher Power',[7] it was a mystical experience. Lord Dawson of Penn was sitting in the congregation with a primed hypodermic syringe concealed in his robes,[8] in case divine sustenance failed. The Bishop of St Albans swore the King and Queen emanated some sort of 'religious radiation' and even Ramsay Macdonald felt that the couple were in states of religious trance at certain points in the ceremony.[9] Be that as it may, Bertie, after being kept awake since 3 a.m. by the testing of loudspeakers and the jubilant din of military bands, 'could eat no breakfast & had a sinking feeling inside'. He was then kept waiting for what seemed hours at the Abbey because one of the Presbyterian chaplains in Elizabeth's procession had fainted (again?). Finally he entered the Abbey and 'negotiated' (the word is very apt) the flight of steps going up to the Sacrarium. He bowed to his mother & the Family in the gallery, and after the Introduction moved to the Coronation Chair where he was eventually got into the white Colobium Sindonis, 'a surplice which the Dean of Westminster insisted I should put on inside out, had not my Groom of the Robes come to the rescue.' When it came to taking the Coronation Oath, the Bishop of Durham stood on one side of him, the Bishop of Bath and Wells on the other, to support him and hold the form of Service for him to follow. Unfortunately neither Bishop could find the right place in the missal. The Archbishop's Higher Power prompted him to hold out his own book for the King to read, but 'horror of horrors his thumb covered the words of the Oath'. It was perhaps at this point that Bertie began to glow.

> My Lord Great Chamberlain was supposed to dress me but I found his hands fumbled & shook so I had to fix the belt of the sword myself. As it was he nearly put the hilt of the sword under my chin trying to attach it to the belt ... The supreme moment came when the Archbishop placed the St Edward's Crown on my head. I had taken every precaution as I thought to see that the Crown was put on the right way round, but the Dean & the Archbishop had been juggling with it so much that I never did know whether it was right or not ... As I turned after leaving the Coronation Chair I was brought up all standing, owing to one of the Bishops treading on my robe. I had to tell him to get off it pretty sharply as I nearly fell down ...[10]

Too many damned parsons, as his father had said. There may even have been moments when Bertie would have seconded Mr G. Hardie's suggestion in Parliament: 'If people want to see the Coronation why can't they wait for a dry day and have it in a big field where everybody could have a chance of seeing it?' His great-grandmother's Uncle, William IV, had much the same idea. If Bertie ever had such an eccentric thought, he kept it to himself.

According to a recent biography by Ann Morrow, Elizabeth 'broke down and cried out: "I can't go through with it. I can't be crowned".'[11] If this is true, it would seem a sufficiently important piece of information to warrant some source or corroboration, but Miss Morrow gives neither. Perhaps it came from that ubiquitous 'member of the household', on unusually intimate terms with the Queen. Perhaps it is common knowledge among the *cognoscenti*, of whom there are so very many. Perhaps it should have happened. Anyway, from all other accounts she sailed through the whole thing with professional, smiling dignity – 'much more bosomy' noted

Chips Channon.[12] Of course she had first-night nerves, but of course she overcame them. Her own family, so unexpectedly and perilously elevated, watched her with pride. The children, in lightweight coronets and purple velvet robes trimmed with ermine, behaved impeccably, apart from Margaret playing rather too noisily with her prayer-book and getting a disciplinary nudge from Lilibet. The Hardinges, unfortunately, were away, recovering from nervous prostration in India, but many of those present at the Abbey must have thought of the Coronation originally intended for this day – a solitary man, childless, standing in Bertie's place, no wifely throne, no peeresses, no one to go home to; or, if that scene was too heart-rending, Wallis Simpson smirking under the Koh-i-Noor: 'O Lord, the giver of all perfection: Grant unto this thy servant Wallis our Queen, that by the powerful and mild influence of her piety and virtue, she may adorn the high dignity which she hath obtained through Jesus Christ our Lord . . .' Even those who had entertained doubts now realized that 'hush-hush and rally round the new King' was the best policy.

The day after the Coronation, the King and Queen drove in an open carriage through the streets of London, their progress unanimously described as 'triumphal'. On the following Tuesday night they made modest history by being the first reigning King and Queen to attend a private dance, if the Duchess of Sutherland's Coronation ball at Hampden House can be described in such terms. 'The Queen was in white,' noted the industrious Channon, 'with an ugly spiked tiara . . . The King followed her, showing his teeth.'[13] 'Everyone' was there: Queen Mary in ice blue, Princess Olga of Yugoslavia wearing her mother's ruby parure, the Queen of Egypt, Prince Ernst August of Hanover, Prince Fritz of Prussia, Mrs Maggie Greville. Only one habitual guest was conspicuous by her absence. It had been suggested by Buckingham Palace that perhaps Lady Cunard might be invited after supper, by which time the King and Queen would have gone home. So Emerald waited by the telephone to be told when she could safely leave Grosvenor Square for Green Street.[14] Such ugly little discords in the National Anthem went almost unnoticed.

Nor did very many people see, or fully understand if they did, the statement in the London Gazette of 28 May:

> The King has been pleased by Letters Patent under the Great Seal of the Realm bearing the date the 27th day of May 1937 to declare that the Duke of Windsor shall, notwithstanding his Instrument of Abdication executed on the 10th day of December 1936, and His Majesty's Declaration of Abdication Act 1936, whereby effect was given to the said Instrument, be entitled to hold and enjoy for himself only the title style or attribute of Royal Highness so however that his wife and descendants if any shall not hold the said title style or attribute.

David had wanted a morganatic marriage – let him have one. Short of giving up his own royal title, he was to live for the rest of his life with a superior social status to Wallis and she – as *The Times* put it when objecting to the original proposal – must 'carry in solitary prominence the brand of unfitness' to be a member of the Royal Family. The ostensible reason for this insult was that if she divorced her third husband, as she had done the previous two, the family did not want an ex-wife wandering about as an HRH. Slightly less cynically, they did not want the same thing to happen if David should predecease her, as in fact he did.

The result was disagreement among the rest of the family, which must have caused Bertie considerable distress. His nephew George – now Lord Harewood – was in his first year at Eton and remembered, 'it was hard for the younger amongst us not to stand in amazement at the moral contradiction between the elevation of code of duty on the one hand, and on the other the denial of central Christian virtues – forgiveness, understanding, family tenderness.'[15] His mother and father had been the first to visit David in his exile in Austria. The Duke of Kent had stayed with him too,* so had Louis Mountbatten, though cousin Louis could always be counted on to keep an even keel once he had ascertained which way the wind was blowing. Queen Mary, of course, could be relied on to support the Throne through thick and thin, regardless of her personal feelings, and Harry was in the comfortable position of having no opinions at all; but for the rest Coronation Year 1937 was an uneasy time for the royal conscience.

*   *   *

Meanwhile Europe, regardless of who occupied the British throne, marched at a brisk pace towards World War II; or more accurately Germany, packed and ready, marched briskly, while everybody else mislaid their bits and pieces and flurried about, nagged by Churchill and delayed by Neville Chamberlain. Guernica was destroyed by Fascist bombers and 4,000 Basque Catholic child refugees arrived at Southampton, only to reveal that they were mostly neither Basque nor Catholic, but Asturian, Galician and Castilian infidels.[16] This put

---

* Alastair Forbes in *The Times Literary Supplement* of 4 January 1980, writes that Marina had received instructions from Queen Mary that, being a foreigner, she must not be 'the first female member of the family to call on her'. This makes no sense, 'she' – the nameless Other Woman – being in the South of France waiting for her divorce absolute. In any case, Princess Mary had been the first to call. On the other hand Walter Monkton's story, as quoted by Frances Donaldson, that Marina stubbornly refused to accompany her husband is almost as unconvincing. The upshot, anyway, was that Marina earned the approval of both Queens and, as Frances Donaldson says, 'a coolness grew up between the Duke of Windsor and the brother who had been so close to him'.

the Catholic Church and the Salvation Army – responsible respectively for the children's spiritual and physical welfare – in a quandary. Germany and Italy left and returned to the Non-Intervention Committee so often that nobody could keep track. As the Committee itself was unable to agree about anything, it didn't seem to matter much. Hundreds of Trotsky sympathizers and hard-line Communists were executed in the Soviet Union. There were pogroms in Poland, strikes and riots in Trinidad, riots in Barbados, a 90-day 'state of war' in Brazil, violence in Palestine and the Sino-Japanese war in China. On 21 August HMS *Leander* annexed three uninhabited islands in the Pacific Ocean for Great Britain.

The rest of the world's royalty was, on the whole, muted. King Alfonso of Spain, exiled in Vienna, was reported to be lunching off boiled beef and apple tart in the Hotel Bristol; the Duc de Guise, Pretender to the French crown, issued a manifesto declaring that he had decided 'to claim the throne of his fathers', after which he relapsed into a profound silence; at Serowe, in Bechuanaland, ex-Queen Bagakgametsi pleaded guilty to trying to harm the Queen Mother by 'mystic potions and incantations'. King George VI sat in his study at Buckingham Palace with the Crown on his head, practising indefatigably for his Opening Address to Parliament. King Leopold of the Belgians came to stay, and at dinner Elizabeth wore 'a *robe de style* of gleaming silver tissue over hooped *carcase* of stiffened silver gauze, with a deep *berthe* collar of silver lace encrusted with glittering diamonds'.[17] A few weeks later Their Majesties toured Cornwall to receive the feudal dues from the tenants of the Duchy. They were presented with a pound of pepper, a hundred shillings, a grey cloak, a brace of greyhounds, a pair of gilt spurs, a salmon spear, a load of wood, a bow d'arbus and a pound of cumin. During the summer they stayed for a quiet weekend with Mrs Greville at Polesden Lacey and had dinner with three dukes, four duchesses, an unspecified number of marquesses, and Osbert Sitwell.[18] On Saturday, 13 November there was a discreet paragraph in *The Times*:

> The King and Queen will attend morning service tomorrow at the parish church of St Paul's Walden, near Hitchin, where the Queen will unveil a stone tablet to commemorate the fact that she was born in the parish and baptized in the church. Their Majesties wish the service to be a very quiet one and the congregation will be limited to the usual worshippers resident in the village. Admission to the service will be by ticket only.

Lady Strathmore was not present at this ceremony and Lord Strathmore is not mentioned. Elizabeth, as she graciously unveiled the tablet, was probably the only person there to know that one line of its tribute – 'BORN IN THIS PARISH' – was untrue. Well, after all, it wouldn't have looked right to put 'BIRTHPLACE UNKNOWN' or 'SOMEWHERE IN LONDON', would it? *The Sunday Times* of 25 May 1980 revealed the discrepancy. The tablet – with God's blessing, one assumes – remains unchanged.

Most of the remaining events of that Coronation year were unremarkable. Compared with 1911 there was less glamour and far less amazement at the achievements of man; consequently there was a general lack of fun. Acts of God were unoriginal – 671,000 homeless and 400 drowned in floods in the Ohio Valley, floods in the Fen country, floods in Syria, forty deaths caused by storms in the Oriente Province of Cuba – that sort of thing. Nobody discovered very much, apart from the only known mummy of a noble of the 1st Dynasty and a new comet of the 7th magnitude. The longest solar eclipse of modern times was visible in the South Pacific, the Moon occultated Mars and the near approach of Jupiter to the earth was noticed in July. Even the air was relatively dull: Flight Lieutenant Adam reached an altitude of 53,937 feet and two Japanese airmen in their aircraft *Divine Wind* flew from Tokyo to Croydon in 94 hours 18 minutes; the German airship *Hindenburg* was destroyed by fire at Lakehurst, New Jersey; the majority of French aviators, however, appeared to survive. There were a couple of attempted assassinations, but the only one that succeeded was that of Bagir-Sidqi, Chief of the Iranian General Staff. William Morris, after giving away millions of pounds to deserving causes, was made a Viscount, and Mr Neville Chamberlain opened a campaign for a Fitter Britain, perhaps as a substitute for the Archbishop of Canterbury's Back To God campaign, which had achieved no noticeable support. In Berlin on 5 July the American journalist William Shirer wrote in his diary, 'The Austrian Minister tells me that the new British Ambassador here, Sir Nevile Henderson, has told Goering, with whom he is on very chummy terms, that Hitler can have his Austria so far as he, Henderson, is concerned.'[19]

★   ★   ★

The wedding of the year was, of course, the Windsors'. For some reason Bertie was responsible for deciding where the ceremony should take place. He and Elizabeth chose the Château de Candé, which they had never seen, owned by a naturalized American called Charles Bedaux, whom nobody knew. However, of the various suggestions put forward, the Château seemed furthest removed from the Riviera and its implications of flightiness. The command went out that nobody should attend the wedding. David Low drew a cartoon for the *Evening Standard* entitled 'Guests to the Duke's Wedding' – Romeo and Juliet, Tristan and Isolde, Abelard and Heloise, Paris and Helen, Antony and Cleopatra, filing into church being filmed by

Great Love Stories Inc. But they were all ghosts.

Three thousand invitations, you may remember, were sent for Elizabeth's wedding. The presents were stacked in crates. Five Lords Spiritual, headed by the Archbishop of Canterbury, joined the innocent pair in holy matrimony. When the former King of England got married he did so in the presence of his wife's Aunt Bessie; his assistant private secretary, Hugh Thomas; George Allen, his solicitor; Lady Selby, wife of the British Minister in Vienna; Walter Monckton, his legal adviser; the Herman Rogerses, friends of Wallis; Charles Bedaux and his wife, whom he had only just met; the Metcalfes and, saving the day for England, Randolph Churchill. Cecil Beaton had been there until the day before taking wedding pictures and had longed to stay, but realized that 'I could scarcely be permitted . . . when so many intimates had been excluded.'[20]

Two days before the wedding Lady Alexandra Metcalfe noticed that George and Harry were the only members of the family to have sent presents. Walter Monckton brought congratulations from the King and Queen in the form of a letter telling the bridegroom that, as an exception to 'the settled general rule that a wife takes the status of her husband', his bride would not. They hoped that this painful action they had been forced to take (by whom and why was not explained) would not be regarded as an insult.[21] The news had been published in the *London Gazette* five days before. The letter appeared to have been timed in order to send them to the altar in a state of humiliation and, perhaps, remorse.

But what altar? The Windsors were simple, conventional souls and they wanted God's blessing. This could only be transmitted through a minister of the Church of England to which, more or less, they belonged. The Church refused to have anything to do with it. A Reverend R.A. Jardine from Darlington wrote and offered his services. The one-time King of England, Emperor of India and Defender of the Faith was naïvely delighted to accept this improbable representative of the Almighty. 'A gallant little fellow,' wrote Lady Alexandra Metcalfe. 'HRH is so pleased to be having a religious ceremony. We found a chest suitable for an altar, put a lamé and horn tablecloth of Wallis's round it & with the aid of Mrs Spry's flowers it looks quite pretty.'[22]

The Bishop of Durham, informed of Jardine's project, lost no time in stating that 'Mr Jardine has no authority whatever to officiate in any other diocese than Durham . . . If the marriage of the Duke of Windsor were taking place in the Diocese of Durham, the Bishop of Durham would consider himself in duty bound to inhibit him or any other clergyman within his jurisdiction from officiating at the marriage.' Under the circumstances, he turned the profligate over to the Bishop of Fulham, who was in charge of the diocese of Northern and Central Europe. The Bishop of Fulham went into a huddle with the Archbishop of Canterbury at Lambeth Palace, the result of which is unknown. Prebendary F. A. Cardew, however, Church of England Rural Dean in France, stated, 'I have discussed the matter with the Bishop of London and the Archbishop of Canterbury and they have been on the telephone to the Archbishop of York and the Bishop of Durham. I have been very worried about the whole thing. Mr Jardine is down there on his own initiative. He represents nobody but himself'.[23] This raises so many philosophical and ecumenical questions that it is simpler to say that it all worked out in the end. David Windsor said, 'I, Edward Albert Christian George Andrew Patrick David, take thee Bessie Wallis to my wedded wife, to have and to hold from this day forward, for better or worse, for richer or poorer, in sickness and in health, to love and cherish till death do us part...' and Wallis, faltering slightly, promised to love, cherish and obey; David endowed her with all his worldly goods and the Revd Jardine blessed them both.

★   ★   ★

At Christmas the King and Queen gathered together their whole family, bar one, at Sandringham. Last year, when their reign was not yet two weeks old, Queen Mary's staff had run everything and the old lady herself had been unwell. This year Elizabeth took charge. The vast fir tree glistened, soft cries of delight welcomed the Fabergé ornaments and diamond trinkets as they were unwrapped, the children in their party frocks danced about with excitement, Bertie wore a paper crown and Queen Mary thoroughly enjoyed herself. On the last day of Coronation Year she wrote, '...a very wonderful and interesting year. We saw the interesting film "Marie Walewska" after dinner & at midnight sang Auld Lang Syne & had a snap dragon – Very nice being altogether.'[24]

CHAPTER
23

'I *will* not have another war,' George V had bellowed at Lloyd George in May 1935, 'I *will not*! The last war was none of my doing, and if there is another one and we are threatened with being brought into it, I will go to Trafalgar Square and wave a red flag myself sooner than allow this country to be brought in!'[1] But would he have waved a swastika? For his son Bertie, the problem of war was more complex in that it demanded an extensive grasp of politics, economics and moral principles. Relations with Germany since his Accession had been complicated by the fact that the Ambassador, Joachim von Ribbentrop, was part of the social set now being ostracized by the two Queens, who were quite ready to believe that Mrs S. had been plotting with him to get Hitler's support for an Edward VIII *coup*. In spite of the fact that they were wholehearted supporters of Chamberlain's appeasement policy, Their Majesties were outraged by the Duke of Windor's efforts to achieve the same end. In September 1937, when they were happily relaxing at Birkhall, they were told that the Windsors were planning to visit Germany 'for the purpose of studying housing and working conditions'. This must, of course, be a cover-up for a more sinister purpose. Directives were sent flying. When David and Wallis arrived in Berlin on 11 October they found that the British Ambassador had unexpectedly been called away and that the Chargés d'Affaires had been told to ignore their presence. A month later Lord Halifax, in his capacity of Master of the Middleton Foxhounds, attended an international hunting exhibition organized by Goering, and visited Hitler at Berchtesgaden. In Chamberlain's view this visit was 'a great success'. There was the right sort of friendliness and the wrong sort of friendliness. The plight of German Jews and Christians, the offensiveness of Nazi beliefs and the unappealing nature of the Reich Chancellor had little to do with it. On 11 March 1938 Hitler accepted Sir Nevile Henderson's offer and took over Austria. 'A pleasant state of affairs!' was the caustic comment from Marlborough House. To Bertie, unable to see things in red, white and blue as his father had done, it was all very confusing.

He was busy trying to keep track, working at his boxes until all hours of the night, constantly anxious. Elizabeth, apart from such duties as going to an exhibition of hand-quilting by unemployed miners and inspecting Air Raid Precaution Centres, was left to her own devices. Kenneth Clark, Surveyor of the King's Pictures, was staying at Windsor Castle that spring and was 'shocked to see how little she, and the King as well, did with their day: she never rose before 11.'[2] Perhaps he included the King out of fairness to Elizabeth, as it seems quite out of character for Bertie to be idle; in any case, public performers are notorious lie-a-beds and Elizabeth didn't have to make the breakfast or get the children off to school. Even so, there is more than a hint of boredom and discontent in Clark's account of her on this visit. 'There were hardly any guests and the place was as dreary at night as it had been under King George V and Queen Mary.' They went for long walks and 'at least spent one evening tasting country wines in one of the lodgekeeper's rooms'.[3] Clark, whose impression on first meeting the Queen had been 'that she was not much better than the kind of person one met at a country house'[4] found that she had a hitherto dormant passion for contemporary art. In fact she was most delightful and congenial, apart from her poor taste in clothes. In fact 'he might have been a little in love with her'.[5] When he talked about their 'romantic friendship' in retrospect, writes his biographer, he said that 'they saw as much of each other as they dared, adding that the King became unreasonably jealous and twice made scenes, once at Windsor Castle and again at Buckingham Palace'.[6] All this would be more convincing if it had not involved Lord Clark, whose ego was phenomenally inflated even without a flirtatious Queen's assistance.

In any case his influence resulted in one of the two positive interests in her life, modern art. The second would be steeplechasing. Clark encouraged her efforts to be painted by Augustus John, but the old man felt unable to capture the essence of the Queen of England. 'She has been absolutely angelic in posing so often and with such cheerfulness,' John wrote to Mrs Cazalet on 13 June 1940. 'But he could make no contact with her – she was not real. He wanted to make her real . . . Good God! It was an impossible situation!'[7] The portrait, first suggested in 1937, was never finished. It was finally discovered in one of the cellars under John's studio in March 1961 and presented to the sitter. Elizabeth, whose approach to reality was somewhat different from the painter's, wrote to him that, 'It looks so lovely in my drawing room, and has cheered it up no end! The sequins glitter, and the roses and the red chair give it a fine glow, and I am so happy to have it . . .'.[8] 'It is not the picture of a queen,' John's biographer writes, 'nor of a woman: but of a fairy princess.'[9] Augustus had hoped to sell it in Hollywood.

Elizabeth had something more melancholy to occupy her mind in the spring of 1938. Her mother had been gravely ill for some time, and on 23 June she died in London in the presence of her husband, her children and her royal son-in-law. Lady Strathmore was a formidable personality. She had brought up nine children and, as she would have said had her circumstances been different, buried four. In her youth, apparently, she was handsome, with large patrician features which were inherited by the elder children but dwindled into winsomeness in her youngest daughter. In old age she looked, from photographs, slightly grotesque, like a distinguished General playing Widow Twankey.

The old lady was taken from London to Glamis where, in pouring rain, they buried her in a grave lined with rhododendrons. Cosmo Lang conducted a Memorial Service at St Martin-in-the-Fields. 'She raised a Queen in her own home,' he said, as though this were a unique accomplishment, 'simply by trust and love.' Among the many mourners were Mrs Arthur James and the Honourable James Stuart, by now Deputy Chief Whip in Chamberlain's government.

After a few days in hiding at Birkhall, Their Majesties returned to London to prepare for their State Visit to France, which had been postponed because of Lady Strathmore's death. Norman Hartnell, taking as his precedent the wedding of Princess Alice and Prince Louis of Hesse in 1862, seven months after the Prince Consort's demise, remade Elizabeth's entire wardrobe in bridal white, which is considered acceptable mourning. They set off with their entourage for Portsmouth on 19 July, only to find that Bertie had forgotten his hot-water bottle: '. . . a frenzied message preceded their arrival telling the ship to provide one,' Diana Cooper was told. 'A child was dispatched to Boot's Cash Chemists on a bicycle before it was realized that he would never edge his way back through the crowds and the guards, but the clever Puck got back in forty seconds.'[10] That crisis overcome, Elizabeth had a very entertaining crossing: 'The Queen had nobbled everyone, naturally, from the Commander-in-Chief to the marine who always occupies on all fours the bathroom. The First Lieutenant, Mr Costabadie, is like the ailing Knight at Arms. I doubt his being able to cast it off. . .'[11] As Their Majesties were using the Admiralty yacht *Enchantress*, Lady Diana and her niece Liz Paget followed on a ferry-boat and joined the merry-making in Paris: 'Each night's flourish outdid the last. At the Opera we leant over the balustrade to see the Royal couple, shining with stars and diadem and the Legion d'Honneur proudly worn . . . At Versailles we lunched in the Galerie des Glaces, with thirteen glasses apiece for thirteen precious wines, all bottled on the birthdays of presidents and kings . . . Later, by the Bassin d'Apollon, we watched from a grassy dell where shepherdesses tended their lambs beneath tall trees garlanded with roses, living nymphs dance round the stone horses of the Sun . . . on the last night the dancing people were allowed near and everywhere. Many times the King and Queen (a radiant Winterhalter) were summoned to the balconies by insistent clamouring . . .'[12] As Walter Bagehot said, 'A Royal Family sweetens politics by the seasonable addition of nice and pretty events.' France and Britain demonstrating their solidarity, fighter 'planes roared in formation over the nymphs and shepherdesses.

★   ★   ★

Hitler was now demanding 'the return' of Sudetenland to the Reich. On Elizabeth's thirty-eighth birthday, 4 August, while she and Bertie and the children were sailing peacefully up the east coast in the *Victoria and Albert en route* for Balmoral, Lord Runciman arrived in Prague to mediate between the Czech government and the Sudeten party. This was a great relief to Bertie. His heart, says his biographer, was lightened. Meanwhile Shirer, in Prague, was writing 'Lord Runciman arrived today to gum up the works and sell the Czechs short if he can . . . [the] whole mission smells. . .'[13] At Balmoral, with Elizabeth's help, Bertie tried to work it all out. 'The German attitude to what you are trying to do to help the Czechoslovakian situation, certainly gives cause for anxiety, & their partial mobilization on the Czech frontier under the guise of large-scale manoeuvres, might mean all sorts of things,'[14] he concluded, writing to Chamberlain on 14 August. On 22 August, together with his house-guests Jack Eldon, Bobbety Cranborne, David Bowes-Lyon and Arthur Penn, the King shot 450 grouse and 4 hares.[15] The weather was fine and still and they were joined by the ladies for a picnic in the heather.

On 4 September President Beneš ceded the Sudetenland outright to Germany so that, in the words of *The Times*, Czechoslovakia might become a more 'homogeneous state'. On 12 September Prince Arthur of Connaught, Bertie's cousin, died, necessitating another plunge into mourning, and Hitler made a violently aggressive speech at Nuremberg. On 13 September Neville Chamberlain wrote a long letter to the King:

> It has been obvious . . . that we must be prepared for a sudden change for the worse and, if then we have any time at all for action, we must know beforehand what action we are going to take. In these circumstances I have been considering the possibility of a sudden and dramatic step which might change the whole situation. The plan is that I inform Herr Hitler that I propose at once to go over to Germany to see him . . .

After putting the pros and cons of this suggestion at some length, the Prime Minister added a hasty PS. saying that he had already contacted Hitler and was ready to leave. 'I trust that my action will have Your Majesty's approval.'[16]

It did, of course. As Bertie had to travel to London to attend Prince Arthur's funeral, he went to the lengths of telephoning his blessing. By the time he arrived at Buckingham Palace on the morning of the 15th, his Prime Minister was off and away.

Bertie had not been idle at Balmoral. With great thought and care, he had prepared a draft of a personal letter to Hitler, appealing to him 'as one ex-serviceman to another' to spare the youth of Britain and Germany from the horrors of another world war.[17] He knew that his father, though a far more militant pacifist, would never have done such a thing; nevertheless, in his diffident way, he thought it would be worth a try. It was disappointing that Lord Halifax was not more enthusiastic.

Over the next fortnight the situation became increasingly serious. Chamberlain had achieved nothing at Berchtesgaden except the promise of a week's grace before the invasion of the Sudetenland. On 22 September, the week being up, the Prime Minister flew off to Godesburg, only to be told that Hitler now demanded an immediate German occupation of the Sudeten areas. Chamberlain again appealed for time, and was granted until 1 October. He returned home very gloomy, and was not greatly encouraged by Bertie's longing to try a personal appeal himself – if not as an ex-serviceman, then how about as King to Führer? No, said Chamberlain. The draft was once more put back in the drawer.

On 25 September the Air Raid Precautions system was put on a war footing and cellars and basements were commandeered as shelters. The following day thousands of children were evacuated from the cities, each one labelled, some snivelling, most larky. It is unlikely that Elizabeth saw much of them on her way up to Glasgow that night to deputize for her husband at the launching of the *Queen Elizabeth*. Her own children, safely tucked up at Balmoral, joined her at Glasgow station next morning and they all crossed over to Clydebank where the huge, inanimate hulk lay in John Brown's shipyard awaiting the breath of life.

Launching a ship is not something you might call part and parcel of daily life. Cynthia Asquith, attended by 'a delightful sailor' holding a bouquet and umbrella, recalls that she had a confused feeling she was being married. 'At the magic moment I pulled the lever and the ship shivered into life . . . and away she slithered like a lovely, lithe animal, very fast and with wonderful grace . . . When she reaches the sea she curtseys deep and settles down in her element . . .'[18] This is how one imagines it, but perhaps the *Champion* was more skittish than the *Queen Elizabeth*. There was a long, awkward pause while the last props were being removed. As though this were something too intimate to be noticed, Elizabeth looked at a book of photographs and the Princesses examined two models of the completed liner with passionate interest. Suddenly there was a cry of 'She's off!' Startled, Elizabeth rushed forward, seized the bottle of champagne, and just had time to say 'I-name-this-ship-Queen-Elizabeth-and-wish-success-to-her-and-all-who-sail-in-her' and swing the bottle before the great thing lumbered away. The bell, which was meant to announce the moment of launching, rang as the ship's stern touched the water; steam-whistles shrieked and drag-chains screamed and the whole thing was enveloped in a rising cloud of red iron dust. Elizabeth had made the usual speech about being of good cheer in spite of the dark clouds and placing entire confidence in the leaders who, under God's providence, were striving their utmost etc. Queen Mary, who had just been fitted for her gas mask, listened on her radio set: 'She made her speech admirably, Bertie's really,' she commented.[19]

Elizabeth returned to London to find that her husband was still persisting in his idea of sending a personal message to Hitler. Chamberlain, at the end of his tether, told him in no uncertain terms to abandon it. Bertie needed sympathy. It was, of course, the most anxious time, but infinitely preferable to that nightmare two years ago. She was in her element; she felt needed, appreciated; she didn't *mind* things so much.

On 28 September Queen Mary and Marina went to the House of Commons to hear Mr Chamberlain's further statement on the crisis. They sat in the Ladies' Gallery and the old Queen listened impassively but intently as the Prime Minister recounted the whole shoddy tale. Suddenly, at twelve minutes past four (Harold Nicolson had just glanced at the clock), there was a flurry on the Government bench and Sir John Simon, a piece of Foreign Office notepaper in his hand, tugged at the Prime Minister's coat. Chamberlain 'adjusted his pince-nez and read the document that had been handed to him. His whole face, his whole body, seemed to change . . . he appeared ten years younger and triumphant. "Herr Hitler," he said, "has just agreed to postpone his mobilization for twenty-four hours and to meet me in conference with Signor Mussolini and Signor Daladier at Munich."'[20] There was silence for a second. Nobody thought of asking why M. Daladier had suddenly become Italian. Then, to switch to Queen Mary's account, 'All the members of the Conservative & National Govt cheered wildly – I was myself so much moved I could not speak to any of the ladies in the Gallery, several of them, even those unknown to me, seized my hand, it was very touching. Let us pray now that a lasting Peace may follow – I went to see Bertie – A most wonderful day – God be praised.'[21]

Two days later Mr and Mrs Chamberlain appeared on the balcony of Buckingham Palace with the King and Queen. Everybody smiled and waved, the crowd cheered, the world had once more been saved for democracy. It was too late for most people to make up for their ruined summer holiday, but they went back to work with renewed vigour. Elizabeth, Bertie and the children returned to Balmoral. Before he left, Bertie 'issued to his peoples a message of sober thanksgiving and gratitude' and wrote to the Archbishop of Canterbury: 'I am sure that some day the Czechs will see that what we did was to save them for a happier future.'[22]

CHAPTER

24

On 10 March 1939 the Prime Minister publicly announced that 'the outlook in international affairs is tranquil'. He had recently been to see Mussolini in Rome – a much more enjoyable visit than those to Godesburg and Munich – and was satisfied that all our troubles were over. On 15 March Hitler and his armies entered Prague. Speaking from the Hradschin Castle, the palace of the Kings of Bohemia, Hitler proclaimed that Czechoslovakia had ceased to exist. Elizabeth, perhaps hoping to see some last-minute drama as her mother-in-law had done, went for the first time to hear for herself what they were saying in the House of Commons. According to one account, she listened to a debate on a Government bill to provide fifty large camps to be used by school children if peace continued, and by evacuees in the event of war. According to another 'the business before the House was not unamusing, for the witty A. P. Herbert was asking leave to bring in a Bill to restore public passenger steamers to the Thames'.[1] Whichever it was, she smiled radiantly down on the Deputy Whip and found it all most instructive.

On Good Friday, just as Their Majesties and family were settling down for a peaceful Easter weekend at Windsor, Mussolini invaded Albania. This was a personal matter, unlike Czechoslovakia: 'We were horrified,' Queen Mary wrote, 'to hear that the Italians had kicked out Zog, King of Albania . . . The poor Queen had to leave with her baby son of 2 days old.'[2] She could sympathize with family dramas Upstairs; what went on Downstairs, among the Hitlers and Mussolinis and Stalins and their like, filled her with incredulous rage. Joseph Kennedy, the American Ambassador, was a guest at Windsor at Easter and they took him to see the Air Ministry's new secret weapons – balloons. Not barrage balloons, but Balloon Squadrons, manned by aviators with telescopes and binoculars. Mr Kennedy was impressed. On 20 April King George sent congratulations to Hitler on the occasion of his fiftieth birthday[3] and the next day Lilibet received a cine camera and projector from her Uncle David on the occasion of her thirteenth.[4]

The previous September Joseph Kennedy had delivered a personal letter to Bertie from President Roosevelt, which greatly pleased Elizabeth. After saying that he had learned in confidence from Mackenzie King that there was a possibility of Their Majesties visiting Canada in the summer of 1939, the President invited them to stay 'for 3 or 4 days of very simple country life at Hyde Park'. '. . . if you bring either or both of the children with you they will also be very welcome, and I shall try to have one or two Roosevelts of approximately the same age to play with them.'

This, at least, was something to look forward to, though of course Bertie had qualms of conscience about going away. 'I feel we must start for Canada on Saturday unless there is any really good reason as to why we should not,' he wrote gloomily to his mother.[5] Keeping Bertie's spirits up was no easy task; he never seemed really convinced that everything was such fun, so long as one kept smiling, or that he would enjoy it when he got there. Queen Mary and the children came to see them off at Portsmouth. Margaret said 'I have my handkerchief' & Lilibet said, 'To wave, not to cry'[6] and as *Empress of Australia* ploughed steadily across the Atlantic towards the New World even Bertie cheered up a little.

Eight days later they were stuck in dense fog in the middle of an ice field ... 'We nearly hit a berg the day before yesterday,' Elizabeth wrote chattily, 'and the poor Captain was nearly demented because some kind cheerful people kept on reminding him that it was about here the *Titanic* was struck, & *just* about the same date!'[7] In the end the crossing from Portsmouth to Quebec took twelve days, but even though Bertie felt revived, it was not without a touch of complaint: '. . . I should not have chosen an ice field surrounded by dense fog in which to have a holiday, but it does seem to be the only place for me to rest in nowadays!!'[8]

Canada fell in love with Elizabeth, of course. By now any attempt to resist her blandishments, let alone to speak of her as though she were a fallible human woman, was tantamount to treason. In their specially built train, in which their private coaches contained a drawing room and dining room, two bedrooms, two bathrooms and an office, they travelled 4,281 miles. Many Canadians, while unanimously doting on the Queen, felt this was not enough. The royal couple visited no universities, schools, charitable organizations or factories. Local officials who had been practising their welcoming addresses for months were told that they were not allowed to present them, 'to save the strain upon the King and Queen'. Those who remembered how the Prince of Wales would clamber down from his observation platform and talk to the people standing beside the track, how he went off into the wilds with Indian guides and bust a bronco at Saskatoon and bought a ranch in Alberta, felt that his younger brother was a decided let-down. Elizabeth, consequently, shone all the brighter, '. . . the Queen,' Lord Tweedsmuir wrote in a letter to a friend, 'has a perfect genius for the right kind of publicity. The unrehearsed episodes here [in Ottawa] were marvellous.' In fact Elizabeth spent ten minutes talking to some Scottish masons 'in full view of 70,000 people' and had a short walkabout among 10,000 veterans after unveiling the War Memorial. Still, it was better than nothing. The official verdict was that the tour had been a triumphant success.

Roosevelt's invitation to stay may have sounded casual but his wife found that formidable preparations were necessary. William Bullitt, the U.S. Ambassador in Paris, sent her a secret memorandum based on the State Visit the previous year. This confidential document contained every detail of the Royal requirements, down to 'a linen blanket for the Queen's couch'.[9] Mrs Roosevelt puzzled a good deal, but was unable to understand what a linen blanket might be, and as Bloomingdales didn't either, the Queen went without. Then the British Ambassador's wife told her that the King must be served at meals precisely thirty seconds before the Queen, the head butler to be provided with a stop-watch for that purpose. But what about the White House rule that the President was always served first? FDR solved the problem by saying that he and the King would be served simultaneously by two butlers and then, after the requisite thirty seconds, the Queen and Mrs Roosevelt in the same manner. But how should they be placed at table? Should the President sit with the King on his right and the Queen on his left and his wife on the right of the King? Or what? It was at last decided that the King should sit on Mrs Roosevelt's right and the Queen on the President's right.[10] This meant that instead of having Mrs R., King, President, Queen, you had Queen, President, King, Mrs R. – much more satisfactory. Ah, but what should they sit on? The White House dining room had only two special high-backed armchairs, one for the President and one for his wife. Should only the King and the President have armchairs? Surely that would be disrespectful to the Queen? They sent somebody out to buy two more identical chairs.[11]

Of course they had to put up the Scotland Yard people as well. Two more chairs were needed, so that messengers could sit outside the Royal bedrooms day and night. Mrs Roosevelt was exhausted. This last demand 'seemed foolish to me, since the rooms were just across the hall from each other'.[12] Also, of course, the White House was equipped with adequate telephones. Nevertheless, chairs were provided and presumably the messengers sat on them. After all this it comes as something of a shock to realize that the King and Queen stayed at the White House for only two nights.

While the Roosevelts hurried off to Hyde Park to make further preparations for Their Majesties' promised 'rest and relaxation', Elizabeth and Bertie sailed for New York on board the President's yacht, escorted for some of the way by their friend J. P. Morgan in his *Corsair*. After a fiercely hot, humid, noisy, ticker-tape New York day they arrived at Hyde Park, hours late for dinner and in a state of collapse. Franklin said to Bertie, 'My mother does not approve of cocktails and thinks you should have a cup of tea.' Bertie said, 'Neither does my mother,' and took a cocktail.[13] For Bertie this was the start of a warm and solid friendship which was to play no mean part in winning the future war. The paraplegic President was thirteen years older than the handicapped King and their lives had been very different; even so, there was much each understood about the other. Their relationship was something David could never have achieved.

On 22 June, seven weeks after their parents' departure, Lilibet and Margaret, in the charge of Crawfie and Clara, sailed out into the Solent on board the destroyer *Kempenfelt* to meet the returning *Empress of Britain*. What Mr Kirkwood M.P. had to say about this joy-ride, if anything, is unknown. The children were safely transferred from one ship to the other, there was kissing and hugging and squeaking and babbling and how they've grown and don't they look well; there was an hilarious lunch in the ship's dining room, the King threw balloons out of portholes, Lord Airlie popped some with his cigarette 'and everyone', says Crawfie, 'was very youthful and gay'.[14] When they all finally landed at Southampton there was another wild welcome from the crowds packed along the dock, and in London the masses, and Harold Nicolson, were hysterical with joy – 'Such fun . . . the bells of St Margaret's began to swing into welcome and the procession started creeping round the corner. They went very slowly, and there were the King and Queen and the two princesses. We lost all our dignity and yelled and yelled. The King wore a happy schoolboy grin. The Queen was superb . . . in truth one of the most amazing Queens since Cleopatra. We returned to the House with lumps in our throats.'[15] In the evening a vast crowd roared like hungry children for a sight of the scrumptious family on the Palace balcony. They had been starved without them, nothing but bread and scrape. Business had been bad; for those who cared about such things the Season had been a flop; nobody had bothered to come to London and Belgravia tradesmen were in despair. Now they were back, the darlings, all pink and white and delectable, even the King in his Admiral's uniform looking good enough to eat. When they disappeared for a while 10,000 voices were raised in 'The Lambeth Walk' and 'Under the Spreading Chestnut Tree'; it was midnight before the last surfeited revellers straggled down the Mall. What had happened? It was most gratifying, of course, but why?

David Duff, in his *George and Elizabeth*, has a theory that it was jealousy. Reading the wildly enthusiastic reports of Their Majesties' visit to Canada and the United States, people suddenly became aware that this amazing couple belonged to *them*. Anything Ottawa and New York could do, they could do better. This seems very likely, but there were other reasons too. Strong sentiments had been stirred up for a week or so during the Abdication, then frustrated; sex had been connected with the Throne for the first time in living memory; religion was fast withering away, and people had learned from the cinema, even from the radio, that not all extra-terrestrial beings were dead saints and inaccessible angels. King George V had been God the Father, rumbling away behind the clouds and occasionally coming out to shine; King Edward VIII, made flesh, was a kind of precursor of James Dean, a meteoric upset; Bertie and Elizabeth, after flickering uncertainly for a time, exactly fitted the roles left empty by Douglas Fairbanks and Mary Pickford – fallible and yet perfect, exalted in themselves but nearly always seen dealing with danger, fluttering in tight corners, winning through. It was not simply that they had been away and were suddenly seen with new eyes; if they had stayed at home inspecting air-raid shelters, the same thing would have happened. 'George the Good' and his Cleopatra were, at that moment, an historical necessity.

Elizabeth was delighted. Stardom suited her perfectly. She must have some new pictures taken right away – what about that nice young man Cecil Beaton, who had photographed the Kents and Princess Olga? He appeared, properly nervous. They discussed what she should wear. 'You know, perhaps the embroidered one I wore – in Canada...? And I thought, perhaps, another evening dress of – tulle? And a – tiara?' All this, Beaton recalled, 'wistfully said, with a smile, and raised eyebrows', as though it was rather daring of her tentatively to suggest what she had already decided on, and he must be the final judge. Beaton was captivated. Snap-snap he went, photographing her 'with monkey-like frenzy'. 'It is so hard to know when *not* to smile,' Elizabeth murmured, tidying her shoulder-straps meticulously and placing her fan just so. She disappeared for a quick costume change. 'I changed the tiara. And these diamonds – are they all right?' She was insatiable. 'Do you mean to say she's gone off to change once more?' asked the superintendent in despair. 'Why, she hasn't had her tea yet, has she? Well, it means the poor King will have to have his tea alone!' Finally, stricken as Lord David Cecil, Beaton bowed himself away. 'But in my pocket was hidden, scented with tuberoses and gardenias, a handkerchief that the Queen had tucked behind a cushion ... I had stolen it. It was my particular prize, one which would have more romance and reality than any of the photographs.'[16]

Meanwhile Bertie, in his own way, was also rising to the occasion. He had made a fluent, powerful speech in the Guildhall, about the ideals of the Commonwealth; it had been hailed as a declaration of beliefs, an indication that Britain was prepared to defend her democratic institutions, a clarion call to mankind. 'A change from the old days,'[17] he commented dryly. The European situation was much the same as before he went away, except that Hitler was now demanding Danzig and Britain's official policy had changed from appeasement to threats – since there was nothing that could be done to implement them, the result was much the same. How could Hitler be made to take Britain seriously? It was no good just parading 20,000 Civil Defence troops in the Park; Hitler didn't take a blind bit of notice. Much encouraged by his new success, Bertie had another of his ideas. His brother George had recently been in Italy and talked with their Nazi cousin, Prince Philip of Hesse, who was also the King of Italy's son-in-law. Philip had served as personal liaison officer between Hitler and Mussolini and was believed to be on friendly terms with the Führer. 'Do you think it would be possible to get him over here,' Bertie wrote eagerly to the Prime Minister, '& use him as a messenger to convey to Hitler that we really are in earnest?'[18] Neither the Prime Minister nor the Foreign Secretary appreciated the idea; they didn't understand the importance of Family in these matters.

It was time for a break. Bertie thought he might take the family to see his old College, so they all sailed on the Royal yacht and dropped anchor in the Dart at the bottom of the College steps and had a very pleasant two days, recalling old times and playing croquet with the cadets, among whom was young Prince Philip of Greece. Lilibet, who would have been at the giggly stage if she hadn't been Heir Apparent, was much taken with him. Then Bertie went to his Boys' Camp, which was held this year at Abergeldie, conveniently near Balmoral. Elizabeth and the girls went over to supper, but Lilibet did not appear particularly taken with any of the 200 selected boys nervously downing their baked beans. Bertie put on his uniform and went to Weymouth to inspect the Reserve Fleet. 'It is wonderful the way in which all the men have come back for duty at this time,' he wrote to his mother, '& I feel sure it will be a deterrent factor in Hitler's mind to start a war.'[19] Thus reassured, he returned to Balmoral to prepare for the shooting season.

This was the happiest time of his year:

Punctual to the minute he would come from his room where he had already conferred with Gillan as to the day's plan ... his face ... displaying his pleasure at what lay before him ... In one hand would be a long walking-stick, in the other, very often, some special article of apparel of his own planning for combating any possible trick of the weather: a cap, a scarf, or some ingenious kind of coat, for he was always a great contriver. We would all clamber into the bus, which at once became full of chatter, and about once a week whoever was nearest the door would lower the window a little, in order to inspire the storm of imprecation which instantly followed an act of such suicidal folly, for the King always unshakeably maintained that the exhaust and the window were fatally conjoined, and always had been...

On driving days most of the house party joined the guns for luncheon, which was always in the open ... The luncheon baskets were desposited in some favourite situation, plaid rugs would be spread about the heather and bog-myrtle, and since by one of the most hallowed of shooting conventions the ladies were usually on the spot before the guns had descended from the hillside, they had often already removed from the hampers the delicious contents which nobody who had enjoyed them could ever forget...

On Sunday afternoons there might be an expedition to the far end of Loch Muick for tea in the Glassalt and some light-hearted trout-fishing, or perhaps they would all go to 'the Queen's charming little cottage. There a more serious and less reputable form of fishing often produced some salmon, bearing mysterious marks almost suggestive of foul hooking...'[20] As the days went by and the sun shone and the grouse fell in their hundreds it began to seem that Hitler had taken the lesson of Weymouth to heart.

On 22 August news of the Soviet-German Non-Aggression pact burst into this idyll. The King returned to London, leaving Elizabeth in Scotland. 'I feel deeply for you,' Queen Mary wrote,[21] knowing what it was like to be left sitting on a mountain. Bertie lost no time. Make friends with Japan – that was the answer. Alec Hardinge (restored to health and now King George's Private Secretary) wrote to the Permanent Under-Secretary of State for Foreign Affairs, 'His Majesty wonders ... if it would help in any way if, at an opportune moment, he were to send a friendly message direct to the Emperor ... he feels that, when dealing with orientals, direct communication between Heads of States may be helpful.'[22] The Foreign Office politely declined the offer. Well, then, *what* about a personal appeal to Hitler? The King must do *something* – King Leopold had sent one, and President Roosevelt and Prime Minister Mackenzie King and the Pope ... Chamberlain promised that he would keep it in mind, but clearly wasn't convinced. Elizabeth came down from Balmoral, which was a help, though he hardly had time to see her what with meetings of the Privy Council, audiences to Ministers, visits to the War Office, the Admiralty, the Air Ministry and the Central War Room, keeping track of Ambassador Henderson's comings and goings, the promises, the threats, the rumours (Goering is going to get rid of Hitler and restore the Hohenzollerns – ah, if only that were true). It was almost a relief on Friday when Germany invaded Poland. Elizabeth felt she must return to Balmoral and try to explain it all to the children, so Bertie went to bed alone that first night of the blackout.

She came back next day, thank God. The British Government's ultimatum received no reply. On Sunday morning Queen Mary went to the church of St Mary Magdalene at Sandringham, where the rector had installed his radio in the nave. She and tens of millions of her countrypeople heard Neville Chamberlain declare war somewhere between the Absolution or Remission of Sins and the Benedicite. Anthony Eden, Harold Nicolson, Bob Boothby and Duncan Sandys listened to the housemaid's radio in Ronnie Tree's house, since the Trees didn't have one themselves. 'The P.M.,' Nicolson commented laconically, was 'quite good and tells us that war has begun.'[23] This was the first time that radio had been used for such a purpose. Barely a quarter of an hour later, when the air raid sirens sounded over most of Britain, everyone, except the insensible and the indifferent, knew why.

Whether Bertie and Elizabeth dived for the air-raid shelter, I don't know. The Churchills went up to the flat roof of their house to see what was going on. 'Around us on every side, in the clear, cool September light, rose the roofs and spires of London. Above them were already slowly rising thirty or forty cylindrical balloons ... [Then] as the quarter of an hour's notice which we had been led to expect we should receive was now running out we made our way to the shelter assigned to us, armed with a bottle of brandy and other appropriate medical comforts,'[24] wrote the man on whom the King and Queen, together with half the world, would rely for the next five years.

CHAPTER
25

'A foolish woman said to me, "How gracious she is – every inch a Queen,"' A. C. Benson recalled after meeting Queen Mary just before World War I. 'Now that is *exactly* what she was not . . . She looked a hard-worked and rather tired woman . . . doing her best to be civil to nervous people. It made me feel a sort of affectionate admiration . . . I should like to meet her again, and I feel a curious kind of personal regard for her, and a warmth about the heart.'[1] Elizabeth never allowed herself to look over-worked or tired. That was not her style. Her idea of identifying with the common people in wartime was to change her image from Fairy Queen to a sort of exalted Mrs Miniver. Norman Hartnell designed clothes for her which looked as though they might have come straight out of the window of any provincial drapers. The hats became stiff felt haloes, perilously worn on one side and secured, one imagines, with hat pins. The fringe had gone long ago and she now wore a Madonna-like coiffeur, not unlike Wallis Simpson's, but bushier. She began to grow quite stout, in a comfortable sort of way, and by some effort of will or artifice managed to look remarkably plain. Almost half a century later, recalling the Queen's visit to their Women's Institute, two excited old ladies had the following conversation on television:

> *First old lady:* But she really settled in *just* like a W.I. member!
> *Second old lady:* She *is* a W.I. member!
> *First old lady* (incredulously): But she *behaved* like one!

There is no better summing-up of the intrepid gentility, the shining faith in God and home-made jam, that was the image of our wartime Queen. It was just what people wanted.

There were plenty of domestic problems in the first few weeks – Crawfie had to be recalled from her holiday and was arranging sewing parties at Birkhall and seeing that the children went to the dentist, Buckingham Palace had to be packed up and the staff reorganized, but the Queen found time to send the Foreign Secretary a copy of Hitler's *Mein Kampf*, in case he was not clear what the country was fighting for. 'I . . . do not advise you to read it through, or you might go mad, and that would be a great pity ... Even a skip through gives one a good idea of his mentality, ignorance and obvious sincerity.'[2] Since nothing happened it seemed safe to bring the Princesses down to Sandringham for Christmas. In the New Year of 1940 they and Miss Crawford moved to the Royal Lodge.

It is appropriate here to mention the amazing fact that the Royal Family remained in Great Britain for the duration of the war. The Cabinet formally advised the King that the children should be sent to Canada out of harm's way, but their mother is reported to have said, 'The Princesses would never leave without me, and I couldn't leave without the King, and the King will never leave.' For some reason this plain statement of fact has never ceased to strike the British public – most of whom had no alternative – with almost incredulous awe. 'We Stay With Our People! We Are Not Afraid!' ran the headlines, implying that any other Royal Family would have scuttled off, pale with terror, clutching the Crown Jewels. It was transparently specious, but it worked. Elizabeth – so often accurately dubbed 'a real trouper' – entered into the spirit of her new rôle: 'I shall not go down like the others!' she declared, and when Buckingham Palace was bombed she made the outrageous assertion that she was glad, because 'It makes me feel I can look the East End in the face!' The people of the East End, huddled in their flimsy Andersons, crammed into Underground stations, searching for Mum and the kids through last night's rubble, were much impressed. Mass Observation tracked down a few sceptics, but that organization was known to have a left-wing bias and was therefore unreliable. If there really was a housewife who complained 'It's all very well for them traipsing around saying how their hearts bleed for us and they share all our sufferings, and then going home to a roaring fire in one of their six houses'[3] she deserved all she got.

Elizabeth's main concern, however, was Bertie. His role in the war requires a chapter to itself. As he told his wife everything and relied heavily on her judgement, it was a role which she not only supported but actively shared. This was her contribution to history. Visiting bombed cities, re-laying foundation stones of blitzed churches and hospitals, doing her duty as Commander-in-Chief of the WRENS and the WRAFS and the WAACS, inspecting munition factories, entertaining Royal refugees, having 300 land-girls to tea, were all secondary occupations. Nevertheless, it is by those that she is remembered. The anecdotes have filled many books. They are all curiously similar, and these two will give the general picture: 'She enjoyed a threepenny lunch with other people's children [sic] evacuated from London. She ate jam tarts and drank water from a bakelite mug. "This is all very good," she told one of the children around her in the calm of the countryside.'[4] And another: 'At an old people's home, when word got round that the Queen was coming, one old lady was seen by Matron down on her knees touching up the seams of her old red carpet with red ink on a toothbrush. The Queen was told, and as she went into the old lady's room and shut the door behind her she was heard to say, "What a *lovely* red carpet!"'[5] Tripping across bomb-sites in her high heels, always modestly decked in three rows of pearls and the unobtrusive diamond, she appeared to be constantly amused and sympathetic.

Or almost constantly. Very occasionally – but so seldom that the onlookers felt they must have been mistaken – the smile froze and the voice slapped out hard and cold: 'Visiting a factory [she] was shown the spot where nineteen workmen had been killed by a bomb. "Poor things," she said, and walked on.'[6] In Lancashire, presented with an enormous civic lunch which had quite possibly used up all their catering rations for a month, she snapped acidly at the Mayor that 'we don't have any more food on the table at Buckingham Palace than is allowed to the ordinary householder according to the rations for the week.' 'Ah well then,' the Mayor replied amiably, 'thou'll be glad of a bit of a do like this.'[7] A newsreel camera inadvertently caught for posterity 'the expression of distaste . . . as she picked her way through a group of dejected and no doubt smelly citizens huddled in some public building the day after their homes had been destroyed in an air-raid'.[8] The writer was quick to add that the Queen's expression no more indicated contempt or dislike than the grimace of a mother mopping up her baby's vomit, but even so the story made a welcome change. It may be considered unjust to quote such incidents when the unanimous impression was one of radiant and indefatigable concern; but 'affectionate admiration' and 'a warmth about the heart' can only be felt for fallible human beings. Blind and uncritical acclaim is, when it comes to the crunch, worthless.

One of Elizabeth's nephews was killed in action, another taken prisoner of war. At the end of 1944 her father died. David Bowes-Lyon was sent to New York to take over the political warfare and propaganda work of British Security Co-ordination.[9] Apart from her knowledge of State affairs through the King, Elizabeth must have been able to keep track of many devious schemes unknown to the public, including those that affected the Duke and Duchess of Windsor. Bowes-Lyon's appointment was not very successful or popular, though many Americans were impressed by his royal connection and his charm. 'Both are wasting assets,' wrote Sir Robert Bruce Lockhart, 'because David has a poor mind and no knowledge of Europe. Moreover, he is full of suspicions and is quite incapable of "playing straight". In Jack's opinion [John Wheeler-Bennett, official biographer of George VI] he is a bad man.'[10] Although Bowes-Lyon quickly established a powerful social position in Washington, it was soon reported that he was exceeding his powers and trading on his social status to assume functions far beyond the limited range of his ability. Brendan Bracken thought him 'an intriguer' and wanted to get rid of him, but Lord Halifax (by now British Ambassador in Washington, but still touched by Elizabeth's timely gift?) supported him, so nothing could be done. By the end of 1944 things sound serious: 'Jack Wheeler-Bennett, who has an intimate knowledge of David Bowes-Lyon, has a low opinion of David's character and thinks that his capacity for intrigue and untruthfulness has almost no limit ... Young Miall [R. Leonard Miall, a BBC executive], a former protégé of David's ... told Jack today that David, whom Halifax allows to see the most secret telegrams, including those of the Prime Minister and the President, has a photographic apparatus in his Washington office and takes photostats of important secret documents which he is permitted to see and not to keep ... These photostats he used to send to Miall in New York, although they had no bearing whatever on his work. If this were known in London, David would be sacked, King's brother-in-law notwithstanding.'[11]*

One can only surmise how much of this Elizabeth knew. She and her brother had always been considered 'alike as two pins'; their close intimacy had survived both their marriages; he was a constant visitor at Sandringham and Balmoral and no doubt she would not hear a word against him.

* When Sir David Bowes-Lyon KCVO died on 13 September 1961, his obituarist in *The Times* went no further in explaining Sir David's work as head of the Political Warfare Mission than to say, 'some of [this] work has remained secret. Certainly Bowes-Lyon's range went much farther than his ostensible brief and beyond the terms of reference that have been made public...'

CHAPTER

26

Elizabeth was thirty-nine and Bertie just coming up to his forty-fourth birthday when the war started; by the end of it they were middle-aged, with two grown daughters and a backlog of family problems which were all the harder to solve for being royal. As I said, Elizabeth's most significant role during those years was as Bertie's confidante, adviser and support. She was largely responsible for the fact that he did his job so well; it is inconceivable that he could have done it without her.

What was his job? All he actually swore to do, in the Coronation service, was to be merciful and just and support the clergy. In practice he had to endorse the routine machinery of government, process papers and bestow his warrant on the decisions of the government; he had personally to meet senior public servants, ambassadors, administrators and the recipients of all titles bestowed in the investitures, to appear as a figurehead on national occasions and in times of crisis, visit all aspects of the nation at work and at war, represent the country, Commonwealth and Empire to the rest of the world and fulfil his commitments as Head of the Armed Forces.[1] The only things he could do on his own initiative were to advise, encourage and warn the government in the event of there being any controversy, this inalienable right being known as the Royal Prerogative and a great bore to many politicians, since it meant the King had constantly to be told what was going on.

Apart from all that, he had to embody the indefinable mystery of monarchy and so on. It was a fairly demanding job in peace-time, for those who, unlike David, took it seriously. In war it was non-stop. Whether any of it was really necessary is beside the point. Bertie thought it was, and with his wife and helpmeet by his side he tackled it in his own conscientious way.

'After 3 weeks of war,' he wrote in his diary on Sunday, 24 September 1939, 'many strange things have taken place. It is an amazing puzzle.' He then neatly summarized Russia's invasion of Poland, its possible effect on Italy, the unacceptability of Hitler's peace terms and the puzzling fact that 'Germany has not interfered with our mobilizations in any way, & has not raided us from the air. Why? We must wait and see.' Waiting, as he said in his Christmas broadcast, was a trial of nerve and discipline. He occupied himself by inspecting the Maginot Line (his equerry wrote a glowing report to Elizabeth), and placating the Turkish military mission, which had been about to go home in disgust at the British government's parsimony. The Christmas broadcast, in which he quoted a poem by Miss Marie Louise Haskins, was received extremely well. It also turned Miss Haskins into a bestseller which, since she had lived in total obscurity since 1908 when her one and only collection of verse was privately printed, pleased her a great deal.

Mrs Belloc Lowndes tells an improbable story of a young officer, remanded in prison for a week for assaulting a special constable, being let out of prison to join the King's shooting party at Windsor;[2] if true, it is overlooked by Aubrey Buxton – and anyway what would they have been shooting at Windsor? No, my impression is that Bertie slogged away at his desk at the weekends, occasionally shouting for Elizabeth to come and listen to this, or look at that, or what did she think of the other. 'We have been at War for 6 months today,' he wrote on Sunday 3 March 1940 '. . . There have been several "peace" moves, & "scares" that Germany would invade Holland & Belgium...'[3] Chamberlain dismissed the 'scares'. 'Hitler has missed the 'bus!' he declared triumphantly on 4 April. On 9 April Germany invaded Denmark and Norway and the war began.

Everything and everyone leaped into action, particularly the critics of the Prime Minister. Bertie, as a mere King, felt thoroughly left out. 'I have spent a bad day,' he wrote that evening. 'Everyone working at fever heat except me.'[4] British troops landed at Namsos and Andalsnes a week later, but they had no support against German air power and had to be withdrawn. Bertie chafed while Parliament debated the disaster and finally turned Chamberlain out. Then, with some apprehension, he sent for Winston Churchill. 'He looked at me searchingly and quizzically for some moments,' wrote Churchill, 'and then said, "I suppose you don't know why I have sent for you?" Adopting his mood, I replied, "Sir, I simply couldn't imagine why".'[5]

The wartime triumvirate was now complete: Churchill supplied the fiery personality, Bertie the reliable image, Elizabeth the perfumed oil to throw on troubled waters. She got on with the old man very well, though sometimes he punctured her effusiveness with mild irony and he couldn't tolerate her passion for charades and word-games. Perhaps as a sly rebuke for these awful pastimes he gave her Fowler's *Dictionary of Modern Usage* for Christmas in 1940.[6] Bertie, who had received one of Winston's specially designed siren suits, was not above doing a little puncturing himself: 'At last the Army has come into its own,' he wrote to his Prime Minister in November 1942, '. . . ably helped by the forces of the air, & of those that work under the surface of the sea . . .'[7] Everything was made even jollier by the fact that Churchill had appointed James Stuart as his Chief Whip. Jamie, now very much a family man, still had his dry humour and his lackadaisical charm. There were a lot of laughs along with the blood, toil, tears and sweat.

At five o'clock in the morning on 13 May 1940 Bertie was woken up by a police sergeant informing him that Queen Wilhelmina of the Netherlands was on the 'phone. 'It is not often one is rung up at that hour,' Bertie commented mildly, 'and especially by a Queen. But in these days anything may happen, & far worse things too.'[8] The Queen, who had recently threatened Hitler, '*Touchez à mes pays bas et je vous inonde!*,'[9] wanted him to send some aircraft to defend Holland. Bertie passed this message on to everyone concerned and went back to bed.

Later in the morning Queen Wilhelmina telephoned again, this time from Harwich. The sixty-year-old royal lady, realizing that her earlier request might not be treated with proper urgency, had left The Hague and embarked in the British destroyer *Hereward* at Rotterdam. She sat herself down in the deckhouse after inquiring, 'I suppose this is bomb-proof?' The commander did not disabuse her, but asked her to wear a helmet, which she put on top of her hat. Then she told him to take her to Zeeland so that she could join her remaining army. The commander obediently set his course, but on the way received a message that the place was in flames and overrun with Germans. Wilhelmina told him to sail further south, and on being informed that the Germans were there also she replied, 'Then take me to England.'[10] It seemed that her intention was to have a few words with King George and the British Government and return to Holland in the evening.

Bertie dissuaded her, with difficulty, from this plan and told her to catch the next train for London. He met her at Liverpool Street – though he had never seen her before, she was instantly recognizable – and took her to Buckingham Palace. Her mind being on other things, she had not packed so much as a toothbrush and only possessed the clothes she so firmly sat down in.

Elizabeth, naturally, took this problem in hand and arranged for her own dressmakers to come in. None of their regal confections appealed to Wilhelmina. She had once been the prettiest and most sought-after Queen in Europe* but now all she wanted were a few aeroplanes and a

---

* From the *Illustrated London News*, 4 August 1900: 'It is announced that Queen Wilhelmina is not engaged to be married. This seems to have relieved the anxiety of many bosoms. Queen Wilhelmina is a most attractive young woman, and there are

couple of sensible tweed suits. Boxes of hats were unpacked, but she scorned them all. At last, noticing the plain black felt worn by one of the cringing underlings, she declared firmly, 'There you are. That is the hat for me!'[11] Thus garbed, she marched off to conduct the Dutch resistance from her rooms in the Palace. 'She has little S.A.', commented Field Marshal Wavell.[12]

Just over a fortnight later the Belgian army capitulated and the evacuation of Allied troops from Dunkirk began. Bertie was in a ferment of anxiety. Every day he wrote down the number of soldiers brought back, until finally he could record on Monday, 3 June, '... the last of the BEF have been evacuated.' By 5 June the operation was complete – 335,000 troops had been rescued, including 111,000 French. On 10 June Italy declared war on Britain and France: 'Mussolini gave no reason,'[13] the King, baffled, wrote in his diary, and on 16 June France surrendered.

King Haakon and Prince Olav of Norway had by now joined Queen Wilhelmina, Prince Bernhard and Princess Juliana at the Palace. The foreign royals were not unnaturally sensitive to the possibility of German invasion, and felt that perhaps more than Elizabeth's target practice with her .303 rifle and .38 revolver[14] was necessary. Haakon, as spokesman for the refugees, asked Bertie what precautions the Palace had taken against a parachute attack. Bertie explained the method of alerting the guard, but since his Norwegian uncle was clearly sceptical he pressed the alarm signal and they all went out into the garden to observe the magnificent result. There was no result. It seems that the police-sergeant on duty had told the officers of the guard that no attack was impending 'as he had heard nothing of it', so the guards had gone back to filling in their racing forms or reading 'Jane' in the *Daily Mirror*. Shortly afterwards a number of guardsmen entered the gardens at the double and, to the horror of King Haakon, 'proceeded to thrash the undergrowth in the manner of beaters at a shoot rather than men engaged in the pursuit of a dangerous enemy'.[15]

The precautions were soon looked into, and just as well. On 16 July 1940 Hitler issued 'War Directive No. 16', known as Operation Sealion: 'As England in spite of her hopeless military position has so far shown herself unwilling to come to any compromise, I have decided to begin preparations for and, if necessary, to carry out the invasion of England...'[16] The date decided on was 15 September. Meanwhile the *Luftwaffe* was to obliterate Channel shipping and demolish south coast ports and airfields. The German Naval Staff

stories of obscure and hopeless adorers who go about with many of her portraits next to their hearts. When the inevitable wedding comes at last, these gentlemen will probably attend it clad in some kind of sad raiment to signify their forlorn condition.'

estimated that 1,722 barges, 471 tugs, 1,161 motor-boats and 155 transports would be needed to ferry the 16th and 9th Armies across the Channel. By mid-August the barges were assembling in the estuaries of the Maas and the Scheldt while the *Luftwaffe* and Fighter Command fought the Battle of Britain over deserted holiday beaches and towns.

★ ★ ★

It is difficult, even now, not to romanticize this sky-high battlefield. 'Many a young Englishman,' wrote Wheeler-Bennett (who, as we know, was safely in Political Warfare), 'made the discovery in sacrifice that "Death opens unknown doors. It is most grand to die".' 'Just ordinary young men,' wrote Bertie more sanely, 'who come from all trades & professions [and] are now flying & using the most intricate & modern inventions.'[17] Unfortunately there weren't enough of them. By 6 September, although they had made enough trouble for Hitler to postpone the invasion for a further week, the resources of Fighter Command were stretched to the limit and things looked bad.

Bertie's Royal Prerogative, remember, meant that he had to be told everything that was going on, and most of his information was undoubtedly discussed with Elizabeth. After the first fierce daylight raid on London on 7 September, there must have been anxious speculation about the imminent invasion, news of which had been issued that evening by GHQ Home Forces under the curious code-name CROMWELL, a name to give any monarch a sleepless night. The following day, Sunday, was ominously peaceful. The Germans had, in fact, been surprised and unnerved by the fighter opposition over London. On Monday the 9th the *Luftwaffe* attacked London again – nearly half the bomber formations were turned back and the rest scattered. The invasion was postponed for another three days. British bombers and guns pounded the embarkation ports in northern France. Hitler postponed the invasion until 27 September. 'Even though victory in the air should not be achieved before another ten or twelve days,' he declared, 'Britain might yet be seized by mass hysteria.'[18] Perhaps it was, hysteria being a concomitant of war, but it was not the sort that Hitler had in mind. On 15 September a German bomber flew straight down the Mall and dropped two bombs in the forecourt of Buckingham Palace, two in the quadrangle, one on the Chapel and one, carelessly, in the garden. Bertie and Elizabeth had lunch in the air-raid shelter, which Elizabeth had furnished with gilt chairs, a regency settee, a large Victorian mahogany table and a supply of glossy magazines.[19] 'A magnificent piece of bombing, Ma'am, if you'll pardon my saying so,' one of the police constables remarked to the Queen.[20]

The following Sunday, Goering attacked London with everything he had – five fighters for every bomber, flying thick as hornets. The battle raged for an hour. The lethal German formations were scattered and hunted home. That night and the following night Bomber Command destroyed or damaged 12 per cent of the invasion barges and transports due to cross the Channel after the *Luftwaffe* had disposed of the RAF. The rest, as the German navy knew, would soon follow. On the afternoon of the 17th the War Diary of the German Naval Staff recorded Hitler's decision: 'The enemy air force is still by no means defeated; on the contrary, it shows increasing activity. The weather situation as a whole does not permit us to expect a period of calm. The Führer has therefore decided to postpone Operation Sealion indefinitely.' On 19 September the remainder of the invasion force skulked ignominiously away, without even attempting so much as a raid on the coast of Britain.[21]

★   ★   ★

The possible invasion of Hawkhurst and Petersfield became material for 'Dad's Army' as war erupted over the entire world. Bertie went through long periods of depression and bewilderment. The whole position in North Africa was an enigma to him;[22] ploughing through his daily reading of Cabinet papers and Foreign Office telegrams, he found it 'almost impossible to keep a clear mind on all that is going on'.[23] The endless arguments about the conduct of the war were quite incomprehensible: 'I do wish people would get on with the job and not criticise all the time, but in a free country this has to be put up with.'[24] It had never been easy for Bertie to put up with things. In the early days, when he knew most of the people involved – Boris of Bulgaria, Leopold of Belgium, George of Greece, and of course the Yugoslavs – he felt he was doing something useful by writing letters ('I send you my best wishes for the happiness and prosperity of your Majesty and of Bulgaria during these troublous times'),[25] but after Pearl Harbor the whole business got out of hand. 'Anything can happen,' he wrote, feeling helpless, '& it will be wonderful if we are lucky anywhere.'[26] His natural pessimism was perhaps the hardest thing Elizabeth had to cope with during the entire war. 'He feels so much not being in the fighting line,' she wrote to Queen Mary.[27] Gloomy and frustrated, for two nights a week at 6 p.m. on the dot Bertie put on overalls and worked at a bench for three hours making parts for RAF guns.[28]

One thing that comforted him was his friendship with Roosevelt. They went out of their way to be personally amiable to each other's Ambassadors and never wrote to each other without recalling those happy days at Hyde Park. But when Roosevelt died in 1945, though everything was looking much more hopeful, nobody knew that the war would be over in four months, and anyway by that time Churchill was taking all the credit. There was no longer a King or a President left anywhere with whom Bertie could chat on equal terms.

By the spring of 1943 it seemed safe for His Majesty to take a trip to North Africa – the first time he had set foot out of England since he inspected the Maginot Line in 1939. Bertie was unable to view even this exciting prospect without the usual doubt and conjecture: 'As the time draws nearer for my departure on my journey, I wonder if I should go, but I know I shall be doing good ...'[29] Travelling incognito as 'General Lyon' he set out with attendant aircraft in Churchill's luxurious transport 'plane on the evening of 11 June 1943. Elizabeth saw him off at Northolt and went home to wait for news. 'I have had an anxious few hours,' she wrote to Queen Mary next day, 'because at 8.15 I heard that the plane had been heard near Gibraltar, and that it would soon be landing. Then after an hour & a half I heard that there was thick fog at Gib. & that they were going on to Africa. Then complete silence until a few minutes ago, when a message came that they had landed in Africa & taken off again. Of course I imagined every sort of horror, & walked up & down my room staring at the telephone ...'[30] (As Queen Mary must have been equally anxious for news it seems strange that Elizabeth didn't use this convenient telephone to inform her of Bertie's arrival.)

Harold Macmillan, Minister Resident at Allied Headquarters, was one of the party welcoming 'General Lyon' at Algiers. It was his job to go through the programme of the tour with the King, which was not easy: 'Unfortunately, he was very tired from the journey and had not slept at all. So I had a good deal of difficulty in getting him to agree to the various items ... The real trouble is that the courtiers are deplorable. Joey Legh does his best, and, although looking quite half-witted, is not so. But Alec Hardinge seems to me beyond the pale. He is idle, supercilious, without a spark of imagination or vitality. And his whole attitude to the visit makes one wonder why he advised the King to undertake it at all. However, after a lot of cajoling and so forth, we got the first two and a half days agreed...'[31]

After a bath and a sleep at the Villa Emma, Bertie recovered his spirits and his temper. The tour was a genuine success and he enjoyed every minute of it, particularly the stately entry into Valletta harbour on the cruiser *Aurora* when he stood alone in his white naval uniform on the bridge acknowledging the thunderous welcome of troops, sailors, airmen and civilians lining the cliffs, packed into the narrow streets, perilously perched on rocks, lamp-posts, bollards and row-boats while choirs sang and bands played. The King was piped ashore like a conquering hero and that night, sailing over a calm sea to Tripoli, he felt like one. 'Mussolini called the Mediterranean *Mare Nostrum*,' Macmillan wrote in his diary. 'The King, in a cruiser with four destroyers, has crossed it twice in thirty-six hours.' Alec Hardinge, who according to Macmillan 'would have been out of date in the 1900s', resigned a month later, ostensibly because of another bout of exhaustion and ill-health. It is safe to say that he was not greatly missed.

A year later, as D-Day approached, Bertie passionately wanted to repeat this experience. A King could not be expected to lead his invading troops from an office desk. Rather to his consternation he found that Churchill had the same idea. Not content with flying to Tehran by way of Cairo and having interesting conversations with Roosevelt and Chiang Kai-shek and Stalin, the old man glibly informed Bertie that 'he hoped to see the initial attack from one of the bombarding ships'. Bertie was reduced to suggesting that he should go with him, though it wouldn't be quite the same thing. Two years before, the King had noted with some asperity that Churchill 'likes getting his own way with no interference from anybody and nobody will stand for that sort of treatment in this country'[32] and now he was going to steal what should be the Sovereign's thunder. It was a bit much, but since he wanted so badly to be involved in the invasion he would have to put up with it. 'I told Elizabeth about the idea & she was wonderful as always & encouraged me to do it.'[33]

Alan Lascelles, his new Private Secretary, was, however, appalled at the suggestion. Who would the fatherless Lilibet choose for her Prime Minister if both Bertie and Churchill were killed? And what about the commander of any vessel who found himself trying to fight a major battle and look after his King and Prime Minister at the same time? Bertie, a sensible man, reluctantly agreed to sleep on the idea. In the morning he wrote to Churchill asking him to reconsider; 'the right thing to do', he advised through gritted teeth, 'is what normally falls to those at the top on such occasions, namely, to remain at home and wait.'[34]

Next day Bertie and Lascelles went to see Admiral Ramsay, the Allied Naval Commander-in-Chief, at the Downing Street Annexe. Churchill was there, looking ominously smug. Admiral Ramsay, who had no idea that the King might be involved in this absurd enterprise, told Churchill that apart from risking mines, torpedoes, air attack and shells from shore batteries, he wouldn't be able to see a thing anyway. Ramsay was asked to withdraw for a few minutes and there was a quick conference. When he was called back, it was to be told that the King, actually, rather wanted to go as well.

The Admiral, almost literally, blew his top. Churchill blandly said that of course he would have to seek Cabinet approval for the King joining the expedition, but that he would unfortunately be unable to recommend them to give it. Fair enough, said Bertie, until it rapidly became clear that the Prime Minister had no intention of applying this wise decision to himself. Churchill, once more, was making sure that he would have all the glory.

Lascelles and Ramsay tried everything. Churchill sat plumply smiling.

'Your face is getting longer and longer,' Bertie said to his Secretary.

'I was thinking, Sir, that it's not going to make things easier for you if you have to find a new Prime Minister in the middle of "Overlord".'

'Oh, that's all arranged for,' said Churchill, 'and anyhow I don't think the risk is a hundred-to-one.'[35]

Lascelles said that he had always understood that no Minister of the Crown could leave the country without the Sovereign's consent. He would be on a British man-of-war, said Churchill, and therefore on British territory. Bertie and his Private Secretary finally left, defeated.

Bertie was very angry, but controlled himself to write Churchill a long, reasonable letter: 'Please consider my own position. I am a sailor, & as King I am head of all three services. There is nothing I would like better than to go to sea but I have agreed to stop at home; is it fair that you should then do exactly what I would like to do myself? You said yesterday afternoon that it would be a fine thing for the King to lead his troops into battle, as in the old days; if the King cannot do this, it does not seem to me right that his Prime Minister should take his place . . . I have been very worried & anxious over the whole of this business & it is my duty to warn the P.M. on such occasions. No one else can & should anything dreadful happen I should be asked if I had tried to deter him.'[36]

He waited for a reply. Churchill, having received the letter and read it, nipped quickly into his special train and sped to General Eisenhower's headquarters near Portsmouth. With mounting fury, Bertie 'phoned Lascelles and threatened to drive to Portsmouth himself to prevent Churchill embarking. Lascelles rang up Churchill's train. The Prime Minister, knowing when he was beaten, gave in with a bad grace. If only the train had left half an hour earlier, he would have got away with it.

Churchill, whose own account of the drama understandably differs slightly from the above, sat down in the early hours of the morning and dashed off a letter to the King which he sent at once by dispatch-rider to Windsor:

> Sir, I cannot really feel that the first paragraph of your letter takes sufficient account of the fact that there is absolutely no comparison in the British Constitution between a Sovereign and a subject . . . as Prime Minister and Minister of Defence I ought to be allowed to go where I consider it necessary to the discharge of my duty, and I do not admit that the Cabinet have any right to put restrictions on my freedom of movement. I rely on

my own judgement ... I must earnestly ask Your Majesty that no principle shall be laid down which inhibits my freedom of movement when I
judge it necessary to acquaint myself with conditions in the various
theatres of war. Since Your Majesty does me the honour to be so much
concerned about my personal safety on this occasion, I must defer to Your
Majesty's wishes, and indeed commands...'[37]

Thinking it all over in later years Churchill, perhaps unwittingly,
expressed Bertie's own feelings about the war: 'A man who has to play
an effective part in taking, with the highest responsibility, grave and
terrible decisions ... may need the refreshment of adventure. He may
also need the comfort that when sending so many others to their death
he may share in a small way their risks...' Bertie, by his position and
personality, was more frustrated than his Prime Minister but he put up
with it, for once, with more grace.

Three days later Allied forces landed in Normandy. The business of
the House of Commons concerned a question as to why a disabled
soldier had been refused a permit to open a shop in Wimbledon and a
request from Lady Apsley, Conservative Member for Central Bristol,
for an issue of berets to the ATS. Sir James Greig, the War Minister,
replied that this was no time for new hats for the ATS, and Sir
Archibald Southby, Conservative member for Epsom, made a short
and moving appeal for the right of women to new headgear in spring-
time.[38] That night the King broadcast to his people: 'If from every
place of worship, from home and factory, from men and women of all
ages and many races and occupations, our intercessions rise,' then,
provided they were all on the right side, God would see that the war
was won. The problem of the Germans interceding just as unanimously was not one to trouble Bertie. He had a simple, filial belief in the
Almighty, and never doubted which side He was on. 'I am glad you
liked my broadcast,' he wrote to his mother. 'The Bishop of Lichfield
helped me with it.'[39]

CHAPTER

27

Prince Henry, Duke of Gloucester, was gazetted as Chief Liaison Officer with the BEF. 'My role as I see it,' he said, 'is to keep my wicket up for a time and just take the edge off the bowling until the star-turns on the side are ready to go in.'[1] Unfortunately the star turn in France turned out to be his brother David, Duke of Windsor. Junior in rank to Harry, he took all the salutes and left Harry plodding along behind. The Duke of Gloucester, 'without knowing quite what he could have done, did feel that perhaps he ought to have done something.'[2]

His Duchess was pregnant again after suffering several miscarriages. Her X-rays were duly forwarded to Harry at the front, who desperately wanted the opinion of his commanding officer, Brigadier Fanshawe. 'The latter, not unnaturally, did not feel competent to give an opinion, and . . . was so anxious to avoid doing so that he slipped off to bed. Before he had undressed, however, he heard the Duke's foot on the stair and presently his knock at the door. Fanshawe, still in uniform, jumped smartly into bed. Prince Henry entered; Fanshawe feigned sleep; Prince Henry shook him . . .' The Duke was so taken up with the X-rays that he failed to enquire why his commanding officer had gone to bed in full uniform.[3] They sat for hours puzzling over the Duchess's pelvis.

Harry's next job was a diplomatic mission to the Near and Middle East and India, which ended with much hilarity bicycling along the passages of the Viceregal Residence in Delhi and squirting Billy Ednam and Andrew Elphinstone with a fire hose.[4] The Duchess of Gloucester gave birth to two sons during the war, and at the end of 1944 the Duke, accompanied by his family, set off to be Governor-General of Australia.

★   ★   ★

This post had been intended for George, Duke of Kent, but on the outbreak of war it was decided to keep him at home, presumably 'in case', a phrase constantly uppermost in royal minds. He was attached to the naval intelligence division of the Admiralty and spent the first

17. The Duke and Duchess of York, Princess Elizabeth and Princess Margaret at the Circus, Olympia, 1935.

18. The Duke of Kent, the Duke of York, the Prince of Wales and the Duke of Gloucester follow King George V's coffin from the church at Sandringham to Wolferton Station on its way to London, 23 January 1936.

19. LEFT The Duke of York returning to 145 Piccadilly on the evening of 10 December 1936, the day on which Edward VIII abdicated.

20. BELOW The Duke and Duchess of Windsor at the Château de Candé after their wedding on 3 June 1937.

21. ABOVE King George VI,
Queen Elizabeth and David
Bowes-Lyon visit the church of St
Paul's Walden Bury, 1937.

22. RIGHT The Duke and Duchess
of Kent, 1939.

23. LEFT King George VI and President Franklin D. Roosevelt in Washington, 1939.

24. BELOW King George VI and Queen Elizabeth inspect a bomb crater in London, 1940.

25. King George VI, Queen Elizabeth, Princess Elizabeth and Princess Margaret with Winston Churchill on the balcony of Buckingham Palace on VE Day, 1945.

26. A visit to the Strand Theatre, 1946. (*left to right*) Princess Margaret, King George VI, Queen Elizabeth, Group Captain Peter Townsend and Princess Elizabeth.

27. BELOW The Queen and Queen Elizabeth the Queen Mother leaving the funeral train which brought the body of King George VI to London.

28. LEFT The last newsreel pictures of King George VI were taken at London Airport as he waved goodbye to Princess Elizabeth and Prince Philip as they left for East Africa in 1952.

29. RIGHT Princess Margaret and Group Captain Peter Townsend, 1953.

30. BELOW The Queen unveiled a Memorial plaque on 7 June 1967 to mark the centenary of the birth of Queen Mary. (*left to right*) Prince Philip, the Queen, Queen Elizabeth the Queen Mother, the Duke and Duchess of Gloucester, and the Duke and Duchess of Windsor.

31. LEFT The Queen Mother at the Cheltenham Races in 1985.

32. BELOW The Queen Mother was taken for a short gondola ride on her first visit to Venice in 1985.

year visiting naval establishments in Britain, finding plenty of time to rearrange his 'rich treasures . . . gold boxes, *étuis* and pretty, expensive objects' at Coppins and idly strum Debussy while Marina occupied herself with backgammon.[5] The Kents might not have enjoyed Australia very much, but the decision to keep him at home had tragic consequences.

In 1940 George was appointed Staff Officer in the training command of the RAF and a year later toured Canada and the United States, where he hoped to be able to meet his brother David, now Governor of the Bahamas. This was not permitted. His brother-in-law, Prince Paul of Yugoslavia, was also in disgrace, having given in to the Axis and escaped with his wife to Greece, leaving the eighteen-year-old Peter (he who nearly drowned in the font) in charge. The Kents hurried off to Chequers to try and persuade Churchill to be merciful to Paul and Olga, and perhaps he was – they were sent to Kenya as 'privileged prisoners', which was certainly better than being captured by the Germans, but extremely distressing and embarrassing to the Kents. Their elegant, brittle world was falling apart – David and Wallis, Paul and Olga, all banished; their friends cold-shouldered by the family; Elizabeth – who long ago had been one of them – unapproachable.

The Kents' younger son, Michael, was born on 4 July 1942. On 25 August George started out from Invergordon in a Sunderland Flying Boat *en route* for Iceland. Half an hour later the 'plane crashed into a mountain-side and he and his entire crew, bar one, were killed outright. 'He was killed on Active Service,' Bertie wrote in his diary. It was the only consolation. After the misery of the funeral at Windsor, he returned to Balmoral and went to the site of the crash: 'I met Dr Kennedy, who found him, the farmer Morrison & his son who led search parties . . . the ground for 200 yds long & 100 yds wide had been scored and scorched by its trail & by flame. It hit one side of the slope, turned over in the air & slid down the other side on its back. The impact must have been terrific as the aircraft . . . was unrecognizable when found. I felt I had to do this pilgrimage.'[6]

Queen Mary, desolate, went immediately to Coppins to try and comfort Marina. Bertie sent off a cable to Princess Olga in Kenya asking her to return immediately. Her journey, via Uganda, the Cameroons, Nigeria, Portugal and Ireland, took a week. She used almost every known form of transport and, on the King's instructions, was given priority all the way.[7] Nevertheless, a month after her arrival a furious attack was launched against her in the Commons by Captain Alec Cunningham Reid, Conservative M.P. for Marylebone: 'We have deliberately brought this sinister woman over to the British Isles and have allowed her, to all intents and purposes, complete freedom ... If you are a quisling and you happen to be royalty, it appears that you are automatically trusted and forgiven.'[8] Again and again during the autumn of 1942 Captain Cunningham Reid tried to get Princess Olga incarcerated or sent back to her 'dangerous tiger ... traitorous rat' of a husband. Nor was he entirely without supporters in this curious obsession.

One night that summer Marie Belloc Lowndes, another indefatigable diarist, and know-all, dined 'with an airman friend' who 'seemed worried about the Duke of Kent's accident and said it should not have occurred, that the pilot should have been much higher in the sky. He told me a most curious secret, that an exactly similar accident had befallen a whole Air Mission going back to Russia. Every man was killed and apparently Russia thought it had been done on purpose.'[9] There were many curious 'accidents' during the war.* But why should one of them have befallen the harmless and insignificant Duke of Kent?

★   ★   ★

On 12 May 1940 Elizabeth telephoned Miss Crawford at the Royal Lodge and said, 'I think you had better go to Windsor Castle, anyway for the rest of the week.' Churchill had taken over the Government and war had begun. Clara, still unable to understand any crisis that wasn't to do with dill-water, packed enough socks and knickers for a weekend and the two young Princesses were taken to the Castle for five years.

Windsor Castle itself covers something like thirteen acres. Lilibet, aged fourteen, slept with Bobo the nursery maid, Margaret with Clara. All the paintings had been taken down and all the valuable furniture removed; every room was lit only by one bare light bulb; there was no heating and electric fires were seldom used, partly out of patriotism, partly because of power cuts. Crawfie's bathroom was out on the roof and the air-raid shelter was a hastily converted dungeon.

A company of Grenadier Guards, whose war-work was to defend the Princesses from possible kidnap or worse, soon arrived to liven things up. Daddy and Mummy came at weekends. Lilibet wore her Mickey Mouse gas mask for precisely the recommended period every day and carefully cleaned the eyepieces every evening with the ointment provided. She was a conscientious, worried girl. Crawfie and Margaret were distressingly frivolous. There was hide-and-seek and

---

* On 4 July 1943 General Sikorski, premier of the Free Polish Government exiled in London and C-in-C of the Free Polish forces, was killed in an unexplained air crash over Gibraltar, together with Colonel Victor Cazalet M.P. ('his hobbies were Poles and Jews, and his phobia was Russia,' writes Chips Channon) and Lt. Col. Whiteley M.P., among others.

'sardines' with the young Guardsmen, and treasure hunts and the Madrigal Society and the Girl Guides and, of course, the pantomimes. The first of these, in 1941, was Cinderella, featuring Lilibet as Prince Charming and Margaret as poor deprived little Cinders; we don't know, I think, who played the Ugly Sisters or Buttons, but it all ended with a chorus of tall Guardsmen unfurling a Union Jack and everyone, Bertie and Elizabeth included, singing their heads off. For this production Lilibet wore white satin knee-breeches, but the following year, for Sleeping Beauty, she persuaded them to order a classic Principal Boy costume of jerkin and tights. 'Lilibet can't possibly wear that – the tunic is too short,' her father snapped. She had very reasonable legs, and ought to have sulked. By 1943 and Aladdin, Lilibet was seventeen, Philip of Greece was in the audience and the costumes (as far as I remember my Aladdin it is a knock-about rather than a romance) were decorous if not particularly becoming. This was compensated for by what Lady Longford terms 'the Princesses' aptitude for rollicking satire'.[10]

Widow Twankey: There are three acres and one rood.
Princess M.: We don't want anything improper.
Widow Twankey: There's a large copper in the kitchen.
Princess E.: We'll soon get rid of him.[11]

Not to be outdone, Elizabeth went through her music-hall repertoire and sang 'A Sailor's Wife a Sailor's Star Must Be' in duet with Philip's Aunt Edwina, accompanied at the piano by the skilful young Margaret. The Queen was also very fond of the songs of Vera Lynn and gave some poignant renderings of 'We'll Meet Again' and 'The White Cliffs of Dover'.

The girls' education suffered, of course, from their confinement at Windsor. Elizabeth was not particularly concerned, but agreed to Miss Crawford taking on a Mrs Montaudon-Smith to help out with French, while Lilibet studied constitutional history with Henry Marten, the Vice-Provost of Eton, who never looked directly at her and addressed her, when necessary, as 'Gentlemen'.[12] In 1942 Lilibet was confirmed by old Archbishop Lang, his last act before his resignation took effect. 'The night before I spent at the Castle and had a full talk with the little lady alone ... though naturally not very communicative, she showed real intelligence and understanding. I thought much, but rightly said little, of the responsibilities which may be awaiting her in the future...'[13]

Lilibet joined the ATS as No. 230873 Second Subaltern Elizabeth Alexandra Mary Windsor four months before the war ended, but slept every night at Windsor, possibly still with Bobo. On VE night, 8 May 1945, both girls were set free for half an hour in the Mall – chaperoned by Crawfie, Mrs Montaudon-Smith and a Major Phillips, 'they weren't allowed to go to Piccadilly Circus but ran wildly down St James's Street and shouted outside the Palace "We want the King! We want the Queen!"' Then they went back into Buckingham Palace by the garden gate and were given sandwiches by their mother. 'Poor darlings,' was Bertie's perplexing entry in his diary that night, 'they have never had any fun yet.'[14]

★   ★   ★

Princess Mary must have spent her war much like tens of millions of other women, worrying about her sons, both of whom were active soldiers, and trying to make ends meet. She and Lord Harewood did, however, frequently go to stay with the Beauforts at Badminton in Gloucestershire, where her mother, under the guise of being a guest, conducted what amounted to a court in exile. Queen Mary, apart from Georgie's death and the bombing of Marlborough House and her constant anxiety for the royal relations, had a wonderful war. On 4 September 1939 she set out, with most of her staff of sixty-three persons and their dependants, and drove via Peterborough, Oundle and Northampton to Althorp, where she had lunch with Lord and Lady Spencer – who presumably provided for the retinue as well – and on through Oxford, Chippenham and Swindon, 'a lovely drive'.[15] Greeted at Badminton by her niece, the Duchess of Beaufort, with a certain degree of apprehension – the convoy sweeping up to the house seemed endless – the Queen lost no time in organizing herself and the entire household. She selected a bedroom on the first floor, with an adjacent sitting room and bathroom and splendid outlook across the park. She also chose a dining room, and decided that the Beauforts' large dining room – which they never used, after all – would do very nicely for receiving guests whom she did not invite upstairs. 'Pandemonium was the least it could be called!' the Duchess wrote to Osbert Sitwell. 'The servants revolted, and scorned our humble home. They refused to use the excellent rooms assigned to them. Fearful rows and battle royals fought over my body – but I won in the end and reduced them to tears and pulp . . . I can laugh now, but I have never been so angry! . . . The Queen, quite unconscious of the stir, has settled in well, and is busy cutting down trees and tearing down ivy. Tremendous activity.'[16]

Queen Mary passionately hated ivy. She was not a country-woman, she had never learned to ride and had seldom owned a dog and her gardening really consisted of tours of inspection; but she detested ivy. 'Lovely morning which we spent clearing ivy off the trees . . . while Jack Coke [Major the Hon. Sir John Coke KCVO] hacked off branches of 2 chestnut trees & an elm . . . & the gardeners began to clear a wall of ivy near Mary B's bedroom,' she wrote on 25 September; and on 26 September, 'Lovely morning which we spent clearing ivy off trees – We watched a whole wall of ivy of 50 years standing at the back of Mary B's bedroom being removed – most of it came down like a blanket.'[17] When most of the ivy had been demolished – she learned to destroy the roots after realizing that Nature niftily replaced the rest – she turned her attention to Wooding, setting off in her old green Daimler every afternoon with hacksaws and other lethal implements tied to the back.[18] The Queen personally conducted the operations, poking at recalcitrant branches with her walking stick. The casualty list was formidable: two chauffeurs were knocked out, quite apart from the splinters, wounds, sprains and fractures.[19] The Duke narrowly escaped having his ancient and historic cedar tree felled to the ground. Luckily, the Queen's attention was diverted to Scrap.

Scrap may have helped to satisfy her craving for collecting – a piece of bone left by a fox, fragments of old iron, bottles galore, tins and wire and shards of china, she pounced on it all. The story goes that she returned in triumph from a walk one day, dragging behind her a large piece of rusty old iron to add to the royal dump. It turned out to be a plough belonging to a neighbouring farmer – 'and will Your Majesty graciously give it back to him, please, at once, as he can't get on without it'.[20] The alternative version is that the plough was quietly returned to its owner without the Queen's knowledge, which seems rather more likely.

There were constant air-raid warnings, because of Badminton's proximity to Bristol and Bath. Until she learned to disregard the tiresome things she was always first in the shelter, composed, perfectly dressed and sitting bolt upright doing the crossword while everyone else shuffled in half asleep.[21] Her reaction to the news, which she followed with passionate interest, was very personal – 'What a vile enemy, I feel very bitter – Poor Christian of Denmark and poor Charles of Norway!'[22] and gives the impression that she would have set about Hitler with a rolling pin had she been able. One of her greatest pleasures was giving lifts to pedestrian soldiers, sailors and airmen, particularly Americans. There was no condescension in her interest, no need to exert her charm. In her stately way, she was humble, eager to learn about the people from whom she had been segregated so long. On VE day she listened to Bertie's speech, and dear Mr Churchill's, and then went to the local pub, where the village was celebrating – 'We sang songs, a friendly affair and amusing.'[23]

At last she could go home, back to her pedestal. For the first time in her life, Queen Mary wept in public. 'Oh, I *have* been happy here! Here I've been anybody to everybody, and back in London I shall have to begin being Queen Mary all over again.'[24] She was seventy-five, and too old to abdicate; perhaps the delights of Wooding and Scrap and even waging war against ivy would have palled in peace-time; nevertheless, it is sad to see her disappearing once more into her calm, doomed world of privilege.

CHAPTER

28

There have been countless books and much controversy about the Duke of Windsor's war, and it would be convenient to be able to say that it only concerns this book in so far as it affected Elizabeth. Unfortunately it doesn't work like that. The important question, as far as her biographer is concerned, is what effect did Elizabeth have on the Duke of Windsor's war.

As yet there is no satisfactory answer. Evidence seeps out here and there, but it is nearly always exploited in the interests of the people who use it. Those who are still in love with the Prince of Wales' image ('in love' may seem a curious term, but it most accurately describes their feelings), can have it proved to them chapter and verse that he was a petulant ne'er-do-well, but they won't believe it. Conversely, those who despise him for giving up the throne and frittering his life away are deaf to any argument to the contrary, however well substantiated it may be. David Windsor and Hamlet are the two princes in history who provide topics of inexhaustible speculation.

The general attitude to Elizabeth is, on a different level, much the same. Over the last decade various writers have implied, or quoted sources that have implied, that far from being the darling little creature she appeared – and the old dear she now appears – she conducted a single-handed vendetta against the Windsors and ruthlessly, without a tremor of pity, destroyed them; nevertheless, even if this could be proved, it would not be believed by those who find it more comfortable to adore her. Nor would it have made the slightest difference to Wallis, or to others on the receiving end of British policy towards the Windsors at that time, if they had been given irrefutable evidence of Elizabeth's sweet nature and generosity of heart. In matters of this kind people believe what they want to believe; and what they believe is not based on fact, but on their own personalities and experience.

Begging the question as to why David was in exile at all, and certainly why he had to be humiliated over his wife's title and so thoroughly ostracized, there seems little doubt that it was he who made the first wrong move. On 1 September 1939 Walter Monckton telephoned the Duke to say that the King would send a 'plane of the

King's Flight the next day to pick up the Duke and Duchess and take them back to England. This could not have been an easy decision for Elizabeth to advise Bertie to make. War was about to be declared. They were up to their eyes in problems. David himself might be kept busy in some fairly remote corner of the British Isles, but what about Wallis? Even so, they couldn't just abandon them – it would look so bad – and Queen Mary presumably agreed.

David seemed unable to grasp the situation. He refused to go unless he and the Duchess were put up at Windsor Castle, with a personal invitation from Their Majesties. Monckton stupidly repeated this to Bertie and Elizabeth. The 'plane was cancelled. Four days after war was declared Monckton arrived at Antibes in a small, dilapidated-looking Leopard Moth, clearly impractical for transporting the Windsors, let alone their luggage and dogs. He brought the news that David would only be allowed to return if he agreed to become either Deputy Regional Commissioner in Wales or Liaison Officer with the Howard-Vyse Mission in France.[1] David agreed to these conditions and on the night of 12 September, in the pitch blackout, he and Wallis arrived at Portsmouth from Cherbourg. Churchill had organized a guard of honour and a Royal Marine band to play God Save the King, but otherwise they were met by two people – Walter Monckton and Lady Alexandra Metcalfe. There was no representative of the family, no message, no car, and nowhere to stay. 'Officially,' writes Stephen Birmingham, a quotable but biased author, 'the Royal Family had decided to treat the ex-King, as much as possible, as though he were a dead person.'[2]

David had decided to take the first job – he felt vaguely responsible for Wales, since he had been its Prince and, as King, had rashly promised that something would be done about it. On 14 September he went to see Bertie at the Palace – a meeting Monckton had been able to arrange only by 'the exclusion of women'. The brothers were together for an hour – 'He seems very well,' Bertie wrote to Chamberlain, '& not a bit worried as to the effects he left on people's minds as to his behaviour in 1936. He has forgotten all about it.'[3] (If David had insisted on discussing the matters 'gnawing at their souls', Bertie would have been even more surprised – but that was not the royal way, for either of them.) Something, anyway, must have been said or implied that worried the King. After discussing it with his closest adviser, he wrote to the Minister for War, Leslie Hore-Belisha, that his brother would be most suitably employed in France and not in Wales. Hore-Belisha informed David of this the next day. He agreed, but asked whether he could first be attached to various Commands in England, so that he could get to know soldiers again – and, he added, he would like to take Wallis with him.

The reply was inevitable. 'The King sent for me at 11 a.m.,' Hore-Belisha wrote on 15 September. 'He was in a distressed state. He thought that if the Duchess went to the Commands she might have a hostile reception, particularly in Scotland. He did not want the Duke to go to the Commands in England. He seemed very distressed and walked up and down the room. He said the Duke had never had any discipline in his life . . . 2.30 p.m.: I went to the Palace with Ironside. HM remarked that all his ancestors had succeeded to the throne after their predecessors had died. "Mine is not only alive, but very much so." He thought it better for the Duke to proceed to Paris at once.'[4]

What had happened between David's visit the previous day, which Bertie told Chamberlain had been 'very friendly', and this anxious summons? Does the neat remark about the ex-King being very much alive sound like Bertie? He was not much given to epigrams. Anyway, the result was that on 27 September Major-General HRH The Duke of Windsor sailed for France. General Sir Alan Brooke, Chief of the Imperial General Staff, noted in his diary that Major-General Howard-Vyse 'has instructions to guard against his endeavouring to stage any kind of "come-back" with the troops out here.'[5] This, however, was in vain.

David was back at work (something which his younger brother should have understood), and he was happy – 'full of go and interest', noted General Brooke enthusiastically.[6] The troops, both British and French, gave him an uproarious welcome; his reports were valuable; on 9 October 'Fruity' Metcalfe, now the Duke's ADC, wrote to his wife, '. . . we passed into Br. Sector & went to our GHQ and there met Gort and his chief-of-staff also the Duke of Gloucester. Everyone here was delighted to see HRH & the visit could not have gone better. It was very important to HRH as you can well imagine . . .'[7] It was shortly after this meeting that David automatically returned the salute of a company guard intended for his senior-ranking brother Harry. The two men may have found this quite a joke, but some days later the one-time King was severely reprimanded for violating military etiquette. As a soldier, this was bad enough; as an ex-Monarch it was appalling; as the senior brother, it was intolerable. 'David shrugged the incident off,' wrote Wallis, but '. . . we had two wars to deal with – the big and still leisurely war, in which everybody was caught up, and the little cold war with the Palace, in which no quarter was given.'[8]

According to Michael Bloch, secret instructions now went out from the Court to ensure that the Duke in future acquired no personal publicity or prestige. He was to be 'punished' by a period of in-activity.[9] Mr Bloch gives no source or authority for this information, but Wallis wrote to her Aunt Bessie on 3 December, 'My brother-in-law [the King] arrives in France tomorrow, but competition still exists in the English mind – so one must hide so there is no rivalry. All very childish except that the biggest men take it seriously. Anyway the Duke can leave the front and spend those days with me so that the cheers are guaranteed.'[10] Once Bertie was safely back in England, David set off again to visit the Second French Army, from which he sent a very prescient report, which was disregarded.

On 9 April Germany invaded Denmark and Norway and, as we know, Bertie had a frustrating day. Harry was winched out of Boulogne and flown back to England in advance of the retreating British Army,[11] but the Duke of Windsor was given neither instructions nor information. On 28 May he went to the British Embassy and asked Sir Ronald Campbell if he could be temporarily seconded to the Armee des Alpes, where he could inspect the French forces drawn up along the Italian frontier and pack up his possessions at La Croe.[12] For once, his suggestion was accepted. On the same day that the British Army began leaving Dunkirk, the Windsors arrived at Antibes.

Ten days later the French Government fled from Paris to Tours and on the following day Italy declared war on France and England. The Riviera emptied, but still there was no word from England as to what the Windsors were expected to do. France surrendered on 16 June. The Germans were at Dijon and heading for the Rhône Valley. David 'phoned the British Embassy, temporarily encamped at Bordeaux, and asked if he and Wallis could be evacuated by the Royal Navy. 'He was told (with "suave but firm politeness") that this was out of the question.'[13]

Finally on 19 June, with the Germans only 200 miles to the north, the Windsors joined a convoy of consular-refugees heading for the Spanish frontier. '*Je suis le Prince de Galles. Laissez moi passer, s'il vout plait,*' the Duke shouted at every barrier;[14] and they did. At the border, he was refused visas on the grounds that he might become a charge on the neutral Spanish government. A 'phone call to the Spanish Ambassador in France finally put matters right, and on 20 June they arrived at Barcelona. David then sent a cable to Churchill: 'Having received no instructions have arrived Spain to avoid capture. Proceeding to Madrid. Edward.'[15]

Only then, with a decisive slamming of the stable door, did Churchill inform him that 'we should like Your Royal Highness to come home as soon as possible,' and two flying-boats were ordered to proceed to Lisbon to pick them up. At the same time Alec Hardinge wrote a furious letter to the Foreign Office saying that 'the King had noted with extreme displeasure that the Duke and Duchess had been referred to as "Their Royal Highnesses". His Majesty's express wish was that steps be taken to ensure that such an official error should never occur again.'

I may be falling into the usual trap, but I am unable to believe that this ceaseless persecution was instigated by Bertie. He was fussy, intensely correct, and could be childish, but there is no indication that he was vindictive, except perhaps towards Lady Sybil Graham's dog. Possibly Alec Hardinge and his cronies acted without consulting the King, but that seems unlikely. He was, after all, the Duke of Windsor's brother; it was a family situation and David, at least, was still a member of the family. Who, then, within the family, had sufficient influence over Bertie to make him behave in this un-characteristically ruthless manner? His mother? His wife?

Even the outsider, investigating the available evidence, can see a number of possible answers. They are all speculation, and some drift up, murkily, from vague suppositions about the psychology of monarchy, which are neither here nor there. Far more than any concrete evidence, it is instinct that sends me off on Elizabeth's track, snuffling among the tuberoses and gardenias, worrying away at the smiling image. On 25 July 1940 the German Ambassador in Madrid reported to the German Foreign Ministry that Miguel Primo de Rivera, leader of the Madrid Falangists, had just returned from Lisbon: 'He had two long conversations with the Duke of Windsor; at the last one the Duchess was present also . . . The Duke and Duchess have less fear of the King, who was quite foolish, (*"reichliche toricht"*), than of the shrewd Queen who was intriguing skilfully against the Duke and particularly the Duchess . . .'[16] This could be Teutonic make-believe, or the Windsors' paranoia. But 'fear' and 'shrewd' are memorable words.

★   ★   ★

The Windsors reached Lisbon on 3 July 1940. That same evening, Churchill was summoned to the Palace. On the morning of 4 July David received a telegram: 'I am authorized by the King and Cabinet to offer you the appointment of Governor and Commander-in-Chief of the Bahamas . . . Personally I feel sure that it is the best open in the grievous situation in which we all stand. At any rate I have done my best.' Back in London, Beaverbrook commented that the Duke would be very relieved. 'Not half as much as his brother will,' Churchill replied.[17]

David had already made arrangements to return to England on the flying-boat of RAF Coastal Command waiting, as promised, in Lisbon harbour. He had dropped every condition for his return except one: that he and Wallis should be received just once by his brother and sister-in-law, if only for a few minutes, and that notice of the fact should appear in the Court Circular. The result had been a rap over the knuckles: 'Your Highness has taken active military rank, and refusal to obey direct orders of competent military authority would create a serious situation. I hope it will not be necessary for such orders to be sent...'[18] Clearly any kind of life they might lead in England would be intolerable. The ex-Liege Lord, by the Grace of God, of Great Britain, Ireland and the British Dominions beyond the Seas, Defender of the Faith and Emperor of India accepted the job. Churchill informed the Dominions. 'The position of the Duke of Windsor on the Continent in recent months has been causing His Majesty and His Majesty's Government embarrassment...' he explained. 'There are personal and family difficulties about his return to this country...'

Perhaps trying to keep some shreds of dignity and self-respect, David made a foolish fuss about getting two servants released from the Army. Vitriolic cables shot back and forth. Britain was expecting to be invaded any day, but there was a long wrangle about how the Windsors were to get to Nassau – the obvious way, via America, was not allowed. Finally, as a representative of the Crown that refused to grant his wife a five-minute audience, the Duke of Windsor sailed from Lisbon on the ss *Excalibur* on 1 August, the ship having been re-routed and insured at a cost of $17,500.

There are worse places to spend a war than the Bahamas. At least David thought that Wallis, as the Governor's wife, would have equal status with him and that – however trivial it may seem – is what mattered. But he had underestimated his persecutors. Senior Government House officials in Nassau had already received a message from the Lord Chamberlain: 'You are no doubt aware that a lady when presented to HRH the Duke of Windsor should make a half-curtsey. The Duchess of Windsor is not entitled to this. The Duke should be addressed as "Your Royal Highness", and the Duchess as "Your Grace".'[19] The Bahamas, as far as the Windsors were concerned, were the uttermost ends of the earth; even so, they were not to be let off the hook, even though the Battle of Britain was said to be exclusively taking up Their Majesties' energies.

Nassau was hot, uncomfortable, and deadly dull. There was time to brood on it all. David wrote long letters in which he protested bitterly about the continuation of 'the mean and petty humiliations in which a now semi-Royal Family' – a direct and snobbish dig at Elizabeth – 'with the co-operation of the Government has indulged itself for the last four years'.[20] Possibly the letters were never sent, but they relieved his misery and anger a little. He did his job competently, even well, but it was not what he had been trained for. His long experience enabled him to put a royal face on it, but as a man he was crumbling.

David heard the news of his brother George's death on the Empire Service of the BBC;[21] telegrams from Queen Mary and Lord Halifax followed, but nothing, as far as we know, from Balmoral. It was a knockout blow. He had supported Georgie through all the early scandals; they understood each other's deviations from the royal norm; their devotion to each other had withstood David's abdication and marriage, even if there had been some tricky moments when George's loyalty had seemed questionable. The fact that they had not been allowed to meet either in Portugal or America added intense bitterness to David's misery. He wanted to share in the grief of his family, but he had no family. He plunged into the darkest depression, and although this lifted with time, it left a permanent sense of deprivation. There was no substitute for his relationship with George, any more than there could be a substitute for Wallis.

Like his brothers, David had never been what is known as a 'strong' character, and he had even less grasp of reality. His best qualities were a naïve, almost childish goodwill, enormous energy and a unique talent for being loved. After George's death, inconsolable, stripped of his confidence, under ceaseless pressure from home, all these qualities began slowly to disintegrate until finally, as an old man, he seemed little more than an empty husk.

Wallis, too, in spite of her efficient work with the Red Cross and Infant Welfare Clinics and her successful efforts to keep up appearances, began to suffer 'an evident moral and physical decline'[22] that would continue for the next thirty years, a long, painful deterioration. Her letters to Aunt Bessie became increasingly agitated and indecipherable – some RAF officers were leaving, 'one hopes there will be more adonises and Don Juans in the new lot'. She was approaching fifty, and in constant pain from various abdominal troubles. The brisk, funny, odd-looking Wallis Simpson, who had coped so admirably with her unlooked-for role in the Abdication, was, by the end of the war, unrecognizable to anyone but her love-blinded husband.

The Duke of Windsor resigned his Governorship on 16 March 1945 and sailed for the United States with Wallis on 3 May. On VE Day they were in Palm Beach, and on 15 September they left for Europe on the U.S. troopship *Argentina*. It called at Plymouth *en route* for Le Havre but the Windsors did not disembark. They appeared on deck and waved at the crowds in the best balcony tradition; David told reporters that, yes, he would very much like a job. On 5 October he flew from Paris to London and, at last, stayed with his mother at Marlborough House – 'at 4 *David* arrived by plane from Paris on a visit to me – I had not seen him for nearly 9 years! it was a great joy meeting him again, he looked very well – Bertie came to dinner to meet him.'[23] On Sunday he went to see Bertie alone, a meeting that seems to have given him much encouragement, for he wrote shortly afterwards from Paris:

Dear Bertie, I was very glad to see you in London after so long an interval and to find you looking so well and vigorous after the strain of the last six years of total war . . . don't forget that I have suffered many unnecessary embarrassments from official sources uncomplainingly in the last nine years, *but I have reason to believe from the spirit of your recent two long talks with me that it is now your desire that these should cease* [My italics].

The truth of the whole matter is that you and I happen to be two prominent personages placed in one of the most unique situations in history, the dignified handling of which is entirely yours and my responsibility, and ours alone. It is a situation from which we cannot escape and one that will always be watched with interest by the whole world. I can see no reason why we should not be able to handle it in the best interests of both of us, and I can only assure you that I will continue to play my part to this end . . .[24]

Bertie did not reply for a month. When he did so, it was to the effect that there was no question of official work for his brother in peacetime, but that everything would be done to facilitate any plans he might have to leave Europe for good and spend the rest of his life in America.

PART FOUR

CHAPTER

29

On 2 August 1945, three months after the end of the European war, Bertie met President Truman on board the battlecruiser *Renown* in Plymouth Sound. Most of the conversation, over a merry lunch, was concerned with the use of the atom bomb. 'It sounds like a professor's dream to me,' growled Admiral Leahy. Bertie, twinkling, replied, 'Would you like to lay a little bet on that, Admiral?'[1]

Four days later Hiroshima, and 200,000 of its citizens, disappeared in a mushroom cloud. Three days after that 150,000 people were wiped out in Nagasaki. Japan surrendered. Services of National Thanksgiving had already been held in St Paul's and St Giles' Cathedrals for the defeat of Germany; there was no point in being effusive, and God received no official thanks for this latest miracle.

A new method of waging war brought with it a new method of conducting peace. The keynote from now on would not be prosperity or equality or the advancement of civilization or having a nice time, but survival. It was, from the word go, extremely dreary.

Anyone who remembers the late Forties and Fifties will recall that everything seemed sludge-coloured. People moved about with a sort of weary caution in clothes which looked as though they had been made out of something else, and frequently were – skirts out of curtains, trousers out of overcoats, nameless garments out of dishcloths and old ribbon. Bread was rationed for the first time in 1946, taxation went up. The Labour Government was in again, showing, Bertie and Elizabeth thought, the country's gross ingratitude to Churchill, and by September 1947 the King was writing to his mother, 'I do wish one could see a glimmer of a bright spot anywhere in world affairs. Never in the whole history of mankind have things looked gloomier than they do now...'[2]

Bertie was, as we know, inclined to look on the black side. What about Elizabeth? David Duff describes her as she appeared in 1946: 'A happy little woman who might easily break into "Lily of Laguna" at breakfast time or while away a motor drive with "Daisy, Daisy" ... Eating what she liked, regardless of her figure. A lover of sweets. A woman who ... referred to her Hartnell creations as "my props" ...

A non-photogenic woman . . . A woman whose courage and love had helped to cure the King's impediment. A woman with a dog. Not smart, not sporty . . . A woman who knew that change was coming, and went with the tide. The woman who knew, when she married "Bertie", that a wife could make or mar him. The woman who had made "Bertie".'[3]

It is a reasonably convincing description of the Queen who bore the family off to Balmoral in the summer of 1945, determined that they should enjoy themselves. It was an indifferent year for grouse, so the King and his party, which included Lilibet, set off on a sort of lethal treasure hunt to see how many sorts of wildlife could be shot or caught. They ended up with nineteen varieties, including one mountain hare, two capercailzie, a heron, a sparrow hawk, three rabbits, one roedeer, six ptarmigan and a stag, which was felled by Lilibet. Meanwhile Lord Eldon, whose friendship with Elizabeth went back to the old Glamis days, was detailed to collect fish; he got two salmon and, after being rowed up and down the loch for two hours by 'one of the ladies', a few small brown trout.[4] In spite of the economic depression and the bewildering lack of any spoils of war it was, Bertie recorded in his game book, 'a lovely day'.

On 2 January 1946 Clara, after four decades of service to the family, died at Sandringham. She was taken to St Paul's Walden Bury where all her various charges, from the middle-aged Elizabeth to the fifteen-year-old Margaret, attended her funeral. 'In loving and thankful memory – Elizabeth R.' was the message attached to the wreath of violets on her coffin.[5]

Shortly after this sad occasion Lady Airlie went to Sandringham for the first time in six years and found many changes.

> In the entrance hall there now stood a baize-covered table on which jigsaw puzzles were set out. The younger members of the party – the Princesses . . . and several young Guardsmen – congregated round them from morning till night. The radio, worked by Princess Elizabeth, blared incessantly . . . One sensed far more the setting of ordinary family life . . . It was in the way in which the King said, 'You must ask Mummy' when his daughters wanted to do something . . . In Princess Margaret's pout when the Queen sent her back to the house to put on a thicker coat . . . In the way both sisters teased, and were teased by, the young Guardsmen to whom Queen Mary referred when we were alone together as 'The Body Guard'.[6]

After six years of being cloistered at Windsor, Elizabeth's daughters were making the most of their freedom – though freedom is, of course, relative, and the most they could make of it was to do jigsaw puzzles and flirt with a carefully selected group of officers and shoot the odd stag. Lilibet, however, had an advantage over her sister: a regular *beau*. 'They have been in love for the last eighteen months,'

Queen Mary told Lady Airlie in strictest confidence. 'In fact longer, I think. I believe she fell in love with him the first time he went down to Windsor, but the King and Queen feel that she is too young to be engaged yet. They want her to see more of the world before committing herself, and to meet more men. After all she's only nineteen, and one is very impressionable at that age.'[7] Whatever his other merits, Prince Philip of Greece was dazzlingly handsome at that time. Unfortunately, however, he was not only a Greek national, but sixth in succession to the Greek throne, the whereabouts of which, at the time, were far from clear.

Philip had spent much of his early life in England and was sent to Cheam preparatory school in Surrey when he was nine years old. Two years later he had a short period at Kurt Hahn's Salem school on Lake Constance. Hahn was arrested by the Nazis, released after a direct appeal from Ramsay Macdonald to President Hindenburg and came over to start Gordonstoun in Scotland on the same spartan and high-minded principles as Salem. Philip was there for four years before he joined the British Navy in 1939. With the invasion of Greece by Italy in 1940 he became an ally and was transferred from convoy duty to active service under the temporary Defence Regulations of 1939. If he wished to have a permanent commission in the Navy, let alone marry the Heir Apparent, he would have to become a British subject. His cousin, King George II, had given his permission; but his cousin was in Cairo, and no one knew whether he would ever return to the Greek throne. If Philip were given British citizenship it might be thought that Britain was supporting the Royalist cause; on the other hand, it might look as though the prospects for the Greek monarchy were so bad that members of the Greek Royal House were leaving a sinking ship. Bertie had therefore been advised that it would be wiser to postpone the question of Philip's naturalization until after the Greek plebiscite on the monarchy had taken place in March 1946.

The plebiscite resulted in a declaration calling on George II to return to Athens. Good news, one might think; but no, there was now a further complication. If Philip, as a Greek royal in direct succession to the throne, were to renounce his nationality immediately after the restoration, it would be very unhelpful to the Greek King's cause. The best thing, again, was to wait.

When a suitable time had passed, the problem was tackled once more. What would the young man be called? He himself decided on 'Lieutenant Philip – R.N.' Excellent, but Lieutenant Philip what? The Royal House of Greece and Denmark had no family name – it had never been considered necessary – so something must be invented. What about 'Oldcastle'? Well, it was an anglicization of 'Oldenburg', and that had been the original name of the House of Schleswig-

Holstein-Sonderburg-Glucksburg. Perhaps not. What about 'Batten-berg', then, already translated into 'Mountbatten'? Splendid. The announcement that Lt Philip Mountbatten R.N. had taken British citizenship was at last made in the *London Gazette* of 18 March 1947, at which time his intended fiancée was in South Africa with her family.

★　　　★　　　★

The South African trip of February 1947 was intended primarily for the opening of the Union Parliament in Cape Town, but it also provided a change for the family after the rigours of war and a breathing space for Lilibet who might, even now, change her mind. It was an unfortunate coincidence that conditions in Britain were at their worst. Sixteen degrees of frost were recorded in London. Iceburgs were observed off the Norfolk Coast. Trains stopped running and froze to their sidings, power stations ran out of coal, there was no electric power for many industries, the export rate was nil. Unemployment rose to 2½ million, cattle and sheep died in their thousands, old people and children in their hundreds. As the entire Royal Family, with an accompanying entourage of ten courtiers, slipped away from Portsmouth in the *Vanguard*, claims of 'We Stay With Our People', 'We Are Not Afraid', had a distinctly hollow ring. It was all very well to share their sufferings in spirit, but the people felt that their King and Queen should be at home, tripping through 14-foot snowdrifts, looking the power cuts in the face.

So, of course, did Bertie. On their arrival at Cape Town one of the first things he did was to cable Prime Minister Attlee expressing Their Majesties' 'sympathy with the people of Britain and their earnest hope for an early alleviation of their present hardships'.[8] In spite of this reassurance, reports of criticism continued to arrive. Attlee felt that it would be bad for morale to curtail the tour, as Bertie had anxiously suggested, especially in the eyes of foreign observers. There was nothing for it, then, but to face the sunshine with courage.

The tour, like all tours, was hailed as a triumphant success. 'At Paarl', Peter Townsend, the King's equerry, wrote, '. . . laughing boys and girls, cool and clean and sunburnt, their fair hair blown by the wind, cheered them through the streets'.[9] In the Rand, 'hundreds of thousands of sweating, screaming, frenzied blacks lined the route . . . and hollered their ecstatic joy at the sight of this little family of four, so fresh and white . . .'[10] As they drove into Benoni Elizabeth smartly attacked 'a black and wiry assailant' with her parasol, breaking it in two. It later emerged that the 'assailant' had simply wanted to give Lilibet a 10/- note for her birthday. 'I hope he was not too badly hurt,' Bertie said kindly.[11]

The Press accompanied them in the aptly named White Train;

among the usual royalty-followers was a rather bemused James Cameron:

> The King kept saying he should be at home and not lolling about in the summer sun; never was a man so jumpy . . . One evening he called some of us Press people along to his dining car, ostensibly because he had a communication to make, but more probably to relieve the deadly boredom . . . We found him behind a table covered with bottles of all sorts of things, with which it would seem he had been experimenting, with some dedication. 'We must not f-forget the purpose of this t-tour,' he said . . . 'trade and so on. Empire cooperation. For example. South African b-brandy. I have been trying it. It is of course m-magnificent, except that it is not very nice. But,' he said triumphantly, 'there is this South African liqueur called V-Van der Humm. Perhaps a little sweet for most. But, now, if you mix half of brandy with half of Van der Humm . . . Please try.

The Pressmen obediently tried, and a hundred or so miles of South Africa passed very pleasantly.

When the train stopped at some wayside halt (the organizers had learned the lesson of Canada), Elizabeth would entreat her agonized husband, 'Oh, Bertie, do you see, this is Hicksdorp! You know we've always wanted to see Hicksdorp! Those people there with the bouquets – they must be the local councillors. *How* kind! And those people at the far, far end of the platform, behind that little fence – I expect they are the Bantu choir. How kind! We must wave, Bertie.' And with a little nudge, the King found himself on terra firma, clearly wishing he were anywhere else on earth, with his wife just as clearly having waited all her life to see Hicksdorp.'[12]

Sometimes, however, the King commanded the train to stop, simply so that he could have a swim. One evening, Cameron remembers, it drew to a halt on the verge of a broad beach near Port Elizabeth. Police appeared on the sands and roped off the vast crowd of onlookers into two halves. 'Down the path from the Royal Train walked a solitary figure in a blue bathrobe, carrying a towel. The sea was a long way off, but he went. And all alone, on the great empty beach, between the surging banks of the people who might not approach, the King of England stepped into the edge of the Indian Ocean and jumped up and down – the loneliest man, at that moment, in the world.'[13]

The Princesses, meanwhile, had horses waiting for them. With Townsend as protector, they galloped along the sands or across the veldt, Lilibet 'competent and classic', Margaret 'pretty and dashing', until Peter beat them by a neck back to the train. Margaret's parents must have known that she had 'a terrific crush'[14] on Bertie's equerry, but they didn't take it seriously. He was nearer her mother's age than Margaret's, a married man, father of a baby son, a thoroughly decent sort, and they were both very fond of him. It was 'rather sweet' that their own sixteen-year-old baby worshipped him – just like a big brother. They returned to England to face the infinitely more significant and complex problem of Lilibet's marriage.

Philip had been invited to Balmoral for a month the previous summer so that they might assess his character, behaviour, habits and prospects. Bertie may secretly have hoped to find him lacking. He passed the test, but certainly not for his ease of expression. Thanks to Basil Boothroyd, we have the story of the courtship in Philip's own words. It is by no means a romantic account and ends, 'I suppose one thing led to another. I suppose I began to think about it seriously, oh, let me think now, when I got back in 'forty-six and went to Balmoral. It was probably then that we, that it became, you know, that we began to think about it seriously and even talk about it. And then there was their excursion to South Africa, and it was sort of fixed up when they came back. That's what really happened.'[15]

On 10 July 1947 an announcement was made from Buckingham Palace that Their Majesties' daughter, the Princess Elizabeth, was betrothed to Lieutenant Philip Mountbatten R.N., son of the late Prince Andrew of Greece and Princess Andrew. On 4 October Philip was received by Geoffrey Fisher, Archbishop of Canterbury, into the Church of England. ('I talked to my beloved old Archbishop Germanos, the representative of the Oecumenical Patriarch in England, a grand man,' recalled Archbishop Fisher. 'He saw the point.')[16] And on 20 November at Westminster Abbey, the couple were married. The bride, it was announced, had been allotted a hundred extra clothing coupons for her trousseau and her bridesmaids twenty-three each. Her mother, playing this role for the first time, was barely mentioned. Chips Channon was rather off-hand about the whole thing, since he had not been 'commanded'. He did, however, go to the reception at St James's Palace to view the wedding presents, which he thought, apart from his own, Queen Mary's and the Nizam of Hyderabad's, 'ghastly'.[17] *Plus ça change...*

★   ★   ★

Bertie, whatever his opinion of Philip, was as miserable about Lilibet's marriage as his father had been about Princess Mary's. Perhaps it says something about royal marriages in general; or, more likely, the relationship of Sovereigns to their daughters. Queen Victoria had much preferred her daughters to her sons, and their wedding festivities had all the sprightliness of funerals. King Edward VII didn't seem to suffer from this intense possessiveness, but his wife did. 'Alix found them such companions,' he explained to his mother, 'that she would not encourage their marrying, and ... they themselves had no inclination for it.'[18] Perhaps this is a common phenomenon, but the isolation that royalty imposes on itself is not common, and Bertie had found a friend in his twenty-one-year-old daughter; they were very alike; practical, conscientious and pessimistic. Margaret, and Elizabeth at her best, were what Queen Mary called 'espiègle' – mischievous, roguish, arch, perpetually playing games. He was going to miss Lilibet dreadfully. 'I was so proud of you & thrilled at having you so close to me on our long walk in Westminster Abbey, but when I handed your hand to the Archbishop I felt that I had lost something very precious,' he wrote in one of those customary, blighting honeymoon letters.

> . . . I am so glad you wrote & told Mummy that you think the long wait before your engagement & the long time before the wedding was for the best. I was rather afraid that you had thought I was being hard hearted about it . . . Our family, us four, the 'Royal Family' must remain together with additions of course at suitable moments! I have watched you grow up all these years with pride under the skilful direction of Mummy, who as you know is the most marvellous person in the World in my eyes . . . Your leaving has left a great blank in our lives but do remember that your old home is still yours & do come back to it as much & as often as possible. I can see that you are sublimely happy with Philip which is right but don't forget us is the wish of Your ever loving & devoted Papa.[19]

Lilibet, in fact, was never to forget her priorities. The family was, and would always remain, a family of four; the only peripheral additions would be royal grandchildren. 'We keep wondering whether Philip realizes what he's in for,'[20] Bertie had been heard to say at a cocktail party that autumn. So, perhaps, did Philip.

What was Elizabeth's attitude towards her daughter's marriage? On the face of it they had little in common. Lilibet was a chip off the old block – the Duke of Devonshire told James Lees-Milne that 'she is just like the young Queen Victoria with the old Queen's sagacity. She makes it very plain to the Queen [her mother] that whereas she, the Queen, is a commoner, she, Princess Elizabeth, is of royal blood.'[21] If it was necessary for Elizabeth to think primarily of her husband as her King – which according to her mother-in-law it was – then presumably it was equally necessary to think of Lilibet as the Heir Apparent. From that point of view, Philip seemed as suitable, in his way, as Albert had seemed to Victoria, Duchess of Kent (not that the Duchess had much say in the matter). Lilibet and Philip were third cousins through the lineage of Queen Victoria, second cousins once removed through Christian IX of Denmark, and fourth cousins once removed through collateral descendants of George III. Therefore as Prince and Princess they were clearly made for each other.

As a man, he was possibly a little philistine for Elizabeth's taste.

Like young Margaret, she preferred a lean and hungry look, a hint of sensitivity, a touch of rumpled charm. Philip's family, too, presented difficulties. She did not altogether trust the Mountbattens, and Philip's mother, *née* Princess Alice of Battenberg – at one time running neck and neck with Queen Wilhelmina as 'the prettiest princess in Europe' – was definitely odd. A wonderful woman, of course; but odd. Elizabeth, in her baby-blue, with her lilting voice and winsome ways and rippling giggle, was indeed a remarkable contrast to the gaunt, sombre Greek princess in her nun's habit. Twenty years later, when Lilibet was Queen, Alice would make her home in Buckingham Palace where, according to Lord Louis Mountbatten, she had more influence on the Queen than anyone. 'The Queen adored her . . . she is fond of her mother, but got on infinitely better with my sister.'[22] As Elizabeth waved goodbye to her daughter and son-in-law on their way to honeymoon at Uncle Dickie's country estate she was aware that having Mountbattens in the family was not going to be easy.

CHAPTER

30

Apparently forgetting the disaster of White Lodge, Bertie and Elizabeth had chosen Clarence House as a suitable residence for their daughter and son-in-law, who thought it dilapidated and uninhabitable. The Government voted £50,000 for its repair since, as Alexandra of Yugoslavia said, 'even a nation in economic difficulties was not willing to see its heiress presumptive [sic] and her husband housed indefinitely in three rooms in the Palace'.[1] This wasn't strictly the case, as Bertie had also given them Sunninghill Park, near Ascot, for a country retreat. For some curious reason, never disclosed, this burned down while they were on honeymoon. 'Oh, Crawfie, how *could* it have happened?' Lilibet is reputed to have written to her ex-governess. 'Do you really think someone did it on purpose. I can't believe it. People are always so kind to us. I don't for one moment believe it was the squatters.'[2]

Bertie gave them Windlesham Moor in Berkshire to make up for it. In any case Lilibet was going to join Philip in Malta very shortly, where Uncle Dickie would lend them his own luxurious villa. It was no doubt unsettling in the meanwhile not having a permanent London roof over their heads. On the evening of Their Majesties' Silver Jubilee on 26 April 1948 Elizabeth broadcast to her people: '. . . at this time my heart goes out to all those who are living in uncongenial surroundings and who are longing for a time when they will have a home of their own. I am sure that patience, tolerance and love will help them to keep their faith undimmed and their courage undaunted when things seem difficult.'[3]

Unfortunately patience, tolerance and love were not, as Elizabeth herself should have known, inexhaustible. The occasional grumble became more frequent, making itself heard in the strangest places. Many of the old aristocracy disapproved of Mountbatten for 'giving away' India; they had never thought very highly of the 'new' royal family anyway. Even the labourers of Somersetshire, on whose uncritical loyalty the Throne depended, were feeling disgruntled. The loss of India diminished the romance and dignity of the Crown. Where, after all, had their support got them? They were worse off

217

than before – rationed, cold, frequently homeless, and without even an Empire to boast about. The independence of India and Pakistan was declared on 15 August 1947 and that day Lord Listowel, ex-Secretary of State for India, delivered up his seal of office to the ex-Emperor at Balmoral. In return Bertie asked if he could have the flag from the Lucknow Residency as a souvenir of the Empire he had never seen.[4] Queen Mary wrote on the back of the envelope containing her son's latest letter, 'The first time Bertie wrote me a letter with the I for Emperor of India left out, very sad,'[5] and filed it away with the others.

★ ★ ★

At the beginning of 1948 Bertie complained to Elizabeth of an odd sort of cramp in his legs. Too much sitting at his desk, no doubt. Lilibet and Philip were still living at the Palace during the week, so his fears of losing her were calmed for the moment, and Margaret had a crowd of new friends who brightened the place up, even if they did make an awful row. Lilibet was pregnant, and Elizabeth responding charmingly to the inevitable cries of 'I can't *believe* you're going to be a grandmother!' Bertie could well believe he was going to be a grandfather. At the age of fifty-two, he felt old and tired.

Still, there were compensations. Elizabeth's feeling was that they could relax their vigilance a little now the war was over, and although they still had nothing to do with the old 'smart Set' (Lady Cunard, poor old thing, died that summer) they were seen out and about more often, enjoying the invasion of American entertainers like Danny Kaye and Frank Sinatra. Mae West, too, was in England and Bertie might well have enjoyed meeting her; unfortunately she was snapped up by Mrs Sacheverell Sitwell, who invited Lady Cunard (before her demise) to her party, so Miss West was sadly beyond the pale. Princess Marina, however, attended, in spite of Queen Mary's instructions twelve years ago. Marina, poor dear, was still a little difficult.

Both parents were delighted to see Margaret taking her responsibilities seriously, as well as having a lot of healthy fun. In the autumn of 1947 she had flown to Belfast to launch a new liner. On being presented with a bouquet of roses by a young sailor, she immediately plucked one out and presented it to him – just like her mother. A year later she did very well at the Investiture of Crown Princess Juliana as Queen of the Netherlands, supported in Amsterdam by the Duke of Beaufort, Princess Alice, Countess of Athlone and dear Peter Townsend. Her chief *beau* seemed to be 'Sunny', Marquess of Blandford – or was it Johnny, Earl of Dalkeith? Anyway, there was safety in numbers. Young Porchester, Peter Ward, Colin Tennant, Angus Ogilvy, Simon Phipps, Dominic Elliot, Billy Wallace – it was quite hard to keep track.

In October 1942 Mrs Roosevelt had been over to England to see for herself the role that British women were playing in the war. The three British women with whom she had come into closest contact had been Elizabeth, Queen Mary and Mrs Churchill. She had got on very well with the last, but her visits to the first two had been quite a strain. At Buckingham Palace she had been given Elizabeth's bedroom, the windows patched up with wooden frames and isinglass; the almost inedible wartime food had been served on gold and silver plates and after dinner they all had to sit down and watch Noel Coward's *In Which We Serve*, wrapped in every available fur and woolly. At Badminton she almost froze to death and conducted a difficult conversation with Queen Mary, who had retired to bed as the only place where she could keep warm. Impressed though Mrs Roosevelt was with their fortitude, she had caught a terrible cold and earned a scolding from her aunt for 'using those nasty little tissues and wadding them in your hand while the King used such lovely sheer linen handkerchiefs'.[6] All in all, it had been a great relief to get back to Washington.

In the spring of 1948, now a widow, Mrs Roosevelt ventured to England again. This time she stayed at Windsor and found the conditions, though far more comfortable, almost equally strange. At dinner a kilted Highlander marched round the table playing the bagpipes and 'there was, of course, much formality'. She had been reassured earlier in the day by the normal family atmosphere – Margaret and her friends playing the gramophone too loud and being yelled at by Bertie to turn it down, Elizabeth's 'skill . . . in keeping their family life on a warm friendly level' – but after dinner they were all commanded to play 'The Game – a form of charades. Queen Elizabeth acted as a kind of master of ceremonies . . . She puzzled for some time over various words and occasionally turned to Mr Churchill for assistance, but without success. The former Prime Minister, with a decoration on the bosom of his stiff white shirt and a cigar in his hand, sat glumly aside and would have nothing to do with The Game.'[7] Chips Channon, ear to the ground, reported that 'the house party . . . became quite childish with the Queen wearing a beard etc. A wonderful scene it must have been. Mrs Roosevelt was exhausted.'

Perhaps it was reaction from the war, perhaps it was 'her age' or the company of her youngest daughter's friends or the prospect of becoming a grandmother, but Elizabeth certainly seemed to be becoming sillier – or, as Chips Channon phrased it, more 'slack'.[8] She still, of course, presented the public image, making the right speeches in the right places and appearing eagerly interested in the poor and the deprived, but there was more than a hint that after all those years of effort she was out to have a good time. And very good luck to her.

Unfortunately it all went sadly wrong.

In July 1948 they all went into their customary residence at Holy-roodhouse in Edinburgh, where Margaret took ghoulish pleasure in showing Townsend the very spot where Rizzio, Mary Queen of Scots' rather too intimate secretary, had been stabbed to death. One evening Townsend went for a walk with the King up to Arthur's Seat. Normally, the younger man had a job to keep up with that long, dogged stride, but that evening Bertie was clearly in difficulties. 'What's the matter with my blasted legs?' he kept muttering. 'They won't work properly!'[9] By August, Elizabeth knew that her husband was in discomfort most of the time. By October, when they got back to London, his left foot was numb all day and the pain keeping him awake at night. The trouble moved to his right foot, and Elizabeth insisted on calling in Sir Morton Smart, Manipulative Surgeon to the King. Smart was gravely alarmed and requested the second opinion of Sir Maurice Cassidy, the King's general medical adviser. Ten days later both these gentlemen examined him, and also took the opinion of Sir Thomas Dunhill, Serjeant-Surgeon to the King. Their unanimous opinion was that Professor James Learmonth, Regius Professor of Clinical Surgery at Edinburgh, should be consulted. On 12 November Learmonth's examination disclosed early arteriosclerosis, with a danger of developing gangrene. He feared that the King's right leg might have to be amputated.

None of this, apparently, was disclosed to Lilibet on the grounds that it might distress her during her pregnancy. Possibly she thought that her mother's unnaturally glum face was due to her own condition, or to some tactless remark of Philip's, or worry about 'Sunny' Blandford. On the evening of 14 November she was moved into 'the delivery room', which had once been her nursery. Philip changed into flannels and a roll-neck sweater and went off with Michael Parker for a game of squash.[10] Shortly afterward, he received the message that Lilibet had given birth to a boy.

The Palace was in a frenzy. Twelve temporary typists had to be hired to acknowledge the sacks full of letters and presents. Philip rushed about with champagne and bunches of roses, Queen Mary noted the child's remarkable resemblance to the Prince Consort. Elizabeth hurried from husband to daughter to grandson. The doctors issued a bulletin saying that the King was suffering from an obstruction to the circulation through the arteries of the legs and that complete rest and treatment to improve the circulation must be maintained for an immediate and prolonged period, adding that 'there is no doubt that the strain of the last twelve years has appreciably affected his resistance to physical fatigue'.* Nobody mentioned then or later that he had been an exceptionally sickly child or that he had been a chain-smoker for the whole of his adult life. Elizabeth, refusing to believe in the will of God, needed something or someone to blame: she decided on Wallis Windsor. If Wallis had not 'blown in from Baltimore', Bertie would have been perfectly healthy. Perhaps this fantasy helped her to deal with her own anxiety and Bertie's impatience.

He tried hard to be philosophical, but after a fortnight of inactivity told his mother that he was 'getting tired & bored with bed as I am feeling so much more rested which is a good thing'.[11] A fortnight later he was present and correct at his grandson's christening. One of the official photographs of the occasion shows him looking ill and haggard, standing between David Bowes-Lyon and Philip; both Margaret and Queen Mary appear to be in a bad temper and only Lilibet wears a delighted grin. Charles Philip Arthur George, dressed like a bishop, sleeps soundly in a sort of side-saddle position on his mother's knee. Where was Elizabeth? The absence of coquettish grandma, with her talent for looking so pleased with herself and life, gives a sudden realization of what the Royal Family would have been without her – dignified, honourable, and definitely stodgy. Five days later a Dr Jacob Snowman, then in his eighties, made the long trek from Hampstead to circumcise the baby,[12] an event as baffling to contemplate as it must have been for Charles to experience.

* Brigadier Stanley Clark OBE, whose dates in his *Palace Diary* are at variance with John Wheeler-Bennett's, says that the King at this point was diagnosed as having Buerger's Disease: an inflammatory or toxic condition which attacks the arteries and veins in a limb, generally in young men; also known as thrombo-angiitis. It is associated with heavy smoking and often leads to gangrene. Treatment takes the form of exercises to improve the circulation in the affected limb. (RD *Medical Encyclopaedia* 1975).

CHAPTER
31

It is no use, in hindsight, pretending that Bertie's health was not the greatest of Elizabeth's concerns for the next three years. At the time, there may have been short periods when she could put it at the back of her mind, think about something else, even feel optimistic; but no amount of burying her head in the sand or pretending it wasn't happening or retiring with some minor indisposition could convince her that her husband was anything but a very ill man. For the first time in her life she had to live with an uncompromising reality, while at the same time condemned by habit to look as though she was constantly enjoying herself. Thousands of women go through this ordeal. The fact that Bertie was King of England, and his health a matter of national concern, made it no easier.

At the beginning of March 1949 the doctors concluded that either the King must continue to lead the life of an invalid, for which he was temperamentally unsuited, or that they must perform a lumbar sympathectomy. There was a right royal row. Bertie shouted and stormed. So all this treament had been a waste of time,[1] why the hell couldn't the bloody quacks learn their business and so on. When he had calmed down a bit it was tentatively suggested that it might be more practical if he went into the Royal Masonic Hospital. 'I suppose I've a good right to go to a Masonic Hospital,' he said, 'but I've never heard of a King going to a hospital before.'[2] Nobody was going to point out to him that it was high time he did. A complete surgical unit was established in the Palace. The operation was stated to have been successful and newsboys scrawled on their placards a terse, cheerful message: 'He's all right.'

Professor Learmonth said rather obscurely that 'the problem was both psychological and physical' and that Bertie would have to take it easy. On his final visit before leaving his patient in Elizabeth's charge he was perhaps alarmed when the King, after commanding the Professor to hand him his dressing gown and slippers, whipped out a highly polished sword from the bedclothes or other place of conceal-ment, chuckling maliciously, 'You used a knife on me, now I'm going to use one on you.'[3] Before he knew where he was, the Professor had become a knight. He was much relieved and honoured.

Elizabeth, trying to keep Bertie quiet in the intervals between having tea with old ladies in council flats and looking at portraits of war leaders, being seen at serious theatre like *The Wild Duck* (Margaret went to see *Harvey* that night, lucky girl) and smiling at the photographers as she came and went, was under considerable pressure. Fuss about the repairs of Clarence House – made of course by those tiresome Labour people – helped nobody. Lilibet was so excited about everything Philip was doing there. He had studied all the plans with the Ministry of Works architects and told them exactly where they had gone wrong and how it should be put right. Canada had given them the white maple panelling for Philip's study and the City of Glasgow had presented them with all the white sycamore wall fitments for his bedroom. Lilibet herself had mixed the paint to get exactly the right shade for the apple-green walls of the dining room, and Philip had cleverly found someone to make the carved and gilded light brackets which looked for all the world as though they were genuine George III.[4] How could the House of Commons claim that they had spent £250,000 on it, instead of the £50,000 they had been given? True, the Ministry of Works did say that the work would exceed the estimate by 10 per cent, but Philip said that always happened with estimates, and Philip was simply furious with the secretary of the London District Committee of the Amalgamated Society of Woodworkers, who had more or less told those lazy carpenters to go on strike.[5] After all, she and Philip only had £50,000 a year between them – Philip's share of that was shockingly small – and they now had a baby to consider. What were they supposed to do? Commute from Windlesham on the Southern Railway?

By the early summer of 1949 Bertie's condition had improved. The Edinburgh family had survived their troubles and were about to move to Clarence House. Margaret was in high spirits after a European Grand Tour which left the *paparazzi* exhausted. It was time, Elizabeth thought, to show the country that the royal family were not downhearted. In June a memorable ball was held at Windsor to which – there being no problem about Lady Cunard – almost everyone who was anyone came. The rooms were banked with flowers, the chandeliers winked down on diamonds, every woman had a new gown and the men were swathed and studded with honours. After the guests had waited for about twenty minutes the doors were flung open to reveal the King and Queen. 'He seemed brown,' Channon recorded – Bertie had started using heavy makeup to disguise his pallor – 'and she, though unfortunately very, very plump, looked magnificent in a white satin semi-crinoline number, with the Garter and splendid rubies ... Mrs Greville's, I suppose.'[6] The King rested his foot on a stool when he was not dancing. Elizabeth was indefatigable, and allowed Maurice Winnick's band to go on playing until a quarter to five in the morning. Everyone was enchanted with the evening.

Meanwhile the meat ration was reduced to one shilling's worth per person a week and the sugar ration to eight ounces. Bertie, who cared about such things, was plunged into renewed gloom at the prospect of having to deal with another crisis. Balmoral restored his spirits. He improvised a harness with a long trace attached to a pony, so that he could be pulled up hills – it had, of course, a quick-release mechanism in case the pony bolted. In his broadcast from Sandringham that Christmas, he said, 'None of us can be satisfied till we are again standing upright and supporting our own weight and we have a long way to go before we can do that.' Only the most insensitive listener could have thought – as Bertie did – that he was talking about economic aid from America.

★   ★   ★

The General Election of 23 February 1950 brought the Labour Government back with a majority of eight. The King was in a ferment of worry about what he should advise, encourage or warn Clement Attlee to do or not to do if he asked for a Dissolution, but luckily, on Churchill's advice, he didn't. Lilibet was sailing round the Mediterranean in HMS *Surprise*, escorted by Philip in *Magpie* – a cruise only loosely connected with his command in the Navy but never mind, the poor darlings had never had any fun yet. 'Princess full of beans,' *Surprise* would signal to *Magpie* and *Magpie* would signal back, 'Is that the best you can give her for breakfast?'[7] Do listen to this, Bertie, *such* fun, what a blessing he has a sense of humour.

The next blessing was a granddaughter, Anne Elizabeth Alice Louise, born at Clarence House on 15 August. Bertie was alone at Balmoral, worrying about Korea and the deteriorating relationship between his country and America. If only Roosevelt were still alive he could have telephoned him and asked how things were at Hyde Park before mentioning that it might be helpful if America resisted blowing up the world. As it was he felt as useless as he had done in 1940. In November Lilibet went off to join Philip in Malta, leaving the children in the charge of their grandparents. 'Like the wife of any naval officer,' said the Press, 'she is joining her husband on his station.' It was also mentioned that she had sent out her car, forty large cases of clothes and personal effects and a new polo pony for Philip.[8] Bertie missed her bitterly.

The last straw in 1950 was when the Stone of Scone was stolen from Westminster Abbey on Christmas Eve. It had been safely stowed away under the Coronation Throne for six and a half centuries and was, to Bertie, a sacred object. At least this was one occasion when he could make himself heard. Majestic edicts were sent out and all jokes about the heinous crime were cut from radio programmes and variety shows – even *Take It From Here*, Their Majesties' favourite listening, was censored.

Elizabeth also had reasons for distress. She heard that her nephew Timothy, 16th Earl of Strathmore, was opening Glamis to the public, charging 2/- entrance fee, and selling off thousands of acres of family property. She herself had actually been criticized. Some dreadful Sunday rag – which nobody read, one hoped – had been deliberately insulting about her appearance at the Somerset-Thynne wedding: 'Her hat is too large, too heavy and too drooping . . . the pattern of the dress would be better on a furnishing fabric, the skimpy cape is both broadening and shortening, the dark edging makes the dress look like a dressing-gown with the sash undone, the gloves are too heavy-looking and add unnecessary bulk to the figure and peek-a-boo shoes have been considered inelegant for two years.'[9] The King and Queen were not alone in being apprehensive about the future. 'So ends a horrible year with worse to come,' Harold Nicolson wrote in his diary on 31 December 1950. 'It is sad to become old amid such darkness.'[10]

★   ★   ★

On 3 May 1951 Bertie opened the Festival of Britain from the steps of St Paul's. Intended as a commemoration of the Great Exhibition of 1851, to demonstrate British Achievement in the arts, sciences and design, it struck Queen Mary, at least, as 'really extraordinary and very ugly'.[11] Nevertheless she resolutely toured the Dome of Discovery, inspected the sculpture, murals and mobiles by Moore, Hepworth, Piper, Sutherland, Topolski and Epstein, peered up at the Skylon and tested the tree walk. Bertie, the papers said, looked well. In fact he was exhausted. Elizabeth insisted that they should go to Balmoral for a rest, taking only Margaret, Peter Townsend and one lady-in-waiting. She knew Peter's marriage was going through a difficult phase and it would do him good, too, to get away for a week or so.

It was a splendid holiday. 'The sun warmed the scent from the pines,' Townsend remembered nostalgically, 'and the crisp nights were full of stars,'[12] but it wasn't long enough. Bertie went down with 'flu. The doctors found that his left lung was inflamed and put him on penicillin. The King was deeply interested in his own condition and gave a detailed account of it to his mother, explaining the results of his X-rays and the cause of his cough. But as the weeks went by his interest flagged; he was despondent at 'not being able to chuck out the bug'. At the beginning of June eighty-year-old King Haakon came to stay. Bertie being unable to entertain him, Elizabeth met the old man at Westminster pier, took him to the Royal Tournament and laid on a State Banquet at which Lilibet read her father's speech. At Ascot, presumably putting a brave face on it, 'the Queen was in lilac and looked sublime'. Chips 'watched all the real Princesses of the Blood Royal as they kissed and curtsied to her, and really marvelled at her self-possession.'[13] She took Margaret to Ireland to stay with her sister Rose. It was necessary to make people believe that nothing was wrong. Nevertheless, in July Philip was brought home 'on indefinite leave'. The navy lark was over.

At the beginning of August they were back at Balmoral. At first all went well – the weather was good and Bertie could enjoy a full day's shooting. Margaret asked Johnny Dalkeith and Billy Wallace to stay for her twenty-first birthday. One night, when they were making a particularly deafening noise downstairs, Bertie rang for his equerry: 'I . . . found him standing there, a lonely, forlorn figure. In his eyes was that glaring, distressed look which he always had when it seemed that the tribulations of the world had overcome him . . . "Won't those bloody people ever go to bed?"'[14] On the birthday itself he went out with a shooting party that included Philip, Dalkeith and Jack Eldon. They got 300 grouse, some of them not fully grown,[15] but there was a cold wind and the King caught a chill. Elizabeth sent for his doctors, who arrived from London and examined him on 1 September. They insisted that he should go to London for X-rays, so on 7 September he went alone on the overnight train, flying back to Dyce Airport the following day. The first thing he did when he got home was to go to the sand-table model of the moors and ask for every detail of the day's shooting to be explained to him. Elizabeth, anxious to hear the doctor's verdict, had to wait.

The verdict was, in fact, ominous: bronchoscopy for the purpose of removing a portion of tissue from the lung for histological examination. On 14 September he went out with Harry, David Lyon, Eldon, Porchester, Heywood-Lonsdale and Philip, bagged 38 hares, 1 pigeon and a further 302 grouse and took the night train for London. Two days later Elizabeth learned that her husband had cancer.* She flew south with Lilibet and Philip, leaving Margaret and the two grandchildren at Balmoral. Because of the glum crowd staring through the Palace railings they went in through the side gate. An operation for lung resection was arranged for Sunday, 23 September. Early that morning Elizabeth and the family drove to Lambeth Palace to pray with the Archbishop of Canterbury for Bertie's recovery. Bertie, in

* Dorothy Laird writes, 'Those close to Queen Elizabeth – even her own family – were never allowed to know whether she understood the full implications of the doctors' reports upon the King's health.' (*Queen Elizabeth the Queen Mother*, 262). The King himself never knew – or was never told – that he had cancer.

something of the same spirit, gave instructions for three brace of grouse to be delivered to the Duke of Windsor, who was staying in London.★ 'I understand he is fond of grouse,' he said.

The lung resection was performed without a hitch. In the process, however, it was discovered that some of the nerves of the larynx would have to be sacrificed, which might mean that Bertie would never again be able to speak in a normal voice – an appalling prospect. Peter Townsend met the King one day in the corridor outside his room, wearing a blue dressing gown and looking frail and thin. 'He smiled warmly, almost apologetically . . . when he spoke it was not in his firm, deep voice, but in a thin whisper.'[16]

Recovery was slow, but at least there was some good news at last. Lilibet and Philip were having a predictable success on their tour of Canada and the General Election of 25 October brought the Conservatives back. Churchill, aged seventy-six, returned to Downing Street 'with no sign of doubt or anxiety as to his ability to govern on the score of age or any other',[17] and Jamie Stuart became Secretary of State for Scotland. Chips Channon, in pensive mood, consulted the oracle of his diary: 'What will this new Parliament unfold? The deaths of Winston, Queen Mary and the Monarch? A Coronation, some sort of show-down with Stalin? Shall I survive it? Shall I die, or be made a Peer, or just resign?'[18] Elizabeth, equally haunted by possibilities, started work again. She opened an extension of the Royal Free Hospital School of Medicine, saying that she was 'happy that [her] first engagement since the King's illness should be at an institution closely connected with the relief of suffering', and she took Sister Doreen Pearce and Sister Ruth Beswetherwick – both of whom, it was carefully reported, were officially off duty – to the Royal Variety Performance at the Victoria Palace.

By 9 December it was considered safe to hold a National Day of Thanksgiving for the King's recovery. The Commonwealth thanked God, and Bertie knighted some more doctors. Prolonged illness had given his appearance a curious new distinction and grace; what Cecil Beaton described as 'the raw, bony, medieval aspects of that handsome face'[19] had blurred into a kind of haunted gentleness. He longed for the country. 'I have been through a great deal in recent times,' he wrote to Mr R. G. Casey, the Australian Minister for External Affairs, 'but my main task is getting well. I am going to dedicate myself now to that task of getting well. I am a man who likes outdoor life. I love all the things England offers in such wealth outdoors, and one of the

★ The Duke of Windsor's autobiography, *A King's Story,* was about to be published. The royal family had certainly read it by now, and had presumably been responsible for 'a few wisely chosen omissions' in the English edition. Their reaction to the book is not known. The reviews were excellent.

things I do not get is country life. Kingship keeps me in this room, talking affairs of state constantly, even when I am not quite up to it. I just yearn for the country.'[20] To his relief, it was soon time to go to Sandringham. The vigilant doctors allowed him to go shooting again, provided he didn't stay out too long and always moved about in his Land Rover. At Christmas Elizabeth gathered together every member of the family, except the Windsors. Queen Mary supervised the arrangement of all their presents in the ballroom, though she was plagued with rheumatism in the dank Norfolk climate.

Dr Malan, South Africa's strongly reactionary Prime Minister, had offered them his official residence in Natal so that Bertie could escape the worst of the winter. They decided to accept the offer, and Peter Townsend was sent out to look it over. Although the King was now, in Rebecca West's words, 'esteemed to the point of tenderness'[21] by the public, this projected visit came in for much criticism both in Parliament and the Press. Elizabeth ignored it. 'If the dividing lines in South Africa go deep,' Mr Morrah had written in his delightful book about their visit in 1947, 'the reconciling appeal of royalty goes deeper still.'[22] Peter sent a very encouraging report on Dr Malan's house and they looked forward to leaving on 5 March.

At the end of January 1952 they returned to London from Sandringham. Bertie was very worried about the trouble in the Suez Canal and what he called 'our unhappy relations with Egypt', which was something of an understatement considering that the day before they left Sandringham, Shepheards Hotel, Barclays Bank, the BOAC offices, four cinemas and a number of petrol stations in Cairo had been set on fire. The Edinburghs were replacing Their Majesties on another tour – this time to Australia and New Zealand, calling in at East Africa on the way – so as a farewell celebration, and to distract Bertie, they all went to see *South Pacific* at Drury Lane on 30 January. It was a most enjoyable evening. The entire company on stage sang the National Anthem, the audience cheered, Margaret went home singing 'I'm gonna wash that man right out of my hair'. The next day they went to London Airport to wave goodbye. The television cameras were there – something which neither Bertie nor Elizabeth could ever get used to – and tens of thousands of viewers watched the King, bare-headed, gaunt, his hair blown about by the January wind, 'almost mad-looking',[23] staring after his daughter's 'plane until it was no more than a speck in the sky. When they got back to the Palace Queen Mary came to tea, after seeing a very pleasant exhibition of French drawings from Fouquet to Gauguin at the Arts Council. That evening Elizabeth went to Finsbury Barracks to visit the City of London Squadron of the Royal Auxiliary Air Force, of which she was honorary Air Commodore. It seems a bleak thing to have to do under the circumstances, but she was a great success in the officers' mess and carried it off with her usual aplomb.

The following day, 1 February, they all went back to Sandringham, taking the grandchildren with them. *The Times* provided a lot of entertainment: Nairobi had given Lilibet and Philip a right royal welcome; they were now at the Sagana Hunting Lodge taking pictures of elephants, and a lion eating a wildebeest – there was a very waggish leader under the title *Leo Sapiens* – and they were going on to Tree-tops, where baboons had just eaten all the new lampshades. It took Bertie and Elizabeth back to those happy days – 1924 was it? gracious, how time flies – when they had hunted with guns, not cameras.

There was no such milksop feeling here, thank God. 5 February was 'Keepers' Day' at Sandringham. All the tenants, estate workers, neighbouring small farmers and local worthies joined in the shoot with the King to pick up the remains of the game left at the end of the season. Elizabeth and Margaret had taken the opportunity to go to lunch with the painter Edward Seago at Ludham; after looking at his paintings and sketches, and choosing some to take back to Sandring-ham, Seago took them out on Barton Broad in a hired motor-cruiser and on to tea with some friends at Barton Hall. It was late when they got back. Elizabeth hurried straight to Bertie's room, relieved to find him in topping spirits. Seago's pictures had been propped up in the hall, so they went down to look at them and Bertie, although his knowledge of art could have been considerably greater, was enchanted with them all. They had 'a truly gay' dinner[24] and the King, exhausted but happy, went to bed. A valet took him a cup of hot chocolate and he read until around midnight, when a watchman in the garden saw him fastening the latch of his bedroom window.[25] The next morning, while Elizabeth was drinking her tea, Sir Harold Campbell, the equerry-in-charge, came to tell her that Bertie was dead.

CHAPTER

32

'The King is regarded in law as both a body politic and body natural. The death of the body natural is termed the demise of the Sovereign; the body politic is immortal.' Lilibet inherited the body politic on the night of 5-6 February when, it seems, she was sitting in a tree with Philip and her cousin Pamela Mountbatten, watching elephants by artificial moonlight.[1] From that moment (whenever, precisely, it was) she was Queen of England, and it is as 'the Queen' I shall refer to her in future.

The Queen, then, and the Duke of Edinburgh, arrived at London Airport from Entebbe at 4.19 p.m. on Thursday, 7 February, where they were met by the Duke of Gloucester, Winston Churchill, the Mountbattens, Anthony Eden and Clement Attlee. On the same day the Duke of Windsor sailed from New York on the *Queen Mary*, leaving Wallis behind. Royal persons and dignitaries all over the world cancelled their engagements and prepared to set out for London. The weather was appalling.

The King still lay in bed, where he had died. Sixteen years ago, at the same lowest ebb of winter, he had waited downstairs with David, Harry and George while Cosmo Lang delivered his father's soul. Elizabeth had been ill then; now, with Margaret, she walked through the rain to the parish church of St Mary Magdalene and back again to the house, where Seago's paintings were still propped against the wall. The Sebastopol bell in the Round Tower at Windsor tolled once for every year of the King's life. The great bell of St Paul's tolled for two hours over the drenched City of London.

The following day, 8 February, the Queen attended her Accession Council: '. . . I pray that God will help me to discharge worthily this heavy task that has been laid upon me so early in my life,' she said in her high, certain voice. (David had asked for support 'in this heavy task'; Bertie had 'taken up this heavy task' – was there ever a Sovereign who took the job on with optimism?) During the few hours that it took to read the Proclamation over the length and breadth of Britain, mourning for the dead King was suspended and everyone was offici-ally jubilant.

We, therefore, the Lords Spiritual and Temporal of this Realm ... with the Principal Gentlemen of Quality ... do now hereby, with one Voice and Consent of Tongue and Heart, publish and proclaim that the High and Mighty Princess Elizabeth Alexandra Mary is now, by the Death of our late Sovereign of Happy Memory ... become Queen Elizabeth II, by the Grace of God, Queen of this Realm, and of her other Realms and Territories, Head of the Commonwealth, Defender of the Faith ... God Save the Queen!

The Queen made history by watching herself proclaimed on her black and white television set. The relatively few people who were watching it 'live' in the rain croaked their response, the band played the National Anthem, the guns boomed out from Hyde Park and the Tower and nobody, as far as is known, said or did anything significant. Chips Channon, however, writing his diary on 11 February, supplied the necessary note of joy: '*Mirabile dictu* ... The young Queen has invited Paul over for the funeral ... Princess Olga rang me from Coppins to tell me ... I rejoice in the new reign and welcome it. We shall be the new Elizabethans ... '[2]

The Queen and the Duke of Edinburgh with their children drove to Sandringham, where her mother and sister were waiting for them. Queen Mary, devastated by her son's death, had made a point of going to Clarence House to do homage to the new Sovereign: 'Her old Grannie and subject,' she said, 'must be the first to kiss Her hand.'[3] We do not know whether Elizabeth did the same. At five o'clock that evening Bertie was moved into his coffin, and taken the short distance to the church. There a series of workers on the estate – gamekeepers, foresters, carpenters, in tweed knickerbocker suits and polished boots – guarded him, four at a time, until the following Monday.

On Sunday morning Elizabeth and her family went to the church, which was temporarily closed to the public, for early service. The doors were then unlocked and all day employees and tenants from the late King's villages and farms filed past the coffin. Bertie had been 'in a real sense, father of his family in this village and, indeed, in all the villages which make up the Sandringham estate,' said the Revd H. V. Anderson, the local cleric. 'He cared most deeply for its people, its homes, its woods, its fields and farms ... ' Many of them were the same men who had guarded his father's coffin; there were still some who remembered Prince Albert shooting his first woodcock, his first partridge and his first grouse in King George's Coronation Year. Rain changed to snow. The added chill of a Royal death made it a typical Sandringham winter.

On Monday morning almost exactly the same cortège that had accompanied King George V from Sandringham to Wolferton Station accompanied his son's coffin: the Queen replaced her grandmother, and there was no riderless pony, but the gun carriage rumbled slowly along the lanes, the muffled clopping of horses, the crunch and shuffle of feet, emphasized the winter silence. I can find no mention of a piper. If there was a pheasant careening free across the sky, no one noticed it.

At King's Cross the Imperial State Crown, under a purple covering, was waiting on a pedestal on the red-carpeted platform. The train pulled in, the doors of the funeral coach slid open revealing purple curtains and draperies. Lieutenant-Colonel Sir Terence Nugent, Comptroller of the Lord Chamberlain's Office, lifted up the crown and carried it into the funeral coach. There was a long pause. Then, shrouded in black, Elizabeth and her daughters stepped out on to the platform, followed by the Duke of Edinburgh and the Duke of Gloucester. Another pause. None of them moved. Perhaps a few sparrows chirped in the roof; the sound of traffic going about its business in the Euston Road. Then, with alarming care eight lofty Guardsmen shouldered coffin and crown out of the train and slow-marched to the waiting gun carriage. Harry and Philip fell in behind them. The women were left alone.

They waited. They seemed uncertain what to do. Finally Elizabeth and the Queen moved together to speak to the attendant Nugent. Given his signal, the royal car drew up into its proper place. The Queen and her mother graciously acknowledged the salute from the guards of honour and disappeared inside the car, followed by Margaret. The guards marched off. The props were cleared away.

Among the many eulogies delivered that day in Parliament, Viscount Samuel's was the most realistic: 'What is needed in a constitutional monarchy,' he told the House of Lords, 'is not brilliance, or mere cleverness or eloquence, but a sincere good will and a sound common sense.' As he grew more familiar with death, Bertie seemed to be outgrowing even those sterling qualities. He had taken on the magical 'look of Weltshmerz'; he had finally acquired the talent to be loved. James Cameron was in Westminster Hall waiting for the cortège to arrive. Cameron had strong feelings about many things, but he was not often choked, as are so many other writers, with emotion. The piece he wrote for the *Illustrated London News* is choked: 'While the King lived we spoke of him as this, and as that, endowing him with all the remote virtues of an infallible man; such men do not die. But the King died; and we found somehow a different thing: that we loved him ... the sudden shadow fell momentarily across the heart of every man; loyal men and cynics, the rich and the dispossessed, reactionaries and radicals...'[4] Apart from a few Royalty-climbers like Chips Channon, this was true. Nothing in this King's life became him like the leaving it.

Reports of Bertie's lying-in-state are almost interchangeable with those written sixteen years before. 'The public ... began to arrive in numbers so astounding that every plan was upset, every traffic arrangement entangled ... By the afternoon of the third day 80,000 people were waiting in what was almost certainly the longest queue the world has ever seen ... a vast strip of humanity over three miles long, stolidly facing a five-hour wait in the toothed wind...'[5] The Kings and Queens of Norway, Sweden, the Hellenes and the Netherlands were staying at Buckingham Palace. Together with various members of the British Royal Family they crept in and out, trying not to be noticed. Queen Mary, erect but tottering, heavily veiled, came with her eldest son. 'The Queen was courageous,' Cameron wrote. 'That we have been told five hundred times, but she *was*.' He found it 'strange – almost incredible – to see these opaque veiled figures and recognize them for the ladies whose professional uniforms – that they may fulfil their duty and be conspicuous – are light pastels. It was difficult to adjust oneself to the new titles: Queen, Queen Mother. And those who photographed them ... did a strange thing: they found for the first time perhaps in twenty years a picture of the King's widow without a smile.'[6]

David and Harry, the only survivors among Queen Mary's sons, did not stand guard over the coffin. Neither did Elizabeth's son-in-law, peaky with anxiety. ('I never felt so sorry for anyone in all my life,' Michael Parker said, when he told Philip about the King's death. 'He looked as though you'd dropped half the world on him.')[7] However desolate Elizabeth felt, she was caught up in the frantic rush of hospitality at the Palace. The young Queen was being whisked from engagement to engagement with barely time to speak to her husband, let alone her mother: Churchill brought a deputation from the House of Commons, she received the Prime Minister of New Zealand, gave lunch to the Swedens and the Netherlands and the Mountbattens, received the High Commissioners of Commonwealth countries, Ministers, Ambassadors and Foreign Ministers, and the representatives of Ireland, received the President of the French Republic at 6.30 p.m. and the President of the Turkish Republic at 6.45 p.m. and the President of the Praesidium of Yugoslavia at 7. On Wednesday, 13 February, according to Brigadier Clark, the Duke of Windsor was entertained to tea by the Queen, Prince Philip and the Queen Mother.[8]

On 15 February Elizabeth's standard flew over Buckingham Palace. The day of Bertie's funeral, at least, was hers. The long, melancholy cortège lumbered from Westminster Hall to Paddington. David, in the uniform of Admiral of the Fleet, followed the coffin with Harry on foot; behind them marched Philip, Edward Kent and a battalion of minor royalties; the women, shadowy in their nylon veils, swayed like sea-grass behind the windows of the funeral carriages. Queen Mary asked Lady Airlie to keep her company at Marlborough House. 'We sat alone together at the window, looking out into the murk and gloom,' wrote Mabell. 'As the cortège wound slowly along the Queen whispered in a broken voice, "Here *he* is" . . . I could not speak to comfort her. My tears choked me . . . We held each other's hands in silence.'[9]

Queen Mary watched the coffin arrive at Windsor, the procession to St George's Chapel and the interment in the vault on her television set.[10] She had not been present at Queen Victoria's funeral because George had German measles, but she remembered how beautiful she thought 'beloved Grandmama' looked after death, 'like a marble statue'; her father-in-law's funeral had been, for her, an agitated affair, with Alexandra insisting upon a precedence which was not hers by right and George and herself, as the new King and Queen, 'very busy with dull things of all kinds';[11] then 'that terrible day of sadness' of her George's funeral when, dressed in the peaked coif and thick crêpe veils of German royal mourning, she stood alone at the foot of the coffin as her daughter-in-law did now. It must have been strange to see from such a distance her son being lowered into that same vault to lie for the present with his ancestors; almost as though she were already with him, on the Other Side.

PART FIVE

The death of the Prince Consort was the central turning-point in the history of Queen Victoria. She herself felt that her true life had ceased with her husband's . . . Nor is it possible that her biographer should escape a similar impression. For him, too, there is darkness over the latter half of that long career. The first forty-two years of the Queen's life are illuminated by a great and varied quantity of authentic information. With Albert's death a veil descends . . . the rest is all conjecture and ambiguity . . . We must be content in our ignorance with a brief and summary relation.

Queen Victoria, Lytton Strachey

CHAPTER

33

Oh, Mabell, if only you knew how hard it has been; how
I have struggled with myself. All through the years the
King always told me everything *first*. I do so miss that.
Queen Mary to Lady Airlie after the death of King George V.

Elizabeth had spent nearly thirty years creating a King out of
unpromising material – a King she had intended to last, to become a
habit with his people, to grow old with dignity. But her artefact had
fallen to pieces. She was fifty-one years old and (apart from two
daughters, two houses, and a considerable income for life) she had
very little to show for it.

More than that, in the process of building a King she had brought
up, as it were, a man to whom she could respond and on whom she
could rely. He had learned to apply his mind to problems, to take
decisions. He had smoothed her path and surrounded her with comforts. Their roles in the relationship were not exactly reversed over the
years, but they had merged into what seemed a more mutual depen-
dence. Like millions of other women, she had never been alone, or
responsible for her future. Like millions of other women, in mourning
her husband she was, however unconsciously, mourning her own life.

Grief is often alleviated by anger; a furious sense of injustice makes
waking up in the morning easier to bear. Elizabeth is said to have
convinced herself that if Bertie had not been forced on to the throne he
would not have got lung cancer and he would not have died from
coronary thrombosis. Whether or not this argument is medically
viable, considering his history, one also wonders whether a longer life
as Duke of York, subservient to his elder brother and occupied with
the minor, tedious duties that came his way, would have given Bertie
the opportunity to become the man he did. Was he, in fact, not more
fulfilled, if not happier, with greatness thrust upon him than he would
have been without any greatness at all? 'He loved you all, every one of
you, most truly,' Elizabeth said in the personal statement she issued
after the King's funeral. She would not have been able to say that as the
widowed Duchess of York.

It's true, however, that she would have gone on being Duchess of York. As Queen Consort, with a clearly defined status in the Constitution, she ceased to exist the moment her husband died. The title itself went into cold storage. Elizabeth, technically, was now Queen Dowager, with fewer prerogatives (it is, for instance, impossible to be 'treasonable' towards a Queen Dowager).[1] Disliking the connotations, perhaps, she chose to be called 'Queen Elizabeth the Queen Mother'. Though in this way she managed to be called 'Queen' twice over, it made not a jot of difference. She was demoted. The Sovereign to whom she now owed allegiance was her twenty-five-year-old daughter Lilibet.

There is, of course, no such title as King Father – in the unlikely event of a King abdicating in favour of his son they would presumably have to invent one – and 'Queen Mother' automatically implies the lonely eminence of a widow, a solitary female relic of the previous reign. If her son takes over, she can continue, in a way, to be his feminine counterpart – his wife, as Queen Alexandra made so clear, is always in a subservient position. If, however, the successor is a daughter, what role does her mother play? There is no room for two women on the throne. The natural relationship, based as it is on identification and rivalry, is thrown awry. *'Il n'y a plus d'avenir pour moi,'* Queen Victoria's mother wailed to Madame de Lieven after her daughter's Accession; *'Je ne suis plus rien.'* There must have been long stretches, during those first months of her widowhood, when Elizabeth could have said the same.

It is not surprising that for the rest of the year her mood seems to have been unpredictable. 'My only wish now is that I may be allowed to continue the work we sought to do together,' she had told her daughter's people. But what work, exactly? 'The great task of service' sounded more than ever amorphous. Was she now to become a vaguely endearing old nuisance, like Alexandra, or a formidable matriarch, like her mother-in-law? She was too young for the part. Or should she quietly return to the obscurity she was reputedly so reluctant to leave thirty years before? A bitter prospect. A Queen Consort is powerless without a King; a wonderful wife is useless without a husband; 'a man's woman', as Elizabeth was – and is still – wilts and shrivels in the no-man's-land of respectable widowhood. She was not only grief-stricken; she was frightened. Reliable sources say that it was a surprise visit from Churchill that refired her enthusiasm for life. A great director, he was able to make her see a new approach to the role of Queen Mother.

At the beginning of May 1952, three months after Bertie's death, she flew from Windsor to Fife to inspect the First Battalion of the Black Watch before they left for Korea. In telling them that she knew that whatever they were facing they would win new honour for the Black Watch and for Scotland it may have sounded as though she were sending them off with drum and fife to attack Napoleon's army, rather than sniping at Communists in the Korean jungle, but the cheers were just as rousing. A few weeks later her old friend 'Bobbety' Cranborne, Marquess of Salisbury, arranged a joy-ride for her in a brand-new Comet.* Margaret, Peter Townsend and two of Elizabeth's chauffeurs were in the party which flew 1,850 miles to Bordeaux and back, picnicking over the Alps. At one point Elizabeth took over the controls of the taxpayers' priceless machine and, according to Sir Miles Thomas, 'the mach needle crept towards the coloured danger sector and suddenly the Comet began to porpoise . . . had that gone on much longer, the wracking on the structure could well have precipitated a rupture of the skin of the kind that caused subsequent tragedies.'[2] Elizabeth was so pleased with her performance that she sent a telegram to the City of London Squadron of the RAAF to tell them about it.[3]

The following month she went to stay with her friends the Vyners on the remote coast of Caithness. As always, she responded promptly to her surroundings. Perhaps dignified, if gradual, retirement was the answer. Go back to her roots. So she bought Barrogill Castle, a dilapidated property overlooking the Pentland Firth. Though there was no tongueless girl or hidden Monster, there were said to be shoals of mermaids disporting themselves in the warmth of the Gulf Stream along the Caithness coast and sea-serpents, too, surging in great stately hoops from Dunnett Head to Hoy. It was a bleak landscape, barren moors, desolate lochs, towering cliffs, whirlpools. The castle itself had the requisite bricked-up rooms and dungeon. It may have seemed her spiritual home, but unfortunately, since it needed three years' work to make it habitable, it was physically inadequate. Having changed its name to the Castle of Mey, she left it in the architects' and builders' hands and returned to London.

Peter Townsend, whom she had made Comptroller of her Household, was supervising repairs and redecorations at Clarence House, for which Parliament had voted an inadequate £8,000 on the grounds that at a conservative estimate £100,000 had been spent on it for her daughter three years before. Elizabeth was permitted to stay in her own suite on the first floor of Buckingham Palace while this work was being done. The Queen and her husband took over the Belgian Suite

---

* Peter Lane (*The Queen Mother,* 205) dates this jaunt in May 1953. Considering that Elizabeth was in mourning for the King, this would seem more probable. However, Helen Cathcart (*The Queen Mother Herself,* p 180ff), David Sinclair (*Queen and Country,* 179) and David Duff (*Elizabeth of Glamis,* p 316) say that it took place in May 1952. Miss Laird does not mention the occasion.

on the ground floor, Charles and Anne lived in the nursery suite on the second floor and Margaret, sensibly, had the suite at the opposite end, over the Visitors' entrance. Elizabeth had modernized the place considerably since she and Bertie went there in 1937, when all the food had to be transported from the kitchens at Buckingham Palace Road to the dining rooms at Constitution Hill, but nothing could be done to make the royal tenement more cosy. There were messengers, of course, to sprint down miles of corridor with messages; there was the telephone; there were antique lifts to crank them up and down when they went calling. Even so, at the end of the day, with the grandchildren asleep and Margaret entertaining her friends and Lilibet either working or preoccupied with her family, the new Queen Mother must have been lonely and dejected. The Sultan of Brunei brought her some silver candlesticks from Borneo, though she might have preferred one of the gold sarongs he had presented to Margaret and Queen Mary (after all, imagine Queen Mary in a gold sarong – ridiculous), but there seemed precious little else for a woman who had been accustomed to the constant love and attention of a King.

She returned to Scotland. Edith Sitwell sent her an anthology of poetry she had recently published. Writing to thank her, Elizabeth said that she had read it sitting by the river, 'and it was a day when one felt engulfed by great black clouds of unhappiness and misery'. She found hope in George Herbert, she said, and 'thought how small and selfish is sorrow. But it bangs one about until one is senseless.'[4] This letter was dated 15 September.

Barely two months later she went with the Queen and Margaret to see Freddie Lonsdale's *Aren't We All?* at the Haymarket Theatre. They sat in the Royal Box, which was hideously decorated with small bronze and yellow chrysanthemums. The Queen and her mother both wore tiaras. People were curious to see Elizabeth. The Press had gone on for months about how heartbroken she was. What a relief to find, as Cecil Beaton did, that she 'was in her most jovial mood, enjoying every nuance of the play's humour with a hearty relish, and alert to all the twists of the mechanical plot. She was having a 'night out' and in such good spirits that she chuckled at many things that the audience would take for granted, and roared at the things that amused her most.' The Queen sat 'relaxed and hunched, with head cocked backwards to listen concentratedly to the play', or to think about opening Parliament, or having the Archbishop to lunch, or whether the design for her Coronation gown was quite right, and Margaret, with 'straight neck and back' was miles away.[5]

In the interval, Beaton asked Elizabeth whether she had enjoyed her holiday, though any newspaper would have told him that this was a tactless question.

'"Oh, I've bought a villa in the most remote part of the world!"

'"How brave of you to have nothing between you and the Atlantic," babbled Beaton.

'"I've taken this villa to get away from everything but I don't expect I shall ever be able to get there." Everyone roared with laughter. It was that kind of evening.'[6]

In December 1952 Peter Townsend divorced his wife on the grounds of adultery with John de Laszlo, son of the man responsible for the most idealized and popular portrait ever painted of Elizabeth. The Royal Family was discreetly sympathetic. At Christmas they stayed at Sandringham as usual. Queen Mary, eighty-five years old, felt unequal to the jollifications and remained in her room. She had recently made a new Will, leaving everything previously bequeathed to Bertie to her eldest granddaughter. Now she thought how tiresome it would be to spoil Lilibet's Coronation by dying in the middle of it: 'How careless of him to die in the middle of the season,' she had once remarked on hearing of the death of some public figure. She would make a memo: Coronation not to be postponed or upset in any way because of mourning.

CHAPTER
34

Queen Mary became in her later years the most regal of matriarchs. Elizabeth would soon be faced with taking over that role, but she would have to play it quite differently. Unlike Queen Mary, she had no sons to support her; her brother-in-law Harry, though immensely conscientious in his duties, was hardly a shoulder to lean on; her son-in-law was a Mountbatten, not at all what she needed. There were friends, of course, but they were all outsiders. She must have the support of a completely trustworthy man in her inner circle, a man *in the know* who would complement her femininity in public; not a lover – that went without saying – but a confidante, a protector, someone who would look after her while she worked out the best way of tackling the future. She had made Peter Townsend Comptroller of her Household in order that he might soon fulfil this role. Peter's affection for Bertie and stabilizing influence on Margaret, his rather melancholy good looks, his efficiency in dealing with all the boring trivia and the good fortune that he was no longer married were perfect qualifications for a lifetime as *chevalier servant* to a Queen Mother.

The more worldly Queen Mary (who had danced the Hokey Cokey with Peter at Balmoral and thought him a nice young man) would have seen the dangers in a trice. Something would have been done to stop, or at least deflect, the course of human nature. Elizabeth, having a more optimistic and complacent personality, never thought about such things. She must have known how painfully Margaret missed her father, that she was jealous of her sister and piqued by her boy-friends' precipitate dashes to the altar with other people and generally bored and lonely. She must have sensed, at least, that Peter was deeply unhappy about his divorce. Perhaps her inability to see the outcome was due to simple ignorance. While her own sexual approach seemed to work wonders, her actual experience was extremely limited for a woman of fifty-two. Whatever the explanation, she was not aware that both Townsend and her daughter were in that vulnerable state in which falling in love or off a high building seem the only solutions. Left alone at Sandringham or Windsor, they found it easier to fall in love.[1]

Now, surely, Elizabeth must have noticed what was going on. It is impossible for a normal mother to sit smiling placidly while sexual fireworks explode over the Canasta and zip across the dinner table. If Elizabeth noticed a change in the atmosphere it seems, according to Townsend's account, that she must have put it down to the weather. Margaret eventually confronted her mother with the situation, but even then, according to Townsend's autobiography, he could only imagine Elizabeth's reaction.[2] The subject gnawing at their souls was not one she would discuss with the Comptroller of her Household. She made no sign that she felt angered or outraged or, on the other hand, that she acquiesced. She didn't say 'I thought so' and she certainly didn't send for Mr Churchill and greet him with, 'Well, Prime Minister. *This* is a pretty kettle of fish!' As a mother she appeared to opt out completely. Lilibet, head of the family and realm, must deal with it.

Although Townsend was a perfect Comptroller of a royal household, he was ineligible as a member of the Royal Family because of his divorce. It made not a jot of difference that he had been 'the innocent party'. As far as Margaret was concerned, she was in any case bound by the Royal Marriages Act of 1772 which stipulated (and still does) that until the age of twenty-five all potential successors to the throne must have the Sovereign's permission to marry; for the subsequent two years they have to ask the approval of Parliament; not until they are twenty-seven can they do what they like. Margaret was twenty-two, Townsend forty. Five years of enforced celibacy did not appeal to either of them.

So the Princess asked the Queen and the Queen asked the Prime Minister. Churchill, who had burned his fingers over the Abdication, maintained that it was quite impossible for Margaret to marry a divorced member of the Household. She must wait until she was twenty-five and apply again. In the meanwhile Townsend should depart for the equivalent of Oklahoma. The Queen took the first part of his advice, but not the second. She insisted that Townsend should keep his position in her mother's ménage – a well-meant but naïve gesture from an elder sister who seems to have felt that if she herself had a husband and children and the Crown, Margaret could at least have Townsend. The couple were even invited to dinner in the Belgian Suite as a further sign of goodwill. Philip, to whom the consequences must have seemed obvious, amused himself with witticisms about the affair, but otherwise it was a pleasant enough evening.

★   ★   ★

It is to be hoped that Queen Mary was unaware of these deplorable events. She did not venture out in the bitter weather of early 1953 and by March it was clear to those around her that she was dying. On the night of 24 March the crowd waiting in fog and darkness outside Marlborough House watched in awestruck silence as the Queen's personal standard was lowered from the masthead. 'The glorious old girl', as Chips Channon had called her, was dead. She was buried in St George's Chapel on 31 March. That night there was a dinner party for twenty-eight members of the family at Windsor Castle. Prince Paul of Yugoslavia, his wartime treachery forgiven and forgotten, sat between the Queen and the Queen Mother. The Duke of Windsor, who had followed his mother's coffin and watched it lowered into the familiar vault, was not invited.

The Queen and her family remained at Windsor while a large army of workmen moved into Buckingham Palace to refurbish it for the Coronation. During this time Cecil Beaton went to take more pictures of Elizabeth and found that in her daughter's absence the Queen Mother was being given 'quite casual treatment' by the remaining staff. If Margaret and Townsend were there, they were not in evidence. Elizabeth's old rooms were bare, the furniture taken away; the whole place smelled of paint, electricians whistled in the Picture Gallery, it was bitterly cold. Some of the staff complained to Beaton's assistants that they 'couldn't think why the Queen Mother stayed on here so long – not that she will relish the move to Clarence House for there won't be the number of servants there that she's accustomed to'.[3] When he asked for a vase of flowers he was told there wasn't a flower in the place. Beaton was concerned for himself, as well as the Queen Mother. The photographer Baron was a friend of Prince Philip's and had been taking recent pictures of the family; he might get the job of doing the Coronation, which Beaton badly wanted. When the session was over he stopped at his favourite florist and ordered a huge bouquet of spring flowers 'to be sent to that adorable human being living in that cold, bleak Palace'. Beaton got the job, and meeting Elizabeth at the American Embassy ball a few days later thanked her for helping to bring this 'coup' about. 'She laughed knowingly with one finger high in the air.'[4]

On 18 May the Queen Mother, together with her Household and Margaret, finally moved into Clarence House. Townsend's own account of this period is concerned with the hostility of the Queen's Private Secretary, Tommy Lascelles, and the negligence of her press secretary, Richard Colville. He says nothing about his curious status but presumably he divided his time between mother and daughter, hoping for the best. Rehearsals for the Coronation were taking up much of their time. This would be the first TV Coronation and it must not only be right, but be seen by millions of viewers to be right. The Earl Marshal of England, the Duke of Norfolk, whose job it is to reproduce history on these occasions, is, rather charmingly, a Roman Catholic. The Archbishop of Canterbury, Geoffrey Fisher, was full of ideas, such as reintroducing the Armills (or bracelets) which had been used in the Coronation of Elizabeth I. The Duke of Norfolk got on with his job of co-ordinating, planning, choreographing and rehearsing the operation while Archbishop Fisher took great delight in instructing the Press about mysteries such as the Recognition, the Oath, the Anointing, the Investiture, the Crowning and the Enthronement, not forgetting the Ampulla, the Spoon and, of course, the Armills. The Press transferred the information, suitably adapted, to the pagan hordes who for the first time would participate in these ancient Anglican ceremonies. He also released little confidences, such as that Elizabeth I's Armills were much too cumbersome for Elizabeth II, so it had been suggested to the Commonwealth that it might give her enough gold to make daintier ones;[5] also that George VI had used up all the anointing oil, so a Bond Street chemist was busy concocting some more from King Charles I's recipe. In order that his sense of smell should not be impaired the good man had given up smoking for a month.

Meanwhile the Queen, a large sheet pinned to her shoulders, rehearsed in the Buckingham Palace Ballroom, which was marked out with posts and tapes, to the accompaniment of gramophone records of her father's coronation. Presumably she had read his account, and was on the lookout for accidents. On 28 May Elizabeth and Margaret rehearsed the procession to their seats in the Abbey, and on 29 May there was a final dress rehearsal with stand-ins for the principal performers. The Queen's understudy was the Duchess of Norfolk, the first time in history that a Roman Catholic had taken the role. Her husband said that she gave 'a superb performance'.[6]

★   ★   ★

In she came, glittering from top to toe, diamonds everywhere, a two-foot hem of solid gold on her open dress – the Queen Mother playing second lead as beautifully as she had played the first. On she came up the aisle with a bow here to Prince Bernhard, a bow there to a row of ambassadors, and up those tricky steps with no looking down like the Duke of Gloucester – no half turn to check on her train like the Duchess of Kent, no hesitation at the top like Princess Margaret, no nervous nod of the head like Princess Mary...[7]

Or so it seemed to Ann Edwards, a young journalist on the *Daily Express*. Channon, not for the first time, but extraordinary in the context, was cruel: 'Queen Mum was ok, but compared badly with Queen Mary's entry last time.'[8] Cecil Beaton saw 'The Mistress of the

Robes to the Queen Mother, of towering height . . . minimized by the enormous presence and radiance of the petite Queen Mother. Yet in the Queen Widow's expression we read sadness combined with pride.'[9] Harold Nicolson watched it all on television in the comfort of the Travellers' Club, but went outside to see the procession. It was pouring with rain and he expressed no particular sympathy for Elizabeth and Margaret, drenched in their open carriage, but commented that 'the procession characteristically . . . ended by an ambulance for any horses that might get hurt'.[10] Brigadier Clark, in the Abbey, saw a grandmother managing her four-and-a-half-year-old grandson. Charles, in an oyster-coloured satin suit with a Coronation medal pinned to his shirt and his hair slicked down with brilliantine, hung perilously over the Royal Gallery until Elizabeth hauled him back; then he disappeared altogether. Elizabeth, searching for him with one foot and muttering entreaties, meanwhile kept devotedly looking at the crowning of her daughter. At last the child emerged, triumphantly holding her handbag aloft.[11] He was, I hope, congratulated. From then on he pestered his aunt and grandmother with questions. Someday in the next century, a different world, he would be in his mother's place. In the meanwhile, and maybe for the next sixty years, Charles must be kept quiet.

News arrived that day that Hillary and Tenzing had reached the summit of Everest. By early evening the international Press were on to a story of far greater significance: Princess Margaret had picked a piece of fluff off Peter Townsend's uniform in full view of the Royal Family and Coronation guests. This astounding gesture was headlined in the New York papers the following morning. As in 1936 the British Press, seething, kept silent for ten days. Then, on Sunday, 14 June, the *People* opened fire:

> It is high time for the British public to be made aware of the fact that newspapers in Europe and America are openly asserting that the Princess is in love with a divorced man and that she wishes to marry him. The story is of course utterly untrue. It is quite unthinkable that a royal princess, third in line of succession to the throne, should ever contemplate a marriage with a man who has been through the divorce courts.

The power of the Press over our inviolable Royal Family and their Establishment is remarkable. A paragraph such as this can change their lives and cause their policies to be reversed overnight. The next day Townsend, who had been due to leave for Rhodesia with Elizabeth and Margaret on 30 June, found himself posted as air attaché in Brussels. Patrick Plunket, the Queen's equerry, replaced him in the Queen Mother's entourage.

★   ★   ★

A promise had been given that Townsend need not leave for Brussels until Margaret returned from Rhodesia on 17 July, so in fact it was to be only just over two weeks parting. The Princess and the Queen Mother accompanied by Lady Hambleden, Lord Plunket, Elizabeth's Private Secretary Captain Oliver Dawnay and Margaret's lady-in-waiting the Hon. Iris Peake,* flew to Salisbury on 30 June as planned. After a State drive down Third Street – known as Royal Mile since Bertie and Elizabeth drove down it in 1947 – they relaxed, or discussed their problems, and on the following morning visited the farm of a Mr Miller, one of the leading cattle breeders in the country, and took morning tea with Mr Miller and his friends.

That night they boarded their train – which had changed its name from 'White' to 'Ivory' in the past six years – and arrived at Bulawayo at half past ten the next morning, where Elizabeth opened the Rhodes Centenary Exhibition before a crowd of 25,000 people. The Queen Mother's feelings for the black Africans were maternalistic. 'She loved them,' according to Lady Longford, 'as a Queen Mother should.'[12] I suppose this means, as Rebecca West said of Rhodes, that she 'wanted Africa to be a paradise where Englishmen tenderly cared for the black boys whose souls were white'.[13] In her speech, the Queen Mother said that the impulse which drove Rhodes on to the north was no mere desire for territorial expansion. It was something more than political. It was in its essence a spiritual motive. The Exhibition, she said, showed the 'wonderful progress' that had taken place in Central Africa. 'The whole development has been that of a tiny white community, surrounded by primitive Africans, growing into a young and flourishing nation.' *The Times* leader was considerably more ironic. 'Starting from the current Victorian agnosticism [Rhodes] chose to believe in God upon a balance of probabilities, and found it "obvious" that God was trying to produce a type of humanity most fitted to bring peace, liberty and justice to the world. He did not doubt that the race into which he had been born was alone on the earth in fulfilling the qualifications. This was his justification of Empire.' The next day, to prove her whole-hearted support for Rhodes's opinions, Elizabeth made a last-minute decision to join the procession to his grave in Matapos. Wreaths were procured for the Queen Mother and Princess Margaret to lay on the hallowed spot. Photographs show Elizabeth with the inevitable fur stole and peep-toes looking merry, Margaret glum. Perhaps to cheer her up, Elizabeth suddenly decided to give a party at Government House for Pressmen and broadcasters and local journalists. Sad to say, Jim Cameron was not among them. The only creature in which Margaret appeared to take the slightest interest was a leopard cub.

* Captain Dawnay was divorced in 1962 and married the Hon. Iris Peake in 1963.

From Bulawayo by train to Gwelo, where there was a triumphal arch proclaiming GREETING GREAT WHITE QUEEN AND GREAT WHITE PRINCESS and a choir from Johannesburg singing an anthem in praise of 'all descendants of Queen Victoria'. A night run through Salisbury, Marandellas and Rusapi to Umtali in Southern Rhodesia, a town comprising 7,000 whites and 18,000 Africans. Here Elizabeth unveiled a memorial to Kingsley Fairbridge, originator of the Fairbridge farm schools, ominously said to be 'one of the most successful child migration schemes'. Then they went off for a day's break to the Leopard Rock Hotel in the Vumba Mountains, and received the news that Townsend had been told to report for duty in Brussels on 15 July, two days before they were due to return.

Anyone who has been a spoiled girl in love – or the mother of one, come to that – can imagine the scene. Margaret raged, wept, and took to her bed. Her mother explained that she had a bad cold. Two days later Margaret was flown back to Salisbury in the Prime Minister's Dakota, where she was attended by a Dr Michael Gelfand, 'a specialist in the Government medical service'.

By the time her mother joined her there on 12 July Margaret had recovered sufficiently to attend a display by the British South African Police, enlivened with Highland dancing performed by the local Caledonian Society. It appears that she couldn't face the Harare African Township, about which Elizabeth was so enthusiastic. Meanwhile in Kenya, a thousand or so miles to the north, the Mau Mau had stolen binoculars, blankets and tins of food from 'Tree Tops Hotel' and attacked Royal Lodge at Sagana, where only last year the Queen had been watching floodlit elephants.

For all the benevolent smiles and bland speeches, it couldn't have been a very enjoyable trip. A ball at Government House in Margaret's honour sounds one of the worst ordeals. It was attended by 850 'young guests' from all over the colony, some chosen by ballot. Margaret was as sophisticated as her social drawbacks would allow, and by no means stupid. If she put a brave face on that evening she was, after all, a chip off the old block. The next day they drove to the village of Mrewa 'in the heart of the native area' and were much diverted by Chief Mangwande's welcoming address: 'Welcome, mother of our gracious Queen and British Empire, in which space and distance have become of small account when words and works may encircle the globe as does the sun, so that no part of the Empire may brood in darkness ... Welcome also to the daughter of our honoured Empire!' An eighty-year-old chief with a long white beard did an impromptu caper for their benefit and collapsed with the strain. On 15 July, while mother and daughter were attending a tobacco auction in Salisbury, Peter Townsend arrived in Brussels.

Three days later they were at Ascot with the Queen and Philip. Elizabeth looked flourishing enough, but the stress of the last few months suddenly required her to take to her bed. Margaret toured the gardens of Stoke Newington, Holloway and Finsbury in her place.

★   ★   ★

This was Elizabeth's fourth Coronation Year. Apart from the Atom Bomb and television and the fact that machines went faster and higher, there was little change in the basic pattern. God was still active, drowning 307 people in British floods in January and 1,794 in the Netherlands; there were earthquakes in Persia and the Greek islands, tornadoes in Texas, Michigan and Ohio, tremors in Ethiopia. The Russians exploded an H-Bomb in Siberia, the United States dropped the biggest ever Atom Bomb over Nevada and the British dropped a couple more on Woomera, Australia. A very ancient method of warfare was revived by the United Nations Command in Korea with the offer of $50,000 reward for every Communist 'plane delivered intact to non-Communist territory and a further bonus of $50,000 to the first Communist pilot to arrive. The jackpot was won by a North Korean pilot who flew his MiG-15 to an air base near Seoul and retired a rich man. The Korean war ended on 27 July after three years and twenty-five days.

Practically nobody was assassinated, except the heir to the Bey of Tunis and the vice-chairman of the Tunis municipal council. Even the revolutions didn't come off, though they were attempted in Bolivia, Bulgaria and Cuba. There were the usual riots, skirmishes and emergencies – (the situation in Kenya was known as the latter). On 8 April Jomo Kenyatta was sentenced to seven years' hard labour. Stalin died from cerebral haemmorrhage and was succeeded, briefly, by Malenkov. Eisenhower took over from Harry Truman. Marshal Tito was voted President of Yugoslavia by 568 votes to one. British royalty was in the limelight with the Coronation, Queen Mary's death, the Townsend affair and the Queen's trip to Australia and New Zealand at the end of the year, during which time the Queen Mother was one of the five Counsellors of State and deputized for her daughter as Queen. Carol of Rumania died in Portugal, King Ibn Saud died in Riyadh. King Faysal II took the oath in Baghdad, King Husain took it in Jordan. King Norodom Sihanouk of Cambodia fled to Siam on 13 June, but returned on 21 June; the Shah of Persia fled to Baghdad on 16 August, but returned on 22 August; King Sisavang Vong of Laos fled from his capital of Luang Prabang on 10 May and never returned. The Egyptian monarchy was abolished. Prince Jean of Luxemburg married Princess Josephine Charlotte of Belgium and Princess Ragnhild of Norway married Erling Lorentzen, a commoner. Apart from the

Coronation, it was all relatively poor stuff.

Accidents were unspectacular: eleven people killed in a collision on the Central Line, forty-three in a BOAC Comet crash near Calcutta, twenty-seven in a BEA Viscount crash in Belfast, a hundred and thirty-three drowned when the mail ferry *Princess Victoria* foundered off the coast of County Down. Julius and Ethel Rosenberg were executed as spies on 19 June, John Halliday Christie sentenced to death on 25 June for the murder of six women. More happily, Dilys Cadwaladr won the Bardic Crown at the national Eisteddfod at Rhyl, and the International Court of Justice found unanimously that sovereignty over the islets and rocks of the Ecrehous and Minquiers in the Channel Islands belonged to the United Kingdom.

We don't know if any member of the Royal Family summed up the year in their diary. Our grandchildren will know more what they thought of it than we do, and I doubt whether our grandchildren will care much. One of the last entries in Channon's published journal* was, for him at least, a happy valediction: 'Goodbye, wonderful Coronation Summer. I have revelled in you and drunk your pleasure to the dregs.'[14]

* Chips was knighted in 1957. He died two years later at the age of sixty-one.

CHAPTER
35

Though Margaret's love life, or lack of it, would concern her mother for the rest of her days, the Townsend affair, coming so soon after Bertie's death, was perhaps particularly aggravating. It was also an indication of the emotional pattern to which the Princess still seems condemned in her mid-fifties. To conjecture who or what was responsible – her parents, her environment, her Maker? – is inappropriate. These, more or less, were the facts of the matter, and the nine out of ten readers who know them already can skip to the next chapter.

By 1954 Margaret had taken up again with the friends she had temporarily abandoned for Townsend – Billy Wallace, Peter Ward, Henry Porchester, Colin Tennant, Judy Montagu, the Fifties equivalent of the Bright Young Things. She was smoking her cigarettes through an exaggeratedly long tortoiseshell holder (Queen Mary's idea, she said), staying out late at insalubrious nightspots, behaving with a flamboyance unsuited to a twentieth-century British princess, however unremarkable in anyone else. The Press never tired of her. A lot of other people did, which was not her fault.

In June of that year Judy Montagu put on Edgar Wallace's *The Frog* at the Scala Theatre 'in aid of charity' (waifs and strays? unmarried mothers? the RSPCA? we don't know). The lead parts were played by Lords Porchester and Norwich, Billy Wallace and Mrs Gerald Legge, (now Countess Spencer), with *vignettes* from Elsa Maxwell and Douglas Fairbanks. Margaret, ironically not allowed to perform in public, was Associate Director. 'The whole evening was one of the most fascinating exhibitions of incompetence, conceit and bloody impertinence that I have ever seen in my life,' wrote Noel Coward, a close friend of the Kents and Mountbattens and seldom disposed to criticize the *haut monde*. '. . . In the dressing room afterwards, where we went civilly to congratulate Porchy, we found Princess Margaret eating foie gras sandwiches, sipping champagne and complaining that the audience laughed in the wrong places. We commiserated politely and left.'[1] The Queen Mother, on the other hand, appeared to enjoy it very much.

Margaret would soon be twenty-four – one more year to go and she would be free of her sister's veto on marriage with Townsend. It would be nice to think that at this juncture she had a moment of active rebellion and sent him an SOS. It is more likely that it was Townsend who rebelled against not seeing his young sons (he was given custody of them in the divorce – why weren't they with him in Brussels?) and decided that exiled or not he was going to visit England. He arrived under the name of 'Carter' and after an elaborate cloak-and-dagger scheme involving Harrods bookshop was reunited with Margaret at Clarence House. A month or so later Margaret spent the night at Balmoral, unchaperoned, in the proximity, if not the company, of Colin Tennant. This, and the newspaper headlines, frightened Tennant so much that he fled to Venice. 'Dominic Elliot took over with Princess Margaret,'[2] he said laconically.

21 August 1955 was the crucial birthday. Crowds converged expectantly on Balmoral, perhaps hoping to see Townsend descend by parachute. All they saw was a Sale of Work at Abergeldy in aid of Craithie Church, with the Queen, her children, her sister and her mother selling the work. On 1 October Anthony Eden, himself divorced and remarried, arrived at Balmoral with the extraordinary news that certain members of the Cabinet, headed by the Marquess of Salisbury – that same 'Bobbety' who had provided the Comet for Elizabeth's entertainment – threatened to resign if the Princess married the divorced Group Captain; also, if she persisted, it must be made clear that she would forfeit her right to succession, her Civil List allowance and her domicile in the United Kingdom. Lord Salisbury would not have contrived such an ultimatum without consulting Elizabeth. It was, perhaps, the nearest she came to making a pronouncement on the matter.

Whatever her reaction to this, Margaret had already arranged to meet Townsend in London on 13 October. On 9 October Elizabeth flew off to the Castle of Mey for three days, returning to London on the 12th. On the 13th, as arranged, Townsend turned up at Clarence House.[3] The following day the couple went to stay the weekend with Elizabeth's niece, Jean Wills, and her husband at Allanby Park, Binfield. On Sunday Margaret and her cousin drove to Windsor to attend morning service in the Chapel Royal and Margaret went for a forty-minute walk with her mother round the gardens of the Royal Lodge. Anyone who has spent forty minutes walking round the garden with their daughter or mother knows that something more than the floribundas is being discussed. On Monday Townsend and Margaret seem to have had a normal evening out with the Mark Bonham Carters in Kensington – normal, that is, apart from being followed by ravening packs of reporters. On Wednesday they didn't meet; Margaret had dinner at Lambeth Palace with her mother, her sister, her brother-in-law and Archbishop Fisher. On Thursday the Cabinet assembled to discuss a Bill of Renunciation which would free the Princess of her responsibilities under the Royal Marriages Act and enable her to marry Townsend in a civil ceremony. The consequences, of course, were unaltered. Apart from Lord Salisbury's resignation, which might considerably weaken Eden's government, she would have to live abroad, possibly for five years, on an air attaché's pay. The example of her Uncle David was not encouraging.

On Friday, in driving rain and bitter wind, the family gloomily gathered together for the unveiling of King George VI's statue in Carlton Gardens. What would Bertie have thought of all this? 'He was the living symbol of our steadfastness,' said the Queen. '. . . Much was asked of my father in personal sacrifice and endeavour . . . He shirked no task, however difficult, and to the end he never faltered in his duty to his peoples.' She took her sister off to Windsor Castle for the weekend, and their mother went too.

On Monday, *The Times*, right on cue, provided a flourishing cadenza. More hurt than angry, it pointed out that the Royal Family is a reflection of our 'better selves', and that if the Queen's sister entered into a union which our better selves could not 'in conscience regard as a marriage', that reflection would become distorted. As for the young woman's happiness, we must not forget 'that happiness in the full sense is a spiritual state and that its most precious element may be the sense of duty done'. Meanwhile the Church was bellowing for its strayed lamb with phrases like 'an affront to religion' and 'contrary to the law of Christ'.

Given the personalities and circumstances of the couple concerned, the result was inevitable. Margaret, or Townsend, or both, decided that the game wasn't worth the candle. On the evening of the day of *The Times* leader they gave up. For some inexplicable reason 'the royal advisers' were against making the decision public. On Thursday Margaret went to see Archbishop Fisher and return herself officially to the fold, but it was not until the following Monday evening that the BBC broke into its programmes to broadcast her renunciation statement:

> I would like it to be known that I have decided not to marry Group-Captain Peter Townsend. I have been aware that, subject to my renouncing my rights to succession, it might have been possible for me to contract a civil marriage. But, mindful of the Church's teaching, that Christian marriage is indissoluble, and conscious of my duty to the Commonwealth, I have resolved to put these considerations before any others. I have reached this decision entirely alone, and in doing so have been strengthened by the unfailing support and devotion of Group-Captain Townsend. I am deeply grateful for the concern of all those who have constantly prayed for my happiness.

Even though, she might have added, those prayers have been unavailing.

Elizabeth had doubtless interceded on her daughter's behalf – if not necessarily on behalf of her happiness – and was heartily grateful for the result. She had always been a pious Christian, and since entering the Royal Family had made many friends in the upper echelons of the Church of England. The support of Archbishop Fisher in this sad business must have seemed, at the time, a direct sign of God's co-operation and concern.

The Archbishop, however, was unable to leave well alone. He may have been haunted by the spectre of his predecessor, Cosmo Lang, but it clearly didn't warn him. He prattled about the Townsend Affair to Richard Dimbleby on a television programme that purported to be about Lambeth Palace. Feeling that he might have been indiscreet, he followed this up with a letter to *The Times* the following day:

> Of course she took advice. She got plenty of advice, asked for, and a good deal more unasked for ... She was seeking all the time what God's will was, and when it became clear what God's will was, she did it, and that is not a bad thing for people in general to take note of ... she especially thanked those who had prayed for her. Only people who have been praying for her can really understand the decisions demanded of her, the problems she had to face, and the tearing of the heart one way or another. Those who prayed for her know what she has been through, and those who have not do not.[4]

This arrogant gobbledegook got the Press on the raw. On 4 November the *Daily Sketch* accused the Archbishop of throwing words 'like a bundle of incendiaries on a dying fire' and suggested that the disestablishment of the Church would be no bad thing. The *Daily Mirror* positively demanded it: 'CRISIS HAS COME TO THE SERENE CLOISTERS OF THE CHURCH OF ENGLAND – Slowly a wave of anger mounts against the Primate, bringing with it a tide of doubt about the teachings of the Church on divorce . . .' The *Daily Express* merely said that the Princess's romance and heart had been 'broken by ecclesiastical influence'.[5] The Archbishop, an ebullient gentleman, survived. Like many survivors, he was masterful with the truth. When asked in Capetown whether the fuss had been justified, he replied cheerily, 'The whole thing – and you can quote me – was purely a stunt.'[6]

Five years later, on 6 May 1960, Margaret married Antony Armstrong-Jones in Westminster Abbey. The marriage lasted for eighteen years and produced two children, David, in 1961, and Sarah, in 1964. Apart from the attendant publicity, it followed much the same course as innumerable other wealthy, upper-class marriages. Elizabeth was fond of her son-in-law – she had been fond of Townsend – and unhappy as the relationship deteriorated. On 24 May 1978 Margaret was granted a decree nisi and on 15 December her ex-husband married a girl called Lucy Lindsay-Hogg, who soon afterwards gave birth to a daughter.

The only constructive result of all this as far as the country was concerned was that the official attitude to divorce was forced to become less rigid, the Church lost much of its authority and the divorce laws themselves, eventually, were made more humane. The image of a King who sacrificed the throne for the woman he loved had been replaced in the mythology of the New Elizabethans by the Princess who sacrificed the man she loved for the sake of duty, a title, and £15,000 a year. This was exactly what Elizabeth had prayed for. How perplexing, then, to see David Windsor devotedly faithful to Wallis until his death; Peter Townsend married to a beautiful young Belgian, living happily ever after; her divorced son-in-law contented with his family and his work; and her dutiful daughter, brought up on the highest moral principles, with her mother's shining example always before her, growing older alone, unloved, unappreciated and angry. Most of us would ask ourselves where we went wrong. Elizabeth must have had the fearful suspicion that God Himself had blundered.

CHAPTER

36

In October 1954 Elizabeth went abroad for the first time by herself, to receive the fund collected to commemorate King George VI in the United States. It is one thing to drift, smiling radiantly, in the wake of a King; quite another to take the responsibility alone. She accepted the cheque at a banquet at the Waldorf-Astoria, wearing one of Hartnell's crinolined creations and smothered in priceless jewellery. She unveiled a couple of portraits, met Senator McCarthy and Richard Nixon at the British Embassy and had an animated conversation with Vyshinsky at the United Nations, bestowing her smile impartially. She received an honorary Doctor of Laws degree at Columbia ('a noble Queen, whose quiet and constant courage in time of great stress sustained a nation and inspired a world . . .'), trudged through forty-four galleries of the Metropolitan Museum of Art, expressed much admiration for the Guggenheim, stayed with the Eisenhowers in Washington, was received by Congress.

But it was her lack of nobility that endeared her to the American people. At the Commonwealth Ball she requested the band to play 'Hey there (you with the stars in your eyes)' and 'Hernando's Hideaway'. She adored the Empire State Building, bought a steam shovel and a dolls' plastic teaset at F.A.O. Schwarz and jewelled cashmere sweaters for Margaret and Lilibet at Hammacher Schlemmer, a magnetic bottle opener, a Scrabble set on a turntable, a decanter equipped with an automatic measure – gifts for the Castle that had everything. A New York taxi driver, stuck in a traffic jam on Broadway, watched her arriving to see *Pajama Game*, all sparkles and graciousness and royal fun. 'If she wasn't a Queen there's many a man who'd like to marry her,' he said, and added, after profound consideration, 'She'd be a pleasing handful at playtime.'[1]

Fired by the success of this first solo performance abroad, Elizabeth decided to go on tour. Between 1956 and 1985 she played Northern Rhodesia and Nyasaland twice, Southern Rhodesia four times, Canada nine times, Australia, New Zealand, Honolulu and Fiji twice, Uganda twice, Kenya, Tunisia, the Caribbean, Jamaica, Germany,

Rome, Cyprus, Iran, Venice and Paris, as well as frequent guest appearances in the French provinces, the Channel Islands, the Isle of Man and Northern Ireland. Little Indian, Sioux or Crow, she brought them hope and joy and a glimpse of a better world. To the black peoples – now known as the Third World – she presented herself as *Mambo Kazi*, entertaining them with suitably simple, if incomprehensible, metaphors about oxen and ploughs and harvests.★ To those of her own class, creed and colour she brought reassurance that everything was still as it should be and that they were not forgotten. The indefatigable old lady's latest transatlantic engagement was a month before her eighty-fifth birthday, when she went to Canada on an eight-day official visit and made even larger headlines than usual by dropping her glove and picking it up. Between the 12th and 22nd of July she toured Ontario, Saskatchewan and Alberta, opened the fifth World Angus Forum, watched the 126th running of the Queen's Plate, insisted on being taken up the 850 foot C.N. Tower in Toronto in spite of the fact that the view was almost totally obscured by smog, and made a number of charming speeches.

Some trips, naturally, have been more fun than others. One of the most enjoyable was to Jamaica in 1965. The eighty-two-year-old Princess Alice, Countess Athlone, who had marched Elizabeth up a Scottish mountain so long ago, was, at that time, Chancellor of the University College of the West Indies. Every January, sharing a small cabin on a banana boat and accompanied by only one maid, the old lady would sail to Jamaica to fulfil her various duties. One of these, in February that year, was to confer an honorary Doctor of Letters on the Queen Mother. The ceremony was hilarious. Princess Alice had a fit of the giggles and nice Mr Adlai Stevenson, their distinguished speaker, was most droll. 'Well, Mr Stevenson,' Elizabeth said, cocking her head on one side, twinkling up at him, 'we were together at Oxford six weeks ago, and now we meet here. Where shall it be next?' 'You name the place, Ma'am, and I'll be there,'[2] he replied, the perfect gentleman.

A few days later she and her entourage drove what seemed like hundreds of miles to lunch with her dear friend Noel Coward. They had bullshots on the verandah and then delicious curry served in steaming coconuts, followed by strawberries and rum cream pie. 'I am at her feet,' Coward wrote in ecstasy. 'She has infinite grace of mind, charm, humour and deep-down kindness, in addition to which she looks enchanting . . . The houseboy – by his special request – wore white gloves and a white coat. It was all tremendous fun . . . and she

★ 'When one ox pulls this way and the other that, nothing is achieved. It may even be that the yoke is broken. But when all bow their yokes the plough moves and the work for the harvest has begun.'

left behind her five gibbering worshippers.'³★

★ ★ ★

At home, the Queen Mother's favourite roles over the last thirty years are said to have been as Chancellor of London University and as Lord Warden of the Cinque Ports, neither of which parts had previously been played by a woman. The first, which she took over in 1955, lasted until 1980 and was a resounding success. The second, which among many other honours entitled her to any flotsam and jetsam washed up between Shore Beacon, Essex, and Redcliffe in Sussex, had since World War I been performed at various times by Sir Robert Menzies, Sir Winston Churchill (he wore his costume to the Coronation of Elizabeth II) and the one-time Liberal Leader, Earl Beauchamp KG, although it is unlikely that this particular Warden was mentioned, as in June 1931 he absented himself in a great hurry after being accused of homosexual practices by his brother-in-law the Duke of Westminster. 'I thought fellows like that shot themselves,' King George V exclaimed in astonishment. Anyway, the Earl was certainly not in Elizabeth's thoughts when she said, 'I feel both proud and humble to follow these great men,' while a nineteen-gun salute boomed through the sea mist and the new flag was broken above Dover Castle.

She is associated either as President or Patron with 312 organizations, ranging from the Royal Agricultural Society to the Dachsund Club, Colonel in Chief of 18 regiments, Commandant-in-Chief of the Women's Army, Navy and Air Force and Master of the Bench of the Middle Temple. She is a Lady of the Order of the Garter, a Lady of the Thistle, a Lady of the Grand Cross of the Royal Victorian Order, a Lady of the Grand Cross Order of the British Empire and Imperial Order of the Crown of India and is eligible to act as a Counsellor of State. Her engagements for 1985 were perhaps slightly less arduous than in previous years. She sailed to the Isles of Scilly but only went abroad, officially, three times; for the rest it was mainly jobs like visiting a supermarket, stirring a celebratory cake for the Royal Navy,

★ On 28 March 1984 the Queen Mother unveiled a memorial stone in Westminster Abbey to 'Noel Coward, Playwright, Actor and Composer'. The Address was given by Sir Richard Attenborough CBE, flowers were laid at the foot of the stone by The Lord Olivier OM and at its four corners by Miss Joyce Carey OBE, Sir John Mills CBE, Miss Evelyn Laye CBE and Dame Anna Neagle DBE. Penelope Keith gave The Toast from 'Cavalcade' and the ancient Abbey, home of the Lords Spiritual, coronation place of Monarchs, shrine of Shakespeare and Milton, was filled with the nostalgic melodies of 'Someday I'll Find You' and 'I'll See You Again'. It was a triumphant marriage of Show Business and the Establishment, which only Elizabeth could have arranged. By the time the Ambrosian Singers had finished with 'London Pride' there wasn't a dry eye in the house.

christening a new railway train and scattering a trowelful of token
gravel on the roof of King's College Hospital. The impression, nevertheless, is one of a hectic succession of commitments that could not
possibly be fulfilled by any other woman of her age. How, people ask,
aghast, does she do it?

Mainly by helicopter. Sometimes in the Royal Yacht. Wherever she
goes a lady-in-waiting goes with her, and she is nearly always
accompanied by her faithful Private Secretary, Sir Martin Gilliat.
Their responsibility is to dispose of all the minute difficulties that
might impede the royal progress, to keep their eyes peeled, their ears
to the ground, their noses to windward. The organization is impeccable, though sometimes upset by the lady's vagueness about time.
The Queen Mother Image is dressed, coiffeured, made up, transported, deposited. When the performance is over it is fetched,
transported, deposited, fed, cleaned and put carefully away for the
night. If the Queen Mother beckons, someone notices; if she calls,
someone comes. All she has to do when she drops fresh as a daisy from
the sky is to generate love, delight and enthusiasm. As this is her
nature, anyway, and she thoroughly enjoys it, it is not most people's
idea of work, which is usually associated with effort and often with a
dragging reluctance. Public ceremonies when she is one of the royal
crowd come very low on her list of priorities.

★   ★   ★

If one asks people what, if anything, they think lies behind this
appearance of ceaseless activity, many hazard a guess at suffering:
'She's been through it,' they say knowingly. The Queen Mother has
an instinctive distaste for disease, maiming, malformation of any
kind,[4] which must make her patronage of the British Home and
Hospital for Incurables one of her more trying duties. Fortunately in
her own life she has encountered less physical unpleasantness than
most women. In the first decade of her widowhood she was prone to
stumbling or walking into unexpected furniture: in 1956 she fell down
at Clarence House and twisted her ankle, in 1960 she knocked her leg
at the Royal Lodge, in 1961 she fell during an Ascot houseparty at
Windsor and broke a bone in her foot, in 1962 she 'stumbled' at
Birkhall and broke it again; she then seems to have kept her balance
until just before her grandson's wedding in 1981, when she stumbled
at Ascot and wounded herself so severely that she ran a high tempera-
ture. (There is no available photograph of her wearing glasses, though
in 1971 Loelia, Duchess of Westminster snapped her holding a pair.) In
1982 she choked on a fishbone during a dinner party at the Royal
Lodge and had to be whisked to hospital to have it removed under a
general anaesthetic. She had her appendix out in 1964 and a colostomy

in 1966. This – the removal of a major part of the bowel, which is replaced by a plastic bag with a special adhesive for making a comfortable, leak-proof joint to the skin – was referred to as 'major abdominal surgery' for the next thirteen years. The Colostomy Welfare Group was delighted when 'Helen Cathcart', one of the Queen Mother's numerous biographers, eventually revealed the truth. 'We always knew about the Queen Mother,' they said. 'The fact that it has now become public knowledge will encourage the 20,000 or so people who have this operation every year . . . what a pity they don't talk about it.' To be widowed at the age of fifty-one, to have to deal with a difficult daughter, to undergo major surgery in one's mid-sixties and to find oneself in old age the sole survivor of eight siblings may not be the sunny side of life, but it is not uncommon. One of the penalties of Elizabeth's chosen profession was to have to suffer her misfortunes in the public eye. She would not have preferred the public ward.

There have been less tangible discomforts. Her niece Anne Anson – Jock's eldest girl, and Patrick Lichfield's mother – was divorced from her husband in 1948 and married Prince Georg of Denmark two years later. Another niece, Nancy Moira – twin sister of Timothy the 16th Earl – was divorced in 1950 and remarried in 1954 while Margaret and Townsend were enduring their enforced separation. In 1967 Lord Harewood, the Queen's cousin, was divorced; in a few months he married Patricia Tuckwell, by whom he already had a two-year-old son. In 1978 another royal nephew, Michael of Kent, married the divorced Roman Catholic Baroness Marie-Christine von Reibnitz, who was immediately accorded the title of Her Royal Highness. Elizabeth's ostensible reason for the embargo on Wallis Windsor could no longer be justified.

The Queen Mother gently but firmly dissociated herself from all these problems 'When her niece married a Danish Prince,' Archbishop Fisher explained to James Pope-Hennessy, 'she didn't disapprove; but she wouldn't go. Didn't want to get muddled up in it, if you see what I mean.'[5] Neither did she want to get muddled up in the sad life of her nephew Timothy. Timothy Bowes-Lyon's mother died while preparing to move to Glamis after her husband's succession. His sister, Lady Harrington, who was to have taken Lady Strathmore's place as first lady of Glamis, died in Switzerland very shortly afterwards. His elder brother, John Patrick, was killed in action in 1941. Crushed by these disasters added to his inherited melancholy, Lord Strathmore became a recluse. He died in 1949 and his sister Elizabeth, then Queen, went to his funeral. In June 1958, nine years after his own succession, Timothy married a nurse at the Home where he was having treatment for alcoholism. Mary Bridget Brennan was a Roman Catholic, but at least she had not been divorced. There was no just cause or impediment why she should not be the Countess of Strathmore. Elizabeth ignored the wedding. So, therefore, did everyone else. On 8 December 1959 the Countess gave birth to a daughter in London. The baby died of bronchopneumonia at Glamis three weeks later. On 8 September 1967 the Countess committed suicide.[6] Elizabeth sent a wreath. This was her sole acknowledgment of Timothy's existence from the day of his marriage until she attended his funeral on 18 September 1972.

Then, of course, there were the Windsors, chronic discomforts. In June 1967 the Queen invited Wallis to accompany the Duke to the unveiling of a Memorial plaque to Queen Mary – the first official recognition the Duchess had ever received from the royal family and the first time that she and Elizabeth had come face to face for over thirty years. The three elderly stars of 1936 – Elizabeth nearly sixty-seven, Wallis almost seventy and David seventy-three – greeted each other in public with undimmed antipathy and fierce smiles. Elizabeth and David brushed cheeks for an instant. Wallis would not curtsey, but accepted and dropped the Queen Mother's proferred hand. She did curtsey to the Queen who, no doubt for some good reason, looked furious throughout the ceremony. It was left to Marina, the Dowager Duchess of Kent, to give the Windsors lunch before they returned to Paris. Elizabeth and her daughter and son-in-law went to the Derby.

To quote the Archbishop once more: '. . . the Queen Mother's attitude to life is to make everything as easy as possible.'[7] Jealousy and anger are not easy emotions. The Queen's official acceptance of Wallis, the fact that Charles had actually visited her and that Wallis was said to be very fond of him, the possibility of a reconciliation after all these years, was hard to take.

In November 1971 the Duke of Windsor was found to have inoperable cancer of the throat. Six months later the Queen, Prince Philip and Charles visited the old man in Paris. David was dying, happy that his request for Wallis to be buried next to him at Frogmore had been granted. He died on 28 May. His coffin was flown home in a VC 10 jet, met by a Royal Guard of Honour, the Duke and Duchess of Kent and members of the Government. For two days he lay in state while 57,000 people filed past the catafalque. On 2 June Wallis, to whom Elizabeth had refused so much as a cup of tea or a petit-four, was flown from Paris in an aeroplane of the Queen's Flight, met at Heathrow by Lord Mountbatten and driven to Buckingham Palace, where she was given the State Suite. The Duchess was heavily drugged for this first visit to her husband's family. On 5 June, after the burial at Frogmore, she wandered among the guests asking 'Where's the Duke? Why isn't the Duke here?' According to Bryan and Murphy, who were certainly not present, Elizabeth took the Duchess's arm and said, 'I know how you feel. I've been through it myself.'[8] This could have been construed as a pointed reminder, but of course it was not meant as such. Wallis flew back to Paris that afternoon. Although Elizabeth would frequently visit France in the future, she has never seen her again.

Whether the Queen Mother has 'forgiven' the Windsors or not is a sentimental speculation. They never harmed her. There is nothing to forgive. It would be more appropriate to wonder whether she has ever felt any remorse; any indication, if only between herself and the Almighty, of sackcloth and ashes. It is improbable. Even her most fervent admirers don't list humility among her many virtues. The Windsors are among the subjects that are never, even obliquely, mentioned in her presence. They may be corpses in her wake or they may be unfortunate spectres, for which she is not responsible; in either case she says 'Poor souls', and walks buoyantly on.

Certainly Wallis, had she remained *compos mentis*, could never have forgiven the Queen Mother. As it is, forgiveness and repentance are meaningless to her. Wallis has arteriosclerosis and is in an advanced state of senility but, protected from all secondary infection, is unable to die. She is four years older than her sister-in-law. It would be easier for the Queen Mother not to have to endure her funeral in St George's Chapel. It would, in fact, be easier for us all.

★   ★   ★

> The Duchess of York
> Said bother the stork!
> But the Kents cried with joy
> It's a boy, it's a boy!

Whether I have quoted this doggerel correctly, or where it comes from, I have no idea; but it must mean that in the distant past somebody, somewhere, was concerned about the Yorks not having a son. Ironically enough, it is men who find Elizabeth so overwhelmingly maternal; or, conversely, she has qualities which bring out the little boys lurking in their hearts. This may be the reason why her closest friends and greatest admirers, as well as the members of her personal staff, have nearly always been bachelors disinclined for marriage. 'The great mother figure and nannie to us all, through the warmth of her sympathy bathes us and wraps us in a counterpane by the fireside...'[9] 'Regal, yet maternal, hers is the constitutional bosom upon which weary millions would gladly rest their heads...'[10] I have read volumes of female mawkishness on the subject of the Queen Mother, but none of them have tugged at this particular heartstring.

If she did, in fact, feel deprived at not having a boy, the Prince of Wales has reaped the benefit. 'Ever since I remember my grandmother has been the most wonderful example of fun, laughter, warmth, infinite security and, above all else, exquisite taste in so many things,'[11] he wrote in 1978 – qualities which were not, perhaps, conspicuous in his immediate family. It is said that he reminds her of Bertie – perhaps the same diffidence, and reluctance to be royal – but from the time he was a baby he was much more promising material. Elizabeth made no secret, for once, of her disapproval of the choice of Gordonstoun, with its emphasis on surviving physical hardship, as a school for the sensitive lad. It was a typical Mountbatten idea. What was wrong with Eton?[12] No one could have been more appalled by his ordeal of being ducked, fully clothed, in a cold bath; no one could have sympathized more with his loneliness and fears.[13] On his frequent visits to Birkhall from Gordonstoun Charles implored her to persuade his parents to take him away, but Elizabeth wouldn't do that. She would, she said, help him face it.[14] This was the way she had made one King; now, happily, she was making another.

Charles was thirty-two when he married Diana Spencer, grand-daughter of Ruth, Lady Fermoy, one of the Queen Mother's few close women friends and, since 1960, her Woman of the Bedchamber. As far as the two grandmothers were concerned it was a highly suitable match, though it was understandable that Elizabeth should have dabbed an eye at the wedding. The production of two great-grandsons over the next three years proved that their hopes had been well founded. If a remote observer senses a deepening melancholy in the Prince of Wales or catches a look that seems to cry 'Help! I am a prisoner in the British Royal Family!', it is probably only the Coburg in him coming out. It is typical that on his grandmother's eighty-fifth birthday he escorted her to the King's Lynn Festival to hear Rosto-povitch, while Radio 4 plodded through an evening's entertainment of her own choice – the Crazy Gang, ITMA and Noel Coward. Whatever frustrations or inchoate longings Charles may or may not suffer from, his relationship with the Queen Mother is clearly one of mutual admiration and devotion.

Perhaps it is not so necessary to be an example of 'infinite security' to girls. Princess Anne seems to have no memory of being wrapped in a counterpane of love. Her reaction to her grandmother is female, like her great-aunt Marina's: 'Sometimes when I think of her I find it depressing because I can't see any way that I could do what she's done,' she told Kenneth Harris in 1980. 'I'm not the best person to talk about her; it wouldn't be the same as the Prince of Wales talking – there is a rather special relationship between the eldest grandson and a grandmother, I think, which is not true of grand-daughters...'[15] Anne 'volunteered'[16] to go to Benenden at the age of thirteen; she got very respectable A-level results and made up her mind that she would become the best eventing rider in the world – which she did. Anne is definitely not *espiègle*. Nor is she happy to be a royal figurehead. Now the most articulate and seemingly the least neurotic of the family, her work for the Save The Children Fund – never wasting time on her image, sensibly dressed, scowling if she feels like it, business-like and brusque – attracts attention to her cause rather than her performance. It is unlikely that the Queen Mother feels that she could never have done what her eldest grand-daughter has done.

Next to Charles, it looks as though Margaret's son and daughter, Viscount Linley and Lady Sarah Armstrong-Jones, are the favoured grandchildren. They belong to a milieu – artistic yet definitely top-drawer, a touch raffish yet a credit to the Queen's Lawn at Ascot – in which during her widowhood the Queen Mother has come to feel very much at home. Queen Mary might not have approved; neither, perhaps, would Bertie. But the snubbing of Lady Cunard and the rejection of Peter Townsend as a suitable son-in-law are both very long ago and Elizabeth has metaphorically loosened her stays a good deal since then. She has fun with David and Sarah and their friends, and they have fun with her, the old darling.

The Queen Mother's only surviving contemporaries in the family, apart from Wallis Windsor, are her brother David's wife, Lady Rachel Bowes-Lyon, and Princess Alice, Duchess of Gloucester. Lady Rachel Bowes-Lyon, a woman who gives the impression of quiet – indeed almost inaudible – courage and endurance, lives modestly at St Paul's Walden Bury among grandchildren and dogs, and cares deeply about her garden. Sir David Bowes-Lyon KCVO died in 1961 while they were staying with Elizabeth at Birkhall. The Duchess of Gloucester, sixteen months younger than Elizabeth, is the antithesis of the Queen Mother – thin, simply dressed, with a face one can study with pleasure, as though reading a long and absorbing story. Her autobiography, published in 1983, is discreetly honest and displays a wry humour, but it is an edited version of that story. The Duke, after suffering two strokes in 1968, lived on for six years, incapable of speech and almost incapable of understanding. Their eldest son, William, was killed in a flying accident in 1972.

As well as the grandchildren and great-grandchildren, there are scores of great-nephews and great-nieces – Bowes-Lyons, Elphin-stones, Granvilles, Cecils, Tetleys, Colmans, and a crop of young Windsors. It is safe to assume that most of them adore her. Whatever family discords there may have been, however many skeletons are neatly packed away in the royal cupboard, Queen Elizabeth the Queen Mother, compared with her contemporaries, is a remarkably fortunate old lady.

ENVOI

'To me,' the Duchess of Gloucester writes of her home, Barnwell Manor, 'it is an abode of quiet peace and contentment and trust. I pray that it may remain so for my family for the years to come.'[1] If this was the Queen Mother's fantasy for the Castle of Mey, it somehow hasn't worked out. For the few weeks in the year she is there she fills it with people, busily organizes fishing expeditions, mock pigeon shoots, trips to the Orkneys, sightseeing, endless picnics, charades, games, anything to keep life going at top speed. From there she may fly to Birkhall, then back to Mey, then back to Birkhall; a day or two at Glamis, perhaps a flit to the Isle of Man, to Rosyth, to Aberdeen, then down to Clarence House for a month or so, with weekends at the Royal Lodge; Christmas at Windsor, January at Sandringham, back to Clarence House for a couple of months, then off again.

How, after all, would she occupy her time if she settled down in Mey? She is frequently described as 'a true countrywoman'; nevertheless, Dorothy Laird writes that 'she seems to have no compulsion to identify herself with nature in the practical, detailed or creative ways which draw most people of such intelligence and personality'. She is said to be a knowledgeable gardener; but again Miss Laird writes that she does not 'plant and sow, weed and grub in the soil'.[2] She owns a herd of Aberdeen Angus (and 'makes a decent living from them', according to Anthony Carthew)[3] and a flock or so of Cheviot sheep; but great though her interest in them may be, she is no more a practical farmer than she is a practising horsewoman. As far as hobbies are concerned, 'she neither paints nor photographs nor collects wild flowers';[4] she does not sew, knit or embroider, cook or write or polish the furniture, drive a car or ride a horse or – as far as I know – play Bingo. She collects paintings and antiques and *objets d'art* – a good investment – and fishes and goes for very fast walks and plays the piano occasionally. Even her dogs are not country dogs. Their meat and cabbage has to be cut up in identical pieces, their beds [sic] neatly made up with plumped pillow and smooth blankets.[5] There are a few endearing pictures of her wearing waders and gum-boots, an old felt hat and a Burberry; but as farmer and squire she appears in the familiar uniform, high heels picking their way over the mud, off-the-face hat firmly clamped, gloves and handbag, pearls and pastels.

She has, of course, a dedicated passion for horse-breeding and racing, and is known as the most successful owner in the land. The racing world worships her. When one of her horses died, the Exchange Telegraph's broadcast service to the nation's betting shops was interrupted by the solemn announcement. One racing correspondent was foolish enough to suggest that the punters resented this – millions of pounds, after all, could have been lost. He was as good as lynched – 'If there is a shorter cut to a bloody nose in Tattersall's than to criticize the Queen Mum in any way, I do not know it!' one editorial raged.[6] It is a man's world in which she is protected, cosseted, and genuinely admired. At the same time, the mating of those splendid stallions and quivering mares holds a strong attraction for many women, and the pounding of hooves on the track, the straining muscles and flaring nostrils can make many a ladylike heart beat faster and bring a flush to the most discreetly powdered cheek. Both the Queen Mother and her eldest daughter are at their least self-conscious on the race-track, giving themselves up to an ecstasy which they appear to feel under no other circumstances. There aren't many race courses in the Highlands. The Royal Stud is at Windsor. The reception on the Bookies' Blower, which she listens to so intently at Clarence House, might be poor on the coast of Pentland Firth.

The fact is that what might mean 'quiet peace and contentment' to some people would be a negation of the Queen Mother's *raison d'être* which is, according to Miss Laird, 'to bring her personality and add it to yours, making your aims higher, your achievement greater, your courage brighter and your spirit happier'.[7] To do this, of course, she needs *you*, the audience; she needs the support of the rest of the cast; she needs the brief, safe relationships and glancing contacts, the people who are waiting to welcome her, the people who were sorry to see her go. As for the final curtain, her favourite scene from Noel Coward's *Private Lives*, which she chose for her eighty-fifth birthday radio programme, is very revealing:

> *Elyot:* You mustn't be serious, my dear one. It's just what they want.
> *Amanda:* Who's 'they'?
> *Elyot:* All the futile moralists who try to make life unbearable. Laugh at them. Be flippant. Laugh at everything – all their sacred shibboleths. Flippancy brings out the acid in their damned sweetness and light.
> *Amanda:* If I laugh at everything, I must laugh at us too.
> *Elyot:* Certainly you must. We're figures of fun all right...
> *Amanda:* And what happens if one of us dies? Does the one that's left still laugh?
> *Elyot:* Yes – yes, with all his might.
> *Amanda:* That's serious enough, isn't it?
> *Elyot:* No. No, it isn't. Death's very laughable – such a cunning little mystery. All done with mirrors.

Amanda: Darling. I believe you're talking nonsense.
Elyot: So is everyone else, in the long run. Let's be superficial and pity the poor Philosophers. Let's blow trumpets and squeakers, and enjoy the party as much as we can, like very small, quite idiotic school children. Let's savour the delights of the moment. Come and kiss me, darling, before your body rots and worms pop in and out of your eye-sockets . . . [8]

'I suppose,' Queen Mary asked Lady Shaftesbury suddenly one day, 'one must force oneself to go on to the end?'[9] Sooner or later the image of 'Queen Elizabeth the Queen Mother', also, will be lowered with pomp and ceremony and lamentation into the Royal Vault, before it lies beside Bertie in his own Memorial Chapel for ever. But the implacable end anticipated by Queen Mary is not part of Elizabeth's itinerary. It may be increasingly difficult for an octogenarian to climb into the helicopter, but once air-borne the flight is effortless, skimming over the dull pedestrian world, skimming over empty spaces and uneasy silences, over neglect and indifference, landing only where the lights shine and the climate is entirely dependable. One day she will simply spin out of sight, emerging God knows where to carry on with the angels.

August 1985

NOTES

INTRODUCTION

1 Cynthia Asquith, *Haply I May Remember* (London, 1950), 192
2 Dorothy Laird, *Queen Elizabeth The Queen Mother* (London, 1966), 9-10

CHAPTER 1

1 *Forfar Herald*, 24 August 1900
2 Philippe Julian, *Edward and the Edwardians*, 224
3 Leonard Woolf, *Sowing* (London, 1970), 55
4 *The Memoirs of Princess Alice, Duchess of Gloucester* (London, 1983), 12
5 *Daily Express*, 5 November 1908
6 Lady Cynthia Asquith, *Queen Elizabeth* (London, 1937), 51-2
7 *Chips: The Diaries of Sir Henry Channon*, edited by Robert Rhodes James (London, 1967), 484
8 Asquith, *Queen Elizabeth*, 77
9 James Wentworth Day, *The Queen Mother's Family Story* (London, 1967), 135
10 *Ibid*.
11 Asquith, *Queen Elizabeth*, 62
12 *Daily Express*, 1 July 1909
13 Asquith, *Queen Elizabeth*, 49-51
14 *Daily Express*, 1 July 1909
15 Asquith, *Queen Elizabeth*, 51

CHAPTER 2

1 Christopher Hibbert, *Edward VII: A Portrait* (London, 1982), 300
2 Kenneth Rose, *King George V* (London, 1983), 76
3 David Duff, *Alexandra, Princess and Queen* (London, 1980), 255
4 HRH the Duke of Windsor, *A King's Story* (London, 1951), 79
5 *Ottoline, the Early Memoirs of Lady Ottoline Morrell*, edited by Robert Gathorne-Hardy (London, 1974), 96
6 Asquith, *Queen Elizabeth*, 60
7 The Duchess of Gloucester, *Memoirs*, 43
8 Frances Donaldson, *King George VI and Queen Elizabeth* (London, 1977), 22

9 Helen Cathcart, *The Queen Mother Herself* (London, 1979), 42

CHAPTER 3

1 Rose, *King George V*, 166
2 *Ibid*, 168
3 Asquith, *Queen Elizabeth*, 82
4 James Stuart (Viscount Stuart of Findhorn), *Within the Fringe, An Autobiography* (London, 1967), 6
5 *Ibid*.
6 *The Duchess of Gloucester, Memoirs*, 44
7 Asquith, *Queen Elizabeth*, 83
8 Lady Cynthia Asquith, *Diaries, 1915-1918* (London, 1968), 86
9 Stuart, *Within the Fringe*, 16
10 A. J. P. Taylor, *English History, 1914-1945* (London, 1970), 156
11 Elizabeth Longford, *The Queen Mother* (London, 1981), 16

CHAPTER 4

1 John Wheeler-Bennett, *King George VI* (London, 1958), 6
2 J.G. Lockhart, *Cosmo Gordon Lang* (London, 1949), 143
3 Wheeler-Bennett, *King George VI*, 18
4 *Ibid*, 22
5 HRH the Duke of Windsor, *A King's Story*, 17
6 *Ibid*.
7 Wheeler-Bennett, *King George VI*, 21
8 Mabell, Countess of Airlie, *Thatched with Gold* (London, 1962), 113
9 Wheeler-Bennett, *King George VI*, 25
10 *Ibid*, 28
11 *Ibid*, 32
12 Frances Donaldson, *Edward VIII* (London, 1974), 29
13 Wheeler-Bennett, *King George VI*, 45
14 *Ibid*, 58
15 *Ibid*, 69
16 *Ibid*, 71
17 *Ibid*, 63
18 *Ibid*, 74
19 *Ibid*, 76
20 Donaldson, *Edward VIII*, 50

21 Wheeler-Bennett, *King George VI*, 87
22 *Ibid*, 85
23 *Ibid*, 93
24 *Ibid*, 97
25 *Ibid*.
26 *Ibid*, 93n
27 *Ibid*, 100
28 *Ibid*, 103
29 *Ibid*, 116
30 *Ibid*, 120

CHAPTER 5

1 Stuart, *Within the Fringe*, 14
2 Wheeler-Bennett, *King George VI*, 119
3 *Ibid*, 131
4 Longford, *The Queen Mother*, 17
5 *The Lady*, June 1920
6 Longford, *The Queen Mother*, 18
7 Robert Graves and Alan Hodge, *The Long Weekend: A Social History of Great Britain, 1918-1939*, 118
8 Airlie, *Thatched with Gold*, 166
9 Channon, *Diaries*, 68
10 Longford, *The Queen Mother*, 18
11 Channon, *Diaries*, 157
12 Stuart, *Within the Fringe*, 42
13 Longford, *The Queen Mother*, 18
14 *Ibid*.
15 Sencourt, *Edward VIII* (London, 1962), 18
16 Barbara Cartland, *We Danced All Night* (London, 1970), 126
17 Stuart, *Within the Fringe*, 53-4
18 Cathcart, *The Queen Mother Herself*, 66
19 *The Tatler*, 13 October 1920
20 Robert Lacey, *Majesty* (London, 1977), 55
21 Airlie, *Thatched with Gold*, 166-7

CHAPTER 6

1 David Sinclair, *Queen and Country* (London, 1979), 47
2 Airlie, *Thatched with Gold*, 163
3 Wheeler-Bennett, *King George VI*, 150
4 *Ibid*, 163
5 *Ibid*.
6 *Ibid*, 166
7 James Pope-Hennessy, *Queen Mary* (London, 1959), 472
8 Ann Edwards, *Matriarch* (London, 1984), 292
9 *Tatler*, 16 March 1921
10 Richard Hough, *Edwina* (London, 1983), 64
11 *Tatler*, 10 August 1921
12 *Ibid*, 23 March 1921
13 Airlie, *Thatched with Gold*, 155
14 Aubrey Buxton, *The King in his Country* (London, 1955), 28
15 Airlie, *Thatched with Gold*, 167

CHAPTER 7

1 Lacey, *Majesty*, 56
2 Sinclair, *Queen and Country*, 54
3 Helen Hardinge, *Loyal to Three Kings* (London, 1967), 39
4 *Tatler*, 21 September 1921
5 Cathcart, *The Queen Mother Herself*, 69
6 Pope-Hennessy, *Queen Mary*, 520
7 *Ibid*, 521
8 Brian Masters, *Great Hostesses* (London, 1982), 10
9 Edwards, *Matriarch*, 291
10 Wheeler-Bennett, *King George VI*, 145-6
11 *Memoirs of a Conservative: J.C.C. Davidson's Memoirs and Papers 1910-1937*, edited by Robert Rhodes James (London, 1969), 19
12 *Ibid*, 109
13 *Ibid*, 110
14 *Ibid*.
15 Sencourt, *Edward VIII*, 18
16 HRH the Duke of Windsor, *A King's Story*, 182
17 Donaldson, *King George VI and Queen Elizabeth*, 34
18 Rose, *King George V*, 311-12
19 Airlie, *Thatched with Gold*, 167
20 *Ibid*, 48
21 *Ibid*, 54
22 *Ibid*, 59
23 *Ibid*, 62
24 *Ibid*, 168

CHAPTER 8

1 HRH Princess Alice, Countess of Athlone, *For My Grandchildren* (London, 1980), 108
2 Pope-Hennessy, *Queen Mary*, 486
3 Rose, *King George V*, 151
4 Theo Aronson, *Royal Family: Years of Transition* (London, 1983), 72
5 Rose, *King George V*, 37
6 *Ibid*, 71
7 *Ibid*, 151
8 *Ibid*, 20
9 *Ibid*, 84
10 *Ibid*, 55
11 Channon, *Diaries*, 575
12 Pope-Hennessy, *Queen Mary*, 424
13 *Ibid*, 431
14 Airlie, *Thatched with Gold*, 128ff
15 Pope-Hennessy, *Queen Mary*, 517
16 J. Bryan III and Charles J. V. Murphy, *The Windsor Story* (London, 1979), 99

17 Pope-Hennessy, *Queen Mary*, 113
18 *Ibid.*
19 Rose, *King George V*, 302
20 Wheeler-Bennett, *King George VI*, 26n
21 Airlie, *Thatched with Gold*, 113
22 *Ibid*, 145
23 Donaldson, *Edward VIII*, 40
24 Pope-Hennessy, *Queen Mary*, 513
25 Truman Capote, *Esquire*, March 1983
26 HRH the Duke of Windsor, *A King's Story*, 188
27 *Ibid*, 203
28 Donaldson, *Edward VIII*, 40
29 HRH the Duke of Windsor, *A King's Story*, 130
30 Donaldson, *Edward VIII*, 103
31 Noble Frankland, *Prince Henry Duke of Gloucester* (London, 1980), 63
32 *Ibid*, 28
33 Duff and Diana Cooper, *Durable Fire: The Letters of Duff and Diana Cooper 1913-50* (London, 1983), 136
34 Frankland, *Prince Henry*, 26
35 *Ibid*, 161

CHAPTER 9

1 Rose, *King George V*, 311-12
2 *Daily News*, 16 January 1923
3 *The Star*, 17 January 1923
4 *Daily Sketch*, 18 January 1923
5 *Ibid*, 16 January 1923
6 *Ibid*, 17 January 1923
7 *Ibid*, 19 January 1923
8 *The Illustrated London News*, 3 February 1923
9 J. A. Frere, *The British Monarchy at Home* (London, 1963), 110
10 HRH the Duke of Windsor, *A King's Story*, 187
11 Airlie, *Thatched with Gold*, 166
12 Cathcart, *The Queen Mother Herself*, 84
12 *Ibid*, 74
14 *Ibid*, 72
15 Hardinge, *Loyal to Three Kings*, 40
16 *Ibid*, 30
17 *Ibid*, 31
18 *Ibid*, 32
19 HRH the Duke of Windsor, *A King's Story*, 186
20 Rose, *King George V*, 319
21 HRH the Duke of Windsor, *A King's Story*, 185
22 *Ibid*, 186
23 Asquith, *Queen Elizabeth*, 149
24 Dorothy Laird, *Queen Elizabeth The Queen Mother* (London, 1966), 50
25 Rose, *King George V*, 312

26 *The Lady*, 26 April 1923

CHAPTER 10

This chapter is based on reports in *The Times* of 26 and 27 April 1923.

CHAPTER 11

1 Brian Masters, *Great Hostesses* (London, 1982), 87
2 *Ibid*, 88
3 HRH the Duke of Windsor, *A King's Story*, 14
4 Pope-Hennessy, *Queen Mary*, 567
5 HRH the Duke of Windsor, *A King's Story*, 38
6 Hardinge, *Loyal to Three Kings*, 41
7 Wheeler-Bennett, *King George VI*, 192
8 Buxton, *The King in his Country*, 32
9 Sencourt, *Edward VIII*, 36
10 Wheeler-Bennett, *King George VI*, 194
11 *Ibid.*

CHAPTER 12

1 Wheeler-Bennett, *King George VI*, 195
2 J. R. Clynes, *Memoirs*, vol. II (London, 1937), 343
3 Rose, *King George V*, 332
4 Harold Nicolson, *King George V* (London, 1952), 389
5 Harold Nicolson, *Diaries and Letters 1930-1939* (London, 1967), 246
6 Taylor, *British History*, 291
7 Wheeler-Bennett, *King George VI*, 198
8 *Ibid*, 199
9 *Ibid*, 203
10 *Ibid*, 205
11 *Ibid*, 208
12 *Ibid.*
13 Athlone, *For My Grandchildren*, 181

CHAPTER 13

1 Nicolson, *King George V*, 410
2 *Ibid*, 429
3 Cathcart, *The Queen Mother Herself*, 91
4 Elizabeth Longford, *Elizabeth R* (London, 1983), 27
5 Rose, *King George V*, 343
6 Wheeler-Bennett, *King George VI*, 213
7 PD Vol 202, 1231
8 Wheeler-Bennett, *King George VI*, 218
9 *Ibid*, 220
10 *Ibid*, 230
11 Dermot Morrah, *The Work of the Queen* (London, 1958) 14
12 Wheeler-Bennett, *King George VI*, 232

13 Laird, *The Queen Mother,* 115
14 Cooper, *Durable Fire,* 245, 246, 249, 252
15 Pope-Hennessy, *Queen Mary,* 542
16 Donaldson, *Edward VIII,* 137
17 Wheeler-Bennett, *King George VI,* 235
18 James Lees-Milne, *Harold Nicolson: A Biography 1886-1929,* (London, 1980), 365
19 Airlie, *Thatched with Gold,* 197
20 Rose, *King George V,* 367
21 Wheeler-Bennett, *King George VI,* 236

CHAPTER 14

1 David Duff, *George and Elizabeth* (London, 1983), 97
2 *Time* Magazine, 11 June 1923
3 Aldo Castellani, *Microbes, Men and Monarchs: Autobiography* (London, 1963), 116-17
4 Lord Harewood, *The Tongs and the Bones* (London, 1981), 15
5 Castellani, *Microbes, Men and Monarchs,* 117
6 Airlie, *Thatched with Gold,* 183-6
7 HRH the Duke of Windsor, *A King's Story,* 235
8 Rebecca West, *1900* (London, 1982), 116
9 André Maurois, *Memoirs* (London, 1970), 179
10 HRH the Duke of Windsor, *A King's Story,* 242
11 Pope-Hennessy, *Queen Mary,* 550
12 Rose, *King George V,* 378
13 Wheeler-Bennett, *King George VI,* 258

CHAPTER 15

1 Morrah, *The Work of the Queen,* 16
2 *Ibid.*
3 *Ibid,* 17
4 Sir Robert Bruce Lockhart, *Diaries* (London, 1973), Vol. 1, 215
5 Gloria Vanderbilt and Thelma Furness, *Double Exposure* (London, 1959), 281
6 *Ibid,* 282
7 *Ibid,* 280
8 Longford, *Elizabeth R,* 51
9 Bruce Lockhart, *Diaries,* 326
10 Stella King, *Princess Marina: Her Life and Times* (London, 1969), 135
11 Channon, *Diaries,* 37
12 Rose, *King George V,* 395
13 Duchess of Gloucester, *Memoirs,* 103
14 Rose, *King George V,* 390
15 The Duchess of Windsor, *The Heart Has Its Reasons* (London, 1956), 216

CHAPTER 16

1 HRH the Duke of Windsor, *A King's Story,* 261
2 Nicolson, *King George V,* 530
3 Wheeler-Bennett, *King George VI,* 265
4 Lockhart, *Cosmo Gordon Lang,* 391
5 *Ibid.*
6 *Ibid,* 392
7 Rose, *King George V,* 303
8 Hardinge, *Loyal to Three Kings,* 61
9 HRH the Duke of Windsor, *A King's Story,* 265
10 Marie Belloc Lowndes, *Diaries and Letters 1911-1947* (London, 1971), 146
11 Donaldson, *Edward VIII,* 179
12 HRH the Duke of Windsor, *A King's Story,* 266
13 The Duchess of Windsor, *The Heart Has Its Reasons,* 221
14 Channon, *Diaries,* 71
15 *The Times,* 28 January 1936
16 HRH the Duke of Windsor, *A King's Story,* 267
17 The Duchess of Windsor, *The Heart Has Its Reasons,* 221
18 Marion Crawford, *The Little Princesses* (London, 1950), 32
19 HRH the Duke of Windsor, *A King's Story,* 270

CHAPTER 17

1 HRH the Duke of Windsor, *A King's Story,* 292
2 Wheeler-Bennett, *King George VI,* 271
3 Channon, *Diaries,* 76
4 Nicolson, *Diaries,* 245
5 *Ibid,* 238
6 Nicolson, *King George V,* 366
7 Francis Watson, *Dawson of Penn* (London, 1950), 285
8 The Duchess of Windsor, *The Heart Has Its Reasons,* 225
9 Hardinge, *Loyal to Three Kings,* 54
10 The Duchess of Windsor, *The Heart Has Its Reasons,* 224
11 *Ibid,* 225
12 *Ibid.*
13 *Ibid.*
14 Crawford, *The Little Princesses* (American edition, 1950), 72
15 *Ibid.*
16 *Ibid.*
17 *Ibid* (British edition, 1950), 36
18 Channon, *Diaries,* 563
19 The Duchess of Gloucester, *Memoirs,* 113
20 Hardinge, *Loyal to Three Kings,* 102

21 *Ibid.*
22 *Ibid,* 103
23 *Ibid,* 102
24 Nicolson, *King George V,* 516n
25 Wheeler-Bennett, *King George VI,* 274
26 Pope-Hennessy, *Queen Mary,* 568

CHAPTER 18

1 Hardinge, *Loyal to Three Kings,* 112
2 *Ibid.*
3 Belloc Lowndes, *Diaries,* 148
4 Hardinge, *Loyal to Three Kings,* 113
5 Frere, *British Monarchy,* 109
6 Keith Middlemas and John Barnes,
Baldwin: A Biography (London, 1969), 982
7 Hardinge, *Loyal to Three Kings,* 116
8 *Ibid,* 117
9 *Ibid.*
10 Donaldson, *Edward VIII,* 224
11 Hardinge, *Loyal to Three Kings,* 119
12 HRH the Duke of Windsor, *A King's
Story,* 316
13 *Ibid,* 318
14 *Ibid,* 319

CHAPTER 19

1 Donaldson, *Edward VIII,* 228
2 Hardinge, *Loyal to Three Kings,* 120-4
3 *Ibid,* 124
4 *Ibid,* 131
5 HRH the Duke of Windsor, *A King's
Story,* 323
6 *Time,* 9 November 1936
7 *Ibid,* 7 December 1936
8 HRH the Duke of Windsor, *A King's
Story,* 326
9 Hardinge, *Loyal to Three Kings,* 133
10 *Ibid.*
11 HRH the Duke of Windsor, *A King's
Story,* 327
12 The Duchess of Windsor, *The Heart Has Its
Reasons,* 243
13 Donaldson, *Edward VIII,* 237
14 Middlemas and Barnes, *Baldwin,* 991
15 Donaldson, *Edward VIII,* 241
16 Channon, *Diaries,* 103
17 Donaldson, *Edward VIII,* 238
18 The Duchess of Windsor, *The Heart Has Its
Reasons,* 244-6
19 HRH the Duke of Windsor, *A King's
Story,* 329
20 The Duchess of Windsor, *The Heart Has Its
Reasons,* 246
21 Donaldson, *Edward VIII,* 247
22 *Ibid,* 248
23 Nicolson, *Diaries,* 279

24 *Ibid,* 280
25 The Duchess of Gloucester, *Memoirs,* 113
26 Donaldson, *Edward VIII,* 249
27 The Duchess of Gloucester, *Memoirs,*
113-14
28 HRH the Duke of Windsor, *A King's
Story,* 333
29 Middlemas and Barnes, *Baldwin,* 996
30 HRH the Duke of Windsor, *A King's
Story,* 335
31 *Ibid.*
32 *Ibid.*
33 Diana Moseley quoted by Alastair Forbes,
Spectator, 4 January 1980
34 Laird, *Queen Elizabeth,* 25
35 Wheeler-Bennett, *King George VI,* 283
36 Pope-Hennessy, *Queen Mary,* 577
37 Channon, *Diaries,* 111

CHAPTER 20

1 Evelyn Waugh, *Diaries,* edited by Michael
Davie (London, 1976), 415
2 Channon, *Diaries,* 119
3 *Ibid,* 224
4 Wheeler-Bennett, *King George VI,* 286
5 *Ibid.*
6 *Ibid,* 287
7 Wheeler-Bennett, *King George VI,* 284-7
8 *Ibid,* 288c

CHAPTER 21

1 Nicolson, *Diaries,* 298
2 Wheeler-Bennett, *King George VI,* 293
3 Laird, *Queen Elizabeth,* 155
4 Philip Ziegler, *Crown and People* (London,
1978), 39
5 Wheeler-Bennett, *King George VI,* 310
6 *News Chronicle,* 11 February 1937
7 *Sunday Referee,* 28 February 1937
8 Denis Judd, *King George VI* (London,
1982), 155
9 PD Vol. 319, 1812
10 Bryan and Murphy, *The Windsor Story,*
264
11 Channon, *Diaries,* 131
12 *Ibid,* 132
13 Alastair Forbes, *Spectator,* 4 January 1980
14 Nicolson, *Diaries,* 283
15 Cecil Beaton quoted in Masters, *Great
Hostesses,* 88
16 Nicolson, *Diaries,* 309
17 Middlemas and Barnes, *Baldwin,* 1008
18 *Ibid.*
19 Channon *Diaries,* 122
20 Middlemas and Barnes, *Baldwin,* 1011

21 HRH the Duke of Windsor, *A King's Story*, 380
22 PD Vol. 318
23 *Sunday Mirror*, 3 August 1980
24 Channon, *Diaries*, 114
25 Diana Cooper, *The Light of Common Day* (London, 1959), 191
26 Philip Ziegler, *Diana Cooper* (London, 1981), 209
27 Winston Churchill, *The Gathering Storm* (London, 1948), 197-8
28 Donaldson, *King George VI and Queen Elizabeth*, 84

CHAPTER 22

1 HRH the Duke of Windsor, *A King's Story*, 296
2 Lord Gorrell, *One Man Many Parts* (London, 1956), 69
3 Crawford, *The Little Princesses*, 43
4 Donaldson, *Edward VIII*, 317
5 Pope-Hennessy, *Queen Mary*, 582
6 Janet Flanner, *London Was Yesterday; 1934-9* (London, 1975), 71
7 Lockhart, *Cosmo Gordon Lang*, 421
8 *Ibid*, 423
9 Lacey, *Majesty*, 146
10 Wheeler-Bennett, *King George VI*, 312-13
11 Ann Morrow, *The Queen Mother* (London, 1984), 93
12 Channon, *Diaries*, 157
13 *Ibid*, 59
14 Masters, *Great Hostesses*, 143
15 Harewood, *The Tongs and the Bones*, 17
16 Flanner, *London Was Yesterday*, 90
17 David Duff, *Elizabeth of Glamis* (London, 1973), 198
18 Masters, *Great Hostesses*, 106
19 William L. Shirer, *Berlin Diary* (New York, 1941), 76
20 Cecil Beaton, *Self Portrait with Friends* (London, 1979), 58
21 Donaldson, *King George VI and Queen Elizabeth*, 322
22 *Ibid.*
23 *Cavalcade*, 5 June 1937
24 Pope-Hennessy, *Queen Mary*, 589

CHAPTER 23

1 Frances Stevenson, *Lloyd George* (London, 1971), 309
2 Meryle Secrest, *Kenneth Clark* (London, 1984), 119
3 *Ibid.*
4 *Ibid*, 118
5 *Ibid*, 119

6 *Ibid.*
7 Michael Holroyd, *Augustus John* (London, 1974), 491
8 *Ibid*, 492
9 *Ibid*, 489
10 Cooper, *The Light of Common Day*, 224
11 *Ibid.*
12 *Ibid*, 222-3
13 Shirer, *Berlin Diary*, 120
14 Wheeler-Bennett, *King George VI*, 344
15 Buxton, *The King in his Country*, 72
16 Wheeler-Bennett, *King George VI*, 347-8
17 *Ibid*, 348
18 Asquith, *Diaries*, 33
19 Pope-Hennessy, *Queen Mary*, 590
20 Nicolson, *Diaries*, 370
21 Pope-Hennessy, *Queen Mary*, 591
22 Wheeler-Bennett, *King George VI*, 355

CHAPTER 24

1 Cathcart, *The Queen Mother Herself*, 137
2 Pope-Hennessy, *Queen Mary*, 593
3 Andrew Barrow, *Gossip 1920-1970* (London, 1978), 98
4 Lacey, *Majesty*, 154
5 Pope-Hennessy, *Queen Mary*, 594
6 *Ibid.*
7 Wheeler-Bennett, *King George VI*, 378
8 *Ibid.*
9 Eleanor Roosevelt, *Autobiography* (London, 1962), 155
10 *Ibid*, 156
11 *Ibid,*
12 *Ibid*, 155
13 *Ibid*, 159
14 Crawford, *The Little Princesses*, 57
15 Nicolson, *Diaries*, 405
16 Beaton, *Self Portrait*, 68-71
17 Wheeler-Bennett, *King George VI*, 394
18 *Ibid*, 396
19 *Ibid*, 400
20 Buxton, *The King in His Country*, 75-6
21 Wheeler-Bennett, *King George VI*, 401n
22 *Ibid*, 402
23 Nicolson, *Diaries*, 420
24 Churchill, *The Gathering Storm*, 364

CHAPTER 25

1 Pope-Hennessy, *Queen Mary*, 472
2 Morrow, *The Queen Mother*, 120
3 Andrew Duncan, *The Reality of Monarchy* (London, 1970), 101
4 Morrow, *The Queen Mother*, 122
5 Laird, *Queen Elizabeth the Queen Mother*, 222
6 Duncan, *The Reality of Monarchy*, 101

7 Johnston, Sir Eric St., *One Policeman's Story* (London, 1978)
8 Ziegler, *Crown and People*, 36
9 Michael Bloch, *The Duke of Windsor's War* (London, 1982), 32
10 Bruce Lockhart, *Diaries*, 241
11 *Ibid*, 364

CHAPTER 26

1 Lacey, *Majesty*, 21
2 Belloc Lowndes, *Diaries*, 191
3 Wheeler-Bennett, *King George VI*, 435
4 *Ibid*, 438
5 Churchill, *The Gathering Storm*, 599
6 Martin Gilbert, *Finest Hour: Winston S. Churchill, 1939-1941* (London, 1983), 961
7 Wheeler-Bennett, *King George VI*, 553
8 *Ibid*, 450
9 *By Safe Hand: Letters of Sybil and David Eccles 1939-1942* (London, 1983), 43
10 The Countess of Athlone, *For My Grandchildren*, 248
11 Crawford, *The Little Princesses*, 68
12 Channon, *Diaries*, 436
13 Wheeler-Bennett, *King George VI*, 459
14 Cathcart, *The Queen Mother Herself*, 146
15 Wheeler-Bennett, *King George VI*, 464
16 Chester Wilmot, *The Struggle for Europe* (London, 1952), 26
17 Wheeler-Bennett, *King George VI*, 466
18 Wilmot, *The Struggle for Europe*, 51
19 Laird, *The Queen Mother*, 213
20 Wheeler-Bennett, *King George VI*, 468
21 Wilmot, *The Struggle for Europe*, 52
22 Wheeler-Bennett, *King George VI*, 559
23 *Ibid*, 618
24 *Ibid*, 537
25 *Ibid*, 491
26 *Ibid*, 538
27 *Ibid*, 611
28 Alan Jenkins, *The Forties* (London, 1977), 52
29 Wheeler-Bennett, *King George VI*, 567
30 *Ibid*, 601
31 Rt. Hon. Harold Macmillan, *War Diaries* (London, 1984), 120
32 Wheeler-Bennett, *King George VI*, 538
33 *Ibid*, 601
34 *Ibid*, 603
35 *Ibid*, 604
36 *Ibid*, 605
37 *Ibid*, 606
38 James McMillan, *The Way It Happened 1935-1950* (London, 1980), 201
39 Wheeler-Bennett, *King George VI*, 608

CHAPTER 27

1 Frankland, *Prince Henry*, 139
2 *Ibid*, 143
3 *Ibid*, 160
4 *Ibid*, 169
5 Channon, *Diaries*, 339, 402
6 Wheeler-Bennett, *King George VI*, 549
7 King, *Princess Marina*, 170
8 PD Vol. 385 1894
9 Belloc Lowndes, *Diaries*, 232
10 Longford, *Elizabeth R*, 90
11 Alexandra of Yugoslavia, *Prince Philip*, 74-5
12 Longford, *Elizabeth R*, 78
13 Lockhart, *Lang*, 443
14 Wheeler-Bennett, *King George VI*, 626
15 Pope-Hennessy, *Queen Mary*, 596
16 Osbert Sitwell, *Queen Mary and Others* (London, 1974), 34
17 Pope-Hennessy, *Queen Mary*, 600
18 *Ibid*, 601
19 Sitwell, *Queen Mary*, 45
20 *Ibid*.
21 Pope-Hennessy, *Queen Mary*, 603
22 *Ibid*, 604
23 *Ibid*, 609
24 *Ibid*.

CHAPTER 28

1 Donaldson, *Edward VIII*, 347
2 Stephen Birmingham, *Duchess* (London, 1981), 204
3 Wheeler-Bennett, *King George VI*, 417
4 Hore Belisha, *Private Papers* (London, 1960), 236-9
5 Bloch, *The Duke of Windsor's War*, 30
6 *Ibid*, 40
7 Donaldson, *Edward VIII*, 353
8 The Duchess of Windsor, *The Heart Has Its Reasons*, 329
9 Bloch, *The Duke of Windsor's War*, 41
10 *Ibid*, 45
11 Frankland, *Prince Henry*, 155
12 Bloch, *The Duke of Windsor's War*, 41
13 *Ibid*, 71
14 Donaldson, *Edward VIII*, 358
15 Bloch, *The Duke of Windsor's War*, 74
16 Donaldson, *Edward VIII*, 367
17 Gilbert, *Finest Hour*, 699
18 *Ibid*, 613
19 Bloch, *The Duke of Windsor's War*, 127
20 *Ibid*.
21 *Ibid*, 272
22 *Ibid*, 329
23 Pope-Hennessy, *Queen Mary*, 614
24 Bloch, *The Duke of Windsor's War*, 365

CHAPTER 29

1 Wheeler-Bennett, *King George VI*, 645
2 *Ibid*, 666
3 Duff, *Elizabeth of Glamis*, 264-5
4 Buxton, *King in His Country*, 82
5 Lane, *The Queen Mother* (London, 1979), 24
6 Airlie, *Thatched with Gold*, 223-4
7 *Ibid*, 227
8 Wheeler-Bennett, *King George VI*, 686
9 Peter Townsend, *Time and Chance* (London, 1978), 171
10 *Ibid*, 177
11 *Ibid*, 178
12 James Cameron, *The Best of Cameron* (London, 1981), 328
13 *Ibid*, 46
14 Nigel Dempster, *Princess Margaret* (London, 1981), 8
15 Basil Boothroyd, *Philip* (London, 1971), 24
16 William Purcell, *Fisher of Lambeth* (London, 1969), 170
17 Channon, *Diaries*, 510
18 Christopher Hibbert, *Edward VII: A Portrait* (London, 1976), 179
19 Wheeler-Bennett, *King George VI*, 754-5
20 James Lees-Milne, *Caves of Ice* (London, 1983), 239
21 *Ibid*, 129
22 Richard Hough, *Mountbatten, Hero of our Time* (London, 1980), 273

CHAPTER 30

1 Alexandra of Yugoslavia, *Prince Philip*, 107
2 Crawford, *Little Princesses*, 123
3 Geoffrey Wakeford, *Thirty Years A Queen* (London, 1968), 214
4 Peter Townsend, *The Last Emperor* (London, 1975), 321
5 Wheeler-Bennett, *King George VI*, 716n
6 Eleanor Roosevelt, *Autobiography*, 189
7 *Ibid*.
8 Channon, *Diaries*, 516
9 Townsend, *The Last Emperor*, 182
10 Lacey, *Majesty*, 209
11 Wheeler-Bennett, *King George VI*, 765
12 Anthony Holden, *Charles, Prince of Wales* (London, 1979), 55

CHAPTER 31

1 Wheeler-Bennett, *King George VI*, 766
2 *Ibid*, 767
3 *Ibid*, 768n

4 Alexandra of Yugoslavia, *Prince Philip*, 107-8
5 Brigadier Stanley Clark, *Palace Diary* (London, 1958), 38
6 Channon, *Diaries*, 533
7 Boothroyd, *Philip*, 145
8 Clark, *Palace Diary*, 53
9 *Sunday Pictorial*, 6? July 1950
10 Harold Nicolson, *Diaries 1930-64*, edited by Stanley Olson (London, 1980), 347
11 Pope-Hennessy, *Queen Mary*, 617
12 Peter Townsend, *Time and Chance*, 188
13 Channon, *Diaries*, 561
14 Townsend, *Time and Chance*, 190
15 Buxton, *The King in His Country*, 133
16 Townsend, *Time and Chance*, 190
17 Stuart, *Within the Fringe*, 162
18 Channon, *Diaries*, 562
19 Beaton, *Self Portrait*, 105
20 *The Times*, 12 February 1952
21 Rebecca West, *1900* (London, 1982), 180
22 Dermot Morrah, *The Royal Family in Africa* (London, 1947), 34
23 Channon, *Diaries*, 563
24 From a letter from Queen Elizabeth to Edward Seago, quoted Longford, *The Queen Mother*, 121
25 Lacey, *Majesty*, 219

CHAPTER 32

1 Lacey, *Majesty*, 223
2 Channon, *Diaries*, 564
3 Pope-Hennessy, *Queen Mary*, 619
4 James Cameron, *The Best of Cameron* (London, 1981), 47
5 *Ibid*, 46
6 *Ibid*, 45
7 Boothroyd, *Philip*, 104
8 Clark, *Palace Diary*, 75
9 Airlie, *Thatched with Gold*, 235
10 Pope-Hennessy, *Queen Mary*, 619
11 *Ibid*, 423

CHAPTER 33

1 Laird, *Queen Elizabeth*, 271
2 Lane, *The Queen Mother*, 205
3 Sinclair, *Queen and Country*, 179
4 Victoria Glendinning, *Edith Sitwell: A Unicorn Among Lions* (Oxford, 1983), 299
5 Beaton, *Self Portrait*, 240
6 *Ibid*, 241

CHAPTER 34

1 Townsend, *Time and Chance*, 197
2 *Ibid*.

3 Beaton, *Self Portrait*, 249
4 *Ibid*, 251
5 William Purcell, *Fisher of Lambeth* (London, 1969), 241
6 Clark, *Palace Diary*, 110
7 Ann Edwards, *Daily Express*, 2 June 1953
8 Channon, *Diaries*, 578
9 Beaton, *Self Portrait*, 256
10 Nicolson, *Diaries*, 360
11 Clark, *Palace Diary*, 118
12 Longford, *The Queen Mother*, 141
13 West, *1900*, 61
14 Channon, *Diaries*, 581

CHAPTER 35

1 Noel Coward, *Diaries* (London, 1982), 236
2 Dempster, *Princess Margaret*, 27
3 Townsend, *Time and Chance*, 226
4 Purcell, *Fisher of Lambeth*, 245
5 *Ibid*, 246
6 Townsend, *Time and Chance*, 219

CHAPTER 36

1 Cecil Beaton, unpublished diary, October 1954
2 Aronson, *Princess Alice*, 260
3 Coward, *Diaries*, 593
4 Laird, *Queen Elizabeth*, 26
5 James Pope-Hennessy, *A Lonely Business* (London, 1981), 241

6 *Forfar Dispatch*, 21 October 1972 and the *Daily Express*, 30 August 1977
7 Pope-Hennessy, *A Lonely Business*, 241
8 Bryan and Murphy, *The Windsor Story*, 555
9 Beaton (Selected Diaries), 259
10 Donald Zec, *Nova*, August 1979
11 Geoffrey Talbot, *Country Life Book of Queen Elizabeth the Queen Mother*, 7
12 Holden, *Charles*, 109
13 *Ibid*, 116
14 *Ibid*.
15 Kenneth Rose, *Observer Review*, 17 August 1980
16 Princess Anne, interviewed by Terry Wogan, BBC1, 22 March 1985

ENVOI

1 The Duchess of Gloucester, *Memoirs*, 201
2 Laird, *Queen Elizabeth*, 27
3 *The Queen Mother at Eighty Five*, ITV, 3 August 1985
4 Laird, *Queen Elizabeth*, 27
5 Morrow, *The Queen Mother*, 172-3
6 Frank Keating, *Guardian*, 30 April 1984
7 Laird, *Queen Elizabeth*, 27
8 Noel Coward, *Collected Plays* (London, 1979), 56-7
9 Pope-Hennessy, *Queen Mary*, 619

Acknowledgments

We wish to thank the following for permission to quote extracts: *The Best of Cameron* by James Cameron (reprinted by permission of New English Libarary Ltd); *Edward VIII* by Frances Donaldson (Weidenfeld & Nicolson); *Elizabeth of Glamis* by David Duff (Muller, Blond & White Ltd); *Loyal to Three Kings* by Helen Hardinge (William Kimber & Co); *Queen Elizabeth The Queen Mother* by Dorothy Laird (reprinted by permission of Hodder & Stoughton Ltd); *Queen Mary* by James Pope-Hennessy (George Allen & Unwin); *King George V* by Kenneth Rose (Weidenfeld & Nicolson); *Kenneth Clark* by Meryl Secrest (Weidenfeld & Nicolson); *Within the Fringe* by James Stuart (The Bodley Head); *Time and Chance* by Peter Townsend (Collins Publishers); *King George VI* by John Wheeler-Bennett (by kind permission of the Trustees of the Sir John Wheeler-Bennett Settlement); *The Heart Has Its Reasons* by The Duchess of Windsor (Michael Joseph); *The King and His Country* by Aubrey Buxton (Longman).

SELECT BIBLIOGRAPHY

Airlie, Mabell, Countess of, *Thatched with Gold*. London, 1962.
HM Queen Alexandra of Yugoslavia, *Prince Philip: A Family Portrait*. London, 1949.
Alice, HRH Princess, Duchess of Gloucester, *Memoirs*. London, 1983.
Aronson, Theo, *Princess Alice, Countess of Athlone*. London, 1981.
  Royal Family: Years of Transition. London, 1983.
Asquith, Lady Cynthia, *Diaries, 1915-18*. London, 1968.
  Haply I May Remember. London, 1950.
  Queen Elizabeth. London, 1937.
Barrow, Andrew, *Gossip 1920-70*. London, 1978.
Beaton, Cecil, *Self Portrait with Friends: the Selected Diaries*. London, 1979.
Birmingham, Stephen, *Duchess*. London, 1981.
Bloch, Michael, *The Duke of Windsor's War*. London, 1982.
Boothroyd, Basil, *Philip*. London, 1971.
Buxton, Aubrey, *The King in His Country*. London, 1955.
Byran, J. and Murphy, Charles C.V., *The Windsor Story*. London, 1979.
Cameron, James, *The Best of Cameron*. London, 1981.
Cartland, Barbara, *We Danced All Night*. London, 1970.
Castellani, Aldo, *Microbes, Men and Monarchs*. London, 1963.
Cathcart, Helen, *The Queen Mother Herself*. London, 1979.
Channon, Sir Henry, *Diaries*, edited by Robert Rhodes James. London, 1967.
Churchill, Winston S., *The Gathering Storm*. London, 1948.
Clark, Brigadier Stanley, *Palace Diary*. London, 1958.
Cooper, Diana, *The Light of Common Day*. London, 1959.
Cooper, Duff and Diana, *Durable Fire: Letters of Duff and Diana Cooper*. London, 1983.
Coward, Noel, *Diaries*. London, 1982.
Crawford, Marion, *The Little Princesses*. London, 1950; New York, 1950.
Clynes, J. R., *Memoirs*. London, 1937.
Davison, J. C. C., *Memoirs and Papers 1910-37*, edited by Robert Rhodes James. London, 1969.
Day, James Wentworth, *The Queen Mother's Family Story*. London, 1967.
Dempster, Nigel, *Princess Margaret*. London, 1981.
Donaldson, Frances, *Edward VIII*. London, 1974.
  King George VI and Queen Elizabeth. London, 1977.
Duff, David, *Alexandra, Princess and Queen*. London, 1980.
  Elizabeth of Glamis. London, 1973.
Duncan, Andrew, *The Reality of Monarchy*. London, 1970.
Eccles, Sybil and David, *By Safe Hand: Letters of Sybil and David Eccles 1934-42*. London, 1984.
Edwards, Ann, *Matriarch*. London, 1984.
Flanner, Janet, *London Was Yesterday*. London, 1975.
Frankland, Noble, *Prince Henry, Duke of Gloucester*. London, 1980.
Frere, J. A., *The British Monarchy at Home*. London, 1963.
Gilbert, Martin, *Finest Hour: Winston Churchill, 1939-41*. London, 1983.
Glendinning, Victoria, *Edith Sitwell: A Unicorn Among Lions*. Oxford, 1983.

Gorrell, Lord, *One Man Many Parts*. London, 1956.
Graves, Robert and Hodge, Alan, *The Long Weekend*. London,
Hardinge, Helen, *Loyal to Three Kings*. London, 1967.
Harewood, George, Earl of, *The Tongs and the Bones*. London, 1981.
Hibbert, Christopher, *Edward VII: A Portrait*. London, 1976.
Holden, Anthony, *Charles, Prince of Wales*. London, 1979.
Hore-Belisha, *Private Papers*. London, 1960.
Holroyd, Michael, *Augustus John*. London, 1974.
Hough, Richard, *Edwina*. London, 1983.
   Mountbatten, Hero of our Time. London, 1980.
Jenkins, Alan, *The Forties*. London, 1977.
Johnston, Sir Eric St, *One Policeman's Story*. London, 1978.
Judd, Denis, *King George VI*. London, 1982.
Julian, Philipe, *Edward and the Edwardians*. London, 1967.
King, Stella, *Princess Marina*. London, 1969.
Lacey, Robert, *Majesty*. London, 1977.
Laird, Dorothy, *Queen Elizabeth the Queen Mother*. London, 1966.
Lane, Peter, *The Queen Mother*. London, 1979.
Lees-Milne, James, *Caves of Ice*. London, 1973.
   Harold Nicolson. London, 1980.
Lockhart, J.G., *Cosmo Gordon Lang*. London, 1949.
Lockhart, Sir Robert Bruce, *Diaries*. London, 1973.
Longford, Elizabeth, *Elizabeth R*. London, 1983.
   The Queen Mother. London, 1981.
Lowndes, Marie Belloc, *Diaries*. London, 1971.
Macmillan, Harold, Rt. Hon., *War Diaries*. London, 1984.
MacMillan, James, *The Way It Happened*. London, 1980.
Masters, Brian, *Great Hostesses*. London, 1982.
Maurois, André, *Memoirs*. London, 1970-7.
Middlemas, Keith, and Barnes, John, *Baldwin: A Biography*. London, 1969.
Morrah, Dermot, *The Royal Family in Africa*. London, 1947.
   The Work of the Queen. London, 1958.
Morrow, Ann, *The Queen Mother*. London, 1984.
Nicolson, Harold, *Diaries and Letters 1930-39*. London, 1967.
   Diaries 1930-64, edited by Stanley Olson. London, 1980.
   King George VI. London, 1952.
Pope-Hennessy, James, *A Lonely Business*. London, 1981.
   Queen Mary. London, 1959.
Purcell, William, *Fisher of Lambeth*. London, 1969.
Roosevelt, Eleanor, *Autobiography*. New York, 1961.
Rose, Kenneth, *King George V*. London, 1983.
Secrest, Meryle, *Kenneth Clark*. London, 1984.
Sencourt, Robert, *The Reign of Edward VIII*. London, 1962.
Shirer, William, *Berlin Diary*. London, 1941.
Sinclair, David, *Queen and Country*. London, 1979.
Sitwell, Osbert, *Queen Mary and Others*. London, 1974.
Stevenson, Frances, *Lloyd George*. London, 1971.
Stuart, James, Viscount Stuart of Findhorn, *Within the Fringe*. London, 1967.
Talbot, Geoffrey, *Country Life Book of Queen Elizabeth the Queen Mother*. London, 1978.
Taylor, A. J. P., *English History 1914-45*. London, 1965.
Townsend, Peter, *The Last Emperor*. London, 1975.
   Time and Chance. London, 1978.

Vanderbilt, Gloria and Furness, Thelma, *Double Exposure*. London, 1959.

Watson, Francis, *Dawson of Penn*. London, 1950.

Waugh, Evelyn, *Diaries,* edited by Michael Davie. London, 1976.

West, Rebecca, *1900*. London, 1982.

Wheeler-Bennett, Sir John, *King George VI*. London, 1958.

Wilmot, Chester, *The Struggle for Europe*. London, 1952.

Windsor, The Duchess of, *The Heart Has Its Reasons*. London, 1956.

Windsor, HRH the Duke of, *A King's Story*. London, 1951.

Woolf, Leonard, *Sowing*. London, 1970.

Ziegler, Philip, *Crown and People*. London, 1978.

   Diana Cooper. London, 1981.

INDEX

280

The Royal Family

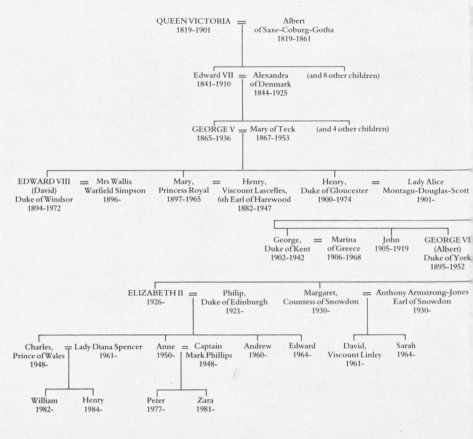

QUEEN VICTORIA = Albert
1819–1901   of Saxe-Coburg-Gotha
  1819–1861

Edward VII = Alexandra   (and 8 other children)
1841–1910   of Denmark
  1844–1925

GEORGE V = Mary of Teck   (and 4 other children)
1865–1936   1867–1953

EDWARD VIII = Mrs Wallis   Mary, = Henry,   Henry, = Lady Alice
(David)   Warfield Simpson   Princess Royal   Viscount Lascelles,   Duke of Gloucester   Montagu-Douglas-Scott
Duke of Windsor   1896–   1897–1965   6th Earl of Harewood   1900–1974   1901–
1894–1972   1882–1947

George, = Marina   John   GEORGE VI
Duke of Kent   of Greece   1905–1919   (Albert)
1902–1942   1906–1968   Duke of York
    1895–1952

ELIZABETH II = Philip,   Margaret, = Anthony Armstrong-Jones
1926–   Duke of Edinburgh   Countess of Snowdon   Earl of Snowdon
  1921–   1930–   1930–

Charles, = Lady Diana Spencer   Anne = Captain   Andrew   Edward   David,   Sarah
Prince of Wales   1961–   1950–   Mark Phillips   1960–   1964–   Viscount Linley   1964–
1948–   1948–   1961–

William   Henry   Peter   Zara
1982–   1984–   1977–   1981–